Literature-Based Instruction with English Language Learners, K–12

Nancy L. Hadaway
University of Texas at Arlington

Sylvia M. Vardell
Texas Woman's University

Terrell A. Young
Washington State University

Allyn and Bacon

Boston ■ London ■ Toronto ■ Sydney ■ Tokyo ■ Singapore

To our families:
Boyd and Mable Hadaway; Boyd, Dana, Erin, and Ryan Hadaway
Russell, Emily, and Alex Vardell and Ingrid Mergeler
Christine, Jonathan, Natalie, Emilee, and Jeffrey Young; Patricia Young, John Young,
Janet Coats, Lisa Moeder, Stacey Briggs, Jennifer Glynn, and Lori Beard.

To all those teachers and students who shared their ideas,
responses, and enthusiasm in the preparation of this book.

Series Editor: *Aurora Martínez Ramos*
Editorial Assistant: *Beth Slater*
Editorial Production Administrator: *Kathy Smith*
Composition Buyer: *Linda Cox*
Editorial Production Service: *Chestnut Hill Enterprises, Inc.*
Electronic Composition: *Peggy Cabot, Cabot Computer Services*
Manufacturing Buyer: *Julie McNeill*
Cover Administrator: *Kristina Mose-Libon*

Copyright © 2002 Allyn & Bacon
A Pearson Education Company
75 Arlington Street
Boston, MA 02116

Internet: www.ablongman.com

Library of Congress Cataloging-in-Publication Data

Hadaway, Nancy L.
   Literature-based instruction with English language learners, K–12 /
Nancy L. Hadaway, Sylvia M. Vardell, Terrell A. Young.
        p.   cm.
Includes bibliographical references and index.
   ISBN 0-321-06401-1
   1. English language—Study and teaching—Foreign speakers.   2.
Literature—Study and teaching.   I. Vardell, Sylvia M.   II. Young,
Terrell A.   III. Title.
   PE1128.A2 H24 2002
     428.0071—dc21   2001053767

Printed in the United States of America

10 9 8 7 6 5 4 3   06   05

CONTENTS

PREFACE

The title of this book, *Literature-Based Instruction with English Language Learners, K–12,* reflects our basic belief about the power of literature and its potential in the classroom. We believe that literature offers the most effective instructional tool for English language learners in Kindergarten through grade 12. Yet, little attention has been focused on the use of literature with English language learners. Thus, this book will focus on the use of literature with English language learners in grades K–12. The theory and research that supports literature-based instruction, especially with English language learners, will be coupled with hands-on activities, lessons, and units, and extensive professional references as well as children's and young adult literature lists.

Who Is This Book For?

The three of us—Nancy, Sylvia, and Terry—are university professors with a primary emphasis in literature and literacy instruction. Convinced about the power of children's and young adult literature, we left our university classrooms to conduct demonstration lessons using children's literature in K–12 English as a second language (ESL) classrooms and to collaboratively plan literature-based units with teachers of grades K–12. The student and teacher response was tremendous. Thus, this book attempts to meet our goal of informing all teachers who work with English language learners about the potential for implementing literature-based instruction to foster literacy development.

This text fills a tremendous void in several ways. First, little attention has been focused on literature-based instruction with English language learners. In addition, many texts addressing instruction of linguistically diverse students focus on the elementary-age student and/or the bilingual classroom. Yet, English language learners are an increasing population, and given recent legislative changes in California and Arizona marking a move away from bilingual education, a focus on ESL is overdue.

This book is appropriate for preservice and inservice teachers pursuing coursework related to certification for ESL or for reading with special populations. Given the increasing number of grade-level teachers who will encounter English language learners, we have designed this book to meet the needs of all teachers who may work with English language learners. Beyond its use as a textbook in formal courses, this text serves as an excellent personal reference tool for K–12 teachers, administrators, and teacher educators. Finally, this book would be ideally suited for school district staff development.

Terminology

As with any profession, this book uses some terms that may be unique to teaching and working with English language learners. To begin, we use the terms **first language,**

native language, and **home language** interchangeably to refer to the language children first learned from their parents. The term **limited English proficient (LEP)** is commonly found in federal legislation and other official documents. This term has drawn criticism for its emphasis on the deficits the individual brings to the language learning situation. We have chosen to use the terms **English language learner** and **nonnative English speaker** to represent individuals in the process of learning English after learning a first or other language. While second language learner is another name often used, we avoided this term since English may not be the second language to be learned by the individual. However, ESL is used to refer to instructional settings, not just individuals; therefore, we will use **English as a Second Language (ESL)** to denote the instructional period during school in which a teacher has only English language learners. **Bilingual education** is a program of dual-language instruction (e.g., English and Spanish) usually provided in the elementary grades.

Generally, English language learners may range from totally non-English speaking (beginners) to high intermediate or early advanced English speakers almost ready for the grade-level classroom. We wanted to avoid the negative image of "fixing" the English language learner to move into the "regular" (all English) classroom setting, so we chose **grade-level classroom** to refer to K–12 classes that are not bilingual classrooms or ESL only classes.

Finally, **literature-based instruction** is an instructional approach for language teaching that uses authentic materials, including children's and young adult literature cutting across genres (e.g., poetry, fiction, nonfiction, fantasy). In literature-based classrooms, teachers choose from countless strategies not only to teach language but to also concentrate on cognitive development and affective issues.

Organization of the Book

The basic question we explore in this book is: How can teachers utilize children's and young adult literature to foster the literacy development of English language learners? In the first section, "Beginning the Journey," we offer an overview of English language learners, establish a rationale for using literature in grades K–12 to foster language acquisition, walk the reader through the process of setting up a literature-based classroom, and introduce the many diverse genres of literature. The second section, "Growing in Language Ability," focuses on the development of oral language, reading, and writing with English language learners and offers specific examples of children's and young adult literature to be used at various grade levels and linguistic proficiency levels. Specific strategies for incorporating authentic materials in the classroom are provided with actual examples of student work related to those techniques. "Responding to Culture and Language," the third section of the book, highlights the area of culture that is intertwined with language. The use of multicultural literature, folklore, and poetry are discussed, and specific literature-based activities and units of instruction are described. Finally, because academic language is crucial to any English language learner's eventual success in school, the last section, "Exploring Content," addresses the use of literature, particularly nonfiction literature, as a means of supplementing content textbooks and teaching content concepts.

Each chapter includes several elements to assist the reader in understanding the range and possibilities of using literature with English language learners. Within each chapter, readers will find the following elements:

- Reflective questions at the beginning.
- Review of research/theoretical base.
- Scenarios from K–12 classrooms with English language learners.
- Sample activities with examples of children's and young adult literature.
- Assessment issues.

Finally, we offer a complete bibliography of children's and young adult literature cited in the text. These books span a wide variety of genres and themes that effectively meet the needs of both language and content instruction across the curriculum and grade levels. In addition to listing each book, at the end of each citation we provide a guide to help teachers choose books best suited for their classrooms, considering the age and English proficiency level of the students. We have coded each book with an indication of the type of book (picture book, chapter book, nonfiction, and poetry) as well as an indication of the English language proficiency level(s) (beginning, intermediate, and advanced) that each book seems best suited for. We chose this coding scheme because using grade levels to indicate an appropriate reading level seemed somewhat narrow. Among English language learners, we have beginning readers at every grade level. Therefore, the type of book is a better indication of approximate reading level. Our coding scheme is merely an approximation; many of these books can be used across the entire K–12 curriculum depending on the objective of the lesson.

Coding Scheme for Children's and Young Adult Books in the Bibliography

Proficiency level is indicated by B, I, or A.

B=Beginning (non-English speaking to some).
I=Intermediate (limited to average fluency).
A=Advanced (average fluency to ready to be mainstreamed).

The **type of book** is indicated by PB, CB, NF, or P.

PB=Picture book.
CB=Chapter book.
NF=Nonfiction.
P=Poetry.

Coding scheme example: B/PB (Beginning proficiency/picture book).

We would like to thank the following reviewers for their helpful comments and suggestions: Naomi Migliacci, University of Delaware; Karen Sakash, University of Illinois at Chicago; and Stephen Stryker, California State University at Stanislaus.

SECTION ONE

Beginning the Journey

He who has help has hope, and he who has hope has everything.
—Arab proverb

The first section of this book provides an overview of English language learners in our schools today, noting changing immigration patterns. We also highlight the many different educational settings that students may encounter during kindergarten through twelfth grade. Next, we establish a rationale for using literature in grades K–12 to foster language acquisition; we walk the reader through the process of setting up a literature-based classroom; and we introduce the reader to the many diverse genres and types of literature that are available to implement in any classroom. This section contains three chapters.

- **Our Changing Classrooms**
- **Language Acquisition and Literature-Based Instruction**
- **Organizing for Literature-Based Instruction with English Language Learners**

1 Our Changing Classrooms

We must become the change we want to see.
—Mahatma Ghandi

Immigration has changed the face of American society and American schools. Until the 1950s, the majority of immigrants still originated from Europe, but by the 1980s, this pattern had changed dramatically, with 85 percent of more recent immigrants coming from developing countries (Crawford, 1992). This shift in immigration has in turn altered not only the look but most importantly the sound of classrooms. Carlos Cortes (1994), in his chapter for *Kids Come in All Languages: Reading Instruction for ESL Students,* describes the range of differences among children who come to school with a home language other than English.

> Students come to school speaking different languages. They bring varying home values and behavioral patterns. They have diverse learning styles. They have undergone different and sometimes soul-shattering experiences. They live in unequal socioeconomic conditions. Their prior education varies. They have different knowledge bases and experience-honed perspectives. They often lack self-esteem. Many have little vision of future careers or awareness of what educational steps they must take in order to transform dreams into possibilities. (pp. 30–31)

In this chapter, we begin our examination of this growing population of students within our schools, English language learners. We will address the following questions.

- **Who are English language learners?**
- **What types of programs are designed to help English language learners in American schools?**
- **What backgrounds do English language learners bring to the classroom?**
- **How can teachers become more aware of English language learners?**

Let's begin by describing our diverse schools in terms of linguistic diversity and considering the need for educators who are prepared to work with the English language learners.

3

Who Are English Language Learners?

More than 7.5 million school age children in the United States come from homes where a language other than English is spoken (NABE, 1992, p. 3). At the beginning of the twenty-first century, these students accounted for 35 percent of all schoolchildren across the nation. In short, immigration changes mean that English language learners are the fastest growing group in our schools today (McKeon, 1992). Furthermore, these figures do not even begin to paint an accurate picture of the many schools and districts where a concentration of English language learners virtually overshadows the native English speaking student population. Nonnative English speakers in some school districts represent 25 to 60 percent of the entire school population (Porter, 1990).

To view the reality of this diversity, let's listen to some typical teachers describing their classrooms in Box 1.1. These vignettes were drawn from teachers who participated in a series of workshops that Nancy conducted recently. To sum up the diversity reflected in these teachers' classrooms, they reported students from at least twenty-two different ethnic groups and even more countries of origin, such as Mexico, Haiti, Vietnam, Bosnia, India, Ethiopia, Iraq, China, Japan, and Africa.

Are we prepared to deal with this dramatic change in our classrooms? Not really. The critical shortage of teachers actually prepared to work with the growing number of children with a first language other than English has been well documented (Crawford, 1995; Delpit, 1995). The Association of School, College, and University Staffing (ASCUS) conducted a nationwide survey of teacher placement officers in 1988. The results indicated that the greatest shortages existed in English as a second language (ESL) and bilingual education (Gonzales, 1993).

What happens to English language learners when they enter school? Generally, they receive most, if not all, of their instruction in grade-level classes. Waggoner and O'Malley

---

B O X 1.1

Voices from the Field: Diversity in Today's Classrooms

- I have twenty-two students, seven of whom are ESL students. Their ethnic backgrounds include Vietnamese, Chinese, Japanese, Hispanic, and Middle Eastern. My ESL students speak English ranging from proficient to limited. One student is beginning his first year in an English-speaking public school. He comes from a Hebrew private school. (grade 4)
- I teach some eighty-nine students math in an ESL setting everyday. Mostly, they are Hispanic, but I also serve children from Bosnia, Albania, Vietnam, Russia, and Africa. (middle school)
- I teach three classes—one middle school (grades 6–8) and two high school classes (grades 9–12). All of the students are ESL, and all are recent immigrants. There is great diversity in national/ethnic backgrounds, but primarily the student population is Hispanic. My class size averages twenty-two students. However, I have taught as many as thirty-five students in a class. (International Newcomer Academy)
- I teach in a high school language center—math and science. My classes range in size from seven to twenty-five students. Most are Spanish speakers, but some come from Pakistan, India, and Bosnia. (high school)

(1985) reported that 25 percent of all public school teachers had English language learners in their classrooms, yet 70 percent of these same teachers remarked that they had received no academic preparation in bilingual or ESL methods. Given the current teacher shortage and continuing immigration patterns, the lack of personnel trained to work with English language learners is unlikely to change. As a matter of fact, the teachers in Box 1.1 were involved in a four-day training program to provide the background and skills to work with English language learners. Each year, two hundred such teachers in that district will receive ESL training; these teachers already have English language learners in their classrooms but have no previous training in ESL instruction.

What Types of Programs Are Designed to Help English Language Learners in American Schools?

Given the fact that American schools have been steadily changing over the last few decades, some individuals might question the need for focusing on English language learners. Indeed, we are serving more students of color and more children living in poverty than ever before, and these trends will continue as the twenty-first century progresses (Au, 1993). Yet, the range of diversity that English language learners bring to the school moves well beyond ethnic and socioeconomic lines, adding another layer of complex diversity— English language proficiency—which is directly related to school achievement.

In response to the language proficiency issue, the government and the courts turned their attention to English language learners. As a result of a series of legislative acts and court rulings, including the Fourteenth Amendment of the U.S. Constitution, Title VI of the Civil Rights Act of 1964, the 1974 U.S. Supreme Court case of *Lau* v. *Nichols,* and Title VII of the Improving America's School Act of 1994, federal policy has evolved to protect the rights of English language learners (Ovando & Collier, 1998). With the force of legislation and court rulings, special language programs have evolved over the last few decades. Depending on students' ages, previous schooling, and proficiency in home languages and English, a variety of K–12 programs are now available to assist students to acquire English and move forward in school. Following is a brief overview of the types of programs available.

Program Configurations

Self-Contained Bilingual Classrooms with ESL Instruction.   The population of non-native English speakers in many school districts and individual campuses is so large that bilingual education programs are possible. Bilingual education is a program of dual language instruction including students' first languages and English. Given the shortage of bilingual education teachers, however, many students receive ESL instruction through one of the following program configurations.

Pullout ESL.   For elementary schools with smaller populations of English language learners, the typical option is a pullout ESL program. The pullout ESL teacher removes the children from grade-level instruction classrooms during the day and works with them on English language development for a limited amount of time. The rationale for such programs is to provide extra language instruction so students can better understand the content when they return to grade-level classes. Common criticisms of pullout programs center on the fact that children miss valuable content instruction when they have gone to another setting and that, when they return to the classroom, the grade-level teacher lacks the training to effectively address their needs.

Push-in ESL.   In response to criticisms leveled against pullout programs in relation to lost content exposure and the lack of training of the grade-level teacher, push-in programs present another option. Mainly for elementary grades in schools with a smaller number of English language learners, a teacher trained in ESL techniques visits grade-level classrooms and works with teachers and students learning English as a new language within the grade-level setting. Theoretically, such programs allow grade-level teachers to learn the skills needed for effectively working with English language learners as they team with the push-in ESL teacher. Often, the implementation of push-in resembles one-on-one and small-group tutorials as English language learners are still pulled aside from the normal classroom interaction, and the grade-level teacher does not see the strategies that the push-in ESL teacher uses.

Self-Contained Elementary ESL.   In elementary schools with large populations of English language learners, self-contained ESL classrooms are the norm. Given the number of English language learners, especially in some urban school districts, grouping all the English language learners in classrooms with teachers who use ESL methods to convey all the subject areas seems logical.

Grade-Level Elementary Classrooms.   To avoid pullout programs and to respond to the need for English language learners and native English speakers to work together on a daily basis, grade-level elementary classrooms supply an alternative. In the grade-level setting, there is a mix of English language learners and native English speakers led by a teacher responsible for teaching all subject areas *and* meeting the needs of the various linguistic proficiency levels of both English language learners and native English speakers in the classroom.

Self-Contained ESL (Secondary Level).   In secondary schools, students may receive their language arts instruction in a self-contained ESL class. Generally, this class, composed solely of English language learners, would occur during a normal instructional period. Beyond this one class period, students might have the balance of their classes (biology, history, algebra, etc.) within the normal school schedule with native English speakers.

Sheltered Content Area Instruction.   English language learners at a more basic proficiency level may have the option of sheltered content area instruction in some schools. This type of instruction is generally offered at the upper elementary and secondary level to classes composed only of English language learners. Sheltered content area teachers provide content instruction in math, history, science, and the like using ESL methods to make the concepts more understandable to the students.

Grade-Level Language Arts. In an attempt to integrate native English speakers and English language learners, secondary schools may mix students learning English as a new language and native English speakers together for their English and language arts instruction. As in the elementary grade-level classroom, this configuration creates a classroom of very diverse language proficiency levels that the teacher, hopefully with prior ESL training, must address.

Newcomer Schools. Awareness of the tremendous adjustments faced by recent immigrants led to the creation of newcomer schools. Proficiency levels of students at a newcomer school generally range from totally non-English speaking (or preliterate) to very limited English proficiency. These schools provide not only a full day of instruction in language and content to new immigrants learning English, but they also offer support during the first months of transition to a new country and a different culture. Once students acquire a basic understanding of English in a year or so, they move to a typical school setting.

Newcomer Career Academy. Some older students arrive in the United States with little or no previous schooling. As an option for these students, who would typically struggle in a more academically focused high school, the newcomer career academy offers an emphasis on survival-level English and on school-to-life or work skills.

This section has summarized the various types of ESL settings that might be afforded an English language learner on entry to the U.S. schools. Over time, the types of programs have changed to more closely meet the needs of an increasing student population that brings very diverse backgrounds to the school setting.

What Backgrounds Do English Language Learners Bring to the Classroom?

The variety of special language programs reflects the diversity of English language learners in our school. Many factors contribute to this diversity, and often these factors are interrelated. Teachers in ESL settings and in grade-level classrooms need to be aware of the background that English language learners bring to school and how their personal and family histories can affect their eventual success both academically and linguistically. A word of caution is in order, however. Teachers should not perceive any of the issues we cite as negatives that present dead-end streets for instruction. These factors merely represent starting points the child brings to the classroom.

Student Age

English language learners in the schools may range from four to five years of age to twenty-one years of age. Some children born in the United States arrive at school at age four or five with limited exposure to English. Other children immigrate at various points in their youth through late high school. Complicating children's transition into the schools is the issue of age–grade mismatch if they are placed in lower grade levels to compensate for lack of schooling. This may result in the learner's feeling alienated, and the situation may be further worsened if the learner does not make adequate academic progress and is retained. We knew of one case where a ten-year-old boy from Mexico entered a U.S school. Because he had never attended school, he was placed in the third grade, where he struggled with basic school procedures, literacy, and social issues (e.g., fitting in with younger children). At the end of his first year, he was retained in the third grade for a second year, and the age–grade mismatch grew even worse.

Beyond the age–grade mismatch, the age a student enters the American school system plays a crucial role in the student's becoming competent in English. Younger children have more time in school to catch up. Older English language learners who arrive later, depending on their previous schooling, have a more difficult time because academic language generally takes from five to seven years to develop (Thomas & Collier, 1995). A middle-school math teacher said that he was teaching a young student from Burundi. This young man had never been to school because of the civil war in his country. As an adolescent, he was now making up for lost time, beginning with basic math concepts such as numbers.

Previous Schooling

Ease of transition into U.S. schools is greatly affected by the amount and quality of schooling prior to arriving in this country. Some immigrants come to the English learning situation with a strong native language foundation and a sound knowledge base that can be transferred to English. A consistent educational experience, even in a language other than English, affords English language learners content concepts and linguistic awareness. Indeed, students with a strong educational background from their home country may have additional language study beyond their first language, so they are *consciously* aware of the process of language learning. The extent and nature of an immigrant's previous schooling depends on the country of origin and its socioeconomic conditions. Many immigrants experienced sporadic attendance in school due to political and economic turmoil in their home countries, their parents' jobs (e.g., migrant labor), health and family issues, and so on. Additionally, some children from rural areas may come to the United States later in the K–12 sequence without any exposure to formal schooling in their home country. One urban district near Nancy and Sylvia has experienced a sharp increase in the number of unschooled children entering the intermediate grades (grades 3–5).

Home Ties and School Attendance

Once students are enrolled in U.S. schools, a consistent educational program fosters academic achievement and language development. However, the nature of the parents' work or the family's economic situation may necessitate repeated moves that break up the school experience and delay English language development. Frequent absences arise when children stay home to care for younger siblings due to family illness and emergencies or when they are needed to serve as translators at the doctor's or attorney's office. Furthermore, strong ties to the home country and the proximity of Latin America, often give rise to frequent absences from school, and even to sporadic enrollment in school. One teacher commented, "Since school has begun, I have had ESL students come and go from my classroom. The numbers seem to change on a weekly basis. The trend seems to be to return to Mexico and then back to Texas." Another teacher added, "I have a boy in my class whose parents pulled him out of school for four months last year to go to Mexico. Since their return, his parents have pushed him to catch up on his studies. They have made it clear to me that they wish for him to get a good education."

Family Literacy Background

Closely linked to previous schooling is the issue of family literacy background. The caretakers of English language learners represent a tremendous range of educational backgrounds and thus linguistic diversity in both English and in the home language. According to many ESL teachers with whom we work, the families of their students range from total non-English speakers to individuals studying or teaching at local universities.

Where English proficiency is limited, there may be a rich native language foundation that serves to support English language acquisition. In the case of Rene, a young student from a writing research project, this was the case. Rene obviously came from a home where the native language was well developed, and eventually this was an important factor in his transition to English. His journal entries, written in perfect Spanish with correct spelling and accent marks, referred to checking out books in Spanish from the classroom library to take home and read with his mother. He clearly knew about language and its many uses; a home environment that modeled literacy in Spanish aided his progression to English.

Other parents, who are not literate in their native language, may provide little modeling of reading and writing. In these homes, the oral tradition can supply a rich language experience. Schools then extend the child's oral language development through a focus on storytelling using family stories. Home language literacy is not the only area to consider. Within the family, the proficiency level in English may vary widely based on some parents' contact with English through a work environment, as compared to other caretakers who remain surrounded by the home language. Or the variety of English spoken at home may vary from the model of language that the teacher is working to highlight in the classroom. This last point is also a factor for our native English speakers as well.

In families where little to no English is spoken at home, the children sometimes become the translators and negotiators for the family. In several instances, teachers commented on this crucial role that the children play. One first grade teacher said that "in most families there are older children who read and write English and help younger children with homework." Serving as family translator may push the child toward faster and greater English acquisition. As a fifth grade teacher cited, "I have a very bright and dedicated student from Bosnia. She speaks and understands English very well. She has to translate and interpret English for her mother." This role can also be a pressure as children are called on to take adult responsibilities beyond their age and experience (e.g., speaking to government officials, physicians, and attorneys).

Finally, families learning English often experience a certain level of prejudice because they are not conversant with the language or have heavily accented speech. Concerned that their children not experience any further discrimination, parents may insist that their children speak only English at home, causing an estrangement from older relatives who speak no English and even from the parents themselves who may not yet be fluent in English. Moreover, parents may even refuse special language services (e.g., bilingual education and ESL), fearing that their children may not learn to speak English properly.

Native-Born or Immigrant Status

Literacy background, at times, is a reflection of the family's geographic background—where they have lived, how often they may have moved, and so on. Some English language learners were born and have lived in the United States all their lives before arriving in the K–12 schools. Most likely, native-born English language learners identified for ESL instruction have grown up in homes and closely knit ethnic communities where little if any English is spoken.

Many immigrants have complex issues to deal with. When families immigrate as a result of political turmoil or severe economic hardships, the children often come to school in a state of shock. Because of age or stress during the move, children may not have well-developed coping strategies. In these instances, school often becomes a place where children work out their issues, and teachers may report more frequent acting out or withdrawn behavior, such as remaining in the silent period of language acquisition longer than other English language learners. Transition to a new country is difficult under the best of circumstances, but traumatic reasons for immigration only serve to complicate the adjustment process. Listen again to voices from the classroom in Box 1.2 as various teachers describe some students' traumatic experiences prior to their journey to America.

Difficult Living Conditions

Whether a family has immigrated to or has lived in the United States for some time, often the living conditions at home affect children's attention at school. Many children live with

---

B O X **1.2**

Voices from the Field: Transition Issues for Immigrants

- Two years ago a Hmong student of mine moved to America from Thailand, leaving behind several family members. His brothers and sisters had died due to illness and war.
- The family of one of my students had to flee Iraq or the government would have killed his family. They were a professional family, and the father works in the United States as a dishwasher.
- I have a beautiful Vietnamese student. She lives with her grandparents in public housing. Her father was killed trying to leave the country.
- I have a young student from Bosnia. He is seventeen and anxious to drive, get a job, and do regular teenage activities. He has personally witnessed war atrocities—the deaths of babies and "enemies of the state." He has lived in a refugee camp. His dental health is bad—visiting the dentist is not a survival interest. His older brother still has nightmares about life in Bosnia.

extended family—grandparents, aunts, uncles, cousins. While the family can be a tremendous support system, such a gathering of family can also result in very overcrowded living arrangements. Two elementary teachers mentioned students living in very tight quarters, with twelve to sixteen people under the same roof. Certainly, that might make the morning routine very hectic.

Citizenship status presents another obstacle in the life of some families. When parents come to the United States as undocumented workers, legal status becomes a constant concern. Yet, with or without papers, working through the bureaucratic process to become citizens takes time. A first grade teacher described just such a situation. One of her students had been separated for some time from her parents when they crossed the border to work here as undocumented laborers. The parents spent a great deal of time "trying to get legalized. As soon as this happened, they brought over the children."

In classrooms we have visited, we found that some English language learners are not living with parents or even family members. Sent to the United States to receive an education and to learn to speak English, these students live with extended family members, family friends, and sometimes older siblings. At times, we discovered adolescents as the primary caregivers of younger siblings.

Finally, tremendous economic hardship can result in stark living circumstances. A fourth grade teacher revealed, "One of my students is Bosnian. He is having a very difficult time. He lived in a refugee camp in Bosnia. He now lives with his dad. They are homeless. A pastor from a local church and our school counselor have been trying to help them."

Linguistic Proficiency in the First Language

First language literacy lays a firm foundation for adding another language. The more proficient children are in their home language, the easier their transition to English. Hopefully, our students bring all kinds of knowledge about language to the classroom, such as a well-developed vocabulary, implicit understanding of morphemes (e.g., prefixes and suffixes or verb tense and number markers), and an intuitive awareness of basic syntax. When children possess a basic understanding about issues such as word order in sentences in the home language, they can more easily understand that English has similar principles, even if the syntactic rules are not the same as in English—as for example, where the descriptive adjective precedes the noun (the blue book) compared with Spanish where the descriptive adjective follows the noun (*el libro azul*). In contrast, some children have little knowledge about their home language. The literacy background of parents, previous schooling, and lack of exposure to a print version of the home language all affect knowledge of the first language.

Many children come to the English learning situation with a language similar to English in terms of its sound system, syntax, and its use of the Roman alphabet (e.g., Spanish). Other children speak languages with very different phonological characteristics, that may use a non-Roman alphabet, and that differ markedly from English in terms of structural elements (e.g., many Asian languages do not use articles such as *a, an,* and *the*). Familiarity with the languages that students speak in terms of their comparability with

English helps teachers provide the support needed when students encounter totally new English sounds and structures.

This section has attempted to provide a brief overview of the many factors that can affect English language development. As we move forward in upcoming chapters, we will demonstrate how the language development of English language learners can be positively affected by the use of authentic materials.

How Can Teachers Become More Aware of English Language Learners?

Countless sources of information exist about students in today's classrooms. Colleagues can serve as resources, and professional organizations such as the National Association for Bilingual Education (NABE, www.nabe.org) and Teachers of English to Speakers of Other Languages (TESOL, www.tesol.org) are support systems for educators who work with English language learners. The Internet also provides ready access to Web sites for professional organizations, government data, and teacher resources. Obviously, the students themselves should be an initial source of information. Looking over students' permanent records and talking to them and their families furnish much valuable data to classroom teachers.

However, since this book highlights literature-based instruction, we want to demonstrate that literature is not just for instructional purposes in the classroom. Many current fiction and nonfiction children's and young adult books supply a vast wealth of knowledge that teachers can use to become acquainted with the geographic and linguistic backgrounds of their students, the values that they bring to the classroom, and the cultural conflict that may arise for them in this new home. In short, many of the books we will be recommending for instructional purposes over the next few chapters are not just for children. They can also expand teachers' awareness and prompt self-reflection about their own cultural backgrounds and the potential gap between the experiences of teachers and children. In the following section, we suggest a variety of books that teachers might want to explore for instructional purposes as well as for their own awareness. These books reflect varying reading levels, but we contend that there is much information in books at lower reading levels for both children and adults. We would argue that many of our recommended books are really junior coffee-table books designed for a wide audience of readers from kindergarten through high school.

Students' Geographic Backgrounds

Teachers frequently cite a need for a greater understanding of their students' geographic and cultural backgrounds. Many children's and young adult books are available to address this need. *A Is for Asia* by Cynthia Chin-Lee (1997) uses an alphabet arrangement to furnish a global view of Asia, including the geography, culture, holidays, traditions, and many languages of Asian countries. *D Is for Doufu: An Alphabet Book of Chinese Culture* by Maywan Shen Krach (1997) and *I Is for India* by Prodeepta Das (1996), on the other hand, focus on particular countries, giving readers a bird's eye view of China and India.

Once teachers have read these books, they might choose to share a letter of the alphabet each day with the class and discuss the rich heritage of Asia and the many contributions that Asians have made to our history. We love this alphabet format for providing a quick overview of any area.

Several excellent works provide a panoramic view. For instance *Children Just Like Me* (Kindersley, 1997) and *Children from Australia to Zimbabwe: A Photographic Journey around the World* (Ajmera & Versola, 1996) supply brief snapshots of children from many countries. In *Children from Australia to Zimbabwe*, for example, the alphabet book format is used to present one country per two-page spread for each letter of the alphabet. Photos of children and bulleted lists of facts about each country are extended by brief descriptions. Besides serving as a brief overview to whet the appetites of teachers and students, this book also furnishes a wonderful model of writing. After a teacher-led overview of the book, students in class can use other literature and reference resources to write their own alphabet book highlighting their own home countries and, perhaps, others not presented in the book. Using *Children Just Like Me,* highlighting children from more than thirty countries, the class might produce a class book entitled *Students Just Like Us* that could supply a wealth of information about their peers. Finally, let's not forget the rich diversity within the United States itself and our native-born English language learners. *Kids Explore America's Hispanic Heritage* (Westridge Young Writers Workshop, 1992) might be another good source of information on the Latino population and the Spanish language within our own country. It is also one of a series of books about the microcultures within our own borders.

Stories of Immigration

Numerous books provide perspectives on the process of immigration as well as the transition to the United States and the English language. *Who Belongs Here? An American Story* by Margy Burns Knight (1993) is the fictitious story of Nary, a Cambodian refugee. Written in language accessible to primary grade children, the narrative story runs along the top of each page, accompanied by a nonfiction sentence below providing insights into immigration and the adjustments that modern immigrants face. This nonfiction addition is an ideal way of contrasting narrative and expository text for older readers and provides enough detail to engage older English language learners.

Expanding on the individual perspective, Yale Strom's *Quilted Landscape: Conversations with Young Immigrants* (1996) presents a nonfiction view of twenty-six young people from ages ten to seventeen. Using first-person narrative, the youngsters briefly describe the reasons for immigrating to the United States and provide some background on life in the home country and the many personal changes that have taken place since their move. The introduction by the author offers an excellent overview of recent changes in immigration patterns followed by a world map noting the country of origin as well as the new home in America of each young person interviewed for the book. This wonderful geographic focus begs to be repeated in the classroom. Using a bulletin board or chart paper on the wall, students can construct their own world map with countries of origin for both English language learners and native-English speakers (if they know where their families originally came from). Additionally, students might map any moves they have made within the United States. *Quilted Landscapes* is designed for intermediate grades and intermediate proficiency levels and above. However, a very brief overview of each home country is provided via statistical data in chart form (e.g., size of country, population, capital). Such bite-sized information is ideal for beginning English language learners, supplying a model of writing to scaffold their attempts to reproduce a table with these facts for their own countries of origin.

The tremendous difficulties associated with the refugee experience are chronicled in numerous books. An in-depth focus on the Hmong is furnished in *Dia's Story Cloth* by Dia Cha (1998). Using photographs of a traditional Hmong embroidered story cloth, the author describes her life in Southeast Asia, the family's years in a refugee camp in Thailand, and their eventual immigration to the United States. Pegi Deitz Shea tells a similar story in *The Whispering Cloth: A Refugee's Story* (1995). Written for intermediate grades and above, the example of the story cloth furnishes a wonderful model for a family literacy activity. *My Freedom Trip* (Park & Park, 1998) is yet another example of the struggle and sacrifice refugees make as they flee their homelands. Teachers can send students home to interview family members, and the English language learners can return to class to illustrate and write their own stories. In the hopes of sharing U.S. culture, a connection can be made at this point to the American tradition of quilting and the many rich family stories depicted in this folk art format.

For teachers, older readers, and intermediate proficiency levels and above, we recommend Brent Ashabranner, an award-winning author with numerous books written in a photo-essay style. *Still a Nation of Immigrants* (1993) looks at where the present influx of immigrants come from and how they fit into American life. *Children of the Maya: A Guatemalan Indian Odyssey* (1986) highlights a group of Guatemalan refugees fleeing political upheaval and war to come to America and settle in a small community in Florida. Through heartfelt individual stories and photographs, the issue of illegal immigration to the United States provides the focus of two Ashabranner books, *The Vanishing Border: A Photographic Journey along Our Frontier with Mexico* (1987) and *Our Beckoning Borders: Illegal Immigration in America* (1996). While Ashabranner's books lean toward the intermediate grade levels and above, they will prove to be fascinating reading for teachers, too. The language in these books may be well beyond the beginning proficiency level of an English language learner, but the photographs provide cultural awareness. Teachers can share these powerful photos to spur classroom discussion with students of any age or language level. Also, the photo essay format serves as another strong model of writing. Taking any issue, the class can highlight the topic with original or magazine photos or illustrations and then add text. In one high school ESL class, Nancy and a teacher colleague taught an immigration unit. Students were most interested in the legal issues surrounding immigration such as legislation and quota systems. Such a focus could be the ideal beginning of a photo essay concerning the effect of quotas and legislation on U.S. immigration through the years.

Migrant Life

Various children's books, both fiction and nonfiction, highlight the life of migrant farm workers. For example, primary grade students and beginning-level English language learners will enjoy the beautiful illustrations and text of *Amelia's Road* by Linda Jacobs Altman (1993), *Going Home* by Eve Bunting (1996), *Radio Man* by Arthur Dorros (1993), *The Upside Down Boy* by Juan Felipe Herrera (2000), and *Tomas and the Library Lady* by Pat Mora (1997). Each of these picture books tells the story of youngsters who are part of a migrant family. *Radio Man* and *The Upside Down Boy* are bilingual books with both English and Spanish text, while *Tomas and the Library Lady* is available in both English and Spanish versions. While the previous examples focus on Latino families, *Working Cotton* by Sherley Anne Williams (1992) highlights African Americans also involved in migrant labor. Finally, S. Beth Atkin and Brent Ashabranner furnish powerful photo essays detailing migrant life. Written for older students with more developed language proficiency, *Voices from the Fields: Children of Migrant Farm Workers Tell Their Stories* (Atkin, 1993) and *Dark Harvest: Migrant Farm Workers in America* (Ashabranner, 1997) afford insightful perspectives on the plight of migrant workers, with Atkin's work focusing on the effect of this lifestyle on youngsters. After reading several of these books or surveying the pictures in the photo essays, the class can study statistics related to migrant life, such as longevity, health, and the like. In addition, the text of picture books can spur the development of a readers theater script. We recently used a script for *Tomas and the Library Lady* with a family literacy group to demonstrate the power of books in a child's life.

Language Issues

The diversity of languages around the world, the joy of knowing two languages, and the difficulty of learning English are the subjects of many poems and books. *What Is Your Language?* by Debra Leventhal (1994), *Scripts of the World* by Suzanne Bukiet (1993), and *People* by Peter Spier (1988) remind us about the fascinating diversity of languages around the world with their different alphabets and sounds. Using these books as a springboard for discussion, teachers can have students compare and contrast their languages with English. Comparing alphabets, vocabulary, and syntax issues proves an enlightening experience for the whole class.

In the poem "Spanish" from *Canto Familiar* (1995), Gary Soto paints a joyous picture of bilingualism, arguing that knowing two languages actually enlarges one's world. In contrast, the poem "Elena" from Pat Mora's *My Own True Name* (2000), poignantly portrays a young mother struggling to learn English and beginning to feel estranged from her children, who are now part of an English-speaking world. In "Speak Up" from *Good Luck Gold and Other Poems* (Wong, 1994), we hear a Korean American child teased by classmates about speaking another language. Sharing these poems may prompt students to discuss how they feel about speaking their home languages and how their parents and older relatives feel about their English proficiency levels. Transcending the language barrier, *Sitti's Secrets* (Nye, 1994) describes a young girl's visit to her grandmother in a small Palestinian village. While Mona begins to learn a few words of Arabic, she and her grandmother invent a new language through nonverbal cues and gestures.

Finally, the power and the responsibility of children knowing English when their parents do not is depicted in the picture books *I Speak English for My Mom* by Muriel Stanek (1989) and *Going Home* by Eve Bunting (1996). Both books portray the many roles children must fulfill in order to help their parents negotiate an English-speaking world in the United States.

The Family

Family structure and traditions vary from culture to culture, and such differences furnish great classroom content. For instance, Carmen Lomas Garza depicts traditional Mexican American life in *Family Pictures/Cuadros De Familia* (1990) and *In My Family/En Mi Familia* (1996) with short vignettes about folk medicine cures and legends such as La Llorona, the weeping woman. Making traditional foods is the focus of Gary Soto's *Too Many Tamales* (1993) and his poem "Tortillas Like Africa" (*Canto Familiar*, 1995) while the staples of bread and rice, shared by many cultures, are the focus of *Everybody Cooks Rice* (1991) and *Everybody Bakes Bread* (1996) by Norah Dooley. These last two books include recipes using bread and rice. In the classroom, teachers can encourage students to share recipes from home. In fact, collecting recipes and having children share special stories associated with familiar foods can grow into a wonderful class book project.

Naming practices are very culturally related, and several books focus on this issue. Marilyn Sanders' *What's Your Name? From Ariel to Zoe* (Sanders, 1995) presents an alphabet of diverse names with the stories behind the children and the names. Not too long ago, Nancy collaborated with a high school ESL teacher (Hadaway & Mundy, 1992) using "My Name," an excerpt from Sandra Cisneros' *House on Mango Street* (1984) that describes how the protagonist, Esperanza, feels when the teachers at school mispronounce her name. Moving beyond our given names, *Do People Grow on Family Trees? Genealogy for Kids and Other Beginners* (Wolfman, 1991) has a chapter devoted to surnames. Teachers might consider using these books to encourage English language learners to share their feelings about the mispronunciation of their names by native English speakers and the dilemma of last name differences from culture to culture (e.g., Latinos use both parents' names but in a different order than in English, for example, Juan Garcia [father's surname] Lopez [mother's surname]).

In this section we have discussed the potential of children's and young adult literature to assist not only the students in the classroom but also the teacher. Teachers can glean much useful information about their students' backgrounds from the same trade books they utilize in the classroom.

Checking It Out: Assessment and English Language Learners

At the end of each chapter, we will address issues related to assessment and English language learners in the section "Checking It Out." We have chosen to weave assessment into the text of each chapter since it is a critical component of instruction that teachers sometimes fail to consider. We engage in the act of assessment even before our students enter the classroom. As we plan lessons, we gauge the materials and activities to be used in terms of our audience and determine whether students have the appropriate background knowledge. If they don't, we must take steps to build that background. Then, as we teach, we constantly assess whether our students comprehend the lesson and the materials.

The task of assessing English language learners is even more complex. Part of this is due to language and part to the many regulations that govern instructional programs that serve English language learners. To demonstrate this complexity, we will overview six specific purposes for assessing English language learners in our schools: screening and identification, placement, reclassification or exit, monitoring student progress, program evaluation, and accountability (O'Malley & Pierce, 1996).

Screening and identification is the first purpose for assessing English language learners. In general, school districts follow these initial steps in screening and identifying children's eligibility for special language programs. First, the family or guardians of the student visit the school to enroll the child in school. During the intake interview or registration process, the family completes a home language survey indicating what languages are spoken at home and what languages the child speaks. If a language other than English is spoken in the home or used by the child, that student is identified as a candidate for testing to determine eligibility for special language programs such as bilingual education or ESL.

Once identified as a nonnative English speaker, possible **placement** in bilingual education or ESL becomes the next priority. Under state and federal guidelines, schools have a defined period of time to screen, identify, and test students for placement. Depending on the student's age, placement is generally determined by standardized tests, including an oral language proficiency test to determine oral communication ability in English and/or the reading/language arts portion of a norm-referenced test (e.g., Iowa Test of Basic Skills). Students who score in the "limited English proficient" (legislative terminology) range are eligible for special program support such as bilingual education and ESL. Parental approval for placement in these programs is generally required.

As students become more proficient in their new language, they have the potential for **reclassification or exit.** Again, schools use standardized measures—norm-referenced or criterion-referenced tests or a combination of both—to make this determination. If students score above a certain predetermined score, they are moved to grade-level classrooms and receive instruction in settings not specifically designed for English language learners.

Even when students move to the all English setting of the grade-level classroom, schools continue to **monitor student progress.** While English language learners may score in the exit range, they may still struggle with the academic language needed for school achievement. At times, students may be moved back to special language programs if adequate progress is not made.

Since special language programs generally receive additional funding through state and federal sources, **program evaluation** is an ongoing requirement. So schools continually monitor the effectiveness of their bilingual and ESL programs to determine whether they are meeting students' needs and whether students are making the academic progress needed to eventually graduate.

Finally, because the public eye is constantly focused on education, **accountability** measures are also a part of the assessment requirements. Most states now have educational standards and mandated exit tests for high school graduation. In addition, schools are rated by their scores on norm-referenced assessments, the percentage of students completing college entrance exams, and dropout rates. These high-stakes measures and public scrutiny mean that schools carefully monitor language minority students to ensure academic progress.

Once the child enters the classroom, teachers use additional assessment measures to gauge instructional planning efforts and to monitor language development. Perhaps the most difficult decision initially for ESL teachers is taking any baseline data they may have through initial assessment and determining where to begin. Once children are in the classroom, observation can be coupled with checklists of student behaviors or anecdotal records (e.g., whether the child participated in an activity and at what level). If children respond only during nonverbal activities, they may be in the beginning stages of language acquisition or the preproduction phase. However, teachers cannot discount other factors such as shyness or home difficulties. To assist teachers in their efforts to get to know students, we have taken the factors presented earlier that affect language acquisition and school achievement and constructed a checklist in Table 1.1. Using these points, teachers can collect information along the way and keep a folder of observations about each child in the classroom.

In addition to this survey, many of the trade books and instructional activities just shared also serve as assessment techniques or as sources of information for the checklist. For instance, an All about Me book or a photo essay of the class provides an opportunity for students to merely illustrate or to label or write information about themselves. The level of contribution and the type of language produced can help pinpoint students' language levels.

The importance of determining student background and language proficiency levels is closely linked to the selection of appropriate materials and activities. Most teachers we work with still struggle with an accurate determination of children's language levels. Consequently, they worry about the types of materials they choose for the children. Are the materials too easy, too hard, appropriate in terms of interest and prior knowledge, and so on? In the following chapters, we not only recommend a host of children's and young

TABLE 1.1   Getting to Know English Language Learners

Student name:
Student age:
Home country/born in U.S.:
Language(s) spoken:
How long has the student been in the U.S?
Previous schooling (home country):
Previous schooling (U.S.):
School attendance:
Family information:
List family members or guardians at home/language(s) spoken:
Oral Language Proficiency Test score (or teacher observation of English proficiency):
Level of student knowledge of home language:
Other information and observations:

adult books to use in the classroom, but we will also address the issue of teacher selection criteria.

Summary

In this chapter, we focused on the changing immigration patterns in the United States and the need for trained teachers to meet the linguistic needs in our changing classrooms. In addition, we provided an overview of the types of programs designed to assist English language learners toward proficiency in their new language as well as noting the varied backgrounds that English language learners bring to the language learning process. Finally, we recommended using children's and young adult books as sources of information about children in our diverse classrooms. In the next chapter, we will explore the link between language acquisition and the use of authentic materials such as children's and young adult literature.

2 Language Acquisition and Literature-Based Instruction

A journey of a thousand miles begins with a single step.
—Lao Tzu (604–531 B.C.)

"Your whole person is affected as you struggle to reach beyond the confines of your first language and into a new language, a new culture, a new way of thinking, feeling, and acting. Total commitment, total involvement, a total physical, intellectual, and emotional response is necessary" (Brown, 1994, p. 1). H. Douglas Brown's comments remind us that learning a new language is difficult and very time-consuming work. Yet each year countless children enter our schools in America and are expected to master the curricula of grades K–12 while at the same time learning a completely new language. The increasing number of English language learners encountering the demands of both language and content mastery requires us to closely examine factors that can contribute to their success. Therefore, in this chapter we explore the complex issue of language acquisition and how to use what we know about language and the language acquisition process in the classroom to more effectively teach English language learners. Finally, we also examine the powerful role that literature can play in the language acquisition process. In this chapter, we address the following questions.

- What is language?
- What does it mean to be competent in a language?
- How do individuals acquire a language?
- What strategies are most effective in helping students acquire another language?
- How do the principles of language acquisition support a literature-based instructional approach?
- How do teachers match books to their English language learners?

Let's begin our discussion with a consideration of exactly what language is.

What Is Language?

Defining language is a complicated process. Language is more than the sounds and symbols used to convey meaning; there is an affective and cultural component to language as well. Each of us uses language to communicate, but we don't all sound the same even if we speak the same language. We communicate within different cultures composed of various speech communities that may have varying rules for language usage. For instance, at home we speak one way, but at work or school we adapt to other rules of speech. Moreover, males and females differ in their use of language (Tannen, 1990). In case you are wondering how we ever learn to use language given this complexity, we would add that language is systematic with certain universal characteristics. Language is composed of the following structural elements: phonology, morphology, and syntax (Fromkin & Rodman, 1993; Delahunty & Garvey, 1994; Piper, 1998).

The first element, **phonology,** involves the sound system of a language, including the individual sounds and how they are produced. Children learning their first language have considerable time to become familiar with its sounds as they listen to caregivers and the interactions within their environment (Lindfors, 1987). Through listening they pick up the unique sounds and rhythm of language. With encouragement and sufficient listening, they begin to experiment with the sounds of their language—babbling, cooing, and eventually trying their hand at forming words. Continued support allows all children, barring hearing or speech difficulties, to articulate the individual sounds of the language and to combine these to make words and then to construct sentences.

The second element, **morphology,** deals with the composition of words (Fromkin & Rodman, 1994). Morphemes are the smallest units of meaning. Some morphemes can stand alone, as in the case of free or base morphemes while others are bound to other morphemes but still possess a meaning component, as in the case of affixes (prefixes and suffixes), the past tense marker (*ed*), third-person singular verb markers (*s* and *es*), and noun plural markers ('s' and 'es'). All words are made up of one or more morphemes as in the following examples: helpful = help (base morpheme) + ful (suffix); helps = help (verb and base morpheme) + s (third-person singular marker). Although this sounds quite complex and rather advanced, children actually grasp this at a subconscious level. While they cannot state the rules for combining nouns or verbs with plural or past tense markers or base morphemes with prefixes and suffixes, they manipulate these pieces of language, often creating new and unique words. Shel Silverstein's poem, "The Twistable, Turnable Man" (*A Light in the Attic,* 1981) provides a glimpse of this very process. Along with commonly accepted words, Silverstein combines suffixes with base morphemes to create totally new nonsense words that are highly descriptive—a sort of wordplay that we often see in poetry. Take for instance, the beginning lines with his newly coined words "turnable" and "pullable." This process of affixation, or the addition of prefixes and suffixes, is the most common way that words are added to our language (Andrews, 1998). So, some of the "nonsense" words that our language learners create today via their experimentation with morphemes may become established parts of the language in the future.

Finally, **syntax** involves a combination of words into phrasal groups and of phrasal groups into sentences. While the sentence is the basic syntactic unit, within sentences are other building blocks of sentences. For instance, sentences may contain **phrases,** grammatical equivalents to a single word with no subject or predicate (e.g., the big book), and **clauses,** groups of words with their own subjects and predicates included in a larger sentence (e.g., because the big book had such good repetitive language. . .). Sentences then combine phrases and/or clauses to become the largest unit of grammatical description (e.g., because the big book had such good repetitive language, the teacher chose that book for the read aloud activity with her class of English language learners). Teachers can encourage student awareness of these building blocks of language by utilizing the poetic language of picture books such as Judy Nayer's *A Tree Can Be . . .* (1994) for noun phrases ("A tree can be . . . a place to rest, a place to play" or Douglas Florian's poem "My Robot" (*Bing, Bang, Boing,* 1994) with examples of verb phrases for the chores in store for the robot. For clauses, teachers can turn to cumulative repetition books based on the pattern from "This is the house that Jack built" using works by Madeline Dunphy—*Here Is the Tropical Rain Forest* (1994), *Here Is the Arctic Winter* (1993), and *Here Is the African Savanna* (1999)—that demonstrate strings of embedded clauses.

We see that despite the complexity of language "children exhibit a remarkable ability to infer the phonological, structural, lexical, and semantic system of language" (Brown, 1994, p. 36). This innate sense of language comes into play with works such as Lewis Carroll's classic "Jabberwocky" from *Through the Looking Glass* (1997). Children discern parts of speech and guess the meanings of words even though the author has created a poem with nonsense language. Graeme Base's illustrated version of "Jabberwocky" (1989) is a great resource for this activity. To be sure, some students enter the language learning situation with more awareness, either consciously learned or subconsciously acquired, of the elements of English phonology, morphology and syntax. Students from a Roman alphabet background may find many similarities in the phonological representations of English and their language. However, for students from a non-Roman alphabet background, the home language and English will have numerous differences. Using literature, teachers create an increased awareness of the structural elements of English. Through read alouds, students encounter words with various phonemic patterns, as in Nancy Shaw's series of books about those lovable sheep: *Sheep in a Jeep* (1986), *Sheep on a Ship* (1989), *Sheep in a Shop* (1991), *Sheep Out to Eat* (1992), *Sheep Take a Hike* (1994), and *Sheep Trick or Treat* (1997). In particular, poetry provides an opportunity to talk about different word orderings since authors often use poetic license to create special effects with words. Literature is full of examples of the structure of our language with its infinite range of combinations of morphemes to create words and phrases and clauses to construct sentences.

Why bother with this technical information about the structural elements of language? Moreover, why call students' attention to them? First, most professional organizations recommend that teachers have some knowledge of linguistics and language as part of their professional training. Our knowledge about language helps us understand what the student is learning and, further, how best to implement lessons to help the student acquire English. TESOL (1975), for example, recommends that teachers should understand the nature of language, language varieties including social, regional, and functional—and the structure and development of the English language systems.

Second, and most importantly, Brown (1994, p. 6) notes that "your understanding of the components of language will determine to a large extent how you teach a language."

Perhaps the very structure of language—phonemes, morphemes, syntax—encourages some to view language as discrete bits to be presented in pieces for students to put together; *but* we see language as a whole, not as a discrete set of subskills. Therefore, we support a balanced literacy approach that introduces whole text through literature and other authentic materials to students, and encourages language learners to expand on their subconscious feel for language in a natural way.

What Does It Mean to Be Competent in a Language?

Since our description of language includes so much detail on the structural elements of language, readers may conclude that knowledge of the phonemes, morphemes, and syntax is sufficient to help a student become competent in a language. Yet we have all worked with language learners who understand English structurally but still have difficulty communicating. One reason is related to semantics, or the meaning component of language. Choosing the right word to use in the correct circumstance is an advanced skill. Hence, many young children and English language learners struggle with wording issues. In addition, **linguistic** or **grammatical knowledge** in a language is only part of the journey to becoming a strategic user of a language (Hymes, 1970). **Linguistic performance** requires more than knowledge of the sound system, morphological structures, sentence patterns, and vocabulary. Communicative competence—the ability to communicate in a meaningful fashion with as few distractions as possible—involves juggling several additional components of language, including the following.

■ **Topic.** Knowing what topics are appropriate or inappropriate for various occasions and settings is a critical to language use. Young children learning their first language, for example, share intimate home experiences in public, much to their parents' chagrin. Because each language is shaped by differing cultural norms, English language learners may err in this respect as well.

■ **Setting.** Tied closely to the issue of topic is the setting of language use. Competent language users are aware of how setting affects both the topic and the manner of communication. For instance, the casual interaction style of American schools may surprise or shock English language learners who are accustomed to more one-way, even authoritarian, teacher communication. In American classrooms, we prompt the class for input, concerns, and questions. English language learners may feel awkward with this, and teachers may need to coach them to become active questioners during instruction.

■ **Role of Participants.** Understanding your role in an interaction helps you adopt an appropriate verbal and nonverbal attitude and make wise language choices. Individuals who are equal in status communicate using similar norms or rules of interaction. If two individuals have differing status (e.g., parent–child or teacher–student), the norms of interaction will be different. Peers interact using more informal language and casual nonverbal styles, while individuals with dissimilar status adopt more formal language and nonverbal behaviors. A common example used in training is the issue of eye contact. In mainstream American culture, we expect children to look at us when we reprimand them. However, many cultures consider this nonverbal behavior inappropriate; downcast eyes are instead the norm. Many of Allen Say's picture books portray nonverbal behaviors such as posture and eye contact within Asian and Asian American cultural boundaries. *Tea with Milk* (1999) is one example with illustrations of characters interacting within a cultural context.

■ **Register.** Most of us have different styles of speaking, or registers. In one day, we may shift our style to adapt to the setting, topic, and our role within an interaction. Beginning English language learners are struggling to get any message out and therefore will probably not be able to vary their style of language until they have more language proficiency. Indeed, this may make an English language learner appear more distant, even in casual conversation. Teachers can coach students in the subtleties of language through role plays in language variation after read alouds of books that demonstrate various styles of speech. In Kevin Henke's *Chrysanthemum* (1991), for example, students can see how the protagonist struggles with having a name that is very different, how her classmates tease her, and how her parents reassure her.

Beyond the distinction between knowledge and performance of a language, Halliday (1978) argues that linguistic competence includes the learner's ability to relate the components of a language to the functions for language use. He proposed that our skill in negotiating language functions (e.g., greeting, interrupting, complimenting, reprimanding, apologizing, changing the subject, etc.) is an indication of our competence in a language. We spend a great deal of class time on some of Halliday's functions, such as informing and reporting information, but there are other language uses that we might include in the classroom. These functions could provide students with interpersonal skills along with developing their language. For instance, knowing how to change the subject and to politely interrupt are actually very handy skills to possess. Halliday so influenced ideas about language learning that an approach called the Notional-Functional Syllabus has been based on his work (Wilkins, 1976, 1979). Basically, the Notional-Functional Syllabus is a planning template for second language and foreign language instruction with the curriculum structured around Halliday's functions. Humorous books about manners and etiquette—such as the classic *What Do You Say, Dear?* and *What Do You Do, Dear?* both by Sesyle Joslin (1986), *Perfect Pigs* by Mark Brown and S. Krensky (1993), *It's a Spoon, Not a Shovel* by Caralyn Buehner (1995), and *Manners* by Aliki (1990)—help students learn about social politeness in less didactic and more playful ways.

In summary, we see that communicative competence in a language is a complex task, requiring a combination of grammatical knowledge along with sociolinguistic competence. Beginning English language learners struggle with mastering the grammatical knowledge along with correctly applying the sociolinguistic rules of the language and understanding the myriad of language functions. Packaged programs focused on linguistic knowledge provide only half the answers to the language puzzle. A balanced approach to literacy using authentic materials and encouraging students to read, discuss, and respond to text fosters strategic language users. Let's now examine the road to communicative competence and how we acquire a language and develop proficiency.

How Do Individuals Acquire a Language?

Theories of First Language Acquisition

Language acquisition is an internal cognitive process and, as such, is difficult to observe. We have only the overt linguistic behavior as data for our theories; hence, many disagreements exist about how individuals acquire a language. For teachers to have a better understanding of their English language learners, they must possess some awareness of the language acquisition process that will lead them to the most effective strategies for enhancing student growth. A complete understanding of second language acquisition really starts with the theories surrounding first language acquisition, so let's consider for a moment several of the conflicting theories: behaviorism, innatism, and interactionism.

Behaviorism is a major learning theory grounded in the belief that we learn through stimulus, response, and reinforcement. Behaviorists believe that "language is a set of habits that can be acquired by a process of conditioning" (Brown, 1994, p. 34). This theory of language acquisition has come under a tremendous amount of criticism from those who argue that "such conditioning is much too slow and inefficient a process to account for the acquisition of a phenomenon as complex as language" (Brown, 1994, p. 34). For instance, most sentences used by first language learners are original and have never been heard by the child. Nevertheless, behaviorism led to a major language-teaching approach known as the audiolingual method.

In contrast to the view that language is acquired by responding to external stimuli, **innatists** (or nativists) believe that language acquisition is innately determined and that the linguistic environment surrounding the learner has a minor effect. In other words, "we are born with a built-in device of some kind that predisposes us to language acquisition— to a systematic perception of language around us, resulting in the construction of an internalized system of language" (Brown, 1994, p. 25). Chomsky, a major player in the innatist movement, proposed that we are born with a "language acquisition device" (LAD) that enables us to distinguish speech sounds from other sounds in the environment, organize linguistic events into various classes that can later be refined, understand that only a certain kind of linguistic system is possible and that other kinds are not, and engage in constant evaluation of the developing linguistic system so as to construct the simplest possible system out of the linguistic data encountered (McNeil, 1966). Chomsky's idea of the LAD was further expanded into a system of universal linguistic rules, or universal grammar. Universal grammar research "is attempting to discover what it is that all children, regardless of their environmental stimuli (the language(s) they hear around them) bring to the language acquisition process" (Brown, p. 25).

While innatists would largely discount the effect of environmental stimuli, **interactionists,** on the other hand, argue the importance of input from caregivers. As Berko-Gleason (1982, p. 20) notes, "while it used to be generally held that mere *exposure* to language is sufficient to set the child's language generating machinery in motion, it is now clear that, in order for successful first language acquisition to take place *interaction,* rather than exposure, is required; children do not learn language from overhearing the conversations of others or from listening to the radio, instead they acquire it in the context of being spoken to." Thus, caregivers play a critical role, providing input and modeling language as a means of negotiating one's world. Based on caregiver input, "the child is constantly forming hypotheses . . . and then testing those hypotheses in speech (comprehension). As the child's language develops, those hypotheses get continually revised, reshaped, or sometimes abandoned" (Brown, 1994, p. 26).

Second Language Acquisition Theories

Researchers have considered the relationship of theories of first and second (other) language acquisition and have asked the following questions (Peregoy & Boyle, 2001, pp. 40–41).

- "Is second language acquired the same way as the first?"
- "If so, what are the implications for instruction?"
- "Because first language acquisition is so successfully accomplished, should teachers replicate its conditions to promote second language acquisition? If so, how?"

Keeping these questions in mind, let's look again at the three theories of first language acquisition and see how they relate to second language learning.

As noted earlier, behaviorism had a powerful influence on methods of language learning. The belief that repetition and reinforcement would facilitate second language acquisition led to the development of the audiolingual approach and materials that revolved around the repetition and memorization of dialogues—in other words, stimulus, response, and reinforcement. Students learning via this method soon found that memorized dialogues were not sufficient for spontaneous communication and higher-level interactions.

Rejecting the artificial input of the behaviorist-influenced audiolingual approach, Stephen Krashen (1981) proposed five hypotheses of second language acquisition that fit the innatist theoretical framework, emphasizing the innate process within the learner. A brief description of each hypothesis follows.

First, Krashen makes a distinction between learning a language and acquiring one. In the **acquisition versus learning hypothesis,** he argues that learning is a more formal, classroom-driven process focused on the rules and structure of a language, while acquisition is a natural (or innate) process such as occurs in first language acquisition. All of us have experienced both processes although we know more about language learning since schooling involves heavy doses of learning. On the other hand, we remember little about acquiring our first language because we were engaged in the process at an early age. Others, however, have experience acquiring a second language through immersion, by living in another country and having to communicate on a daily basis to get needs met.

Like the innatist's view of universal grammar, Krashen argues in the **natural order hypothesis** that grammar structures (e.g., passive and active voice) are acquired in a fairly predictable order. This order of acquisition for first and other languages is similar, but not exactly the same. Certain structures (e.g., plural of nouns) are acquired early in the acquisition process, while other structures (e.g., the third-person singular verb) are acquired late. Some structures are acquired in groups, several at a time.

Next, Krashen suggests in the **monitor hypothesis** that we have a monitor or editor that can be put into play in conscious learning situations. However, certain conditions must be present before the monitor, our conscious learning of language, can be used, including adequate time to edit our language, a focus on form or thinking about correctness, and consciousness of rules.

In the **input hypothesis,** Krashen notes that the most critical component for acquiring a language is adequate input that is fine-tuned to a learner's level of proficiency—something Krashen terms **comprehensible input.** The input hypothesis stresses receptive skills because students understand more than they can produce. Consequently, teachers should provide abundant comprehensible input via meaningful activities and reduce formal study with worksheet and skills drill. In addition, Krashen suggests that comprehensible input should include contextualized language a bit beyond students' current level of competence. In this way, teachers continue to push students' language ability forward.

Finally, the affective dimension of acquiring and learning a language is just as important as the cognitive dimension. In the **affective filter hypothesis,** Krashen examines certain attitudinal variables. If the classroom situation is tense, there is a high affective filter, and learners are anxious and less open to input. If the classroom situation is relaxed, there is a low affective filter, resulting in relaxed learners who are receptive to input; hence, greater language acquisition occurs.

Krashen's five hypotheses have been used to shape an instructional orientation labeled the "Natural Approach" (Krashen & Terrell, 1983). Natural Approach lessons provide relaxed acquisition-like situations with rich, understandable input through authentic materials and contextualized vocabulary presentations, gestures, visuals, and hands-on activities.

In a sample lesson from a unit on families using this instructional orientation, for example, teachers can use picture books or poems to introduce vocabulary (e.g., different family members, etc.). Some great sources of poems about families are found in the following collections: *Big Book of Families* (Anholt & Anholt, 1998), *Families, Families* (Hopkins, 1998), and *Fathers, Mothers, Sisters, Brothers* (Hoberman, 1991). Using pictures from magazines or elsewhere showing families of varying sizes and a variety of family members, the teacher holds up each picture, describes it, and points to the various family members: "In this photo, there is a family with five members—mother, father, grandfather, son, and daughter." As each photo is described, the teacher hands the photo to a student. After numerous photos have been described with the key vocabulary items repeated many times, the teacher begins a questioning sequence: Who has a picture of a family with five members? Who has a picture of a family with a mother? A grandfather? Students are able to hold up the photos and respond nonverbally; the teacher can elaborate by repeating the description and key vocabulary. Next, the teacher can describe his/her own family using a diagram of a family tree on the board or overhead and labeling key relationships to reinforce the vocabulary just presented. Then students can draw a family tree and label the relationships, or they can use a sample family tree for a fictional family and place flash cards with the key vocabulary denoting family relationships. Finally, they write a short paragraph or essay describing their family. Beginning English language learners simply draw an illustration of their family and then label or write short sentences and phrases.

The idea of comprehensible input is extended in the last second language acquisition theory, the interactionist perspective (Peregoy & Boyle, 2001). Input is provided by many individuals—parents, teachers, siblings, relatives, and friends. While this input is important, students must move beyond receptive skills and interact in their new language.

Helping students understand input in English and enabling them to respond requires individuals to make adaptations in their speech. Thus, caregiver speech—also called motherese, foreigner talk, and teacher talk (Krashen & Terrell, 1983; Brown, 1994)—provides the support and cues needed to facilitate understanding and to encourage English language learners to interact. According to Patsy Gwaltney, an elementary teacher, "acquiring a second language is the same as the 'teaching' I did for my own children from the time they were born." While interaction is critical to learning any language, English language learners have a particular need for interaction in the classroom since many return home to a first language only setting, resulting in few opportunities to hear or practice English. The interactionists, then, focus on both input and output and the types of speech adaptations needed to foster students' communicative efforts.

A Timeline for Language Acquisition

Our linking of first and second language acquisition theory is easily supported by the wide body of research that indicates the similarity of linguistic and cognitive processes of first and second language learning (Ravem, 1968; Milon, 1974; Natalicio & Natalicio, 1971; Dulay & Burt, 1974; Ervin-Tripp, 1974). For instance, Dulay & Burt (1974) note that children use a creative construction process to learn a second language, just as they do to learn their first language. In addition, researchers have noted a striking similarity between the stages of language acquisition for both the first and another language.

Preproduction, or the listening phase of language acquisition, takes place in the first few months of life. Most children spend up to nine months or more listening and storing up knowledge of the sounds and rhythms of their home language. Individuals demonstrate understanding and growing awareness of language during the preproduction phase by responding nonverbally. Regardless of the age of an individual who is learning another language, there is still a preproduction stage of language acquisition. This silent period (Krashen & Terrell, 1983) of language learning ranges from a few hours or days to many months, as noted by Michelle Marshall, a kindergarten teacher: "I had three students that spoke no English. Little by little they all began to speak at different times. One day the child that would not talk at all just started talking in whole complete sentences."

Daily read alouds to English language learners at the preproduction stage using picture books that provide cues to meaning are an excellent way to give students a jump start on their development of English. Teachers can choose from a variety of titles with simple language and a focus on vocabulary, such as Cathryn Falwell's counting book, *Feast for 10* (1993), Lois Ehlert's alphabet book, *Eating the Alphabet: Fruit and Vegetables from A to Z* (1989), and Tana Hoban's concept book, *Over, Under, and Through and Other Spatial Concepts* (1973) to provide a beginning foundation in English. Many counting, alphabet, and concept books can help provide the reinforcement needed at this stage.

As children listen and become familiar with a language, they eventually move to the **early production** phase. In first language acquisition, children generally progress to this stage between nine months to two years of age or so. In the early production phase, language learners begin to experiment by producing one- or two-word responses. For second (other) language learners, this process may last up to six months, and the vocabulary emphasis during this time centers on basic survival needs. Books with a rhythmic quality and just a few words per page are appealing to individuals at this stage of language development. For instance, Dr. Seuss' *The Foot Book* (1968) highlights all kinds of feet (left, right, wet, dry, etc.) with basic vocabulary that is ideal for this stage in the process of language acquisition. The concept books of Donald Crews, such as *Freight Train* (1978) and *Truck* (1980), are also helpful at this stage.

Speech emergence, the third phase in the timeline of language acquisition, is a period of phrase and short-sentence generation. When learning a first language, this phase extends from approximately two to five years of age. It is a time of great experimentation—trial and error—as children construct their knowledge base through hypotheses about the correct vocabulary and structure of language. For second (other) language learners, the speech emergence stage may take up to one year. Throughout these early phases of acquisition, much of the emphasis is on basic interpersonal communication and context-embedded language (face-to-face language or language accompanied by visual cues to meaning). Simple books with repetitive language patterns such as Eric Carle's *Today Is Monday* (1993) and Mem Fox's *Hattie and the Fox* (1987) encourage children at this stage to chime in with the recurring phrase. Authors like Eric Carle, Mem Fox, Nancy Tafuri, Bruce McMillan, Bill Martin, Jr., Pat Hutchins, Tana Hoban, and Douglas Florian have established repertoires of award-winning titles that provide formulaic language that is still literary and engaging.

By age five, individuals learning their first language reach the stage of **intermediate fluency.** At this point, they are able to verbally negotiate their environment and are prepared to enter school and begin the task of linking their acquisition of language with academic concepts. Second language learners take one to two more years to reach intermediate fluency once the earlier stages have been mastered. However, we need to remember that English language learners may enter the second language acquisition process at any age—from child or teen to adult—and the amount of time needed to reach intermediate fluency is substantial. Using literature that addresses academic concepts with simple language helps pave the way for both English language development and content knowledge. For instance, Mary Lankford's *Is It Dark? Is It Light?* (1991) offers a series of questions and answers that describe the concept in question—the moon. At the end, we learn the equivalent terms for moon in a variety of languages. Ann Morris' simple nonfiction books introduce objects and concepts (such as bread or families) with photographs of examples from around the world.

From the intermediate fluency stage, individuals move to the difficult task of acquiring academic content fluency. Academic language proficiency is the ability we most closely associate with achievement in school. Throughout our lives, additional formal schooling and informal education help us increase our ability to engage in academic discourse. For English language learners in our schools, acquiring a high level of academic language fluency may take from five to seven years. This may not appear to be such a hardship to those English language learners entering American schools in prekindergarten or kindergarten. However, consider that the child learning his/her home language already has a firm grasp of that language by the time of entry into school. This head start is multiplied each day because native English speakers are encountering content concepts in a language with which they already feel comfortable. What children must possess for success in the everyday classroom are the formal listening, speaking, reading, and writing skills needed for academic content (Cummins, 1980). Acquiring that level of language proficiency for the English language learner may take five years or more (Thomas & Collier, 1995). *I Hate English* (Levine, 1995) is a picture book that depicts the struggle of a young girl who is a new immigrant to the United States and worries that she will lose touch with her native heritage, culture, and language. Many students at the intermediate stage of language acquisition may identify with her situation and express similar feelings.

Factors Affecting Second Language Acquisition

Looking at the preceding chronology often prompts individuals to believe that language acquisition is an orderly, uniform, and predictable process for all students. Nothing could be farther from the truth. While we can expect a fairly typical progression of the language characteristics displayed along the way, from a silent period to the one- or two-word utterance stage and then on to short sentences, the timing of that progression and the depth of language ability depend on many variables. Michelle Marshall, a kindergarten teacher, confirms this noting that "there's a great difference in students that have access to models of literacy in the home. They develop literacy skills quicker." We highlighted some of these factors in Chapter 1. Now we examine additional factors, both internal and external to the learner, that affect not only the rate of second language acquisition but also the extent of language ability that a student develops.

In terms of the learner, **age** affects language acquisition. In our schools, English language learners are generally older (at least age four in prekindergarten or age five in kindergarten) when they encounter their second (other) language, and thus they are more cognitively developed than infants and toddlers piecing together their first language. Older students have more world knowledge and, therefore, more information about language in general to bring to the process of second language acquisition. Indeed, Brown (1994, p. 29) notes that "what children learn about language is determined by what they already know about the world."

On the other hand, being older creates some difficulties for English language learners (Krashen & Terrell, 1983; Richard-Amato, 1996). With age come increased inhibitions and anxiety; students feel awkward using a new sound system and are more frustrated with the lack of vocabulary and language structures at their disposal. Also, older students may have poor attitudes and less motivation to learn their new language, depending on their personal and school situations. Finally, in the initial stages of second language learning, the knowledge of the first language may interfere with learning English when items are structurally or semantically similar.

Young children, on the other hand, have few of these concerns. Because they are in the process of experimenting with life in general, the trial-and-error process of language learning seems more natural. Moreover, the sounds of the new language are one more opportunity for the typical wordplay of childhood. Consequently, we find that older students, especially adults, outperform children both initially and in the long run, and that children are more likely to be superior in the area of pronunciation only (Brown, 1994).

Researchers have also studied various **personality factors** of the learner (e.g, self-esteem, inhibition, risk taking, anxiety, empathy, extroversion, motivation, etc.) and their potential relationship to language learning. Self-esteem is an important variable in language learning (Brodkey & Shore, 1976; Gardner & Lambert, 1972). Heyde (1979) found that self-esteem correlated positively with oral production, which represents a higher risk. Inhibitions limit learning, particularly learning a language (Guiora, Beit-Hallami, Brannon, Dull, & Scovel, 1972). Individuals acquiring a language must make mistakes as they hypothesize and move through the trial-and-error process of testing their hunches. It is this very process that causes students to raise their defenses and block out meaningful language input.

Risk-taking behavior is closely related to both inhibition and self-esteem. As we noted earlier, learning a language requires making guesses or taking risks. The silent student who is unwilling to take risks and appear foolish may settle into some permanent patterns of errors in his/her language use (Beebe, 1983). Linked to self-esteem, inhibitions, and risk-taking behavior is anxiety. Language learners might be anxious about the learning situation or their life in general. Whatever the case, high anxiety blocks input. Conversely, researchers have identified debilitative and facilitative anxiety (Bailey, 1983), noting that some anxiety or concern is positive and helps facilitate learning.

Finally, various **external factors** such as the quality of instruction, the classroom environment, and the type of input the learner receives can have an effect on language acquisition. In terms of the quality of instruction, we advocate a balanced literacy approach that integrates listening, speaking, reading, and writing through the use of authentic materials. Such an instructional process comes closest to furnishing students with a real language experience much like learning their first language. Within the classroom environment, the teacher needs to be a role model for the effective use of English and should demonstrate the importance of literacy development by surrounding students with a print-rich environment—bulletin boards, classroom library, learning centers, and so on. The teacher also shapes the classroom environment by accepting and validating students' diverse linguistic and cultural backgrounds.

We have highlighted in this section the many similarities in the process of first and second (other) language acquisition. Yet, there are differences. English language learners bring some special needs to the language acquisition process that are different from—or at least more pronounced than—those of native English speakers (Krashen, 1981; Freeman & Freeman, 1994; Diaz-Rico & Weed, 1995; Gibbons, 1993; Ovando & Collier, 1998). These include four critical differences: a lack of command of English vocabulary, a lack of proficiency in English text structure, a lack of appropriate content background, and a lack of knowledge of American culture. As English language learners begin the process of language acquisition, they master some basic English communicative vocabulary needed to negotiate their environment, but they have wide gaps in the vocabulary required for academic tasks. Alphabet books, survey (nonfiction) books, and browsing books (like the Eyewitness series), in particular, are among the many great resources that assist with vocabulary development.

A fluent English speaker uses the sentences and overall text structure as a means of comprehending; they instinctively know the subordinate ideas. English language learners, on the other hand, get bogged down in text because they do not pick up the cues about what is structurally important and what is unimportant. In content study, English language learners may be dealing with topics about which they have very little background knowledge (e.g., American history). If they have experiences with these classroom topics, their understandings may be different or incomplete in relation to the material. Yet, even when their experiences are appropriate, students often disregard their knowledge, assuming that it has no relevance to the task because of the language difference. Even when English language learners have had some schooling in English in their home country, they lack exposure to American ways and regional language that would help them interpret references in text. Consequently, teachers need to preview material to highlight these items and bring them to students' attention. In the next section, we apply our knowledge about language acquisition to the classroom and explore instructional strategies to scaffold students' literacy development in English.

What Strategies Are Most Effective in Helping Students Acquire Another Language?

When working with English language learners, our instructional strategies should be guided by sound principles of language acquisition. Thus, we begin this section with four important principles teachers should use as starting points when working with English language learners (Krashen & Terrell, 1983):

- Focus on the ability to communicate.
- Comprehension precedes production.
- Production emerges in stages.
- Lower the affective filter of students.

English language learners will not acquire language by practicing speaking or repeating phonics drills or patterned dialogues. "Contextualized, appropriate, meaningful communication in the second language seems to be the best possible practice the second language learner could engage in" (Brown, 1994, p. 69). We see an example of contextualized language in Box 2.1, as an eighth-grade Vietnamese student shares her experiences learning English.

How can we put these guiding principles into play in classrooms? Providing some baseline information on the diversity of linguistic proficiency levels helps teachers plan instruction accordingly, shaped, of course, by the guiding principles of second language acquisition. For instructional purposes in this book, we will refer to three linguistic proficiency levels: beginning, intermediate, and advanced. These terms do not refer to grade levels in school. Rather, they describe the types of language characteristics that students display.

BOX 2.1

Voices from the Field: Contextualized Language

Most of my success goes to my ESL teacher and my cousins for all the extra time they spent with me after school. My teacher turned learning into fun by playing games, taking students on field trips to places where they had to speak English, using music and poetry as a tool for students to learn to communicate, and being understanding when students had a hard day. I don't know how she does it. She just teaches people to speak English. It is really neat.

These are very rough categories, and as with other labels, teachers will see tremendous variation within any one level. For instance, in the beginning level, students may range from newly arrived immigrants who speak no English (beginning beginners) to more advanced beginners ready to move to the intermediate developmental level. Next, we describe student characteristics displayed at each of the levels of language proficiency and suggest some instructional strategies that are appropriate for each linguistic proficiency level.

Linguistic Proficiency Levels

Beginning Proficiency Level.   Beginning English language learners include individuals in the preproduction (silent period), early emergence, and speech emergence stages. The range of language ability may vary greatly, since this category may include recent immigrants along with individuals who have been in the United States for some time, and even native born English language learners. Beginners generally speak and understand little or no English when they enter the classroom; they are silent and not active contributors. Yet even in the silent period, beginning English language learners are acquiring language, focusing on the sound and flow of the target language. They become aware of English intonation, speed, pause patterns, and variation in loudness and pitch, and they begin to discriminate between consonant and vowel sounds. In terms of listening comprehension, beginners can respond to limited English functions such as classroom commands (e.g., Line up), questions (e.g., Who knows the answer?), and directions (e.g., Turn to page 10).

As students become more and more comfortable with their new language, they venture out of their silent period and try to speak. At this point of development, English language learners use very limited language, drawing on their stored knowledge from listening and observing during the silent period. Rarely generating much original language, they most often repeat after the teacher, peers, or other speakers or employ strategies such as telegraphic (using the fewest words possible) and formulaic language (language formulas, which include paired statements such as greetings: Hi! How are you? I am fine.). They also use gestures and facial expressions to indicate the meaning of what they are saying.

Because beginners are new to English and perhaps to school English, they possess limited vocabulary and tend to use egocentric speech—focused on "I/me" that they use to get basic needs met (e.g., I want . . .). Their early speech attempts include literal or factual language using one- or two-word responses and short phrases that typically focus on communicating the most important ideas rather than on elaborating. However, they are experimenting with language and trying out their hunches about how things work. As they interact, they focus on language related to the knowledge and comprehension level—who, what, which, where—rather than analysis level language of how and why. Because they lack fluency or do not understand a question or comment, they may engage in unrelated information sharing, trying to communicate with whatever English words are at their disposal, even if their language repertoire is limited and not germane to the topic at hand. As beginning English language learners become more comfortable with the language, they pick out an increasing number of previously learned vocabulary items from the blur of spoken English and use vocabulary encountered in written form in content areas. Still, misunderstandings abound as students try to decipher spoken and written language and miscue on words or expressions. Finally, writing is very limited, but beginners may write simple sentences with direct assistance.

Observing the preceding characteristics of beginning level English language learners, teachers can fashion instructional opportunities to extend language development. To acquaint students with the rhythm and sound of their new language, teachers can use understandable verbal presentations and demonstrations as well as reading aloud books with very patterned, repetitive language. For phonemic concerns or awareness of the sound–symbol relationship (a symbol has an associated sound), environmental print from logos, labels, and boxtops provides examples of words to solidify sound–symbol relationships. Since beginners focus on the concrete and functional, abstract language should be avoided as much as possible. Lessons should be drawn from relevant language and functions of language (e.g., greeting/leave taking, etc.). Role plays of familiar language situations assist students by providing comprehensible input. Picture books like *Yo! Yes?* by Chris Raschka (1993) or *Today Is Monday* (1993) and *Have You Seen My Cat?* (1987) by Eric Carle provide both visual and textual examples of the conversational use of language.

Beginners are careful observers and gain a great deal of their understanding through recognition of nonverbal body language. Allowing more physical rather than spoken response to lessons helps students feel comfortable and furnishes the needed clues to meaning. One method of creating active nonverbal lessons is through the Total Physical Response (TPR) technique (Asher, 1982), in which students respond to verbal commands (e.g., stand up, sit down, etc.), move throughout the room in response to verbal instructions, and work together at their desks to sequence manipulatives.

In terms of interaction, role plays offer practice in classroom routines and the cultural interaction differences in greetings. For instance, Karen Badt's *Greetings* (1994) can be used to discuss cultural differences in greeting and leave-taking behavior that students can then role play.

During read alouds, teachers can work to help students tolerate the unknown parts of language flowing by. Even native speakers don't need to understand every word to get the gist of a conversation or discussion. Stopping periodically in a read aloud or class presentation to ask students to restate main ideas, focuses student attention on the larger picture rather than getting stuck in too much detail.

As students begin to recognize key vocabulary words learned previously, working with flash cards or pictures at their desks to respond to listening activities provides additional practice. A variation on the flash card technique requires students to perform an action (e.g., washing dishes, brushing teeth) when they hear a certain word, phrase, or situation in a story. Gradually picking up the pace of a read aloud and having students listen for clues in order to perform an action offers a fun and active classroom practice session. Acquiring vocabulary is critical to language fluency. The best techniques involve hands-on methods such as role play, visuals, manipulatives, and illustration. Teachers can use simple techniques combined with quality literature to provide experiences with rich vocabulary.

Intermediate Proficiency Level.   Intermediate students generally fall into the stages of later speech emergence and intermediate fluency on the language acquisition timeline. As with each linguistic proficiency level, learners in the intermediate stage reflect a tremendous range of language ability and often function at different levels in oral communication as compared with reading and writing ability. At this level, students transition to language that is more abstract, but they still use awkward phrases and sentences and experience some interference from their first language. They continue to be actively engaged in hypothesis testing of the language and may overgeneralize language rules. Moving up from the basic retelling of information (what, where, when), students now explain how and why, and they begin to understand the structure of sentences and paragraphs in terms of superordinate and subordinate ideas. Therefore, it is likely that students will begin to experience greater regularization of grammar because their knowledge of words and sentence structure is progressing.

At the intermediate level, students also become aware that we don't use the same types of language all day long and focus on the changing codes or styles of speech (e.g., formal versus informal language). As a result of this awareness, they can analyze language for its purpose and intended audience. Because they will be responsible for the vast vocabulary and concept load of science, math, and social studies, academic or textbook language becomes a critical focus. In addition, students experiment more with writing; they are able to get information out and begin to organize it into some logical sequence. However, the concern is still more with communication, not grammar.

With an increase in the use of textbooks and academic language, students move into language that is context reduced—language that is more abstract due to the lack of visual cues. This presents some unique challenges to English language learners. For instance, as readers, we may not have the author or illustrations present to help us decipher the written text, and this can lead to comprehension miscues.

While language development proceeds, students still need support. There are several instructional considerations for the intermediate level of language proficiency. Wordless picture books, such as Raymond Brigg's *The Snowman* (1978), encourage students to discuss elements of setting and action in a story, and this discussion functions as a powerful prewriting strategy. With more exposure to language, students comprehend a larger number of high-frequency words along with more complex clauses and longer simple sentences. Reading aloud, literature circles, and collaborative activities serve to expand vocabulary recognition and syntax-pattern knowledge.

English language learners may still need to listen to a passage several times before they get a feel for the overall meaning, and vocabulary might need to be highlighted in context prior to discussing the passage. Careful selection of instructional texts is crucial, since listening to the same text can be tedious. Poetry and texts with wordplay to amuse and engage students offer more motivational language input. Classes enjoy choral reading of poems or themed poetry read alouds linked to a specific unit of instruction. Moreover, teachers can enliven the repetition process by reading at different paces and with varying intonation patterns that reflect a range of moods and meaning. To foster content vocabulary knowledge, thematic units that explore a single topic from various perspectives (e.g., the environment is the topic of instruction in science, social studies, and language arts) furnish concentrated input to affect literacy development as the vocabulary is repeated across subject areas and developed at higher and higher levels of understanding. A variety of input of both basic and academic language—such as problem solving, interviews, storytelling, drama, role play, simulation, cooperative games, activities and discussion, illustrated speech (television, movies, real world), and blind speech (telephone, radio)—works to expand language ability (Ovando & Collier, 1998).

For secondary students, instruction in listening and taking notes in class provides an opportunity to practice academic language. Using mini-lessons with environmental print resources, nonfiction trade books, and/or textbooks, teachers can lead students through a procedure to decide on the overall idea or gist, interpret the information for its importance, abbreviate its content, and reword the information for retention and later retrieval. Repeating this procedure with the next piece of the text or explanation teaches students to listen to longer and longer instructional segments. To ease into the process, motivational nonfiction trade books provide an ideal starting point, with a gradual progression toward the more difficult expository textbook. Teachers can provide experience with idiomatic and figurative language. Various trade books can help with this task, including Fred Gwynne's books: *A Chocolate Moose for Dinner (1976), A Little Pigeon Toad* (1988), *The King Who Rained (1970),* and *The Sixteen Hand Horse (1980).*

Lessons should provide opportunities to vary language with different participants, purpose, and topics. This ability to manipulate language for specific situations is a critical language skill. Some formal language study may be helpful at this point. In a writing workshop classroom, the teacher may pull a few students aside to conduct a mini-lesson on some aspect that a group of students are struggling with.

Advanced Proficiency Level.   At the advanced proficiency level, students have finally arrived at fluency with academic content. While English language learners are trying out content language throughout the beginning and, especially, the intermediate levels of proficiency, they are able to more consistently use academic language and negotiate content-laden texts and classroom situations at the advanced proficiency level. At this stage, English language learners are closing in on native English speakers in the grade-level classroom and are close to transitioning to the grade-level classroom. Indeed some English language learners may have already been reassigned to the grade-level classrooms at this point.

Advanced level students understand and employ more complex forms of English and use various functions of English (e.g., informing and persuading) along with more creative use of language—generating ideas and solving problems. Students are able to hypothesize and theorize, engaging in critical thinking skills such as judging their work against a standard. For instance, they can use a rubric and perform some assessment of an assignment. Students use more context free language that helps their attempts at both creative and expository (informational) writing. By the advanced level of proficiency, learners also begin to understand jokes and idiomatic expressions. Appreciating humor in another language is a late-acquired skill because of the cultural dimension—what is humorous in one culture may not be so in another, and our understanding is based on cultural insights and shared knowledge among participants.

As we can see from this discussion of the various proficiency levels, planning successfully for the range of ability levels among English language learners can be a challenging task. Therefore, in Figure 2.1, we present a tool for lesson planning that considers students' proficiency levels and helps teachers consider instructional tasks in relationship to the language demands. The top two quadrants (Quadrants 1 and 3) deal with nonacademic or basic interpersonal language, which makes fewer demands on English language learners. Quadrant 1 involves language that is both nonacademic as well as highly contextualized, or context embedded, while Quadrant 3 addresses easier basic interpersonal language, but without the supportive visual cues that can serve to enhance understanding for English language learners. With beginners, much of our time is spent in these top two categories of language as we teach the basic language and routines of school. Yet, we must also begin to address the academic aspect of language and content concepts, even with beginners. At the bottom of the chart, in Quadrants 2 and 4, we encounter academic language that is more challenging to English language learners but is essential to their success in school. Finally, because the intent of this book is to help teach-

BASIC INTERPERSONAL LANGUAGE (EASY)

CONTEXT EMBEDDED LANGUAGE	**Quadrant 1** ■ Teacher read alouds of familiar stories with illustrations and predictable language ■ Total Physical Response lessons ■ Following along with classroom routines ■ Participating in highly contextualized situations that provide cues to the meaning of language: physical education ■ Literature suggestions: concept and alphabet books with basic/survival vocabulary, fiction with highly repetitive language	**Quadrant 3** ■ Teacher read alouds of familiar stories that have predictable language ■ Using predictable language routines ■ Choral response to poetry ■ Personal reading and writing ■ Literature suggestions: Fiction with predictable language, poetry with repetition	CONTEXT REDUCED LANGUAGE
CONTEXT EMBEDDED LANGUAGE	**Quadrant 2** ■ Participating in hands-on academic lessons: math manipulatives, discovery science, drawing maps ■ Academic presentations with visuals and demonstrations ■ Writing with structured support ■ Literature suggestions: concept and alphabet books with content related vocabulary, nonfiction browsing books that are highly visual	**Quadrant 4** ■ Academic presentations without visuals ■ Textbook reading for the content areas ■ Writing for the content areas ■ Literature suggestions: Chapter books without illustrations, nonfiction literature without illustrations	CONTEXT REDUCED LANGUAGE

ACADEMIC LANGUAGE (CHALLENGING)

FIGURE 2.1   Instructional Planning and Language Demands

Adapted from Chamot & O'Malley, 1987; Cummins, 1981.

ers incorporate literature throughout their instruction with English language learners, we suggest examples of literature that teachers might consider when working within each of the four quadrants.

In conclusion, linking our knowledge of language acquisition with an awareness of the characteristics students display at each of the proficiency levels—beginning, intermediate, and advanced—helps us plan more effectively for their success in the classroom. Beyond the suggested instructional activities that we provided with each proficiency level, there are many popular and research-based language teaching methods. We will explore these next.

Language Methods

As noted earlier, various teaching approaches have emerged from theories on language acquisition. We present a brief summary of several of the most popular methods and techniques including Total Physical Response, drama, the Language Experience Approach, and the literature-based approach.

One of the most popular methods for use in ESL and bilingual settings is the **Total Physical Response (TPR)** method. James Asher (1982) based this method on the premise that learning another language is much like learning your first language as a child. Somewhat like the children's game Simon Says, you listen to commands and respond to them nonverbally. When the whole class is nonverbally responding to commands, students can check each other's responses in order to see if they understand the commands.

Total Physical Response lessons are very active, with the teacher using commands and modeling actions with the whole class, small groups, and individuals. Students do not speak until they have listened and observed the commands many times. First, the teacher demonstrates the meaning of the commands (e.g., stand up, sit down, etc.), saying the phrases and then modeling the physical behavior. In the next phase, the instructor checks on student comprehension using the same phrases again but without the physical demonstration. To move forward, the teacher uses more familiar commands, throwing in some new commands—first with the entire group and then with small groups. Finally, the teacher again uses the phrases but without the demonstration.

Asher suggests that the Total Physical Response method should begin with survival level language or basic content and concepts that beginning level English language learners would need. Table 2.1 furnishes titles of trade books that address basic survival topics.

For instance, Shel Silverstein's poems "Sick" and "Boa Constrictor" (*Where the Sidewalk Ends*, 1974) mention body parts. In addition, one trade book that can be used in a TPR lesson is Byron Barton's (1990) *Bones, Bones, Dinosaur Bones,* a perfect book for beginning English language learners because of its simple and repetitive language. It also has cross-curricular ties to science and social studies. All TPR lessons do not need to focus on the stand-up-and-participate level. Instead, students can match photos or sequence pictures or word and sentence strips at their desks in response to the teacher's commands. Other books with natural links to TPR include *Pretend You're a Cat* (Marzollo, 1990) and *Just Like Me* (Ets, 1978), with vivid descriptions of animal movements and active verbs to pantomime.

TABLE 2.1   Children's Books for Survival Topics

Time and Money

- *26 Letters and 99 Cents* by Tana Hoban
- *Time to* by Bruce McMillan

School

- *School Bus* by Donald Crews
- *Emily's First 100 Days of School* by Rosemary Wells

Numbers and Counting

- *Feast for 10* by Cathryn Falwell
- *100 Is a Family* by Pam Ryan

Colors

- *Growing Colors* by Bruce McMillan
- *Colors Everywhere* by Tana Hoban

Days of the Week; Months of the Year

- *Today Is Monday* by Eric Carle
- *Snowy, Flowy, Blowy* by Nancy Tafuri
- *Cookie's Week* by Cindy Ward

Signs and Symbols

- *I Read Signs* by Tana Hoban
- *I Read Symbols* by Tana Hoban
- *Signs* by Ron and Nancy Goor

Shapes

- *Color Farm* by Lois Ehlert
- *Alphabatics* by Suse McDonald

Self and the Body

- *Here Are My Hands* by Bill Martin, Jr.
- *Two Eyes, a Nose, and a Mouth* by Roberta G. Intrater

Foods

- *The Very Hungry Caterpillar* by Eric Carle
- *Bread, Bread, Bread* by Ann Morris
- *Everybody Cooks Rice* by Norah Dooley

Weather

- *Weather* by Seymour Simon
- *Weather Words* by Gail Gibbons

(continued)

TABLE 2.1   *(continued)*

Clothing

- *Hats, Hats, Hats* by Ann Morris
- *Shoes, Shoes, Shoes* by Ann Morris
- *The Dress I'll Wear to the Party* by ShirleyNeitzel
- *The Jacket I Wear in the Snow* by Shirley Neitzel

Family

- *Family Pictures* by Carmen Lomas Garza
- *The Trip Back Home* by Janet Wong

Homes and Houses

- *Houses and Homes* by Ann Morris
- *Esta Es Mi Casa* by Arthur Dorros

Occupations

- *Who Uses This?* by Margaret Miller
- *Career Day* by Anne Rockwell

Animals

- *Hattie and the Fox* by Mem Fox
- *I Love Animals* by Flora McDonald
- *I Went Walking* by Sue Williams

Manners and Etiquette

- *What Do You Say, Dear?* by Sesyle Joslin
- *What Do You Do, Dear?* by Sesyle Joslin
- *Perfect Pigs* by Mark Brown
- *It's a Spoon, Not a Shovel* by Caralyn Buehner

Drama provides another great language learning approach. The powerful language workout that drama provides also helps student progress, and they therefore feel more secure and less sensitive about rejection. As students plan their dramatic presentations, they are actively involved in the classroom and are able to use their group and social interaction skills. The many possibilities for implementing drama in the classroom include trust walks, pantomime, puppetry, improvisation, storytelling or relating anecdotes, readers theater, and role play. An example of integrating literature and drama is found in Chris Raschka's *Yo! Yes?* (1993), a great book for a creative dramatics interpretation. This picture book illustrates the interaction between two young boys. The plot and their interaction can be performed nonverbally as the teacher reads the book aloud, or students can actually use the words since each boy uses only one or two words per page of action. The level is perfect for the beginning English language learner. Some poems also provide a story line with roles that can be used in a dramatic presentation. "The Library Card" in *My Name Is Jorge on Both Sides of the River: Poems in English and Spanish* (Medina, 1999) involves three characters (Jorge, Mama, and the librarian) and their verbal interchange.

The **Language Experience Approach** (Van Allen & Allen, 1967) offers students an opportunity to participate in an activity and then to verbally reconstruct that experience in a dictation to the teacher. This practice "is predicated on the notion that students can write by dictating to the teacher what they already know and can express verbally, and that they can then read that which has been written" (Richard-Amato, 1996). This is a powerful approach for English language learners, since it capitalizes on their natural language, and their words become the text for their beginning reading. A natural adaptation of the Language Experience Approach is to link the classroom experience to literature. Reading a book aloud and acting out the plot can provide a rich source of data for the child's dictation.

Poetry for choral reading, fiction for role play and readers theater, nonfiction literature for academic language, multicultural literature for cultural emphasis—literature represents a rich source for language development. In particular, a **literature-based approach** offers many benefits for English language learners, creating interest, motivation, involvement, and purpose.

How Do the Principles of Language Acquisition Support a Literature-Based Instructional Approach?

The many genres of literature accompanied by the vast array of subjects and authorial styles provide a rich source of meaningful input for English language learners and serve to push students beyond the normal limits of both home and school language. Such a range of ideas and language levels lend themselves naturally to the diverse linguistic proficiency levels and cultural backgrounds we find in our classrooms. Let's examine carefully the connection between language acquisition theory and the use of literature in classrooms.

First, second language learning is similar to first language learning (Ravem, 1968; Milon, 1974; Natalicio & Natalicio, 1971; Dulay & Burt, 1974; Ervin-Tripp, 1974). Because of these similarities, teachers need to provide acquisition-rich activities like those experienced by young children learning their first language. Literature, in particular, supplies contextualized language that is more meaningful than skill-oriented materials. In addition, classrooms can mirror first language acquisition conditions through listening practice and waiting for students to speak when they are ready (Krashen & Terrell, 1983; Ovando & Collier, 1998). Teacher read alouds furnish an opportunity for students to listen to language, and picture books supply the needed visual cues for understanding. Finally, while the repetition of the audiolingual method is artificial, naturally occurring repetition can be very effective for language acquisition. The long standing favorite *Brown Bear, Brown Bear* (Martin, 1970) uses recurring language that is engaging and invites students to chime in with the reader.

Next, social and affective factors and differences in cognitive learning styles influence second language learning (Brown, 1994). Thus, teachers need to plan for small-group and paired activities to lessen anxiety and promote cooperation among all children;

to vary methodology, materials, and types of evaluation to suit different learning styles; and to build understanding and acceptance of cultural diversity by discussing values, customs, and individual worth. Literature, again, lends itself to use with individual students, partners, small groups, and the whole class. The chance for students to talk about what they are reading is an added incentive to using literature. It is unlikely that students will long to share their workbook activities with each other, but an exciting or interesting reading is always fun to talk about with a friend. In addition, literature provides the ultimate flexibility for instructional purposes. While textbooks are "one size fits all," literature comes in different shapes and sizes—from picture books with just one word on each page to chapter books. Literature adapts to fit all learners, including English language learners.

Finally, appropriate input is necessary for second language acquisition to take place (Krashen & Terrell, 1983). To provide the optimal input for language development, teachers should ensure that they model language that is meaningful, natural, useful, and relevant to children and that they provide language input that is a little beyond children's current proficiency level but can still be understood by them. Michelle Marshall, an elementary ESL teacher, acknowledges the importance of appropriate input, stating, "The reading material must be interesting and at a level that will push the students yet keep them within their comfort zones." Literature provides natural and meaningful language at a variety of levels. Additionally, through illustrations and descriptive language, literature furnishes a model of input that seems tailored to students' individual proficiency levels yet offers something new to stretch toward as well. Steve Jenkin's books, *Biggest, Strongest, Fastest* (1995) and *Hottest, Coldest, Highest, Deepest* (1998), provide reading at two levels. First, the main line of text is a simple, repetitive pattern giving the biggest, strongest, and fastest biology facts or the hottest, coldest, highest, and deepest geographic facts. This line is easily read by the beginning language learner. Second, in the bottom corner of the page are two to three sentences with more information on that animal or geographic area. Some words are repeated from the main text, but the language pushes the reader a bit.

Beyond its obvious connection to language acquisition principles, various researchers have noted the many benefits of using literature. In noting each of these, we also link this benefit to upcoming chapters that will more fully describe the use of literature and how it can foster language growth.

- As discussed in the second section of this book (Chapters 4, 5, and 6), literature creates a meaningful conceptual framework to utilize both oral and written language to learn content (Alvermann & Phelps, 1994).
- Wide reading of literature enhances vocabulary development. In Chapter 5, we highlight how the use of literature helps English language learners encounter vocabulary terms in more authentic contexts that aid in understanding words at a deeper level (Alvermann & Phelps, 1994).
- Literature helps develop fluency and increases voluntary reading. Chapter 5 describes how literature can motivate student reading in class; then, perhaps, that motivation will extend beyond the classroom as students encounter books and topics they wish to explore further (Reed, 1994).
- Literature offers models of many organizational structures, language styles, and techniques used by writers to describe, instruct, persuade, generalize, demonstrate

solutions, and trace events (Moss, 1992). Well-written language serves as a model for students to examine and aim for in their own writing, as discussed in Chapter 6.

- Literature, in particular multicultural literature as noted in Chapter 7, offers a means of meeting the demands of teaching a diverse, rapidly changing audience (Reed, 1994).
- Literature offers great appeal through illustrations. This more visual format especially benefits English language learners, as noted in the section on nonfiction literature (Chapters 10, 11, and 12) (Alvermann & Phelps, 1994; Moss, 1992).
- Nonfiction literature, as highlighted in the last section of this book (Chapters 10, 11, and 12), offers more current, relevant, and interesting information than textbooks that generally take several years to develop (Alvermann & Phelps, 1994; McGowan & Guzzetti, 1991).

In conclusion, literature offers many strong supports for English language learners' literacy development. In the next section, we will explore how to choose wisely from the tremendous variety available in literature and select materials that match the proficiency levels of your students.

How Do Teachers Match Books to Their English Language Learners?

Choosing effective reading material for English language learners is a difficult struggle for teachers. Supportive language environments are fine-tuned to the learner's proficiency level; the input is not too easy or too hard (Krashen & Terrell, 1983). Karla Yarrow, an elementary teacher, notes, "As a first year teacher, I had to learn if the text is appropriate. I use mainly basals but it is hard to gauge the complexity level. It is also a challenge to have all readers find one text interesting."

Our diverse classrooms require the range of language, topics, and style that only literature can provide. Nevertheless, because English language learners are often learning the reading and writing process for the first time while learning English, teachers worry that students will not be able to handle authentic materials such as trade books that they would use with native English speakers. Even when English language learners enter our schools later and have mastered the reading process, teachers often feel more secure with special materials adapted for this population. However, these simplified materials rob English language learners of an authentic language opportunity and often contribute to boredom, frustration, and the feeling that they are being labeled remedial.

In matching literature to English language learners, there are many factors to consider. Allen (1994, p. 112) suggests that materials should

- Encourage children to choose to read.
- Help children discover the values and functions of written language.
- Permit children to use written language for a wide range of purposes.
- Be appropriate for the age and interest level of the children.
- Take into account the children's cultural background.

- Make use of the children's native languages when possible.
- Support the children's acquisition of English.
- Offer a rich array of genres.
- Have text structures that will support children's understanding.
- Take into consideration the children's background knowledge.

We feel that English language learners deserve the opportunity to experience the full range of topics, authors, and authentic language their native English speaking peers have access to. Literature allows this wider choice—one that can be tailored to students' language abilities without diluting the content or the motivational potential. With such variety, students discover the many powerful ways the written word can be used: to inform, to entertain, to persuade. Having a rich model of language encourages English language learners to experiment with their new understandings, to respond orally and in writing, to try their hand at poetry or a folktale.

In addition, literature provides the extension needed to published curriculum materials, which do not necessarily fit individual classrooms. The maturity, backgrounds (family, cultural, language, knowledge), and interests of children in any classroom vary tremendously, and one resource—the textbook—is unable to effectively meet all students' needs. Let's take, for example, the fact that fiction selections predominate in most published reading series. However, we discover in Chapter 3 that fiction may not be the best choice as beginning reading material for English language learners. Literature, on the other hand, offers a wide array of genres to choose from—nonfiction, poetry, and folklore as well as fiction. Among these diverse genres, students encounter different writing styles and patterns of organization, and teachers can select works with text structures that support students' literacy development and take into consideration their unique backgrounds.

Other selection criteria revolve around instructional issues—both cognitive and the affective dimensions. Obviously, when selecting any material, teachers should consider their instructional objectives or goals. Too often, we see the textbook driving instruction, and reading "real" books reserved for free time. Although free-reading time is certainly valuable, literature should not be relegated to that use alone. Moreover, textbook instruction especially dominates the content areas outside the language arts—science, math, social studies—when literature could be easily linked to any lesson or curricular theme within the traditional scope and sequence. Finally, while we advocate that most books are adaptable to many grade levels, there are some affective dimensions to mull over when using children's or young adult literature with English language learners of various ages. Controversial or more mature content themes are not appropriate for younger readers. Conversely, older readers may believe they have outgrown picture books, but numerous illustrated trade books address relevant and mature content issues. Many children's books also offer multiple layers of meaning to explore. The teacher sets the tone in the classroom. When teachers feel secure about their instructional choices, students feel good about their developing language ability. Listen to a high school student's view on this issue in Box 2.2.

Teachers should, however, be prepared to defend their literature choices to students, parents, and administrators. Armed with the research that supports the use of children's and young adult literature across the grade levels and subject areas, teacher's voices carry weight.

BOX **2.2**

Voices from the Field:
Using Picture Books across Grade Levels

My first semester of ESL class was about learning sounds and single words. I learned the sounds and words with picture books and flash cards and a vocabulary list I got each week. In my second semester of ESL, I learned about putting words together and learning to read in English. My teacher read picture books aloud to us. I never felt the books were too immature for class. They were a big part of my learning to read English. There were books I loved that the teacher read and it made me want to read them.

In terms of specific language variables for matching English language learners to books, Table 2.2 presents a valuable checklist for choosing the best materials at the various proficiency levels. The table shows the three levels: beginning, intermediate, and advanced. In addition, we have added a fourth category at the beginning—students with no prior schooling—to reflect those older students entering our classrooms at the intermediate grade levels and beyond who often speak no English and may be preliterate in their home language. In examining this checklist, we see several factors that clearly relate to material selection, including use of illustrations, level of language, and familiar story structure. The more the material deviates from these criteria, the more teacher support will be needed to assist English language learners with the obvious language and structural difficulties. We will return to this chart in upcoming chapters and specifically address issues related to various genres that we present for use with English language learners.

Checking It Out: Assessing Language Acquisition

Assessing language acquisition is a complex task, and accurately evaluating where students are in this process depends on multiple measures. Jennifer Howerton, an elementary teacher, suggests the following methods for assessing students: "keep a journal of observations, gather information on the child through observation and school records, have students share their autobiography created through writing and illustrations."

This teacher's ideas reflect some recent trends in the area of assessment. Herman, Aschbacher, and Winters (1992) cite five major shifts in the way we view the assessment process. First, we have moved from a behavioral to a cognitive view of learning and assessment. This is clearly demonstrated by our focus on not just the product of learning but also the process. In the reading process, we now realize the importance of determining background knowledge before even beginning the assignment. Assessment is not an activity that is loaded at the end of instruction. Rather, it occurs throughout the process of teaching, from beginning to end. In addition, we are interested in how students construct meaning, how they hypothesize about language. We must observe students' backgrounds and behaviors to determine those factors that assist language development and those that serve as barriers.

TABLE 2.2   Matching English Language Learners with Literature

Language Proficiency	Text Features
No prior schooling	Dependent on illustrations, drama, rebus illustrations, and teacher's expressive reading with gestures and props
Beginning	Familiar story or topic Typical story structure Illustrations for each page or opening of text Illustrations support story line or text Illustrations add rich contextualizations to text Simple language Little text on each page Predictable and repetitive text Teacher support with idioms, figures of speech, sophisticated language, and multi-meaning words
Intermediate	**With familiar story or topic** 　Less dependence on illustrations 　More text on page 　Slightly more complex text **With unfamiliar story or text** 　Illustrations support story line or topic 　Typical story structure 　Simple language 　Little text on each page 　Predictable and repetitive text 　Teacher support with idioms, figures of speech, sophisticated language, and multi-meaning words
Advanced	Fewer illustrations in text More complex text Teacher support with idioms, figures of speech, sophisticated language, and multi-meaning words Parodies and fractured fairy tales

Second, we have shifted the end result of assessment from paper-and-pencil measures to authentic assessment tasks that may involve contextualized problems and complex skills, not just regurgitation of information. According to O'Malley & Pierce (1996, p. 4) assessment should "reflect learning, achievement, motivation, and attitudes on instructionally-relevant classroom activities." Most importantly, perhaps, assessment should reflect the individual's pacing and growth. The diversity of language levels among English language learners demands that we consider options other than traditional testing.

Third, a major swing in our thinking has been to move away from a focus on single-occasion assessment to sampling student performance over time, as in portfolios and work samples. To accurately follow language development, we must take a longitudinal view. One measure reflects that point in time. When English language learners visit their portfolios across a semester, they feel more confident that they are indeed making progress. They can see language growth; single-occasion assessments do not allow this possibility.

Next, our view of assessment has broadened, not just to examine progress over time but also to examine achievement in different areas. Rather than looking at one single attribute, such as oral language ability, we now understand the importance of multidimensional assessments. This emphasis recognizes students' many abilities and talents. For instance, in language learning, some students excel in writing, while others are clearly better at oral communication. Our assessment of students should clearly reflect their diverse abilities.

Finally, we have moved from a nearly exclusive emphasis on individual assessment to group assessment. Cooperative learning groups, literature circles, writing workshop—all offer teachers a chance to observe students' interpersonal skills as well as their informal and formal language. Teachers can compare and contrast students' language performance in whole-class, small-group, and individual settings.

Since a new emphasis in assessment includes a focus on authentic language use, in Table 2.3, we offer a checklist to assess students' language acquisition based on the proficiency levels discussed in this chapter. As students interact in the classroom setting, teachers can keep track of the kinds of language behaviors they demonstrate in order to assess their language proficiency level. Thus, we offer some basic characteristics that students at each level of proficiency might display. As teachers use this checklist, they are able to more accurately assess where students are in their acquisition of English and how to most effectively match instructional materials and techniques to students' proficiency levels. Teachers might keep a folder with this checklist for each student in class and, from time to time, note the kinds of language abilities they have acquired.

Summary

Learning a new language is a challenging and time-consuming task. While language is difficult to define, we know that it is composed of structural elements including phonology, morphology, and syntax. Yet, students' language competence requires far more than knowledge of phonemes, morphemes, and syntax. Language users must also comprehend and successfully apply the sociolinguistic rules of language. These rules include the pragmatic and appropriate use of topic, setting, register, and participant roles.

Many theories exist to explain first language acquisition. The behaviorists suggest that language is acquired through imitation. The nativists, on the other hand, submit that children are prewired and develop language through exposure. Finally, the interactionists take the position that the interaction between children and caregivers is paramount to language acquisition.

Acquiring a second language is similar to learning a first language. Krashen suggests that a second language can be acquired by giving students exposure to comprehensible input through interactions with proficient users of the language. Most importantly, teachers need to understand the difference between communicative competence and

TABLE 2.3   Checklist for Assessing Student Language Acquisition

Beginning-Level Proficiency

- Speaks and understands little or no English
- Has a limited English vocabulary
- May produce isolated phrases
- Writing is very limited; writes simple sentences with direct assistance
- Silent; not an active contributor in class
- Generally just repeats after teacher, peers, or other speakers
- Does not generate a great deal of original language
- Uses fewest words possible or patterns
- Uses gestures and facial expressions to indicate meaning
- Dependent on others to translate and negotiate the school environment
- Uses knowledge/comprehension level language—who, what, where
- Language repertoire extremely limited and not germane to the topic
- Language is very literal and factual; vocabulary is survival language
- Uses speech focused on "I/me" to get basic needs met

Intermediate-Level Proficiency

- Still uses some awkward phrases and sentences
- Does more hypothesis testing of the language—i.e., overgeneralizing rules
- Writing involves translation from home language to English
- Begins to use higher-level language, explaining how and why
- Understands the structure of sentences and paragraphs in terms of superordinate/subordinate ideas
- Demonstrates greater regularization with grammar
- Generates information and organizes it into some logical sequence in writing
- Is aware of formal and informal language
- Demonstrates greater awareness of academic and textbook language
- Still more concerned with communication, not grammar
- Begins to understand language that is more context reduced, more abstract
- Still experiences some interference from first language

Advanced-Level Proficiency

- Hypothesizes and engages in critical thinking skills
- Able to judge against a standard—e.g., can use a rubric to assess an assignment
- Able to self-edit language use
- Engages in idea abstraction and talks about topics that are not concrete
- Understands more complex forms of the English language
- Able to do creative and expository writing in English

academic language proficiency. English language learners' proficiency for social purposes often develops in one or two years, while it takes as long as five to seven years to develop the academic fluency needed to learn academic content.

Teachers facilitate English language acquisition when their instruction is guided by sound principles. Instruction should be meaningful rather than based on rote learning of rules and dialogues. Teachers must recognize that their students understand more than they can write and say. Finally, students will learn more and more quickly if they are in a safe environment that encourages risk taking.

Language experience, drama, the total physical response, and literature-based instruction are effective approaches for helping students acquire language. Indeed, the literature-based approach consistently supports the theories of language acquisition. Through literature, students grow to appreciate the many diverse forms and functions of written language, and, most importantly, the use of literature sparks the joy of reading, ideally for a lifetime. To assist teachers in their efforts to incorporate literature into the classroom, we presented guidelines for matching books to students according to their developing English proficiency levels: beginning, intermediate, and advanced.

3 Organizing for Literature-Based Instruction with English Language Learners

We read to know we are not alone.

—C. S. Lewis

"Literature-based, language-rich process classrooms are especially well suited to the second-language learner because there are so many occasions to eavesdrop on and participate in rich natural talk. . . . All day long, in pairs, small groups, and in front of the entire class, children are invited to voice opinions, ask questions, seek clarification, offer criticism, tell stories, and so on" (Harwayne, 2000, p. 364). Such conditions do not just naturally happen; teachers carefully organize their classrooms and literacy programs to enable students' language abilities to grow and flourish as they develop literacy skills and learn curriculum content. Teachers who best meet the needs of their students—especially of English language learners—apply certain principles and practices in organizing students' literacy learning. "The practices are based on research-informed, effective instructional strategies. Though all kids benefit from them, children learning a second language depend on these practices. Without them, school can be a confusing and frustrating place. With these practices, school makes sense for second language learners, and they join their classmates in learning throughout the day" (Cary, 1997, p. 25). In this chapter, we will explore the role of literature in teaching English language learners. We will address the following questions.

- **How do teachers create a literate environment for English language learners?**
- **How do teachers select appropriate materials for literacy instruction?**
- **What approaches are most effective in helping English language learners start reading?**
- **Why use literature with English language learners?**

■ **What books can we use for literacy instruction with English language learners?**

English language learners are found in many classrooms across the nation, and their literacy instruction is organized in a number of ways, as we discovered in Chapter 1. Yet, whatever the instructional configuration, we submit that all teachers can use literature to support their English language learners in developing language, content, and literacy. Let's examine how teachers go about creating a learning environment with literature.

How Do Teachers Create a Literate Environment for English Language Learners?

How do teachers create a productive literacy environment? A review of research indicates four key elements particular to promoting literacy: the teacher, instruction, the physical environment, and resources (Wood & Nurss, 1988; Fisher, 1989; Fortson & Reiff, 1995; Salinger, 1996; Reutzel & Cooter, 2000).

The Teacher

First, teachers shape any learning environment through their knowledge of the content and processes of language and their awareness of students' backgrounds and needs. In the literate classroom, teachers can more fully meet students' needs when they understand the process of language acquisition. As English language learners enter American schools, we assess their knowledge of English. A critical component of that assessment is student understanding of print concepts or knowledge of print in general. Depending on the age and the literacy background, some English language learners bring a well-developed knowledge of oral language and print, even the ability to read in their home language. According to recent research, reading and writing knowledge in the first language transfers well to reading a second language (CIERA, 2000). On the other hand, some students—even older ones—need extensive assistance from the teacher as they encounter the process of reading and writing for the first time in any language and discover that there is a written form of language to process. As a final point, teacher attitude and affect also impact student learning. Listen to one example of a young Vietnamese student's first days in eighth grade in an American school in Box 3.1.

Instruction

Next, the mode of instruction has an effect on the literacy environment. Daily, teachers choose from a variety of organizational patterns for instruction. Whether the teacher chooses whole-class instruction, literature circles, response groups, cooperative learning, guided reading, or another organizational pattern, the idea is to provide multiple opportunities for encountering diverse language experiences and text types and for expressing ideas, thoughts, and feelings by talking about texts. Through the various organizational structures, teachers plan instructional events that integrate the language arts—reading,

BOX **3.1**

Voices from the Field: The Importance of Teacher Attitude

I can recall my first day of school as very scary. My cousin came with me to translate for me, but when I got to ESL class first period, Mrs. Jones sent him home. She said it was her job to teach me and she promised to take care of me. That made me scared but I could tell she was going to teach me well. She really took care of me that day.

On the second day of school in science class, I cried because I couldn't understand anything the teacher was saying. My teacher came over to me after class and told me that she wished she knew how to speak my language and that it wasn't fair that I didn't understand. She said she would help me as much as she could. I decided after that to be brave and not to cry.

writing, speaking, and listening. Using good literature with realistic language, teachers immerse English language learners in reading, illustrating, composing stories from wordless picture books, and responding creatively to text. "The concentrated instruction involved in language development for bilingual and ESL pupils often can be done more effectively with trade books than with a stack of cards or isolated drills" (Savage, 1994, p. 372).

As a case in point, exemplary teachers place a strong emphasis on literature, helping children "explore the experiences" of childhood, of cultures, and so on through good books (Presley et al., 1998). A strong match occurs between the accelerating demands of instruction and students' developing competence, along with plenty of teacher scaffolding. These teachers avoid using reading material at the "frustrational" level of their students. They are good at matching the right books with the right students. They also help students know what to do next, and how and when to use "repair," "fix-up," or "escape" strategies during their reading. They encourage self-regulation on the part of students; children know what they should be doing and what to do next. Exemplary teachers show them how to think strategically. Constantly linking current instruction with previous learning, exemplary teachers make strong connections across the curriculum and throughout the day. Such an instructional emphasis is illustrated in the final chapter of this book with a thematic unit on weather. Additionally, exemplary teachers are expert at helping students use what they already know by providing explicit teaching of skills in meaningful contexts. One of the most striking differences found in this study was that low-achieving students working with exemplary teachers matched or outscored average-achieving students working with average teachers in the assessment of student reading skills (Presley, et al., 1998).

The Physical Environment

Next, the physical environment of the classroom also contributes greatly to literacy development. It is important to provide comfortable working areas for whole-class, small-group, paired, and individual working. Olmstead (1999) suggests the following are essential elements for English language learners.

- Have a quiet class area for English language learners to work independently.
- Provide a listening center and a computer for independent literacy activities.
- Seat students to maximize interaction with others.

The classroom and school environment should clearly exhibit the importance and value of reading and language and celebrate the literacy accomplishments of students. This emphasis on print includes prominent displays of students' written work for children to read and discuss, multilingual labels for classroom items and supplies, a word wall with sight words along with vocabulary drawn from current reading and student nomination, and bulletin boards with postings of the teacher's favorite readings alongside student recommendations and reviews. Reading displays spotlighting a particular author of the month's work and actual books as well as real world print materials linked to current units of study spark student interest and curiosity. Easily accessible and highly visible classroom libraries that showcase a variety of texts reflecting diverse genres, authors, reading levels, and subject areas invite student browsing and encourage the reading habit. Moreover, learning centers supplied with materials (index cards, self-adhesive notes, message pads, paper of assorted sizes and colors, notepads, envelopes, postcards, stationery, pens, pencils, markers, etc.) for responding to reading promote student involvement with text. Finally, room furniture can be arranged to promote small-group interaction, to provide greater child-level access to books and other literacy materials, and to encourage independent reading, writing, and learning. More and more schools are recognizing that they don't have to look like institutions; they can provide touches of home that help students feel comfortable and positive while motivating learning, too.

Resources

Finally, a wide variety of resources for purposeful reading and writing communicates the importance of literacy to students and places materials in English language learners' hands so they can practice and develop as readers and writers. In stocking a classroom library or learning center for independent reading time, teachers might include children's and young adult literature, books on tape, textbooks, pamphlets, magazines, newspapers, cookbooks, empty grocery containers, telephone books, food coupons, business cards, posters and signs, story objects, puppets, drama props, and so on. One essential factor in getting students to read independently is access to books. Students are likely to spend more time reading when they are in classrooms with adequate classroom libraries (Allington & Cunningham, 1996; Krashen, 1998). While there is no readily agreed-upon formula for an adequate number of books, Allington and Cunningham (1996) recommend 700 to 750 books for primary-grade classrooms and 400 books for upper-grade rooms. Moreover, they suggest that it is important to have multiple copies of some books and books appropriate for students who struggle with reading.

Of course, it is not enough to have a classroom library. It is important to think of how books are organized and made accessible to students. Allington and Cunningham

(1996), Chambers (1996), and Routman (2000) indicate that an effective library area has certain characteristics that encourage voluntary reading:

- Attractive, accessible area, large enough to hold five or six students at a time.
- Wide variety of literature, including picture books, nonfiction, and magazines.
- Some books available in students' home languages.
- Featured books displayed open-faced on shelves.
- New books regularly introduced.
- A listening center so students can read along with selected books.
- Simple procedure for checking books out.

Both Hindley (1997) and Routman (2000) recommend involving students in the organization of the classroom library and reading area even when you have a system that works well.

English language learners also benefit from picture dictionaries with illustrations and labels (Jobe & Dayton-Sakari, 1999). These books are helpful tools both for building vocabulary and for writing when students need to find the English label for a concept known in their home language. Finally, it is important to provide students with books in their home language when possible since "developing literacy in the primary language is an extremely efficient means of developing literacy in the second language. To become good readers in the primary language, however, children need to read in the primary language" (Krashen, 1997/1998, pp. 20–21).

Showcasing individual authors and their works in a **featured author center** is one way of helping children discover their favorites (just as avid adult readers do), of leading students to books through interesting personal connections with the authors, and of helping students recognize the individual style of each author's writing. Designate a regular area in the classroom as an author center, and work with the librarian to display a number of books that the author (or illustrator or poet) has created. Teachers should rotate author centers on a regular basis. Intermediate level students can even research and present their favorite authors to the class and post their work in the author center.

More detailed guidelines for matching English language learners to children's and young adult literature based on their proficiency level were provided in Chapter 2. Now that we have considered some of the necessary elements to establish a literate environment, let's examine some of the choices teachers make in organizing materials for instruction.

How Do Teachers Select Appropriate Materials for Literacy Instruction?

Teachers working with English language learners often face many obstacles when it comes to selecting materials for their students. Some teachers are required to use the adopted basal readers and textbooks. Others use a combination of trade books and the adopted curriculum materials. Still others are free to use whatever materials they choose.

Basals and Literature Anthologies

Classrooms that focus instruction on basals and textbooks provide English language learners with the greatest challenges. For instance, basal authors frequently employ "fractured and narrow" language, which many students find unnatural (Goodman, Shannon, Freeman, & Murphy, 1988). These authors often write to formulas that restrict sentence length and word difficulty. "The text is narrowed by the process of revision. The revision may involve shortening sentences, substituting more frequent for less frequent words and phrases, using shorter words, simplifying syntax, eliminating or modifying plot features. Or it may be a synthetic text, one that is produced by the authors and editors of the basals to fit their scope and sequence criteria" (Goodman, Shannon, Freeman, & Murphy, 1988, p. 85).

In general, students find this unnatural text difficult to understand. The language is less predictable, and it is difficult for them to apply their understanding of story structure and English syntax to their reading. For English language learners, such text creates even greater hurdles to their language and literacy development. Reading is often reduced to decoding, since it is more difficult for the students to apply their background knowledge. Literature, on the other hand, provides English language learners with more natural language. The illustrations and other text supports provide rich contextualization that is lacking in the basals and literature anthologies.

The publishing companies that create basal series have been working to improve their products in recent years. However, there are still several advantages in using trade books instead of basal textbooks for classroom instruction. The trade book maintains the author's original language with all his or her distinctive style and phrasing. Many selections in reading textbooks are excerpted or abridged; some are even simplified or edited. This may also be true for the original illustrations published in the trade book. While publishers are making efforts to secure permission from illustrators to reprint some original illustrations, this is not always possible, so they must commission their own artists. Also, rarely is an entire literary work included in a reading textbook at the intermediate level. There simply isn't room to include whole novels in every textbook, so chapters or excerpts are the norm. Students who enjoy a chapter from *Ramona and Her Father* (Cleary, 1977) in the basal reader, for example, are left wondering what eventually happens in Ramona's struggle to help her father quit smoking. In response to this issue, some publishing companies have begun including reprints of trade books alongside the textbook. That leads to another argument in favor of using trade books: the quantity of reading provided. Even the most carefully prepared basal, with high-quality, unabridged literary selections and with original art, is only two hundred or three hundred pages long. Three hundred pages a year is not enough to provide the practice needed to become fluent with reading, much less for students practicing English as well as reading skills. Plus, trade books are "real" books to be taken home, read over and over, and treasured like old friends.

While literature anthologies or reading series used in secondary classrooms are considerably longer, they reflect some of the same issues—condensed, chopped up versions of classics—along with new ones. In general, literature anthologies and reading series emphasize the traditional works commonly known as the canon. With this emphasis on traditional works, anthologies clearly fall short in terms of a multicultural and a contemporary emphasis. In Box 3.2, we hear from high school teachers about anthologies and reading series.

Textbooks

Basals or literature anthologies are not the only textbooks that students encounter, however. Much of the instruction students receive in schools is driven by content textbooks for science, social studies, math, and so on, and these texts present another set of issues. Content textbooks rarely fall into the range of optimal input so needed by English language learners. Vacca & Vacca (1999) note several criticisms leveled at textbooks, including their encyclopedic nature, lack of specificity, avoidance of controversy, datedness, and use of abstract, technical vocabulary and unfamiliar text structure and styles. As a case in point, consider Box 3.3, which describes the dilemma that Eddie Arellano, a third-grade teacher, faced when assigning textbook work to his English language learners.

Teachers can use a variety of fiction and nonfiction trade books to supplement or substitute for content treated in textbooks. A number of benefits can be gained by incorporating nonfiction literature into content study (Young & Vardell, 1993). First, an impressive variety of topics are available. This diversity in trade books is an important element since the range of readability so restricted in textbooks is an impediment for many students—especially English language learners. An array of trade books can provide a better range of reading levels than textbooks. Second, trade books are often more appealing than textbooks. The inviting format, illustrations, access features, and writing style of trade books attract students and render the books more comprehensible to English language learners. Third, nonfiction trade books allow students to study topics in greater depth. Many books on the same topic can be gathered; students can synthesize information, compare viewpoints, and construct semantic maps. Finally, trade books enable students to read material that is as up-to-date and accurate as possible. The next step is how to lead students through books.

B O X 3.2

Voices from the Field: Struggling through Anthologies

"The book might have appealed to my students more if the protagonists had been students and if the situations presented had reflected their own interests and experiences. To assist student understanding, I prepared pre-listening and prereading activities, used pictures in the textbook, and tried to make everything relevant to the students' experiences."—Vera Csorvasi

"As in most anthologies written for native English speakers, much of the literature is difficult for second language learners. Plus, there is too much in the book to cover in one school year, making the book somewhat overwhelming to me as a teacher. Much planning will be needed to cull out and use the 'best' parts. To adapt the text for second language learners, I use read alongs and read alouds and recordings."—Barbara Hackett

---

BOX **3.3**

Voices from the Field:
Integrating Trade Books into Instruction

Day 1: In small groups of four, my classroom of third graders were asked to read and discuss the experience of immigrants coming to America from the chapter section of their social studies text-book. Most of my students seemed disconnected from the material and had difficulty with the end of chapter questions.

Day 2: Based on the experiences of the previous day, I decided to use the social studies text as a resource and provide the students with picture book versions of the same information. The response to the books on immigration was enthusiasm and excitement. This created a beginning foundation for researching the immigrant experience at the turn of the century.

What Approaches Are Most Effective in Helping English Language Learners Start Reading?

There are several avenues for introducing reading and for organizing the classroom for reading instruction, including reading aloud, shared reading, guided reading, self-selected reading, and independent reading.

Reading Aloud

As Jim Trelease, a national advocate for reading aloud to children has said, "We have concentrated so hard on teaching children *how* to read, that we have forgotten to teach them to *want* to read. As a result, we have created a nation of *school*time readers, not *life*time readers." Reading aloud to students offers the highest level of teacher support and allows teachers to demonstrate strategies effective readers employ in their reading. "Reading is the single most important social factor in American life today. . . . We know 82 percent of prison inmates are school dropouts, and 60% are illiterate. . . . If we could focus attention on raising a literate population instead of fixing up an illiterate one, our chance of success would be much greater" (Trelease in Schwartz, 1995).

Most importantly, reading aloud facilitates language acquisition for students new to English (Hadaway, Vardell, & Young, 2001; Olmstead, 1999). Through teacher read alouds, English language learners receive frequent exposure to comprehensible input and quality language models. The inherent support through cues provided by illustrations and authentic purposeful use of language contribute to language growth. Students have opportunities to talk about literature and use English in purposeful ways, and they learn to view reading as a pleasurable and rewarding experience.

Friedberg and Strong (1989) suggest teachers read a poem, a picture book, and a chapter from a chapter book daily to their students. While all this reading may take time in the busy instructional day, Cunningham and Allington (1999) note that reading aloud can help turn reluctant readers into readers. They advise teachers to read daily from nonfiction, poetry, books appropriate for the grade-level readers, and easy reading. It's important for teachers to model reading easy books so students can feel that it is appropriate to read books that are easy for them. In a study of reading aloud practices in more than five hundred elementary classrooms conducted across the United States, Hoffman, Roser, and Battle (1993) described the typical or modal classroom read aloud scenario: "The classroom teacher reads to students from a trade book for a period between 10–20 minutes. The chosen literature is not connected to a unit of study in the classroom. The amount of discussion related to the book takes fewer than 5 minutes, including talk before and after the reading. Finally, no literature response activities are offered."

In departmentalized elementary and secondary classrooms where the push is content coverage and time is short, it is not always possible to use twenty minutes to read aloud on a daily basis. Secondary teachers feel that connectedness and relevance to the curriculum are more important than the amount of time spent in reading aloud. Rather than cutting these types of activities out of their instructional day to cover more material, these teachers may need to focus on read alouds that are closely related to the instructional objective and content for the day. A teacher in a world history course, for instance, may read a five-minute excerpt from Diane Stanley's (1990) *Good Queen Bess* to make a point about Elizabeth I and how she ruled her country. Meanwhile, a physical science teacher might read Seymour Simon's (1994) *Comets, Meteors, and Asteroids* to build background knowledge prior to assigning a difficult reading on the same topic in the textbook. Reading aloud and discussing the selected material with older students, even those in the middle school and high school, is equally as important as for younger learners. In Box 3.4, we see how Colleen Schiebold, a seventh-grade teacher shared one Gary Soto book.

Prior to reading aloud to the class, it is important to introduce students to the book, especially for English language learners. Students can think about what they know about the topic, genre, and author. This is also an opportunity for you to tell students why you chose the book and to share your enthusiasm. Mooney (1994, pp. 90–91) suggests using a variety of ways to introduce books:

B O X **3.4**

Voices from the Field:
Adapting Read Alouds for Involvement

Colleen found that books that interspersed with some Spanish words and phrases were especially interesting to her middle school students. They felt validated by the use of Spanish in published materials used in the classroom. She adopted a dual reader approach when reading aloud to her students from books using Spanish. For instance, in one lesson we observed she read aloud *Chato's Kitchen* (Soto, 1995). While she read the majority of the story, one student held a second copy of the book to show the class the pictures, and a third student chimed in with the Spanish words and phrases as they came along in the text. The students truly enjoyed this technique for sharing books.

- "Do you recall the book about crocodiles and alligators? Here's another book by the same author, Seymour Simon. Let's see what questions we think the author will answer by looking at the cover."
- "Although I first read this book a long time ago, parts of it keep jumping into my mind."
- "As soon as I read this book, I knew I wanted to share it with you because—."

When reading nonfiction, it is important for teachers to demonstrate how to use features such as the table of contents and the index to find information rather than always reading from the beginning to the end (Gonzales et al., 1995). Strategies for doing this will be provided in Chapter 11 when we discuss using nonfiction literature.

Shared Reading

Traill (1999) defines shared reading as the "approach which gives all students access to understanding and information in print. The teacher and students read together, interacting with the print and learning from it and each other" (p. 29). This method was developed by Holdaway (1979) and seeks to emulate the traditional bedtime story in a school setting. The teacher reads a story aloud to students, and they join in the reading or rereading when they feel comfortable. Since the text is read many times, each successive visit involves the students more and more in the text. On these successive visits, teachers often take instructional detours to direct students' attention to new words, punctuation marks, features of text, or applications of skills and strategies (Smith & Elley, 1997; Traill, 1999). Students also respond to the text through writing, art, drama, music, and discussion (Cooper, 2000).

> For older students, shared reading provides support to make difficult texts accessible to all students in a group or class. The emphasis will not be on making anticipations at the word level but rather on supporting students as they interpret and analyze more challenging texts. Shared reading can be used for reading in other curriculum areas, particularly expository texts. In shared reading, all students—including those for whom English is another language—can participate confidently because they are able to construct their own meaning through the illustrations and the shared reading of the text, with the support of the teacher and other students. (New Zealand Ministry of Education, 1996, p. 72)

Guided Reading

In guided reading, described by Mooney (1990) as the heart of the balanced literacy program, the teacher and a small group of students talk, read, and think their way through a piece of text. Traill (1996) notes that "the teacher is in the role of both coach and observer." As a coach, the teacher helps students employ strategies previously taught and modeled during shared reading, encourages self-monitoring, asks questions to help students better understand the text, or models questions that readers should ask themselves (Smith & Elley, 1997; Traill, 1999). As an observer, "each guided reading session provides a context for close observation of the competencies demonstrated by individual children within the group. Each session allows opportunities to gather diagnostic, instructional, and evaluative information" (Traill, 1999, p. 29). This information may be used in grouping and regrouping students, selecting and matching books, and selecting strategies.

Guided reading is effective for a number of reasons (New Zealand Ministry of Education, 1996). First, it provides students with opportunities to talk, read, and think their way purposely through a text with their teacher's guidance. Second, guided reading helps them understand punctuation and other language conventions while developing phonemic awareness. Finally, teachers are able to diagnose their students' reading needs and provide intervention through skill instruction.

Selecting Text for Guided Reading.   Teachers follow certain guidelines in matching books to students for guided reading (New Zealand Ministry of Education, 1996). The books used for guided reading at the emergent and early stages are usually complete little books of up to sixteen pages in length. With older or more fluent readers, short stories, nonfiction pieces, poems, newspapers, magazines, textbook excerpts, and even chapters from longer novels and biographies are used. The New Zealand Ministry of Education recommends the following guidelines for matching students and books for guided reading.

- The level should have enough challenges and supports to allow new learning.
- The material should not be familiar to the students.
- It should be interesting and/or informative.
- It should be suitable for practicing a particular strategy.
- It should be appropriate in length.
- There should be a balance between fiction and nonfiction.
- It should be available in sets so that each student has a copy.

Introducing the Text.   The New Zealand Ministry of Education (1996) recommends a short orientation—no longer than five minutes for fiction. It usually draws on recent experiences, a topic of interest, the title of the text, the illustrations, the author, the main characters, place names, or at the emergent level a picture walk through the book and/or the pattern of the story. The orientation should prepare the students for reading the text silently. Remember, the form of prereading discussion is important. It should be a general discussion of the concepts in the text, not a direct teaching session where vocabulary is pretaught without suitable context.

Reading the Text.   Most books used with young children can be read right through without a break, but in some cases, particularly with more complex text, the reading can be "chunked" with brief discussions to improve comprehension. Students are expected to read silently. Round-robin reading, where each student takes a turn at reading aloud, is not appropriate because it prevents individual students from processing the text and constructing meaning independently. During the silent reading, the teacher listens in, intervening only if necessary to help a student with a difficulty. Students are encouraged to use the strategies they have been learning in shared reading to solve any challenges in the text independently (New Zealand Ministry of Education, 1996).

When students struggle with reading the text, the teacher may choose to work through the text by reading some pages silently and other pages together. The teacher poses questions prior to reading the text (sometimes on a page-by-page basis) to guide comprehension. As students answer questions, the teacher will then ask them to find supportive text to justify their answers. Interesting or difficult vocabulary is discussed naturally as it arises in the text.

When working with more fluent readers, teachers allow students to read fiction by themselves. When using nonfiction, the teacher guides the students through the text in a variety of different ways. Students may read the pages themselves summarizing the main points. A chart, diagram, graph, list, or other visual organizer can be made as a group to demonstrate the main points. Or students may listen and take notes as the teacher reads text with difficult concepts.

More proficient readers with more advanced English proficiency can read the text by themselves. Teacher guidance comes through discussion to help them better understand the text's genre and content.

Discussing the Text.   After reading, students talk about the text and ask questions. The teacher prepares questions to facilitate discussion, but students should be encouraged to ask questions, too. It is a good time to return to the predictions made before students began reading for affirmation. Talking about the difficulties some of the students had and the strategies used to solve them helps reinforce good reading behavior (New Zealand Ministry of Education, 1996). The teacher guides students in examining the text features, plot, characters, setting, and/or theme to help them relate the text to their own experiences. With more advanced students, teachers try to reach a deeper level. For instance, they may compare the theme with that of another story they have read as a group.

Extending the Students' Reading of the Text.   Not every guided reading lesson needs to conclude with follow-up activities. Often, reading the story is sufficient in itself. However, follow-up activities are sometimes used when students especially enjoy a book or need purposeful independent activities to free the teacher to attend to the needs of other children in the class. Typical activities might involve drama, reading aloud in pairs, art, rewriting a portion of the story, vocabulary extension, or other types of response activity (Smith & Elky, 1997). Many more ideas and activities are provided in Chapter 5.

Evaluating the Students' Reading of the Text.   Guided reading provides opportunities to evaluate students' reading development. By observing individual students reading, by keeping running records, and by discussing the ways various students solve word difficulties, the teacher can learn a great deal about their reading behavior. If this information is recorded, it can be used for future lessons to help students use effective reading strategies. In this way, a teacher can monitor students' reading behavior and help them progress through a series of increasingly difficult books.

Self-Selected or Silent Sustained Reading

An important reading mode is self-selected or silent sustained reading (SSR). Known by a host of names—DEAR (drop everything and read), NIB (nose in book), SURF (some uninterrupted reading fun), BEAR (be excited about reading), and WEB (wonderfully exciting books), SSR provides students with the opportunity to practice reading with materials of their own choosing. This time cannot be viewed as optional; SSR has many values to students.

Krashen and McQuillan (1998) reviewed a number of research studies supporting self-selected reading. Their findings were significant: those who read independently in school choose to read more on their own, and this has long-term effects. Students involved in independent reading in school continue to do more leisure reading even six years later than peers who did not have opportunities to read independently in school. Moreover, research evidence exists to illustrate how this type of reading benefits both first and second language development (Elley, 1991; Krashen, 1997/1998). Specifically, students improve in reading comprehension, writing fluency, writing complexity, self-esteem, and attitude toward school (Krashen, 1997/1998).

Guidelines for self-selected reading vary, but the emphasis on self-selected reading must be on helping students to find joy in reading. The following principles are critical to successfully engaging students in reading (Chambers, 1996; Routman, 2000; Tunnell & Jacobs, 2000):

- Self-selected reading occurs in regularly scheduled blocks of time. The amount of time varies based on the age of students and their previous reading experiences.
- Everyone reads, including the teacher. Often, when SSR fails, it is due to lack of teacher participation (Tunnell & Jacobs, 2000). Routman (2000) notes that teachers may be the only adult reading models some students ever see.
- Students select their own reading materials—magazines, newspapers, or books— from home or school.
- Students keep brief records of the titles and genres read, allowing students, parents, and teachers to see reading preferences. Other reports and written responses are not required.
- There is time for sharing and recommending books (Chambers, 1996). Cunningham and Allington (1999) suggest that allowing students to interact with others about what they read improves reading attitudes and achievement.

Independent Reading

Independent reading should not be confused with SSR. Independent reading provides students with an opportunity to read books that are just right for them. Thus, teachers make books students can read successfully available to them in independent reading, while in SSR students read whatever they desire. This approach provides students with opportunities to apply their repertoire of strategies and to build their reading fluency. Moreover, independent reading enables students to see themselves as readers. Margaret Mooney emphasizes that independent reading "should be an integral part of the daily program of every class, even kindergarten. Providing for independent reading at every stage acknowledges children as achievers as well as learners, and allows children to confirm as well as extend their roles as readers and writers" (1990, p. 72).

Whatever the configuration for literacy instruction, our premise is that literature is the most appropriate material for literacy instruction. In the next section, we extend the rationale for using literature with English language learners that was introduced in Chapter 2.

Why Use Literature with English Language Learners?

Roser, Hoffman, and Farest (1990) conducted a study in which children's literature was integrated into a language arts program serving ESL students in economically disadvantaged environments through thematic units in the primary grades. Books were shared and discussed; students talked, drew, and wrote in response to stories; trade books became the focus of formal reading lessons. Roser, Hoffman, and Farest reported that "Our results indicate that a literature-based program can be implemented successfully in schools that serve at-risk students. Further, there is every indication that these students respond to such a program in the same positive ways as any student would—with enthusiasm for books, with willingness to share ideas, and with growth in language and literacy" (1990, p. 559). In another study, Elley and Mangubhai placed hundreds of high-interest trade books written in English into classrooms in rural schools in Fiji. They found that students who were exposed to literature progressed in reading and in listening comprehension at a dramatic rate, demonstrating the role literature can play in helping students learn English as a second or other language (Elley & Mangubhai, 1983). "There are no mystical, magical techniques for helping bilingual and ESL pupils learn to read with literature. Making sure that there is a sound basis of language and understanding; providing a variety of multicultural trade books; using pupils' own backgrounds to build understanding; being aware of points where pupils' language and experience will create problems in understanding; providing well-planned direct instruction in applying effective reading strategies—these are the best procedures for teaching reading to pupils whose first language is not English" (Savage, 1994, p. 374).

Through our experiences working with classroom teachers, we have seen students respond positively to authentic literature again and again. Once teachers understand the importance of literature to the overall literacy experience for English language learners, their attention turns to choosing the most appropriate books. This next section provides many useful recommendations.

What Books Can We Use for Literacy Instruction with English Language Learners?

Special care must be taken to make books available to English language learners that are interesting and engaging, that build on and extend their background experiences. Making books available that interest and engage students is critical and can lead to marked changes in how they view both books and themselves as readers (Samway & Whang, 1995). Moreover, all students need to read books they enjoy and understand in a number of genres. Routman (2000) cautions that students' reading digresses when they have a "steady diet of books that are too hard for them and/or in which they have no interest" (p. 50).

Literature Selection Criteria

In Chapter 2, we presented specific guidelines for matching English language learners with appropriate books in terms of language and readability issues. These guidelines make it possible for teachers to give students books to read that they can comprehend and enjoy. However, when selecting literature for our English language learners, as for all our students, we want to keep in mind the usual qualities of good literature. Temple, Martinez, Yokota, and Naylor (1998) cite the following attributes of a good children's book.

- "Good books expand awareness.
- "Good books provide an enjoyable read that doesn't overtly teach or moralize.
- "Good books tell the truth.
- "Good books embody quality.
- "Good books have integrity.
- "Good books show originality" (1998, pp. 9–11).

Of course, specific criteria vary from genre to genre. Accuracy is enormously important in choosing quality nonfiction, for example. Moreover, we need to consider elements particular to our population of English language learners. These include: "clarity of presentation, use of illustrations, number of new concepts, number of new words, familiarity of subject matter, author's style, and length of book" (Gunning, 2000, p. 38). Bernhardt (2000) further substantiates the value of literature-based learning opportunities for English language learners in her synthesis of second-language reading research: "providing students extended reading experiences over time with authentic, not grammatically sequenced or altered, texts promoted the greatest gains in comprehension over time" (p. 800). The more opportunities English language learners have to look at, read, discuss, and think about real books, the more they are incorporating the language of the literate. "As pupils whose dominant language is other than English begin to achieve more independence in dealing with print, trade books remain essential vehicles for the continuing development of their reading competency" (Savage, 1994, p. 373).

It is not enough for teachers to select books for their students. Students need opportunities to select books for themselves. Effective teachers provide a balance of teacher and student choice. In some situations, teachers determine what students will read. At other times, students have constrained choices, as in the case of literature circles where they can choose one of four available books. Finally, at other times students have total choice in their book selections.

As stated earlier, a well-informed and well-read teacher is essential in promoting wide reading in the classroom. We need to keep up with the latest books being published for children and young adults, learn who students' favorite authors are, and search the Internet for book reviews and lesson plans. It can be especially challenging to know which of the newest books, authors, and trends will be most appealing and suitable for our English language learners. One way to keep abreast of the best literature is to check out the annual awards given to outstanding books. For instance, the Caldecott Award is given every year to the best illustrated picture book in the United States. This is one measure of outstanding literature worth keeping an eye on for the latest good books. However, don't rely on awards alone in selecting books for your classroom. There are many other variables to consider in choosing and using books with English language learners. These will be discussed further in upcoming chapters.

International Literature

As you are busily checking out the best literature to bring into the classroom, don't forget international literature. You may not even realize that some of your favorite titles originated in Britain or Australia. Mem Fox's work is an excellent example; her picture books have traveled well across the ocean and are loved by audiences who don't see the wombats and koalas of Australia daily.

International literature is literature first published in countries outside the United States. More and more of these books are being imported, offering us glimpses into other countries as well as other cultures. Kane-Miller is one outstanding publishing company that seeks out international children's books for republication in the United States. These are not multicultural books, as such. *Multicultural* is the term usually used to refer to books published in the United States about cultures right here in the United States. Multicultural literature will be treated in greater depth in Chapter 7.

International books offer unique perspectives and may provide students who are new immigrants with special affirmation. Sharing international books can be inviting and reassuring for immigrant students. Perhaps they have books from home they can share with the class. Even for students with no exposure to other language backgrounds, sharing international literature opens doors, showing the universal qualities we share as human beings. In addition, bringing in children's books from other lands can teach students about some of the unique attributes of other people and their languages, such as the right to left reading of Hebrew or the unique alphabets of other non-Roman languages.

It can also be interesting to share foreign translations of American classics. Spanish translations of popular American books, like the "Clifford" series, are particularly easy to find. Even if no one in your class speaks Spanish, it can be an eye-opener to discover that Clifford may not be called Clifford in the Spanish translation. Sharing books in a variety of languages can communicate to all your students your openness to and appreciation of many languages.

Genres of Literature

A bird's-eye view of the genres of children's literature, with a special focus on books, authors, and trends relevant to English language learners, may be helpful in planning meaningful and motivating literacy instruction. Therefore, in Table 3.1, we provide such an overview.

Fiction

Fiction is a popular genre with children, and it dominates the textbooks published in reading and language arts. However, it is not necessarily the easiest genre for English language learners to tackle. They may not be familiar with the usual story patterns (beginning, middle, end) or story language ("once upon a time") that dominate American children's

TABLE 3.1   Overview of Genres

Fiction: Picture Books

- ABC and counting books
- Concept books
- Wordless picture books
- Predictable books
- Picture storybooks

Fiction: Traditional Literature

- Folktales (usually in picture book form)

Fiction: Novels

- Contemporary realistic fiction
- Modern fantasy
- Historical fiction

Poetry

- Anthologies and thematic collections
- Individual poet collections
- Poem and song picture books

Nonfiction

- From simple concept books to more comprehensive survey books
- Newspapers, magazines and real-world print
- Biography (including picture book biographies)

literature. It may take longer to engage Coleridge's classic "suspension of disbelief" if English language learners need to focus on comprehending stories at both the word level and story-schema level at the same time. That's one of the reasons we provide an in-depth treatment of nonfiction, poetry, and multicultural literature in the last two sections of this book. Although it may seem counterintuitive, choosing fiction first for English language learners does not necessarily provide them with easier reading. However, with proper preparation, students can enjoy many wonderfully told and beautifully illustrated stories that entertain and enrich. Let's consider where to begin.

Picture Books.   Generally only thirty-two pages in length, picture books are usually intended for young audiences, birth through grade three. Some picture books, however, are so sophisticated and groundbreaking in their content or their art that they are really more appropriate for older readers, even adults. This makes them very useful for sharing with English language learners who can rely on both visual and textual clues for gaining meaning from the story. Sonya Blackwell, a language arts teacher, reflects on her use of picture books to teach literary devices to middle school English language learners in Box 3.5.

BOX **3.5**

Voices from the Field:
Picture Books to Teach Literary Devices

I feel very strongly about the positive benefits of using picture books. Research supports their use, and I have had much success with them in my own classroom. I found them to be a tremendous help in teaching literary devices. For example, I shared *My Life with the Wave* (Cowan, 1997), a picture book based on the story by Octavio Paz. The book, an excellent example of personification, is an enjoyable tale of a boy who brings home a wave from the beach. At first, the wave seems an exciting companion, filling the house with light and air, but her moods are as changeable as the tide.

Readers observe how love transcends language differences in the author's fictionalized recount of her childhood visit to her grandparents in Korea.

Wong, Janet. (2000). *The Trip Back Home,* illustrated by Bo Jia. San Diego: Harcourt Brace.

Whether we're talking about picture books or picture storybooks, there are several interesting trends that bode well for students learning English as well as reading skills. Advanced technology has now made it possible to reproduce full-color book illustrations, leading to very colorful and visually exciting book art. There is also greater openness and experimentation in the content of picture books, from the unusual to the controversial. This means that picture books span broader age and interest levels. Thus, students whom we once may have believed too old for picture books may find these more sophisticated picture books very appealing. For example, *Rose Blanche* by Gallaz and Innocenti (1985) is a story of a "righteous Gentile" during the Holocaust. Finally, more multicultural picture books depicting African American, Asian American, Hispanic American, Native American and other unique multicultural American perspectives are also being published, and more international books originally published in other countries and other languages are being republished in the United States. These offer content that may more closely reflect the lives and families of students learning English.

Major authors and illustrators like Lois Ehlert, Bruce McMillan, Nancy Carlson, Pat Hutchins, Donald Crews, Tana Hoban, and Nancy Tafuri have created picture books ideal for English language learners. Their books are highly visual with clear images and plot depicted in the pictures. Their use of story language is also clear, direct, and simple, without being contrived or didactic. They choose topics and experiences that are either universal or self-contained and self-explanatory within the text and illustrations. Readers do not have to have extensive story knowledge or cultural background to enjoy books like Eric Carle's *The Very Hungry Caterpillar* (1969). Sylvia discovered that this book was immensely popular among English language learners in Zimbabwe.

Choosing books with the possible cultural differences and developing language skills of English language learners in mind is a sensitive business. Although we might often rely on choosing humorous books to share with emergent readers, humor is very much a cultural construct. It can be difficult to get the joke in books like *Alexander and the Terrible, Horrible, No Good Very Bad Day* (Viorst, 1972) if you have not grown up with American stories. Why would running away to Australia, as Alexander wants to do, be funny to a student whose own family members are refugees?

What may be even more helpful when choosing picture books for English language learners is to experiment with the different variations of the picture book format currently available. These include ABC and counting books, concept books, wordless picture books, and predictable books

Perhaps one of the oldest types of children's books of all kinds, the **alphabet book** started off as an attempt to teach the alphabet to very young children. They are sometimes still used for this, but more often than not, the letters of the alphabet simply form a structure to introduce a variety of objects, images, or terms. *Eating the Alphabet* (Ehlert, 1989) introduces fruits and vegetables for each letter of the alphabet, it just begs for a taste test with actual fruits and vegetables. *Illuminations* (Hunt, 1989) is an alphabet book that is really more appropriate for older students. It introduces vocabulary and concepts related to the Middle Ages. The large and vivid illustrations even help secondary school students conceptualize world history facts.

Counting books, like alphabet books, also have a built-in structure. Often this is simply counting from one to ten, but sometimes counting books include zero, sets, multiples, and so on. Making counting books can also be fun for students, and this can incorporate math skills, too. *The M&M's Brand Counting Book* (1994) by Barbara Barbieri McGrath is an enjoyable thematic counting book that lends itself to hands-on eating activities. James Haskins has created several counting books that introduce counting and culture at the same time. For example, students can learn to count from one to ten in Arabic with his *Count Your Way through the Arab World* (1991).

Concept books are really nonfiction books for very young children. The purpose of a concept book is to teach and present information, not to tell a story. The best concept books are very simple and highly visual. They usually deal with challenging concepts for young children, such as color, direction, time, proportion, and the like. Tana Hoban is the acknowledged expert in creating distinctive and useful concept books through the effective use of photographs. Check out *26 Letters and 99 Cents* (1987) for one example that introduces letters, objects, colors, and American coins.

There are some picture books that have no or very few words; the pictures *are* the book. **Wordless picture books** generally tell a story—but through illustrations alone. *Tuesday* (Wiesner, 1991) is a Caldecott award-winning book with an imaginative story about flying frogs. Jeannie Baker's book *Window* (1991) invites prediction, and *Good Dog, Carl* (Day, 1985) is a realistic-seeming story about the perfect canine babysitter. All are told without words and challenge students to create or narrate their own text. This can provide an excellent opportunity for storytelling, writing captions, developing oral fluency, assessing visual literacy, and developing language skills.

The **predictable book** really came on the scene with the now-classic, *Brown Bear, What Do You See?* (1970) by Bill Martin, Jr. So many children have grown up with that book that it has become a staple in kindergarten and even preschool classrooms. English language learners may enjoy comparing it to the very similar, *I Went Walking* (1990) by Sue Williams. "Predictable and patterned stories with repeated refrains are especially appropriate for younger LEP pupils, since these books allow pupils to function quickly as readers of English text. Stories are made comprehensible by illustrations, by repeated language patterns, and by predictable story structure. Good children's literature also provides pupils with models for developing their writing proficiency in English" (Savage, 1994, p. 372).

Traditional Literature. Psychologists tell us that **traditional literature** grows out of our basic human need to explain ourselves and our world. These stories, traditions, customs, and sayings are of such long duration that they cannot be traced to one single person. One distinctive feature of the books in this genre is that there are no known authors for these stories. Instead we identify story adapters or retellers. All cultures participate in storytelling, children's chants, gestures, rhymes, riddles, and proverbs. So all students bring a wealth of background knowledge of this type of language and activity into the classroom, no matter what their general education or level of reading or writing.

Many types of traditional literature published in trade book format are also available to today's students. They can read and listen to the entire range from riddles and rhymes to fables, fairy and folktales, myths, and legends. Moreover, most published traditional literature is in picture book format, with rich illustrations that help cue the reader to important story elements, as well as providing visual cultural details for the story. In Chapter 8, we explore the possibilities of teaching with folklore in depth.

Novels

Longer works of fiction can also be effective with English language learners once their language and reading levels reach the intermediate level of language proficiency. Even with students still working toward that goal, they can be very effective teacher read alouds. Contemporary novels, in particular, hold the same appeal for English language learners that they do for native speakers—the capacity to identify with a protagonist like themselves who is trying to grow up in a confusing world. However, some of the same criteria used for selecting picture books should guide the selection of appropriate novels. Consider the cultural background and prior life experiences of students. Factor in the readability level of the novel, too. Teachers should read the novel and analyze whether the writer provides enough (but not too much) information for students to understand the story, with self-contained chapters and a more linear, episodic plot.

Books that have been made into movies can be especially effective since the reader and viewer has a visual memory for the story's characters and scenes. Thus, watching the video before reading the book can be of great help. Linking the full text to the story excerpt found in the required reading text can also be valuable for promoting better comprehension. Series books can also provide this kind of mental scaffolding. Once the reader is familiar with the characters or the motifs of the series, the next book in the series becomes that much easier to read. The prestigious Newbery award can guide us toward the very best in writing for young people.

English language learners can be just as fickle and independent as native language readers in their developing tastes for books. We need to encourage that individuality and help students find books they like to read, so that they will keep reading. Three types of novels offer different possibilities for intermediate grade-level students and beyond.

Contemporary realistic novels for young people have been some of the most highly acclaimed as well as most popular books in the entire field of children's literature. Newbery award-winners such as *Bridge to Terabithia* (1977) by Katherine Paterson continue to move readers with their stories of growing up in the context of family and friend relationships. Popular novels such as *Are You There God? It's Me, Margaret* (1970) by Judy Blume have also demonstrated their staying power as children read to discover answers to questions about identity, community, and even sexuality. The forms and themes of contemporary realistic fiction vary. They include humor, mysteries, sports stories, survival stories, animal stories, adventure, romance, growing up, dealing with difficulties, and living in a diverse world.

The sophistication level of many of the books in this genre is more appropriate for older students, ages ten to twelve and up. As far as the students themselves are concerned, they generally like to read novels in which the protagonist is their own age or a year or two older. Since they identify so readily with peers and age-mates, the protagonist's age is a major factor in readers' involvement in the story.

Realism is the genre of "reality," and authors in this genre often tackle major societal taboos in their writing, including divorce, death, illness, sexuality, violence, and profanity. For example, in *On My Honor* (1986), by Marion Dane Bauer, two boys ride their bikes down to a river, and one of the boys accidentally drowns. The survivor then tries to pretend that he knows nothing about it. The consequences are unnerving and very realistic. Contemporary realism is subject to controversy; however, we have always argued that the best response to controversial books is not to ban them, but to read the books along with children and talk to them about the issues. It is important to be sensitive to the needs of the students as well as to the norms of the community, and to let parents and administrators know what we're doing with literature. Much censorship can be avoided beforehand by sharing booklists and unit plans and by inviting input before the books and lessons are implemented. The American Library Association is an excellent resource in a censorship situation and can provide guidelines and personnel to help everyone get through the process calmly.

Not all contemporary realism is controversial. Mysteries, survival tales, animal stories, and adventure stories are also realistic novels that appeal to young readers. In addition, it is gratifying to see more contemporary multicultural stories being published, as well as novels about characters struggling with issues of difference, even disability. Gary Soto's novel *Taking Sides* (1991) is very readable for English language learners with intermediate language proficiency; it grabs the reader with its protagonist's conflict between old friends and new, growing up in an all-Hispanic neighborhood, and moving into a middle-class white community.

Fantasy novels present different challenges to English language learners who may struggle with a vocabulary of made-up words (like *tesseract* or *muggle*; "tesseract" is from *A Wrinkle in Time* by L'Engle [1962] and "muggle" is from *Harry Potter and the Sorcerer's Stone* [1998]) and with unreal settings that don't follow the laws of physics. In fact, for students who are recent immigrants, Oklahoma may seem as strange and fantastical as the Land of Narnia. Fantasies range from high fantasy full of concocted characters and places to low fantasy that seems realistic in most respects. The varieties of fantasy include animal fantasy, toys and objects, tiny humans, peculiar characters and situations, imaginary worlds, magical powers, supernatural tales, time-warp, and modern fairy tales.

The characters and themes of many fantasy novels often appeal to students identified as gifted because fantasy protagonists are often especially bright, unusual, and alone. These are attributes with which many English language learners can identify, especially those who are gifted but limited by their ability to communicate in their new language. Students with intermediate language proficiency can begin to tackle shorter fantasy novels such as *Babe the Gallant Pig* (1985) by Dick King-Smith or *The Magic Finger* (1995) by Roald Dahl. Of course, through teacher read alouds, all students can be exposed to fantasy novels and experience the deep appeal of this timeless genre.

Historical fiction dramatizes and humanizes the past for us. This is the genre that tells fictional stories while weaving in historical facts, people, and places. For many readers, it is the best way to learn about history, and it is a natural tool for teaching in the social studies. Like fantasy, historical fiction may be intimidating for English language learners with its use of unfamiliar American historical names, places, events, and language. Fortunately, there are several promising trends in publishing historical books for young people, including historical novels set in other parts of the world that may be home to immigrant students; the creation of historical picture books, such as the powerful story of *Pink and Say* (Polacco, 1994); and more multicultural historical fiction that features the points of view and experiences of growing up on the outside.

There are many creative ways to bring historical fiction to life in the classroom, beginning with choosing to present good historical fiction through teacher read alouds. Dramatic activities such as reenacting historical scenes, inviting guest speakers with historical expertise, and researching primary source documents and artifacts using community resources and the Internet can help English language learners begin to understand the people, places, and events of the past in ways that make their reading even more meaningful.

Poetry

The rich language and short format of poetry sets this genre apart. Poetry does so much for children who are still developing language skills. It has many teaching uses across the curriculum, including building science concepts, reinforcing historical themes, adding zip to math lessons, and as a sponge activity in transition times, among others. We are so convinced that poetry is a natural genre for teaching English language learners that Chapter 9 is devoted to a thorough discussion of approaches and strategies for teaching with poetry.

Poetry books are published in many different formats, including anthologies, individual poet collections, and poem picture books, among others. Each one contains poems students enjoy, especially the perennial favorite, the narrative poem. **Anthologies and thematic collections** are ideal for classroom use in that they are comprehensive and organized by topics that may connect with curricular areas of study. As students develop their taste for poetry, they may also enjoy exploring in-depth **individual poet collections.** Here you will find the poems of only one writer—for example, Douglas Florian in *Bing, Bang, Boing* (1994) or Kalli Dakos in *If You're Not Here, Please Raise Your Hand* (1990). Florian's frequent use of the list poem format and Dakos' focus on school topics have been particularly appealing to English language learners we have worked with.

One other innovative format for poetry book publishing that is particularly effective with English language learners is the **poem picture book** or song picture book. These are picture books that include only the words to a single poem or song. For example, Robert Frost's classic "Stopping by the Woods on a Snowy Evening," beautifully illustrated line-by-line by Susan Jeffers (Frost, 1978), and the rousing anthem, "O Beautiful for Spacious Skies" ("America the Beautiful") by Katharine Lee Bates (1994) help English language learners begin to understand these elements of Americana in both words and pictures.

Multicultural poetry has also gradually made its way onto the scene. Books by Janet Wong, Eloise Greenfield, and Gary Soto include poems with universal themes and experiences, as well as glimpses into growing up as a person outside the mainstream American culture. One of the most exciting new trends in the recent publishing of poetry for young people is the dissemination of bilingual and international poetry. Of course, there are also different kinds of poems, including narrative, lyric, free verse, haiku, and so on. Experimenting with a varied menu of poetry can also add richness to the classroom. Plus, it gives students a variety of formats to try themselves when they want to experiment with writing poetry.

Nonfiction Literature

In our work with teachers of English language learners, we are consistently finding that the genre of nonfiction literature has undeniable appeal to their students. The varied formats for nonfiction literature include activity books, concept books, journals and interviews, photo essays, pop-ups, reference books, series books, social histories, survey books, nonfiction picture books, nonfiction chapter books, and biographies.

Quite often, nonfiction literature finds its way into the classroom first through supplementing content area textbooks or in interdisciplinary or thematic units. Informational literature can evoke responses from students, expand units of instruction, and lead to connections across topics, formats, authors, and genres (Vardell & Copeland, 1992). Whether they read nonfiction books of trivia, such as *The Guinness Book of World Records*, or individual titles by notable nonfiction authors such as Joanna Cole, Gail Gibbons, Seymour Simon, Bruce McMillan, George Ancona, and Brent Ashabranner, English language learners respond immediately to the highly visual look and factual content of nonfiction literature. Here the focus is less on interpretation and more on information gathering. This presents a more level playing field for students whose knowledge of story schema and story vocabulary is still evolving, but whose hunger for facts is equal to that of their native speaking peers.

Most experts group **biography** with nonfiction. This is because biographies are factual books about real people. However, in children's literature, biography has not always been purely factual. Biographies have often been written in a more story-like format. Biographies for children used to be limited to simplistic books mostly about presidents. In addition, these old biographies tended only to glorify the dead white man's achievements, without sharing any of his more human qualities. Biographies for children today are much more varied. One of the major trends now is the availability of biographies about all kinds of people—women, people of color, ordinary citizens, even villains, such as Adolf Hitler. In addition, biographies now include more well-rounded portraits of the subjects, showing the flaws as well as the successes of the person.

There are also different types of biographies for young people, including picture book biographies, which are ideal for English language learners. These shorter books are less intimidating, but they are also more focused in their presentation of information, and they provide illustrations, which help the English language learner begin to visualize the subject and his/her times. A biography such as *Gandhi* (Fisher, 1995) or *Leonardo da Vinci* (Stanley, 1996) provides an excellent introduction to a historical figure that functions well as a read aloud for the whole class or as independent reading for students with intermediate language proficiency.

In summary, this section has spotlighted the many genres of literature that are available for literacy instruction with English language learners. We have provided a brief introduction to these genres as well as some recommended titles for use in the classroom.

However, staying current with the tremendous number of books being published each year is difficult.

Checking It Out:
A Self-Assessment of Reading Teaching

While we generally think of students when we hear the word *assessment,* teachers also need to consider assessing their instructional efforts. Thus, in this chapter on organizing literacy instruction, it seems appropriate to analyze how teachers might reflect on their daily teaching of literacy. At times, we get so caught up in the act of teaching that we forget to really examine what we have been teaching and how we have accomplished our instructional objectives. Indeed, when we do think about our instructional efforts, we sometimes realize that our actions do not match our philosophy. The following simple questions serve as powerful prompts for teachers to check out their literacy instruction.

Did I Take Time to Read Aloud Today?

Reading aloud provides a model of fluent reading, builds children's listening comprehension, exposes them to a variety of books, which they then often choose for silent reading, and shows that reading is a source of pleasure and fun and that there's a real reason to learn to read.

Did I Provide Time for Sustained Silent Reading?

Research clearly indicates that practice in reading silently is essential in developing fluent reading, yet children spend only seven minutes a day engaged in silent reading (and then what do they read?). Provide a variety of materials—books of all genres, magazines, comics, catalogs, and the like. Keep them easily accessible. Read yourself.

Did I Provide Time for Writing?

Why? Engaging in writing allows children to actually manipulate letters, words, and sentences, using their own language in a way that reinforces what reading essentially is—meaning in print. When children act as authors—making choices, controlling the process—they see reading from a powerful perspective as a way of sharing information and experiences with others (also a self-concept builder).

Did I Take Time for Talk?

Children's oral language skills are the foundation for reading proficiency. Second language learners especially need to expand their oral repertoire before attempting to decode print. All children benefit from connecting the spoken with the written, whether in talking about experiences (building schema for reading) or in talking about reading (building comprehension and thinking skills). Stop and listen, too. Find out about their interests; use this in guiding reading choices.

Did I *Show* Instead of *Tell* in My Lessons?

Reading is a process, like cooking. If you want to learn how to make lasagne, you have to do it or see it done, you can't just hear about it. Slow down and show students where the answers to comprehension questions can be found (in the text or in your head) and how you figure out what to do and when. Move from whole to part to whole in teaching (book–sentence–word–sound–word–sentence–book).

Did I Make Connections between Lessons and between Subject Areas?

In any given day, and from day to day, things come up that remind you of something else you've taught. Use it. Refer to it, integrate it, begin to seek out ways to make those connections. In this way, you are providing for transfer of learning and for greater long-term memory based on schematic networking. It sticks.

Did I Provide Opportunities for the Children to Learn from Each Other?

Children understand each other's questions. They can translate for each other and run interference when adult language is not getting through. They also offer the dynamic of friendly persuasion in which peers exert subtle pressure to challenge, encourage, and focus each other. Teachers who guide paired, small-group, and large-group interaction find that a class becomes a community.

Did I Keep Track of Who Is Doing What?

Ongoing assessment is the teacher's most powerful tool for evaluating the effectiveness of her/his teaching as well as of the students' learning. Anecdotal records, notes on what each child is reading and writing, and checklists of discrete skills are invaluable resources for showing each child's progress over time in a way that a single test cannot. The children themselves can be involved in some of this individualized record keeping, noting their own needs, goals, and accomplishments.

Did I Have Fun?

Learning to read is hard work for children, and if they don't have fun doing it, they won't want to work that hard. If you're not having fun, you can bet they aren't. What can you do to make the teaching of reading more fun? Go back to the first question: *Did you take time to read aloud today?*

Summary

Literature-based curricula enable teachers to plan and organize instruction to best support their English language learners' development of English, literacy, and content. While teachers consider many issues in their planning, four key elements, in particular, are important to create an environment for developing literacy skills and a love of reading. These elements include the teacher, instruction, the physical environment, and resources.

Many factors contribute to exemplary teachers' success: knowledge of language, learning, literature, and instruction; classroom management; and instruction congruent with their teaching philosophies. For instance, instruction is organized to provide students with many contexts for reading, writing, and talking. In addition, exemplary teachers' instruction is characterized by high academic engagement, students' reading appropriately selected books, and strategy coaching. They also design the physical environment to enable English language learners to value reading and celebrate their successes. Finally, adequate, abundant, and varied resources promote both reading and language growth.

English language learners benefit from a variety of approaches to reading instruction. These approaches offer students varying degrees of support as they develop both literacy and English. For example, teachers may use a combination of reading aloud, shared reading, guided reading, self-selected reading, and independent reading.

Using a variety of grouping configurations, teachers organize their classrooms so their students can read and learn. Reading aloud, core books, and shared reading work well in whole-class or large-group settings. Meanwhile, small groups are well-suited for guided reading, literature circles, readers theater, interest groups, paired reading, and radio reading. Students read individually in self-selected reading, independent reading, and readers workshop.

Numerous researchers attest to the effectiveness of literature-based instruction with students acquiring English. To best meet the needs of these students, effective teachers utilize a variety of genres of literature, including fiction, nonfiction, and poetry. International and multicultural literature are also important for students in general and English language learners in particular.

Growing in Language Ability

Education is not preparation for life, education is life itself.
—John Dewey

This second section of the book offers an overview of the development of listening, speaking, reading, and writing for English language learners—reflecting on language growth and considering the instructional factors that contribute to language ability. The research base, teaching strategies, and lists and examples of literature will be provided in each chapter. The section contains three chapters.

- **Developing Oral Language through Literature**
- **Reading and Development through Literature**
- **Writing with Literature as a Model**

Although focusing on the language arts areas of oral language, reading, and writing in separate chapters may send a message that we view these as separate skills or processes, nothing could be farther from the truth. We are strong advocates of the integration of reading, writing, speaking, and listening, and within each of the chapters of this book we stress the many ways that language study can be integrated and linked to the other content areas.

4 Developing Oral Language through Literature

Do not only point out the way, but lead the way.

—Sioux Nation

In this chapter, we explore the oral language development—or listening and speaking ability—of English language learners and the ways we can foster that language growth through the use of literature-based instruction. The following two chapters continue with this focus on language development, addressing the areas of reading and writing with English language learners. In our discussion of oral language development in this chapter, we address the following questions.

- What is the importance of oral language to overall literacy development?
- How do teachers create a productive oral language development environment for English language learners?
- What are the stages of oral language development for English language learners?
- How can teachers assist English language learners' listening and speaking development?
- How can teachers provide diverse models of language for students?

Let's begin our discussion of oral language development by considering the many ways oral language contributes to overall literacy development.

What Is the Importance of Oral Language to Overall Literacy Development?

As we observe infants and toddlers and their interactions with those around them, we become aware of the powerful role that oral language development plays in acquiring a language and the foundation it provides for eventually moving on to reading and writing.

Children who come from homes with plentiful opportunities for oral language development have an advantage when they enter school. Through these chances to talk and listen, they gained a great many understandings about language and how it functions—how the language sounds in various circumstances from formal to informal, how sentences are structured, and how different words are used with different audiences and for different occasions. These understandings are essential knowledge for literacy work in school.

English language learners may come from homes that have provided this rich oral language environment. Certainly, a firm background in the home language is a strong indicator of eventual success in learning another language (Collier & Thomas, 1989; Cummins, 1980, 1981). However, at times, students do not bring a well developed oral language background in the native language to school. When we recently administered a survey to two hundred inservice teachers working with English language learners, they reported that students had limited vocabulary in both English and the home language. This lack of word knowledge is a chief indicator of the restricted amount of elaborated language that the children experience at home (Wells, 1986).

When we discuss oral language, we are really referring to listening and speaking as separate from reading and writing. It is hard to factor out reading and writing from oral language, since reading aloud to students involves a focus on print matter as we show children the text and they follow along while we read. As we work with English language learners to foster listening ability in their new language, we can draw their attention to the similarities between listening and reading in preparation for the literacy work ahead. Indeed, children who are struggling with reading often benefit from practice in developing listening skills that help increase vocabulary, story structure knowledge, and even attention span. Often we overemphasize remediating reading when building foundational listening provides greater benefits.

Like reading and listening, writing and speaking share some features (Halliday, 1989). However, writing and speaking also have some distinct differences (Gibbons, 1993; Ovando & Collier, 1998). Spoken language, like written language, is contextual. Spoken language is often **context embedded** or **context bound;** the meaning is very dependent on the immediate situation when speakers are in visual contact and/or there are real-world clues to the meaning (e.g., pointing to an object). Students can see the speaker's facial expressions and gestures or the illustrations and objects to which the speaker is referring. Written language, on the other hand, tends to be more abstract and **context free** or **context reduced.** As readers, we may not have the author or illustrations present to help us decipher the written text, and this can lead to comprehension miscues. Despite the differences, a strong oral language foundation is critical to the development of writing because students' early writing attempts are often just speech written down. Indeed, the exercise of reading one's writing aloud usually helps student writers hear or view their own writing somewhat more objectively. As learners progress, they begin to see how writing often has a formal tone and more academic purposes that may differ greatly from informal conversation (Ovando & Collier, 1998). Given the importance of oral language development, the next section examines how teachers can structure a comfortable yet engaging learning environment to help English language learners with their oral language development.

How Do Teachers Create a Productive Oral Language Environment for English Language Learners?

Oral language development in most English as a second language settings centers around more basic communication or survival skills, and the more academically oriented language lessons focus on reading and writing skills. While reading and writing are the language modes most critical to academic success, the lack of emphasis on more abstract and academically oriented oral language, especially with English language learners, represents a missed opportunity for a natural transition to reading and writing. It is also a necessary step for developing confidence and fluency with all language users.

We never stop developing our listening and speaking abilities throughout our adult lives. So, where do teachers begin to create a productive and challenging oral language focus that fosters not only basic communication skills but also academic language proficiency? Gibbons (1993) offers a description of a supportive classroom for English language learners, and her characteristics especially address the elements needed to foster oral language development among English language learners. The first and most important element needed to support literacy development is a **comfortable learning environment.** English language learners need to feel secure as they experiment with speaking a new language. In addition, comfort level can affect how accurately students hear the English used by the teacher and classmates. When students feel anxious or frightened, this creates a barrier to communication, and less input gets through to the learner (Krashen & Terrell, 1983). Students are less focused on the English input they are hearing and more focused on their own anxiety level.

One means of helping students feel comfortable in the learning environment is to **focus the language used in the classroom on learning about something else.** In other words, don't spend as much time talking *about* language as in using language as a medium to learn about the many content concepts in the curriculum. For example, a lesson on seasons and weather conditions can introduce and reinforce vocabulary and conceptual content related to science as well as extend language knowledge (Chamot & O'Malley, 1989; Hadaway & Mundy, 1999). In this way, students are not focused on the deficits of their own language—what they don't know *about* language—but they are challenged to learn about the world around them *through* language.

As English language learners use language to discover new concepts, they need **planned opportunities for meaningful interaction with their peers.** Collaborative learning through paired and small-group activities provides authentic, motivating listening and speaking opportunities, offers a wide range of language from the teacher as well as from peers at different points in their own language development, and can be used to engage students in discussions of academic content (Scarcella & Oxford, 1992).

The range of language furnished, however, must be **understandable to the learner and also provide new ways of expressing meaning.** Students need to hear models of spoken language that can spur them to increased proficiency and understanding. Yet, English language learners often find themselves in classrooms with only nonnative English speakers and thus experience few models of more proficient English use. Therefore, it is critical that **frequent opportunities exist for quality input from and interaction with native speakers.** A variety of input options (e.g., read alouds by the teacher or guests, books on tape, videos, guest speakers, etc.) could be utilized.

Finally, as English language learners engage in collaborative learning and meaningful interactions with the teacher and peers, they need to be **encouraged to function as problem solvers rather than as information receivers.** While English language learners initially spend some time in a silent period of language acquisition and are thus information receivers, they must move beyond this stage to learn their new language. Students require active involvement with a language: they need to hypothesize and try out their hunches about language. To become English language *users* who speak, understand, read, and write English, they must take responsibility for their own learning.

The classroom environment that we create is critical to fostering a firm foundation of oral language development. A variety of models of spoken English, sufficient teacher feedback, a print-rich setting with quality literature and familiar real world print examples for students to discuss all contribute to the English language learner's literacy development. Beyond understanding the instructional environment needed, teachers also require an awareness of the stages of oral language development in order to plan for effective instruction to engage learners and to choose appropriate materials that motivate rather than frustrate students. So, in the next section we will consider English language learners and the characteristics they may demonstrate as they progress with listening and speaking English.

What Are the Stages of Oral Language Development for English Language Learners?

As toddlers learn their first language, we see the progression from listening to nonverbal responses to one- and two-word answers and then to short phrases and awkward sentences. English language learners exhibit many of the same patterns of language development, as we describe in the following sections about beginning, intermediate, and advanced English language learners (Diaz-Rico & Weed, 1995; Peregoy & Boyle, 1997; Ovando & Collier, 1998).

Beginning English Language Learners

At the beginning level of proficiency, students may appear very passive in the classroom in terms of oral participation. Basically, they are in the silent or receptive period of language learning; they are listening to the noise surrounding them and trying to make sense of it. In general, speaking ability lags behind listening comprehension since comprehension precedes production for the typical English language learner. Therefore, the teacher needs to focus on increased attention to listening comprehension, which will in turn lead to more student output.

At this stage of language acquisition, students focus on the concrete and functional uses of language in order to have their basic needs met. Yet even in the silent period, beginning English language learners are acquiring language. Through listening, learners become aware of English intonation, speed, pause patterns, and variation in loudness and pitch, and they begin to discriminate between gross differences in English consonant and vowel sounds.

As students become more and more comfortable with their new language, they venture out of their silent period and try to speak the language. At this point of development, English language learners tend to use very limited language, drawing on their stored knowledge from listening and observing during the silent period to help them pronounce consonants and vowel sounds understandable to a native speaker. To enhance the silent or receptive period at the beginning level of language development, teachers need to create a low-risk environment where students can experience success and feel comfortable making the natural mistakes that will occur as they learn another language. We need to acquaint students with the rhythm and sound of their new language with easily understandable verbal presentations and demonstrations. Some wonderful books with patterned, repetitive language can assist with this task.

Many authors use repetitive and predictable text in books. This style of writing is ideally designed to enhance the comprehension of English language learners. Beginning English language learners will enjoy *Who Hops?* (Davis, 1998), a fun picture book that tells who hops, flies, slithers, swims, and crawls. Each section begins with a question: Who hops (flies, slithers, etc.)? Then, four answers are given (e.g., birds fly). To add humor, however, the fourth example is always wrong. This book would be a great read aloud that should spur interaction from the audience. Students can supply their own wrong answers on the fourth example, coming up with additional verbs for the sentence "Who _____?" Once students have created their own book, they can perform it for the class.

On a more serious note, Jane Yolen's *Welcome to the Green House* (1993) and *Welcome to the Sea of Sand* (1993) offer lyrical descriptions of the rain forest and the desert. A simple read aloud of these books followed by an examination of the author's repeated patterns can reinforce the use of powerful, descriptive language. While these examples are picture books, the language can be more influential for secondary-age students struggling with descriptive writing and word-choice variety in oral language.

Because their knowledge of the language is limited, students in the beginning level of English proficiency carefully observe and gain a great deal of their understanding of what is said through recognition of nonverbal body language. Allowing physical rather than spoken responses to lessons may help students feel comfortable and furnish the needed clues to meaning. One method of creating active nonverbal lessons is through the Total Physical Response (TPR) technique (Asher, 1982) highlighted in Chapter 2.

As beginning English language learners become more comfortable with the language, they pick out an increasing number of previously learned vocabulary items from the blur of spoken English and use vocabulary encountered in written form in the content areas. During read alouds, teachers should work to help students tolerate the unknown parts of language flowing by. For instance, teachers can first focus on the general topic or situational setting of a read aloud or discussion rather than on specific details. Remember, even native speakers of a language do not need to understand every word in order to get the gist of a conversation or discussion. Stopping periodically in a read aloud or class presentation to ask students to restate main ideas focuses student attention on the larger picture rather than causing them to become mired in too much detail.

As students begin to recognize key vocabulary words learned previously, working with flash cards or pictures at their desks to respond to listening activities provides additional practice. A variation on the flash card technique requires students to perform an action (e.g., washing dishes, brushing teeth) when they hear a certain word, phrase, or situation in a story. Gradually picking up the pace of a read aloud and having students listen for clues in order to perform an action offers a fun and active classroom practice session. A trade book such as *Here Are My Hands* by Bill Martin, Jr. (1985) is a natural for participation and physical movement.

Intermediate English Language Learners

The intermediate level of proficiency brings more purposeful language use, focusing on concept development in English. Students move beyond the survival level and begin to expand their repertoire of language skills and content. While language development proceeds, students still need support. Thematic units and interdisciplinary instruction offer such reinforcement and assistance through extensive listening practice with the same topic focused on vocabulary comprehension and retention. See Chapter 12 for more detailed examples of using thematic links to plan instruction.

At the intermediate stage of language development, English language learners understand and respond to teachers' and classmates' questions and request limited needs and information. Generally, students progress to a point of responding orally with limited vocabulary to visual stimuli or class activities. Wordless picture books such as Raymond Brigg's *The Snowman* (1978) supply an opportunity to encourage students to discuss elements of setting and plot in a story. Such discussion functions as a powerful prewriting strategy. With their sequenced illustrations, wordless picture books are an idea bank to spur student output and creativity, carrying them through the entire narrative structure from beginning to end. Students can work together in groups to create the story; or, working individually, a student might tape-record his/her own version of a wordless picture book, with the finished tape serving as an assessment tool. As part of a research project that Nancy and Sylvia were conducting in middle schools, intern Michael Jarzabski used wordless picture books to encourage oral communication and writing with a class of seventh graders, half of whom were English language learners. Listen to what he has to say about the lesson in Box 4.1.

With more exposure to the language, students comprehend a larger number of identified high-frequency words along with more complex clauses and longer simple sentences. Reading aloud, literature circles, and collaborative activities expand vocabulary recognition and syntax-pattern knowledge, but English language learners still need to listen to a passage several times to get a feel for the overall meaning, and vocabulary needs to be highlighted in context prior to discussing the passage.

Careful selection of instructional texts is crucial since listening to the same text can be tedious. Poetry and texts with wordplay to amuse and engage students offer more motivational language input. In our work with K–12 English language learners, we discovered how much classes at all grade levels enjoy choral reading of poems or themed poetry read alouds linked to a specific unit of instruction. Moreover, teachers can enliven the repetition process by reading at different paces and with varying intonation patterns that reflect a range of moods and meaning.

BOX **4.1**

Voices from the Field:
Using Wordless Picture Books to Develop Oral Language

First, we discussed what a picture book looked like and what it had to offer as literature. The class unanimously decided that picture books were easy and fun to read. They also agreed that picture books (1) have few written words, (2) are usually easy to read, and (3) have lots of pictures. Then, we talked about the elements of a story: plot, protagonist, and conflict. I asked if picture books tell a story. The class agreed that picture books do tell a story. I then divided the class into five groups and introduced the wordless picture books—one to each group. The groups were to discuss the story line and write their version of the story.

The groups spent a good ten minutes leafing through the pages, visiting, and arguing, and then began writing their stories. While the groups liked their books, I had to draw them back into the assignment by prompting them with questions. Eric Rohman's *Time Flies* (1994) was an especially big hit with one group. The students loved this book's dinosaur theme and had no trouble visualizing a story. In fact, they enjoyed the experience more than any other group.

Our time was soon up, and the groups were able to read their stories. At first, the idea of reading out loud was met with great trepidation, but once the readings started, almost everyone wanted to participate. The concept of a wordless book was easily accepted by the class, and after a period of angst the majority of the students seemed to enjoy the exercise. Frankly, I was surprised by how easily the students accepted the assignment. I expected them to reject these types of book as being too young for them. The opposite reaction occurred because it engaged their imagination and creativity. One class period of sixty or seventy minutes is not enough for this assignment. It is evident from the students' reactions that wordless picture books can be very effective tools in improving English language learners' skills.

Poetry performance is one of our favorite oral communication techniques providing opportunities for students to perform as a class, in small groups, or solo. Because our lessons with poetry in ESL classrooms have met with such a favorable student response, we devote Chapter 9 to a more complete examination of the many uses of poetry. Listen to one elementary teacher's experimentation with a choral reading approach in Box 4.2.

While at the intermediate level students understand general spoken English, they still have vocabulary gaps in academic language. To foster content-vocabulary knowledge, Krashen and Terrell (1983) suggest focusing on related vocabulary linked to a theme or concept and presented in context with visual cues and demonstrations to meaning. Thematic and interdisciplinary units that explore a single topic from various perspectives (e.g., the rain forest becomes the topic of instruction in science, social studies, and language arts) furnish concentrated input to affect literacy development as the vocabulary is repeated across subject areas during the day and developed at higher and higher levels of understanding. This integrated approach furnishes the repetitive vocabulary and conceptual content emphasis that English language learners need in order to achieve

B O X **4.2**

Voices from the Field:
Poetry Performance for Oral Language Development

Jennifer Gillard tried the crescendo/decrescendo choral reading technique with her fourth-grade class in order to help her English language learners develop an awareness of English intonation, speed, pause, and variations in pitch. She presented Shel Silverstein poems on the overhead, discussed them with the class, and had the class read the poems together using crescendo (adding more voices) and descrescendo (voices falling out) patterns. While Jennifer planned this activity as a one day mini-lesson, it went so well that she is now doing a poem per day with her class. She notes that the children really look forward to it.

linguistically and academically. Using a variety of trade books also provides more interesting and literary language than might be present in their content textbooks. In addition, these trade books include artful illustrations, which help convey additional information and add the important element of interest and motivation.

As with all linguistic proficiency levels, learners in the intermediate stage reflect a range of language ability, and students often function at different levels in oral communication as compared with reading and writing ability. Variety of input works to expand language ability. Input options include problem solving, interviews, storytelling, drama, role play, simulation, cooperative games, activities and discussion, illustrated speech (television, movies, real world), blind speech (telephone, radio), and one-way, two-way, and more-than-two-way conversation (Ovando & Collier, 1998). One Web site that provides leveled quizzes and activities for various proficiency levels is www. EnglishasaSecondLanguage-lab.com. This site includes Randall's ESL cyber-listening lab (via RealAudio) with activities that reflect a broad range of topics from the practical (e.g., doctors's visits) to the fun (e.g., animal sounds). In addition, each activity has a pre-listening during, and post-listening task to keep students involved.

For English language learners at the middle and secondary grade levels, instruction in listening and taking notes in class provides an opportunity to practice academic language. Using mini-lessons with real world print resources, nonfiction trade books, and textbooks, teachers can lead students through the following procedure after reading or delivering a short presentation: (1) students decide on the overall idea or gist; (2) they interpret the information for its importance; (3) they abbreviate its content; and (4) they reword the information for retention and later retrieval. Repeating this procedure with the next piece of text teaches students to listen to longer and longer instructional segments. To ease into the process, more motivational nonfiction trade books provide an ideal starting point, with a gradual progression toward the more difficult expository textbook. The use of nonfiction to support students' language development and to supplement the textbook is discussed in the final section of this book.

Advanced English Language Learners

In the advanced level of language proficiency, students move to more creative use of language to generate ideas and solve problems. At this stage, English language learners are closing in on native English speakers in the grade-level classroom. While there is no set timeline for progressing through any of these stages, a great deal depends on the many factors that affect language acquisition, as discussed in Chapters 1 and 2. Students' personal and family background as well as classroom instructional factors influence how quickly they acquire English. By the advanced level of proficiency, learners can distinguish consonant and vowel sounds in initial, medial, and final positions; understand and respond both orally and in writing to teachers' and classmates' questions, statements, and requests; and begin to understand simple stories, jokes, and idiomatic expressions. Appreciating humor in another language is a late-acquired skill because of the cultural dimension; what is humorous in one culture may not be so in another, and our understanding is based on cultural insights and shared knowledge between participants.

To put the finishing touches on a students' language development, some coaching in oral language may help—for example, focusing their attention on specific behaviors, suggesting alternatives, encouraging them, and having them practice to improve their ability. Teachers can draw students' attention to the rules for informal oral communication—the sociolinguistic dimension of interaction. As newcomers to American culture, they may not be aware of the more subtle guidelines for speaking the language: when to talk and when not to talk; when to listen to both formal and informal talk; how to speak in the appropriate tone for the situation; what are the right and wrong things to talk about; how to avoid talking too much or not enough; and in group talk, how to stay aware of their noise level.

In this section, we highlighted each of the proficiency levels. Once teachers have a good understanding of where their learners stand in terms of proficiency, they can turn their attention to instructional strategies to help them develop their oral language abilities. In this next section, we explore a variety of instructional strategies to help English language learners develop both listening and speaking skills.

How Can Teachers Assist English Language Learners' Listening and Speaking Development?

Motivating active listening and focused conversation or discussion in any classroom can be challenging. With English language learners, the demands can be even greater since students lack the needed proficiency to easily participate, particularly when they are in the beginning stages of language development. For speaking tasks, they may be very timid about using their new language and taking risks. Speaking in front of the whole class, either formally or informally, can be very intimidating when one is learning another language. To alleviate some students' fears about initially using the language, teachers need to provide means for students to respond nonverbally, then move to small-group or choral responses. Later, before requiring individual speaking tasks, clear goals and a comfortable environment for the assignment need to be provided. In terms of speaking and listening opportunities for English language learners, we suggest that teachers structure classroom activities with the following ideas in mind (Scarcella & Oxford, 1992; Diaz-Rico & Weed, 1995):

- Communicate a clear purpose for the activity and make sure students understand the purpose.
- Choose activities with real, communicative purposes.
- Spend some time initially teaching group conversation and interpersonal skills prior to collaborative tasks.
- Provide for a variety of tasks, and level these according to abilities and interests.
- Build in multiple opportunities for student interaction.
- Integrate listening and speaking activities with reading and writing.
- For listening activities with beginning English language learners, make sure the speaker is visible, that there are real world clues to the meaning, and that no highly specialized vocabulary is used.
- For speaking activities, have students respond in some meaningful, not rote, fashion (e.g., asking a question, discussing a point, following a command).

Given the various stages of the development of listening and speaking just examined, what might be the most effective techniques to foster English language learners' oral communication? All of these ideas can be effectively used for grades K through 12 as well as at all proficiency levels. Remember, many of these techniques also integrate elements of speaking, reading, and writing, a goal all teachers should be working toward.

Matching or Distinguishing

A common task on oral language proficiency tests and other standardized tests involves listening to a passage and choosing an appropriate response. In preparation for such tasks, teachers might select a picture book as a read aloud or tell a story focusing on the setting or an event and then have students place pictures or objects in a sequence that matches the selection or choose a picture or written response that corresponds to the selection. Responses can be completely nonverbal, which is ideal for the beginning English language learner. Additionally, students can discuss in pairs as they match the information heard to some written or visual task.

Poems can also be helpful here. The poem's title is often indicative of the main idea of the poem. Thus, the teacher can read the poem aloud and have students guess or match the poem title from various possibilities. For students at all stages of language proficiency, Lee Bennett Hopkins' poem collection *School Supplies* (1996) provides visual poems about objects familiar in the school environment. For students with intermediate or advanced language skills, Gary Soto's *Neighborhood Odes* (1992) provides excellent poems for this activity.

Transferring

For this activity, students receive information in one form and then transfer all or part of it to another format. After hearing a description of a house, students might sketch what they heard, and then compare their drawing to a partner's and talk through the differences and similarities. Nancy brings poetry into play with the Shel Silverstein poem "Shapes" (*A Light in the Attic,* 1981). First, as a prelistening activity, students draw and brainstorm the names of as many geometric shapes as possible. Then Nancy reads the poem, and students sketch the action that takes place with the personified circle, triangle, and square. Finally, students compare their illustrated versions. As an added bonus, this poem is an easy introduction to the literary technique of personification.

Scanning

While we normally think of scanning as a reading skill, we actually scan both written and verbal input for information. Scanning activities give students permission not to focus on the whole text and remember all the details. Instead of remembering everything, students must target a specific piece of information. For instance, while listening to a news broadcast, students identify the name of the winning party or candidate in an election. To individualize and more effectively address the variety of proficiency levels among the English language learners in many classrooms, teachers can easily create listening centers with oral or written questions and prompts linked to a variety of recorded selections (e.g., commercial or teacher read alouds of trade books, newspaper or magazine articles, radio announcements or advertisements, etc.). The possibilities are endless, and recorded selections can provide the variety of native-speaker models along with input that is fine-tuned to diverse proficiency levels. One helpful resource is the Web site http://grove. ufl.edu/~ktrickel. This site includes listening activities via RealAudio focused on current topics as well as the daily news from CNN.

Extending

While the previous tasks focused on lower-level cognitive tasks—knowledge and comprehension activities—the task of extending moves students to a higher level of language processing as they must go beyond what is provided. Not only do extending activities provide a good comprehension check, they also require some critical thinking. Following a read aloud for instance, the teacher may have students provide a new conclusion for a story or imagine what a character might do in different circumstances. Sharing simple picture books such as *Nothing Ever Happens on My Block* by Ellen Raskin (1966) or Dr. Seuss' classic *And to Think I Saw It on Mulberry Street* (1937) can lead to lively speculation about what we can imagine happening in our own neighborhoods, for example.

Condensing

To condense, students must reduce what is heard to an outline of main points or a very brief summary. To do this requires students to determine what is critical information and what is not. Obviously, teachers need to fine-tune the selection shared to the proficiency level of the students. Read alouds, especially picture books using predictable language and illustrations that provide cues to meaning, are an excellent starting point for beginning English language learners at any grade level. Following the read aloud, students can work together to share their recollections of the selection. Short story collections like *Every Living Thing* (1998) or *Children of Christmas* (1987) by Cynthia Rylant, *Baseball in April* (1990) by Gary Soto, the Frog and Toad books by Arnold Lobel, and the Henry and Mudge series also by Cynthia Rylant can all be effectively linked with this condensing or summarizing strategy.

Predicting

To predict, students must guess outcomes, causes, relationships, and so on. Prediction is a much needed prereading strategy. Teachers can assist students in predicting what a story will be about by reading aloud the title and perhaps the introductory paragraph and showing the cover of the book and other external clues such as illustrations. Even if students know little about a topic, they can still make predictions about what they believe an author will present. Moreover, students' predictions are a great check on the extent of their background knowledge. This technique is useful with any good book, but *The Way It Happened* (1988) by Deborah Zemke is one title that starts students guessing and provides important reinforcement of the value of listening carefully.

Problem Solving

Using logic and deduction is near the top of most taxonomies of listening and thinking. It is one of the most challenging skills even for native speakers. English language learners can benefit from honing their problem-solving skills through listening and speaking activities first, before being asked to apply these higher-level thinking skills to mathematics or reading comprehension. Logic puzzles and brain teasers can be challenging because the vocabulary in these can be very unfamiliar, but George Shannon's story collections *Stories to Solve* (1985), *More Stories to Solve* (1990), and *Still More Stories to Solve* (1990) make this mental activity fun and interesting. Shannon presents classic folktales from around the world in a shortened format as cliff-hangers.

Role Playing

Role play presents a wonderful opportunity to try out oral communication skills and address various speaking situations; but it can prove intimidating to many learners. So it is important to create a low-risk environment for children to test their new language skills. Perhaps nonverbal role plays would be a good beginning point. These silent interactions lend themselves to videotaping followed by class discussion of the appropriate language to use for the action sequence. At this point, some students might be ready to jump into the whole experience—actions *with* words.

Whatever the sequence of events, a critical component of any oral communication activity is the follow-up. Debriefing after a role play, for example, allows the class to analyze the interaction, comparing the actual language used and making suggestions for other language options in future reenactments. Simple folktales provide an excellent resource for role playing. Once the teacher has shared the story orally, students role play or pantomime the various parts. Since the characters and action follow predictable patterns, students usually find this a simple first step. For example, *The Turnip* (1989), a Russian folktale adapted by Pierr Morgan, lends itself to very physical role playing with or without the words.

Show and Tell

This common oral language classroom activity can also be linked to a specific trade book. Mem Fox's *Wilfrid Gordon McDonald Partridge* (1985) provides a perfect show-and-tell opportunity. In this touching story, Wilfrid is a small boy who lives near an old people's home. He befriends the residents of the home and grows concerned because he hears his parents state that his favorite resident, Miss Nancy, has "lost her memory." Curious to know what a memory is, he questions his friends at the home and receives a variety of answers. Read the book to find out what Wilfrid does to help his friend regain her memory.

Choral Reading

When we recite the Pledge of Allegiance at school and make a mistake, no one really hears our blunder. Choral reading offers this same format of protected oral language—the chance for students' individual voices to blend with their peers' voices. Research supports choral reading for a variety of reasons. First, through hearing the language, students become familiar with the rhythm and intonation of English, and when reciting with their peers they are provided an opportunity to work on diction and fluency (Bradley & Thalgott, 1987). Because of the protected format, students feel more enthusiastic and confident about their own language use (Stewig, 1981). Finally, choral reading can tap into any content area and thus expand a student's word knowledge (Sampson, Allen, & Sampson, 1990). Using individual student texts or reading material on the overhead to guide student participation, there are countless response formats for choral reading. These include having the whole class read together in unison, having students echo the teacher's lines, having small groups read specific lines or sections, and dividing the class into two groups, each of which reads a section. The possibilities are limited by your own imagination and creativity.

Chanting

Chants are a type of choral response similar to choral reading. They provide a very easy, structured oral language workout. Unlike choral reading, chants can be presented orally since they are short and very repetitive. Carolyn Graham's *Jazz Chants* and her subsequent work (1978a, 1978b, 1986, 1988) provide very basic language practices focused on specific language patterns and formulas and geared toward beginning level students, in particular. One of our favorites is "Personal Questions," found in the audio program that accompanies the books. This chant presents a somewhat common student–teacher interchange as the class asks the teacher about his/her personal life. In this question-and-answer chant, the students ask questions, and the teacher responds, "I'd rather not say." The rhythmic format of this speaking opportunity draws students into class participation, and the simple format of a chant allows students to brainstorm substitutions, thereby devising their own new version. Even simple singsong playground chants can be used with young children. Traditional examples can be found in collections such as *Juba This and Juba That* (1995) by Virginia Tashjian and *Rocket in My Pocket* (1988) by Carl Withers.

Cumulative-Text Picture Books

Using the format from "this is the house that Jack built," cumulative-text picture books also provide great repetitive language. The teacher can read these books aloud and have students chime in along the way as the repetition becomes familiar. Madeleine Dunphy has created three beautifully illustrated cumulative text picture books that also provide an easy link to science and social studies as they make a point about the interconnectedness of life. The books are *Here Is the Arctic Winter* (1993), *Here Is the Tropical Rain Forest* (1994), *and Here Is the African Savanna* (1999). Other trade books using this format include *The Football That Won . . .* (Sampson, 1996) which addresses sports and the Super Bowl, and *The House That Crack Built* (Taylor, 1992) for secondary students, which puts forth a strong message about the chain of people who support illegal drug trade.

List Poem Read Aloud

In the early stages of oral language development, English language learners tend to use very limited vocabulary and syntax patterns. Formula sentences (e.g., I like _____ , but I don't like _____) offer a basic pattern that students can easily complete with new or familiar vocabulary. While students may find this structure tedious after a while, having students use a read aloud approach with their ideas can be more appealing. Eventually, students can begin to work together to group their completions into list poems and share these with the class. Any sentence starter can work. We drew ideas from the quote books *Live and Learn and Pass It On,* Volumes I and II (Brown, 1991, 1995). These small books offer inspirational completions to the line "I've learned that . . ." volunteered by individuals of all ages. Choosing various sentence completions across the various ages, we put the lines on sentence strips and passed them out to students. When the age of the person who volunteered that completion is read by the teacher, the student stands and reads his/her line. A timeline reflecting age and the sentence completion can also be constructed, and the class can discuss whether age affects what we learn. Finally, students come up with their own completions to "I've learned that . . ." and share them with the class in a read aloud format. This particular sentence starter may be a rich one for English language learners as they share what they have learned since coming to America or beginning to learn English.

Literature Circles

Another technique for developing oral proficiency is group work and peer discussion of reading. Literature circles (Harste, Short, & Burke, 1988) offer a wonderful collaborative opportunity for students to share responses and preferences, read aloud, and talk about reading selections. The small-group atmosphere establishes a safety level that encourages the sharing of more personal opinions and responses, both positive and negative. Often, however, teachers delay such opportunities to read and talk about books until students are older and have mastered the decoding process of reading. However, this delay short-changes students, particularly English language learners, denying them exposure to quality literature and the chance to meaningfully interact about what they are reading. According to Christenbury (1992), group work on literature can be facilitated with the use of assigned roles to question and guide the conversation, highlight important vocabulary and help group members use context to decipher the meaning, and focus on good examples of literary elements to discuss. Perhaps then, the real answer is not to avoid reading literature and talking about books with English language learners, but to begin with a more structured approach to literature circles that supports literacy development.

Audio Publishing

As part of the writing process, a common class activity involves students publishing their work in the form of a class book or paper. Using these published works, students can go one step farther and record their writing on tape. These tapes along with the written version can be housed in the class listening center so that students might listen, follow along, and share in their peers' experiences. We have found that students love to read each other's work and that student-authored books are often the most popular items in the class listening library.

Collaborative Learning Activities

Small-group activities provide a natural place for oral communication development and can extend across the content areas. We find that English language learners are often less reluctant to share and risk making mistakes in a small group. Teachers can develop their own collaborative learning opportunities focused on specifics of the curriculum. There are many professional resources to assist teachers with additional ideas, such as Sloan's *The Complete English as a Second Language/EFL Cooperative and Communicative Activity Book* (1991). For instance, buzz groups provide students with an opportunity to solve a specific problem in a small group. Nancy especially enjoys the poetry collage activity. This is similar to magnetic poetry pieces, but much less expensive. Very short poems can be cut into individual words. Students work together to unscramble the words and massage them into the original poem. The difficulty level of this activity can be increased by removing all capitalization and punctuation clues, or the complexity level can be decreased by cutting the poem into its existing lines. Teachers at all levels are consistently amazed at the very meaningful conversations students have while engaged in this activity and the information their talk provides about their language knowledge.

Round Table

Using a small-group discussion format with three to five participants per group, the class is divided into various stations with a different discussion topic at each table. Students have the opportunity to rotate to different groups to address a variety of topics. This activity offers an excellent review technique for a unit of study or an upcoming exam. Another alternative involves having students contribute their own topics related to a unit of study, a particular theme, or a book currently being read. Another format involves rank-ordering a list of items or options (e.g., given an introductory section from a story, take a set of options and rank-order them in the likelihood of their occurrence in relation to the theme or characters from the story). Even the Choose Your Own Adventure book series or the popular *SimCity, SimTown*, and *SimFamily* computer simulation games can model how selecting various options has ramifications, no matter which path you choose.

Panel Discussion

More formal than the round-table discussion is the panel discussion. It is possible to have an impromptu panel discussion, but in general the topic of the panel is agreed on before-hand. Then, each panel member has a certain facet of the topic to develop, while the class serves as an audience. Panel discussions provide an alternative to teacher talk. For instance, students can be responsible for reviewing the key areas of study in a unit or for supporting an argument. Using a content-area emphasis, each panel member might use a different nonfiction trade book to put together information for an oral presentation that covers all aspects of the topic. Students may even discover that different authors have different points of view on the very same subject. For example, a panel of students might gather several biographies about the same person and present information they find interesting.

Creative Dramatics

Drama provides another excellent oral communication format. Pantomime, puppetry, trust walks, and improvisation all supply opportunities for students to plan, discuss, participate, and reflect. McCaslin (1987a, 1987b, 1990) offers several professional resource books for using drama across various grade levels. Trust walks foster a sense of team play and also foster active listening skills as one student gives directions to the other. Pantomimes allow nonverbal participation but can be discussed before the performance, while improvisation gives English language learners an opportunity for spontaneous language interchanges.

No matter what the age, puppetry is a valuable option, especially with English language learners. Given their varying proficiency levels, the ability to hide behind a sock or paper-bag puppet can increase students' confidence levels about risking using their language. In one high school ESL class that Nancy visited, students constructed paper-bag puppets in the form of insects to perform Paul Fleischman's poems for two voices from *Joyful Noise* (1988). The puppet performances were videotaped, and students analyzed their own pronunciation and delivery of lines.

Readers Theater

The many benefits of readers theater for oral language development include purposeful oral reading, an opportunity for cooperative learning, practice using oral skills, and heightened attention in listening. Because students do not have to stage a scene—they simply read the lines—this simple dramatic technique is easy to implement into any classroom and seems ideally suited to English language learners. One third-grade teacher, Eddie Arrellano, encouraged his students to gather information on immigration from a variety of trade books and then to develop their own readers theater scripts. After completing the unit, these third graders reflected that they learned more from the trade books and readers theater activities than they had from their textbooks.

Students who have had little or no experience with readers theater may need their practices directed by the teacher. A teacher or a child may serve as a director to make suggestions about pacing, clarity, and varying the rhythm, pitch, and volume in speaking. It is important to allow students to experience a variety of formats for script presentation. Also, allowing them to practice reading different parts and to experiment with changes in voice modulation maximizes effectiveness.

As students become more experienced, they can direct their own practices. Videotaping practices helps students prepare for audiences because watching themselves on tapes makes them aware of areas they need to improve. As students perform, they can sit or stand in a semicircle. This arrangement allows students to make eye contact with each other and with the audience. Because, students enjoy performing for more than one audience, they can present their readers theater to other classes, parents, the PTA, a church group, or community groups.

In conclusion, there are countless possibilities to develop listening and speaking ability of English language learners. The suggestions in this section offer the chance for students to work together in low-risk activities to expand their oral language with teacher support. All of these techniques work across grades K through 12 and can be easily adapted to students' varying proficiency levels. Next, we consider how to provide diverse models of oral language for our students.

How Can Teachers Provide Diverse Models of Language for Students?

In addition to furnishing a variety of listening and speaking tasks for the classroom, teachers must offer diverse models of language. We all need to hear different language models. Classroom models may be all the actual exposure English language learners have.

Live or Recorded Interviews

The interview format can be tailored to various proficiency levels and can include a variety of informants. For instance, guest speakers provide diverse models of language and afford an opportunity for students to interview someone outside the class. Speakers might include school personnel like administrators and support staff, community resource people like zoo or museum representatives, local celebrities like newscasters or authors, or even parents and family members. One book that presents this special interview dynamic is *Dear Mr. Henshaw* (Cleary, 1983), a novel that portrays a letter-writing relationship between a boy and his favorite author. In addition, in Chapter 8, we discuss the possibilities for collecting a family history through interviews of family members.

Newscasts

The many varied formats of news reporting can provide valuable comparison and contrast for students. For instance, English language learners might compare and contrast recorded news segments from radio and television along with the printed news in newspapers. Various trade books also utilize a newspaper style format to present information. As part of the focus on the newscast, students can analyze the different news categories (local and national events, weather, sports, entertainment, etc.) for the types of information presented and the typical vocabulary used. Even a simple nonfiction book such as Patricia Lauber's *The News about Dinosaurs* (1989) demonstrates how authors integrate the latest news and research into their writing for children. This book shares what the "old" or "wrong" news was. After watching and discussing many models, students are ready to create their own newscast, either a generic daily news broadcast or one linked to a unit of study such as the discovery of gold in California or the Spanish exploration of the New World.

Speeches

For an example of more formal oral language use, speeches are another option for oral communication in the classroom. Students might consider the tremendous range of speech events (sermons at churches or temples, the State of the Union address, the inaugural address, protest speeches, etc.). Some famous speeches, such as Martin Luther King, Jr.'s "I Have a Dream" and John F. Kennedy's inaugural address, are available on audiotape, videotape, and over the Internet. As a wonderful companion to recorded or historic speeches, some illustrated versions of famous speeches have recently been published, including *I Have a Dream* (King & King, 1997) and Lincoln's *Gettysburg Address* (McCurdy, 1993). One version is even available for the beginning reader in *Just a Few Words, Mr. Lincoln: The Story of the Gettysburg Address* (1993) by Jean Fritz.

Radio and Television Programming.

The media furnish many examples for listening activities: **a news program** can help students focus on who, what, where, when, why, and how as well as on main ideas, examples, and descriptions; **a cooking program** can help students focus on sequence; or **an advertisement** can demonstrate persuasive techniques that grab our attention. An important distinction between radio and television is that radio reflects more context free and reduced language because there are no visual clues to meaning. Television offers a range of context embedded language levels, with cooking shows, advertisements, and children's programming such as *Sesame Street* presenting the most predictable and easy-to-follow language, and with news or talk shows perhaps the most difficult. Peregoy and Boyle (1997) suggest taping a television program, playing it back with no sound, and then having students create their own dubbed version with dialogue and sound effects.

Music

For a motivational language resource that is an intimate part of most students' lives, teachers can check out the many possibilities offered by music. As with literature, the lyrics to music across cultures provide valuable insights into the important values, beliefs, and events of different peoples and eras. Folk songs, in particular, are an interesting link to our history and the issues of various time periods. Since the authors of this book grew up in the 1960s, we still remember the many powerful songs that were written to address social concerns. Many children's books also feature songs that tell of America's past or that reflect diverse cultures. *From Sea to Shining Sea* (Cohn, 1993) is a compilation of American folklore, including the music and lyrics to many folk songs. To assist the comprehension of English language learners, teachers may choose to read the song aloud first and preteach important vocabulary and/or provide copies of the lyrics. Finally, check out the Web site www.globalenglish.com for sing-alongs via karaoke music and other listening and speaking opportunities.

Storytelling or Relating Anecdotes

Don't confuse storytelling with memorizing. True storytelling is an art form with roots deep in our oral tradition. Storytelling activities in the classroom provide both structured and impromptu language opportunities. With practice, children assimilate the concept of story structure—introduction, plot episodes, elaborative details, climax, resolution, and conclusion (Buchoff, 1995). Students can prepare stories or presentations with props—a type of staged performance—or they might simply share unrehearsed personal experiences about family, friends, pets, funny incidents, and current events. Moreover, storytelling can be a whole-group, small-group, or individual-student activity. For instance, beginning with an introductory line (e.g., Suddenly the lights went out and I heard a loud crash . . .) or an intriguing picture or photo, the whole class might work together, with each student adding a line to the story.

In addition, many communities have professional storytellers in their midst. Working through the school or local librarian, teachers can invite a storyteller to teach and perform the storytelling art in person—a memorable experience. Once students have some good models of stories as background, Buchoff (1995) suggests that they collect family stories at home using a variety of "tell me about . . ." prompts, as noted in Table 4.1, and then practice retelling the story to the original teller.

TABLE 4.1   Tell Me about . . . Prompts for Storytelling

- Tell me about something I did when I was little.
- Tell me about a time I got lost.
- Tell me about a neighborhood where you lived as a child.
- Tell me about someone who used to come and visit your house when you were growing up.
- Tell me about your favorite relative when you were a child.

Live Conversation and Dialogue

From classroom discussions to informal chats, spontaneous live conversation provides a needed oral language workout for English language learners. To encourage this format, students might drop ideas (e.g., current theme or controversial topic) into a suggestion box during the month. Then, at the end of the month, students draw a topic and have a chance to talk in small groups, perform a dialogue, or act out a small-group chat skit for the whole class. One book with countless question prompts for lively, real-life discussion is *The Kids' Book of Questions* (1988) by Gregory Stock.

Furnishing diverse models of language for English language learners is critical. We do not all speak the same, and English language learners often have few native speaker models outside their school experiences. This section has highlighted a variety of ways teachers can draw other voices into the classroom and extend listening and speaking opportunities for students.

Checking It Out:
Assessing Oral Language Development

Since oral language is a critical foundation for future literacy development in reading and writing, it is critical for teachers to focus on English language learners' ability to communicate effectively through oral language. Obviously, oral language assessment procedures need to take into consideration the proficiency levels of students. For instance, oral language assessment of beginning level students would involve tasks such as matching descriptions to pictures, responding with a physical response, echo reading, and the like (O'Malley & Pierce, 1996). The more formal uses of oral language, such as oral presentations, should probably be reserved for intermediate and advanced level students. To help in planning the appropriate language assessment tasks for students, teachers might return to the continuum of language discussed in Chapter 2. Students need both basic communicative language and academic language for success in school (Cummins, 1980). Beginning level students, however, may spend more of their time with activities and assessment related to the communicative language functions, while intermediate and advanced students will spend more time with academic language (Chamot & O'Malley, 1994).

Table 4.2 presents a variety of communicative and academic language functions. These may serve as a guideline for constructing oral language assessment activities. For instance, teachers can have students role play a situation where they are using greetings or asking for information.

Oral communication situations in the classroom furnish a rich opportunity to assess students' abilities. For instance, teachers could analyze class discussions, helping students become aware of what's going on during the speaking process and talking about what's going on when one is speaking and listening. The class could analyze a videotape of a class discussion, literature circle, or role play and discuss participation patterns—what enhanced communication efforts and how to improve for future efforts. One example of this technique is the discussion play (Matazano, 1996). Following are some additional options for assessing oral language.

TABLE 4.2   Language Functions

Communicative Language Functions	Academic Language Functions
Greetings	Informing
Requesting information	Comparing
Giving information/directions	Ordering
Describing	Classifying
Expressing feelings	Analyzing
	Inferring
	Justifying/persuading
	Solving problems
	Synthesizing
	Evaluating

Tapes and Videotapes

We presented several options for oral language activities that could be taped or video-taped. The newscast activity could be videotaped and used to assess participants' oral language development. If teachers wish to use videotapes such as these for a grade, they will need to construct a grading rubric with the specific criteria that constitute the evaluation.

Checklists

The teacher can develop checklists tailored to individual activities in the classroom. For instance, during collaborative activities, teachers might simply use a roster with students' names to record how often individual students participate.

Anecdotal Observations

Teachers can also record observations about student performance in class, noting specific dates, topics, activities, language issues, and the like that relate to oral language proficiency.

Dictated Experience Account

Teachers might have a student tell a story based on his/her experiences. The teacher can record this on tape or in written form, and then look for the student's use of elaboration.

Echo Reading

Using a passage of approximately eight or so lines from a source at the appropriate level, the teacher reads aloud a line and pauses. The child echoes the same line.

Story Retelling

Students can also retell a story that the teacher has read aloud. Many story retelling guides exist; most focus on the following elements that should be included in the students' retelling:

- Begins with an introduction.
- Names main characters.
- Describes characters.
- Notes the setting (time and place) of the story.
- Notes the problem to be solved or the goal of the story.
- Highlights the major situations or episodes within the story.
- Tells how the problem is resolved.

These elements can be used as a checklist by the teacher to rate the students' oral language ability. However, teachers should use caution in their ratings because a story retelling reflects more than listening and speaking ability but also is an indication of the student's short-term memory.

Summary

Oral language—listening and speaking—plays an important role in both language and literacy development. Literature-based instruction contributes tremendously to the oral and written language connection. Literacy leans heavily on students' oral language development. That is, oral language provides a foundation for reading and writing. Rich oral language experiences result in well-developed vocabularies, conceptual understandings, and knowledge of language structures. Moreover, oral language proficiency in the home language leads to English language acquisition.

Reading and listening are parallel receptive language acts, while speaking and writing are similar communication processes. Teachers can draw students' attention to these parallels and create productive oral language environments that promote both basic interpersonal language and academic language.

Classrooms offering maximum support for English language learners' oral language development share similar characteristics. These characteristics include a comfortable learning environment, planned opportunities to share with peers, opportunities to use listening and speaking while learning about something else, and opportunities to function as a problem solver as opposed to a receptacle of information.

As with reading and writing, English language learners progress through stages of development in their new language. In order to most effectively plan for instruction, teachers need to have an awareness of the behaviors and abilities at each of the stages of oral language development—beginning, intermediate, and advanced. The teacher and text support needed decrease as students' language becomes more complex.

Teachers draw on numerous strategies to enhance their students' oral language development. Some strategies such as matching, scanning, extending, list poem read aloud, and audio publishing are less common but very effective means for students to apply both listening and speaking. Other better-known strategies work especially well in helping English language learners use their newly acquired language in listening and speaking situations. These include predicting, problem solving, show and tell, choral reading, chanting, collaborative learning activities, round table, panel discussion, creative dramatics, readers theater, using cumulative-text picture books, and working in literature circles. While choosing various oral language development strategies, teachers need to provide a variety of English language models. For English language learners such models of native-like proficiency are crucial. To accomplish this, teachers often utilize live or recorded interview, newscasts, speeches, radio and television programming, music, storytelling, and live conversation.

Classroom oral communication activities provide teachers with many informal assessment opportunities. These assessments include audio and video recordings, checklists, anecdotal observations, dictated experience accounts, echo reading, and story retellings.

5 Reading Development through Literature

Imagination is more important than knowledge.

—Albert Einstein

Comprehending and working with written text are the focus of most school programs. On any given school day, K–12 learners experience reading in many forms, from the expository writing of content textbooks with new concepts in math, science, and social studies to narrative writing in language arts classes. In addition, as students move through the grades, they are increasingly called upon to process text in newspapers, magazines, reference materials, and online sources. This lineup of required reading is daunting for a native English speaker; for those learning English, it can be overwhelming. Thus, for students learning English, the printed page symbolizes another hurdle in their attempt to master a new language and achieve in school. In this chapter, we explore the development of reading with English language learners and how to foster this critical literacy area through vocabulary development. We address the following questions.

- **What is the importance of reading to academic success?**
- **How do teachers create a productive reading environment for English language learners?**
- **What are the stages of reading development for English language learners?**
- **What instructional strategies assist English language learners throughout the reading process?**

Let's begin our discussion of reading and vocabulary development by considering the critical role of reading in the schools.

What Is the Importance of Reading to Academic Success?

The ability to comprehend and work with textual information is the primary emphasis of schooling. Why put so much focus on the printed word? Simply put, once children develop some facility with reading, they are not as dependent on others to deliver information. They have the means to further their learning on their own. They are on their way to becoming independent learners.

Yet, it is exactly this emphasis on print in schools and the empowering potential of reading that puts English language learners at peril. As you read in Chapter 2, language proficiency grows gradually. Infants and toddlers who are learning their first language have time and, hopefully, a nurturing environment on their side. They have five years or so to develop proficiency in their home language—to acquire the sound system and an awareness of morphology and syntax. They have countless contacts with the symbolic representation of the language through home literacy activities and exposure to real world print. Then, these children bring their emerging literacy and its repertoire of linguistic tools to school, where they encounter the academic language of written texts. In short, they are years ahead of the English language learner who enters American schools and subsequently must learn both the sound and the structure—the basic interpersonal English of childhood years—along with the cognitive demands of academic English for math, science, and social studies. English language learners in grades K through 12 don't have the luxury of a long silent period to become acclimated to their new language or an extended time frame for the normal trial and error of language acquisition of early childhood. They experience greater cognitive demands when they are asked to learn both language and content and to learn them quickly if they are to meet the mark on standardized tests and proceed through the grade levels. Given the pressures for English language learners to transition quickly from survival vocabulary and the more basic functions of language to a more academic and print-oriented focus, the next section explores how teachers can most effectively introduce English language learners to the reading process and extend student comprehension of textual material.

How Do Teachers Create a Productive Reading Environment for English Language Learners?

As we have noted, schools emphasize more academically oriented language focusing on reading and writing skills. Indeed, reading and writing are the language modes viewed as the most critical to academic success. Yet, schools face enormous challenges in teaching children to read and write. Meeting these challenges in the twenty-first century requires a fundamental change in how policymakers, parents, and school professionals look at improving schools.

The International Reading Association declares that it is time to build reading programs on a set of comprehensive principles that honor children's rights to excellent reading instruction. The Association believes that the ten specific principles outlined here are the right of every child.

1. Children have a right to appropriate early reading instruction based on their individual needs.
2. Children have a right to reading instruction that builds both skill and the desire to read increasingly complex materials.

A friendly librarian introduces Tomás, a young migrant worker, to the joy of reading. This book was inspired by the real-life story of Tomás Rivera.

Mora, Pat. (1997). *Tomás and the Library Lady*, illustrated by Raul Colón. New York: Alfred A. Knopf.

3. Children have a right to well-prepared teachers who keep their skills up to date through effective professional development.
4. Children have the right of access to a wide variety of books and other reading material in the classroom, school and community libraries.
5. Children have a right to reading assessment that identifies their strengths as well as their needs and involves them in making decisions about their own learning.
6. Children have a right to supplemental instruction from professionals specifically prepared to teach reading.
7. Children have a right to reading instruction that involves parents and communities in their academic lives.
8. Children have a right to reading instruction that makes meaningful use of their first language skills.
9. Children have a right to equal access to the technology used for the improvement of reading instruction.
10. Children have a right to classrooms that optimize learning opportunities.

The Association strongly believes that to honor these rights—that is, to meet our obligation to provide excellent reading instruction to every child—classrooms need to be rethought, sufficient monetary investments must be made, and communities must wholeheartedly support reading reform efforts. In other words, we must work to create a productive and challenging focus on reading and vocabulary development that fosters not only academic language proficiency but also nurtures an enjoyment of reading throughout one's life. The full text of "Making a Difference Means Making It Different: Honoring Children's Rights to Excellent Reading Education" is available online at http://www.reading.org.

Now that we have considered some principles for establishing a productive literacy environment, let's examine the unique needs of English language learners in terms of reading development.

What Are the Stages of Reading Development for English Language Learners?

High-stakes testing in states across the nation has resulted in a heated debate about reading, including how to define reading and how to best instruct students in the process of reading. This dispute has even moved into the political arena, with some states considering legislation regarding the instruction of reading. We define *reading* as "the thinking that is said to occur when a person reads. A reader sees an array of written symbols, associates them with sounds, syntax, and meanings (not necessarily in that order), and comprehends the symbols as facts, information, descriptions, or arguments" (Coles, 1998, p. 4). Often, when working with struggling readers or English language learners, *reading* is more narrowly defined as decoding, which includes the following processes, visual/auditory discrimination, phonemic/alphabetic awareness, understanding of graphophonemic relationships, knowledge of concepts of print, linguistic/structural analysis, automatic recognition of words, use of context clues for word analysis, an established listening and speaking vocabulary, and knowledge of syntactic patterns.

This emphasis on decoding, translated mainly as phonemic awareness and knowledge of the alphabetic principle, has led schools to search for packaged or commercially produced reading programs that help students master the skills of decoding. According to teachers we work with, this highly scripted approach to reading instruction has produced many students who know how to sound out words, but that is where the process of reading ends for them. While the students can decode and even become fluent oral readers, they do not truly comprehend the material; they cannot read between the lines, infer meaning, or detect the author's bias, among other things. Reading, even decoding, is much more complex than simply mastering phonemic awareness and alphabet recognition. It is an incredibly complex psycholinguistic activity involving not only letter sounds, but also comprehension (in all its facets), adjusting reading for varying purposes, literary appreciation, and, most importantly, authentic and lifelong application. Plus, reading requires having a purpose for applying the skills. Am I reading this for pleasure or to prepare for a test, for example? Finally, little of this complex knowledge will be engaged if the student is not interested, motivated, or enjoying the experience. Learning to read is hard work and takes energy and concentration. If it does not seem fun to children, it is difficult to sustain their interest.

Interestingly enough, the processes noted in the definition of reading apply to any language. Whether we are reading in English or Chinese or Spanish, researchers have generally concluded that the processes are similar (Grabe, 1991; Carrell, Devine, & Eskey, 1988; Hudelson, 1981). First, you examine the printed page noting the visual structure of printed words; using your knowledge about the system by which letters or characters represent the sounds of speech, you are able to identify words. These word-identification processes are applied rapidly by fluent readers, but they may hamper readers unfamiliar with a language, especially if that language uses a different alphabet. At the same time the visual word forms are associated with meanings, the reader applies other linguistic knowledge, such as word-order patterns, text structure, and larger meaning issues—semantics—leading to a mental construction of overall textual meaning. This construction of text meaning, however, is subject to continual change and expansion as the reader progresses and engages in a cycle of prediction and confirmation of meaning.

Classroom teachers may be somewhat confused at this point, wondering why, if the process of reading in a first or another language is basically the same, it seems more difficult for English language learners in our classrooms. Simply put, all readers bring different levels of resources to the classroom. Two important resources that affect literacy development for English language learners are their English proficiency and the ability to read and write in their first language (Hudelson, 1987). As we have noted previously, English language learners have a dual task: to acquire English while also learning content and often even the processes of using language such as reading and writing.

When we consider the development of reading, of learning to read, we generally think of emergent literacy and young children. With English language learners, this is not necessarily the case. While some English language learners in our schools have learned to read in their home language before immigrating to the United States, many have not. Among those nonreaders are students of all ages. In our work at newcomer academies and newcomer career academies (described in Chapter 1), we encounter many recent immigrants at the secondary level who are preliterate—not able to read in their first language. Thus, these students are emergent readers despite their age.

Consequently, the twofold process of acquiring English while also learning to read becomes very complex. Our native English speakers have had a chance to master the oral system of language prior to entering school and beginning reading instruction. However, we should not delay literacy instruction with English language learners until they have control of oral language. Research indicates that oral and written English can develop simultaneously (Hudelson, 1984, 1986; Goodman, Goodman, & Flores, 1979; Urzua, 1987).

In order to have a better understanding of our English language learners and the characteristics they may demonstrate as they progress with reading, let's consider the three proficiency levels—beginning, intermediate, and advanced. Remember, there is no magic timetable for progression from stage to stage. English language learners, whatever their age or grade level, move through these stages at different rates based on the many factors that affect language acquisition that were discussed in Chapters 1 and 2.

Beginning Proficiency Level

As highlighted in Chapter 4, strong oral language development is the foundation of reading development. As beginning-level students hear and speak English, they are becoming aware of the sounds of their new language. This phase cannot be underestimated. The next step is to acquaint them with the symbols for those sounds. Unfortunately, at this stage, many ESL teachers turn to packaged programs and phonics readers. These materials focus on letter–sound correspondences and the strategies for decoding printed words into oral words in an attempt to understand the meaning of unfamiliar printed words (Johnson & Pearson, 1984). While such resources seem ideal on the surface because they clearly focus on the letters, sounds, and rules of English, and teachers "know" their students need these skills, some caution is in order.

Phonics should never comprise an entire reading lesson (Hall, 1988). Phonics is a means to an end—the ability to figure out the word and keep reading. Using phonics is only one strategy for helping with unknown words encountered in context in real reading situations. The ultimate goal is independence in word recognition (Johnson & Pearson, 1984). There are many other strategies, such as looking at the whole context for meaning, analyzing parts of the word to see if it looks like another word you know, and so on.

English does not have a very high ratio of symbol-to-sound correspondence; many symbols represent multiple sounds and vice versa (Hamayan & Pfleger, 1987). Like many languages, English is filled with exceptional spellings for many different sounds, as humorously presented in Judith Viorst's (1994) *The Alphabet from Z to A (with Much Confusion on the Way)*. Therefore, it is not a good use of time to teach extended lessons on irregular examples that real readers rarely encounter. Phonics instruction should aim to teach only the most important and regular sound–symbol relationships (Anderson, Hiebert, Scott, & Wilkinson, 1985). Teachers can start with reliable sounds that have a high frequency of occurrence in print.

Phonic rules and generalizations are, at best, of temporary value. Once a child has learned to read the spellings to which they pertain, they are superfluous (Adams, 1990). Once you know how to say and read a word, you don't have to break it down into its parts when you encounter it again.

Packaged programs are designed for whole-class instruction, but within any group of students the diversity is tremendous. Even if all the students are English language learners, the range of backgrounds and abilities is still substantial. Setting up needs groups for skill instruction, therefore, is more efficient and sensible than offering blanket instruction to all children, some of whom may already know what you are teaching (Trachtenburg, 1990).

Adjusting phonics lessons to children's emerging needs, especially with English language learners, is sensible and efficient. Such lessons usually have more effect on learning, as well, because of their timeliness. For instance, certain children can learn to read without phonics; thus, phonics should not be a prerequisite for reading real books (Anderson, Hiebert, Scott, & Wilkinson, 1985). Moreover, if English language learners come from home language backgrounds similar to English (e.g., Spanish), then the transition to the printed version of English is not so different (Odlin, 1989). When this is the case, teachers can link what students know about the sounds and symbols of their home language to English, pointing out the similarities and the differences. Conversely, when students come from a non-Roman-alphabet language, more direct instruction may be required to familiarize students with the sound–symbol correspondence.

Practice to solidify sound–symbol correspondences in English should be meaningful and connected to authentic text, including trade books and real world print (cereal boxes, logos, advertisements, etc.). Moreover, programs for all children, good readers as well as struggling ones, should strive to maintain an appropriate balance between phonics activities and the reading and appreciation of informative and engaging texts (Adams, 1990). When integrated into the learning of reading and writing, phonics can be a big help. Unfortunately, the English language learner who needs extra opportunities to read and write to gain fluency and confidence often gets extra phonics and other skill-only lessons instead. This can be deadly for the struggling student who does not see the purpose in mastering the reading subskills. Finding a way to help these students read *something*—predictable, patterned books, or short magazine articles, for example—is essential.

Immersing students in reading and writing through labeling the room, using big books for younger students, sharing predictable text material with all ages, introducing real world print, and reading aloud may be more powerful long-range strategies to introduce students to the English alphabet and sound system. Indeed, reading aloud regularly appears to be the most crucial activity for building reading knowledge and skills (Adams, 1990). In this way, children hear sounds and words over and over. They hear big words and literary sentences, unlike much of our day-to-day communication. In short, the richer the language environment, the richer the language learning (Cullinan, 1987). This is one of the most basic commandments of a balanced literacy approach. An environment filled with books and other forms of print, with large amounts of time spent on listening to and reading books, and with writing as part of every day is bound to have a powerful influence.

In addition, let's look at how easily real world print can be linked to phonics instruction as well as offering an excellent opportunity for students to share their home language and culture. Focusing on everyday print from their surrounding environment, children can bring food labels and other print examples in their home language to share with the class. At this point, the teacher highlights the similarities and differences between the home language and English in terms of sound–symbol correspondence in these real world print samples. A running record of these examples could be collected, alphabetized, and posted on chart paper along one wall in the classroom. As students bring examples and post these, the key terms (brand name and type of product) could be written in English and the home language. The main sounds in both English and the home language could be highlighted, and attention focused on the sound with the associated symbolic representation. For non-Roman-alphabet examples, students are still provided with sound–symbol opportunities, albeit in only one language.

Reading comprehension at this beginning proficiency level is limited to simple phrases and sentences. Students have not progressed beyond sentence-level text and extract meaning only from short, simple texts. To increase student ability to read simple text independently, teachers can surround students with real world print, the children's own writing, and quality trade books. Patterned, repetitive language is especially effective at this stage of reading development, and examples of this type of language include poetry, songs, and trade books. Authors such as Eric Carle, Pat Hutchins, Tana Hoban, Nancy Tafuri, Denise Fleming, and Lois Ehlert have created award-winning children's books full of lyrical, but simple, language as well as beautiful illustrations.

Predictable books and concept books are also invaluable tools for promoting reading fluency in English language learners. Predictable books are highly formulaic and make extensive use of repeated words, phrases, and stanzas. Although many are designed for younger emerging readers, some lend themselves to use across the grades. The "Very" series by Eric Carle, for example, is appealing in its collage illustrations, patterned language, and interesting content. *The Very Hungry Caterpillar* (1969) is a simple introduction to metamorphosis that appeals to all readers. Concept books go even farther in their informational focus on content. Many of Bruce McMillan's books, for example, help introduce new vocabulary and then visually represent the terms and concepts in concrete ways. See *Eating Fractions* (McMillan, 1991) for an excellent example of the strong match between visual and textual representations of important concepts.

As beginning level students encounter more extensive printed material, the next step is student engagement through various shared reading experiences as well as reader-response techniques, including writing or drawing. Especially for those students who struggle with writing, sketching a summary of the reading with labels for the key points and vocabulary can assist student retention of the information. Illustrating text is an especially useful technique for beginning level students and with more difficult expository reading from nonfiction and content books. Finally, increased encounters with print provide opportunities for shared reading experiences (e.g., choral reading, paired reading, radio reading). More detailed suggestions for shared reading experiences (Vogt, 1992) are highlighted in the next section, which describes strategies for engaging students with the process of reading.

Intermediate Proficiency Level

Intermediate English language learners demonstrate progress toward the goal of using English for both personal and academic purposes. They have increased their facility with printed text. Indications of their transition into the intermediate level include the ability to read cues and sentences orally and to read short paragraphs in stories based on previous oral work in class. This increased fluency in reading and print comprehension is spurred by a command of more vocabulary and an increased number of high-frequency words along with a beginning understanding of different text types (e.g., narrative and expository) and various text structure patterns (e.g., comparison/contrast, descriptive, problem/solution, etc.). Increased comprehension of text provides input for students to verbally negotiate meanings with peers in class discussions and literature circles.

While an introduction to the academic language of the content areas should not be delayed for English language learners, extensive use of the content textbook surfaces more at this intermediate proficiency level. At this point, they plunge in earnest into expository text and the content area vocabulary of science, math, social studies, and language arts. To assist with this information load, teachers may turn to nonfiction authors such as Seymour Simon, Gail Gibbons, and Diane Stanley who have created informational books that are extremely readable and highly visual. Novels by authors like Gary Soto, Karen Hesse, Kevin Henkes, and Mildred Taylor also appeal to intermediate level readers.

Despite the progress with reading at the intermediate proficiency level, extended texts with new vocabulary and content textbooks still present a challenge. Attention-focusing techniques help students move beyond a superficial reading and attend to the reading despite the difficulties that the vocabulary, topic, or format present. For example, graphic organizers allow students to visually represent and map the content of a reading. In addition, lesson frameworks including the directed reading thinking activity (DRTA) and K-W-L address the phases of the reading process (prereading, during, and postreading phases). Both of these techniques will be discussed in detail in Section IV, "Exploring Content," where we offer an in-depth look at the issue of expository text and content reading. The chapters in that section present an overview of the subgenres of nonfiction literature and effective strategies for engaging students with both expository and nonfiction text as well as techniques for linking nonfiction literature with the textbook in order to facilitate student comprehension.

Advanced Proficiency Level

By the time English language learners reach the advanced proficiency level, they may be mainstreamed into grade-level classes or very close to attending all classes with their native English speaking peers. Advanced level English language learners read with comprehension more complex stories and paragraphs based on previous oral work covered in class. More sophisticated picture books like *Animalia* (Base, 1986) as well as Newbery award-winning novels like *Out of the Dust* (Hesse, 1997) are now within their cognitive grasp. In addition, they read orally and silently for comprehension while continuing to expand content area vocabulary in science, math, social studies, and language arts. At this level, teachers often remark that English language learners and their native English speaking peers look much alike in terms of language proficiency. While this may be true, English language learners still struggle with the academic texts required for success in schools, especially with prior knowledge gaps. Thus, grade-level and content area teachers need to assist these students by utilizing the techniques discussed in the next section to prepare them to read, monitor, and extend their reading ability.

What Instructional Strategies Assist English Language Learners throughout the Reading Process?

Within this section, we highlight many instructional strategies that can assist English language learners with reading development. However, our focus will be to present strategies that can be combined with meaningful text not only to help students decode text but, most importantly, to engage them and attain higher and higher levels of comprehension. This emphasis on reader engagement and text enjoyment is a critical factor. In our visits to classrooms, we have seen an alarming increase in the number of packaged programs that seem to reduce the act of reading to a series of skills. Spurred by high-stakes testing and recent state reading reform initiatives, such programs are often highly scripted with little teacher input, and they emphasize direct instruction of phonological skills, phonemic awareness, sound–symbol relationships, and decoding rather than reading for meaning. The reading material used in these programs, and sometimes in reading and language arts texts, leaves a great deal to be desired in terms of motivating and interesting the student.

Moreover, published materials frequently fail to address the tremendous linguistic and cultural diversity present in most classrooms, especially classrooms with English language learners. The rationale behind programmed materials and reading series is to teach the skills first. Interaction with text is often delayed until the sound system has been fully mastered. At that point, students encounter material written for an appropriate grade level. Encountering authentic and meaningful text comes later and may be left up to teacher discretion through the use of supplemental materials. In our conversations with teachers, we have discovered that these approaches tend to turn off students to the joy of reading. They begin to define reading as a tedious act of merely applying a series of skills, rather than as a complex process of unlocking meaning and sifting through information, description, judgment, propaganda, and more to arrive at their own sense of a text. When students equate reading with a joyless act, the task of engaging them with any type of text later proves very problematic.

The Reading Process

Recent descriptions of the reading process have focused on the active nature of reading as learners bring their background knowledge to bear on the printed page. Thus, when we think about assisting the reading development of English language learners, one of the major considerations is working with students at each stage of this interactive process— **prereading, during-reading,** and **postreading.** Attention to each stage of the process helps all readers, especially English language learners, cope more effectively with the text demands presented by varying reading assignments. Thus, we spotlight each phase of the reading process along with specific strategies to help students enter into the text, maintain their comprehension while reading, and reflect back on the text using higher and higher levels of thinking.

Prereading

The two most important resources that all learners possess in terms of the reading process are language proficiency (including linguistic and structural analysis of text, phonemic awareness, recognition of words, etc.) and background knowledge related to the text (including content background as well as knowledge of text structure and features) (Peregoy & Boyle, 1997). While English language proficiency grows gradually, the academic language of the classroom may take five years or more to fully develop for an English language learner (Thomas & Collier, 1995). Yet, building background knowledge related to reading in general and to specific text can be accomplished in the classroom on a daily basis through planning with prereading concerns in mind. Thus begins a cyclical relationship: extending background knowledge enables students to more effectively tackle reading tasks, which leads to increased English language proficiency.

In the past, little attention has been focused on activities before reading. However, research highlights the critical nature of a prereading emphasis. Alverman & Phelps (1994, p. 122) note that "what teachers do before reading to prepare students can be more effective in promoting comprehension than what is done after reading." This is even more true with English language learners in the classroom.

In the prereading phase of the reading process, the teacher needs to activate students' prior knowledge in order to determine whether students have enough background to proceed and to decide whether the knowledge students possess is accurate (Alvermann & Phelps, 1994). If teachers determine that students lack the appropriate prior knowledge, they must carefully consider how to begin, tailoring prereading plans specifically to students and the assignment at hand. After we establish the importance of using *all* information at hand, not just print-based cues, teachers can activate students' visual literacy with illustrations from book covers and within the text itself. As an example, Seymour Simon's books on weather phenomena (*Lightning*, 1997), the solar system (*Comets, Meteors, and Asteriods*, 1994), and natural disasters (*Volcanoes*, 1988) have vivid photos to spark interest prior to content lessons. Using these photos, teachers can lead students into a discussion of their background knowledge and predictions about the upcoming lesson. Remember also that simply talking with students about a topic is a very valuable prereading technique. In addition, poetry can serve as a powerful advanced organizer for a lesson. For instance, reading aloud Lee Bennett Hopkins' poem "Thunder" (*Weather*, 1994, pp. 36–37) can start a discussion about storms that students have witnessed. The teacher can then record student associations about storms, producing a beginning vocabulary bank to use in the upcoming reading.

With the countless options available for prereading, the teacher may wonder where to begin. The choice of strategy really centers around three areas (Graves & Graves, 1994): (1) the students—their cultural background, linguistic proficiency, and content knowledge; (2) the purpose(s) for reading—as a base for class discussion, a cooperative learning activity, or a writing activity; and (3) the material—expository, nonfiction, or narrative text. Some prereading strategies may be more appropriate or necessary for expository text, others for narrative material. Motivational activities include hands-on student participation and involvement. These "direct and concrete experiences facilitate learning for anyone but are essential for English learners" (Peregoy & Boyle, 1997, p. 298).

On the other hand, we assume that narrative text draws students in, offering an entertaining read and holding student attention through plot or description. Nonetheless, within most reading and language arts series, the readability level of stories varies greatly, and English language learners may struggle with unfamiliar cultural and historical settings or character motivation. With this in mind, teachers may decide to focus on building background knowledge as a prereading priority. There are many wonderful techniques for motivating and building background knowledge prior to reading. The premise behind all of these techniques is "to bridge the gap between what the reader already knows and what the reader needs to know before he/she can meaningfully learn the task at hand" (Ausubel, 1968, p. 148).

Building Language Background and Vocabulary.   One of the most important aspects of preparing students for reading is to address their language background, with particular attention to vocabulary. Activities like phonics practice, semantic mapping, and word games may be essential preparation in helping students make sense of text. A part of building background knowledge may include some work on sound–symbol relationships. How might phonics fit into this process? For helping students at beginning proficiency levels, we advocate a balanced stance as an alternative to the reliance on programmed materials. There are several options for emphasizing phonics and the sound–symbol relationship within a balanced literacy environment.

Use the Language Experience Approach to help students see speech–print connections through their dictated writing. As students tell a story, describe an object, or offer a caption for a picture, you write their words down. Read the dictated writing over again as you point to each of the words.

Maximize listening activities to build both auditory discrimination and listening comprehension. For example, use sound guessing games, tapes at a listening center, Simon Says, and so on. Also incorporate oral language activities such as choral reading, rhymes, tongue twisters, and songs to reinforce the sound qualities of language.

Music and art offer opportunities for sound–symbol connections as students draw and write and create captions (using invented spellings that exercise their developing grapho-phonemic awareness). They can sing and write familiar songs, jingles, or finger plays.

Introduce children to real world print around them as they gather pictures and objects whose names begin with a designated letter or sound. Do not proceed alphabetically, but rather begin with regular consonants interspersed with vowels. Show them how much of their environment they are already reading (e.g., stop signs, McDonald's arches, etc.).

Word and letter–sound cards can be a versatile resource for practice and play. Games such as concentration (matching initial sounds/letters and words/pictures), fishing (using magnets and paper clips), and even flash card review (call out a word, hold up a card) can be appropriate and motivating, especially in small groups or with a partner.

Of course, literature is your richest resource for outstanding models of effective language. Read aloud daily, bringing in "sound" books such as *Jungle Sounds* (1989) and *City Sounds* (1989) by Rebecca Emberley; look at ABC books for a variety of sound–letter associations; and seek out books with strong rhyme, predictable patterns, repetition, and alliteration like the classic *Brown Bear, Brown Bear* (1970) by Bill Martin, Jr., or *Each Peach Pear Plum* (1978) by the Ahlbergs. Big books offer these qualities in addition to easier visibility, which invites a shared reading experience. Phyllis Trachtenburg (1990) offers an excellent list of literature that features the repetition of particular phonic patterns.

Building Word Knowledge.   Beyond awareness of sound–symbol relationships, another critical factor in oral fluency and reading comprehension is word knowledge, especially for students at intermediate and advanced proficiency levels. Even if a student successfully navigates the sound–symbol issues, too many unfamiliar words will result in very limited comprehension of the material. If students are unable to understand word meanings as they read, they are simply engaging in mindless decoding (Fountas & Pinnell, 1996). Research documents this critical connection of word knowledge to reading success (Allington & Cunningham, 1996).

Unfortunately, despite research indicating the ineffectiveness of the traditional method of word study, using word lists and requiring students to write the definition of each word and use it in a sentence is still the norm. Because classrooms are filled with diverse learners who learn in a variety of ways—from print-based methods as well as hands-on strategies such as drama—teachers should not limit vocabulary instruction to just one strategy. Furthermore, teachers should recognize that English language learners vary tremendously not only in their knowledge of English vocabulary but also in the depth of their word knowledge in their home language. While many students have a limited vocabulary in their first language and need intensive vocabulary instruction in English, others bring a rich store of first language word knowledge to the classroom that can serve as a foundation for learning new words in English. For students in the latter category, teachers might focus student attention on cognates, words that are similar in English and the home language (e.g., the Spanish *civilizacion* and English *civilization*), and make the link between similar prefixes and suffixes in the languages. In this way, students can feel proud about the knowledge they bring to the classroom.

Finally, we encourage teachers to remember that reading aloud to students and simply having students read often are the most effective ways to build vocabulary. At least two studies have found that students who read learn vocabulary ten times faster than those who receive intensive word-list instruction (Nagy, Herman, & Anderson, 1985; Krashen, 1993). Besides general reading, there are many excellent trade books that focus on word study, including the idiomatic and figurative language featured in Fred Gwynne's picture books and word-specific jargon found in Alexandra Day's books about Frank and Ernest, who try out a variety of professions. Plus, a host of dictionaries or phrase books explain the roots of many of our expressions and colloquialisms in English. For annual lists of books that focus on language and vocabulary in particular, consult the Notable Trade Books in the Language Arts list found on the Web at http://www.childrensliteratureassembly.org.

A variety of instructional activities build word knowledge, including structural analysis, semantic maps, semantic feature analysis, word sorts or categorization, mimes, charades, role plays, games, projects, artwork, word banks, crossword puzzles, and discussion. Teachers can experiment with these, trying them with different content areas, different types of lessons, and so on.

Structural analysis is a simple technique that encourages students to use word parts to determine meaning. Because the addition of affixes (prefixes and suffixes) is the most common means of adding words to our language (Andrews, 1998), increased knowledge about these word parts could become a powerful tool. For example, in Jim Arnosky's *All about Alligators* (1994), the author describes alligators as *semi-aquatic*. Reading on, we discover that *semi-aquatic* "means they spend nearly half their time in water" (unnumbered page). Writing *semi-aquatic* on the board, the teacher can draw students' attention to the prefix *semi* and have them offer other words with the same prefix (e.g., semicircle). This strategy leads to independent word analysis and contributes positively to test-taking skills as well.

Semantic maps or webs (Johnson & Pearson, 1984) link groups of interrelated terms and ideas. Teachers may construct a more convergent semantic map as a preview of a lesson or story, or students may create more open-ended, divergent maps to brainstorm. For instance, in a unit on intergenerational relationships, Nancy worked with a high school ESL class. The students brainstormed their associations for individuals at different age groups—infants, children, teens, adults, and seniors—prior to reading a series of picture books about unique relationships formed between a younger and an older person. This served to start students thinking about the issue of age and stereotypes about age.

Semantic maps work at any point in the word study or lesson: prereading for activating background knowledge, during-reading for focusing student attention, or postreading for review and extension of learning.

Constructing and using a semantic map is simple. Begin by identifying a key topic, word, or concept. Place this in the center of the board, overhead, or chart paper. (For the intergenerational relationships unit, we put "various age groups" at the center of the map). Then identify at least three or four subcategories of subordinate information about the identified concept, and place these on spokes radiating from the center topic. (Again, in the intergenerational unit, we identified various age groups—infants, children, teens, adults, and seniors—as our subcategories.) As a prereading technique, brainstorm with students, asking them to contribute prior knowledge relating to any of the spoke subheadings before reading. During reading, use this graphic organizer as an outline for note taking. After reading, add new information or correct misinformation. Finally, post the class-generated before and after semantic maps to spark discussion.

The **semantic feature analysis** technique (Anders & Bos, 1986; Anders, Bos, & Wilde, 1986; Toms-Boronowski, 1983) helps students categorize and recognize the relationship of interrelated terms. While this strategy can be used at any point in vocabulary study, it is especially helpful as a culminating activity to synthesize information from a unit of study. Teachers might even choose the semantic feature analysis as a means of informal assessment for a unit of study. Creating a semantic feature analysis is as easy as constructing a matrix of columns and rows. When working in elementary classrooms, Terry created the following grid, seen in Table 5.1, with tricksters featured in traditional literature along with their characteristics.

TABLE 5.1   Semantic Feature Analysis for Trickster Tales

Characteristics of Tricksters							
Trickster	**Human**	**Animal**	**Small, Vulnerable**	**Big, Powerful**	**Uses Strength**	**Uses Intelligence**	**Uses Deceit**
Anansi							
Brer Rabbit							
Coyote							
Iktomi							
Reynard							
Sir Whong							
Zomo							

First, create a grid of rows and columns. Place the topic or concept above the grid as a title (Characteristics of Tricksters). Down the first column on the left, place members of your topic or concept (e.g., the tricksters). Across the top row, place the features or attributes of the members of the topic or concept (e.g., human, animal, etc.). It is always good to leave spaces for students to add other topics or attributes. Then have students determine which characteristics belong to each member of the concepts under study, and place Xs in those boxes. Follow up with a discussion, and encourage students to add any other members of the concept to the grid.

Word sorts and **categorization activities** ask students to consider the relationships among various terms. Word sorts can be open or closed. In a **closed sort**, the teacher provides a list of words and a predetermined set of categories, and students simply sort the words into those categories. In an **open sort**, the categories are not predetermined. Students are free to come up with their own categories, and words can be placed in more than one category.

Word sorts can be implemented at various instructional points. For instance, teacher Jolyn Kintner developed a word sort (Table 5.2) for Barbara Bash's (1993) *Shadows of Night: The Hidden World of the Little Brown Bat* to be used before and after reading the book. The prereading sort was an open category, so students could create multiple categories and place words appropriately, with some words used in several categories. The postreading sort was a closed sort with two categories—winter and spring. In addition, word sorts, especially the open sort, are great culminating activities for an entire unit of study.

Categorization activities ask students to choose the word or concept that does or does not belong and often to label the category of words presented. Beyond using words to categorize, teachers could choose more hands-on options, such as providing students with manipulatives to group. For instance, students can group pictures, cards, or objects. Such

TABLE 5.2   Word Sort

Words

birth	pups	females	imitating
clustering	mating	silent maternity	barns
low body temperature	males and females	colony	bat conventions
hunting	warm milk	caves	slow heartbeat

Developed for Bash, Barbara. (1993). *Shadows of Night: The Hidden World of the Little Brown Bat.* San Francisco: Sierra Club.

Prereading: open sort

Postreading: closed sort (categories: spring and winter)

activities are common on standardized tests, and utilizing this vocabulary technique will help students with both word knowledge and test-taking strategies. Words can be drawn from high-frequency lists, from curricular areas, or from children's own suggestions. At regular intervals, the teacher leads students back to real books that use these words in meaningful contexts.

The previous techniques represent just a few recommended strategies to introduce new words and to build student backgrounds. In addition, there are any number of games and activities. For instance, **mime** or **charades** provide opportunities to act out the meaning surrounding a word in a nonverbal manner that might assist the beginning or very shy English language learner. The kinesthetic value of physically participating adds another dimension that enhances learning.

Role play, with or without words, can be used to help students act out the steps for going through a process to solve a math problem or to do a laboratory exercise in science. The brevity of poetry makes it particularly well suited to mime or nonverbal role play. As students participate in the choral reading of poems, they can silently act out the meaning of the words.

Many commercially produced **games,** such as Password, Scrabble, and Pictionary, are also available for classroom use, or teachers can create their own versions of these games tailored to meet the specific vocabulary requirements of their content areas. Hands-on opportunities abound with **projects,** including constructing mobiles with vocabulary words or scrapbooks with related terminology. Another hands-on possibility is **student artwork** in the form of posters or collages that visually demonstrate the meaning of words, such as a family tree. One book that provides input that easily transfers to a family-tree format is Robert Lawson's (1968) *They Were Strong and Good,* which details the author's family story. Using a fictitious source for a family tree may alleviate some of the anxiety that many students feel with a personal activity in the very public school setting.

Word banks, discussed earlier, also provide opportunities for students to write, illustrate, and define a word, while the ever popular **crossword puzzle** offers students a challenge to link meanings with vocabulary terms. Many software programs allow teachers to easily construct crossword puzzles, word searches, and other fun vocabulary-building games with different sets of words each time.

Finally, as students encounter text and work on the sound–symbol relationships and the meanings of the vocabulary in the selection, teachers will want to spark **discussion** related to the material. Talking about new words and hearing new words pronounced and incorporated into daily read alouds help students integrate these new words into their oral and listening vocabularies. The more students talk about words, encounter words in their reading and listening, and engage in meaningful practice with those words, the more likely they are to begin to internalize those words and make them part of their everyday vocabularies.

Prereading Activities.   Vocabulary and phonics activities are just one part of the critical prereading stage of the reading process. Building students' cognitive backgrounds and ensuring their affective connection or motivation are also essential to prereading. Teachers may draw from numerous options to motivate and build background, which we discuss in this section. This is not an exhaustive inventory of prereading techniques; many professional resources provide ideas for this phase of the reading process, including Moore, Readence, and Rickelman's *Prereading Activities for Content Area Reading and Learning* (1989). Many prereading techniques also lend themselves to the other phases of the reading process. As a teacher you are constrained only by your own level of reflection and creativity. While considering these strategies, remember the critical role of the teacher in modeling each technique, talking about the reading process, and constantly reading aloud.

One method the teacher can utilize to prepare students for new reading material is to use **conceptually related readings** through teacher read alouds or demonstrations of visuals or through a student skim-and-scan activity. Indeed, Crafton (1983) found that reading two selections on the same topic had a positive effect on students' comprehension of the second reading. Thus, teachers can foster enhanced achievement when they bring in magazine and newspaper articles, trade books, or other collateral material prior to attacking the assigned reading.

Alphabet and counting books supply a rich source of material to extend students' vocabulary and conceptual base. In one or two pages, a concept related to a specific theme or topic is explored for each letter of the alphabet or each number from one to ten, and often beyond. Functioning as illustrated dictionaries or abbreviated encyclopedias, alphabet books arrange a wealth of information in a very concise format. For instance, *Eight Hands Round: A Patchwork Alphabet* (Paul, 1991) and *The ABC Book of Early Americana* (Sloane, 1995) survey the lifestyle, customs, and traditions of early America and are ideally suited for secondary students as a preview to an American literature selection or the American history textbook. Counting books can also introduce content, as well as reinforce basic mathematical concepts. Excellent examples include Jim Haskins' *Count Your Way through the Arab World* (1991) and *One Good Horse: A Cowpuncher's Counting Book* (1990) by Ann Herbert Scott.

Another picture book format perfect for building background is the question-and-answer book. Again, using one or two pages, one question related to a topic is answered. Many of these books are linked to historical eras or events—*How Would You Survive in the Middle Ages?* (Macdonald, 1995) and *If You Lived at the Time of the American Revolution* (Moore, 1997)—follow a chronological sequence. Indeed, the table of contents for one series of question-and-answer books published by Scholastic is simply a time-ordered listing of questions. Using the question-and-answer book as a prereading link to a specific reading assignment, the teacher uses an overhead transparency of the table of contents to begin discussion. Students brainstorm possible answers to entries in the table of contents, and the class reads an entry to confirm their understanding.

In addition to fiction and nonfiction picture books, poetry—an often overlooked resource—can be used to build background knowledge. For example, numerous books provide brilliant images of various geographic regions using poems accompanied by illustrations or photographs. Used as a prereading tool, these works help students establish a visual image of the setting that can link to a later reading, even as an introduction to an expository selection from the content textbook. For example, Diane Siebert's *Mojave* (1988) and Frank Asch's *Cactus Poems* (1998) offer a rich portrait of the desert.

Prediction is a valuable reading ability and a logical choice for the prereading phase. For instance, teachers can encourage students to make logical extensions or predictions about where a story might go or to make reasonable guesses about the topics the author of an expository text might explore in a particular selection. Using the indicated parts of a text shown in Table 5.3 , a prediction guide could easily be developed for *Sarah, Plain and Tall* (MacLachlan, 1985).

Anticipation guides (Herber, 1978) present a series of statements to tap into what students already know or believe about the upcoming reading. By creating simple anticipation guides, teachers may assess the types of preconceived notions that students have about content and concepts. One excellent purpose of anticipation guides is to serve as "springboards for modifying strongly held misconceptions about the topic" (Dufflemeyer, Baum, & Merkley, 1987, p. 147). For instance, prior to having high school students read an article about euthanasia, you might brainstorm a list of ten statements that students could respond to in terms of what they believe and what point of view they think the author might hold about the issues. This guide would be distributed prior to reading, and

---

TABLE 5.3   Prediction Guide for *Sarah, Plain and Tall*

1. Story/selection title: *Sarah, Plain and Tall,* by Patricia MacLachlan

2. Key words, phrases, sentences: cow pond, hitch, pesky, wail, "Ayuh," hearthstones, dune

3. Incomplete sentences from a story/selection:
   - "Caleb and I looked at each other and. . . ."
   - "A few raindrops came, gentle at first, then stronger and louder, so that. . . ."

4. The setting, place, time, and characters of a selection (to spur predictions of events of the story, etc.):
   - *Characters:* Sarah, Papa, Anna, Caleb
   - *Setting:* The prairies of the American West in the late 1800s

5. Varying portions of text (leading to a prediction about outcomes):
   - "I remember another time when a wagon took Mama away. It had been a day just like this day. And Mama had never come back."
   - "And then Papa drove off along the dirt road to fetch Sarah. Papa's new wife. Maybe. Maybe our new mother."

students would respond to each item. A class discussion of the guide and students' responses prior to reading provide both motivation and content reinforcement. Follow up with the same guide after reading, and have students respond again to see if any of their ideas have changed. In Table 5.4, we see an example of an anticipation/reaction guide drawn from Russell Freedman's *Buffalo Hunt* (1988).

In the **options guide** (Bean, Sorter, Singer, & Frazee, 1986), the teacher instructs students to read up to a specific point in the text. Students then stop and respond to a series of options that refer to how the selection will proceed from that point. For instance, in science, students might read through a lab discussion, stopping to consider options for how the experiment will turn out. The popular "Choose Your Own Adventure" fiction series demonstrates this format clearly and gives students the freedom to "create" the story themselves. Table 5.5 offers an example of an option guide for Phyllis Naylor's *Shiloh* (1991).

Beginning a selection with a what-if scenario can spark students' motivation and engage them with the reading. Teachers can use **problem-solving activities** or **hypothetical situations** (Haggard, 1989) to generate discussion and raise issues and questions, then have students read to seek solutions. The scenario in the options guide for *Shiloh* is just one possibility. Also, consider the problem solving activity in Box 5.1 about a situation that many believe really happened.

In developing and using **attitude inventories** (Vacca & Vacca, 1989), the teacher uses a series of statements to elicit student responses at an affective level. Students are asked to rank items based on their own attitude and belief systems. For instance, prior to reading about a country going to war, a teacher might construct an attitude inventory asking students to respond to various statements about whether it is right to declare war in various situations. It is important to assess students' belief systems prior to readings in which controversial or value-laden information is presented. Students' attitudes may interfere with comprehension of the text when different points of view are presented. If ecology and recycling is the topic, teachers might brainstorm with students to find out what

TABLE 5.4   Anticipation/Reaction Guide for *Buffalo Hunt*

Instructions for Students: Decide whether the statements are true or false. Then discuss your responses with your group. After you have read or heard the book, review your answers.

Before	After	Statement
		1. In olden times, it was said, buffalo used to eat Native American people.
		2. At one time, 60 or 70 million buffalo roamed the plains.
		3. It was a woman's job to skin and butcher the buffalo.
		4. Most Native Americans used guns to hunt buffalo after the white men introduced guns to them.
		5. During a buffalo hunt, marshals and their assistants enforced the rules and regulations of the hunt.

TABLE 5.5   Option Guide for *Shiloh*

Instructions to Students: Read the following scenario. Then circle the option listed below that you believe the young boy will choose.

Suppose a young dog followed you home. You wanted to keep him, but your mother says, "If you can't afford to feed him and take him to the vet when he's sick, you've got no right taking him in." Your parents make you take him back to his owner. The dog's owner angrily kicks the dog and brags how he keeps his hunting dogs half-starved so they will be better hunters. Since the owner mistreats his dogs, you are worried about the one you found. A few days later, the dog returns to your home. What would you do?

Options

- Return the dog to his owner.
- Tell his owner to treat the dog better or you will call the Humane Society.
- Sell the dog to a pet store.
- Give the dog to someone who will take good care of it.
- Hide the dog.
- Take the dog to the pound.
- Buy the dog from his owner.
- Ask your parents to let you keep him.

they know about these important ideas, or they can construct an attitude inventory such as the one in Table 5.6. Then the teacher can use a book like *Trash* by Charlotte Wilcox (1988) to show vivid, realistic photographs and accurate terminology about the multitude of ways we handle garbage in this country. Students might even create their own mini-guide or glossary of terms to guide further reading and research.

All of these prereading techniques furnish opportunities to motivate students and to prepare them to read by building background knowledge in relation to content and language issues. Yet, even after you set students on the course toward their reading with sound prereading strategies, you will still need to support students' reading efforts. So, let's move on to the next phase of the reading process—during-reading.

B O X **5.1**

Problem-Solving Activity for *The Yellow Star: The Legend of King Christian X of Denmark,* by Carmen Agra Deedy (2000)

Suppose you are the King of Denmark, and Nazi soldiers are now occupying your country. You have committed yourself to keep all Danes safe from harm. Now the Nazis have ordered that all Jews must sew a yellow star onto their clothing. The people of your country are frightened. They have heard terrible stories about how Jews who wear yellow stars are taken away and never heard from again. What would you do?

TABLE 5.6   Attitude Inventory: Ecology and the Environment

Directions for Students: Indicate whether you agree or disagree with each of the following statements. Then compare your responses with your group.

1. Separating gross trash from recyclables is a hassle.   Agree Disagree
2. I think we should separate and recycle paper, plastic, glass, aluminum, and even tin.   Agree Disagree
3. Sanitary landfills are the best option for handling trash.   Agree Disagree
4. Creating compost out of garbage is an easy way of dealing with trash.   Agree Disagree
5. Garbage collectors perform an important role.   Agree Disagree

During-Reading

Once you have launched students into their reading through prereading strategies, more decisions need to be made. This is the difficult part of the process, since we can't determine exactly how the student is processing the text. We can only observe outward indications of comprehension and progress. At this point, teachers need to consider how much guidance and what type of guidance to provide during-reading. Questions to ask at this stage of the process include the following:

- Should you allow students to complete the entire reading assignment without any pause or intervention?
- Does the reading assignment need to be divided into chunks that are more manageable and interspersed with discussion of these chunks of text?
- Do students need a reading or study guide to help them focus on the text and recognize the major relationships? What type of guide?

Some texts require little teacher intervention; students can proceed with ease. However, English language learners will require teacher assistance with many assignments, especially content-related ones. The goals for during-reading reflect the types of strategies that good readers bring to the page: activating and utilizing prior knowledge, automatically turning words into meaning, translating ideas into one's own words, and evaluating the author's purpose, motive, or authority (Vogt, 1998). Awareness of these skills assists teachers in providing appropriate during-reading support, modeling the skills for learners, and structuring during-reading plans specifically to individual student needs and the text at hand. For instance, material that is closely linked to students' background and interests may require less active instructional intervention. However, more difficult content selections with densely packed concepts will require techniques to support students while reading. Thus, teachers need to continue modeling strategies such as predicting what comes next and keeping a purpose for reading in mind.

Many of the strategies that skillful readers use while reading indicate metacognitive monitoring—thinking about one's thinking. In other words, skilled readers are thinking about their own processing techniques while reading. They intuitively understand the reading process and the skills involved, and, further, they know how to fix up miscues that may occur during reading. Through an examination of various metacognitive strategies, teachers can develop effective during-reading plans to assist students toward enhanced comprehension. Teachers might consider using think-alouds (Vogt, 1998) to systematically model what good readers do to make sense of text. The process would look something like this: "When I began reading this paragraph, I thought. . . . Then, when I read this part, I realized that. . . . It all didn't make sense to me until I . . ." (Vogt, 1998). Teachers with beginning English language readers can link read alouds to this process to model the strategies that students will eventually be using in their silent reading. Using high-interest, motivational materials to practice helps students get the knack of the process. Then students can apply these strategies with their own self-selected texts during independent reading time.

Reading Options.   To assist English language learners at their various proficiency levels, teachers should search for meaningful reading material, set the stage through prereading strategies, and work to involve the student in the during-reading phase. During-reading allows for a variety of grouping techniques beyond just having students read silently. For instance, the teacher might use whole-class read alouds for students at the beginning proficiency level, stopping periodically to discuss and informally assess student understanding. Additionally, teachers can use audio and video recordings of books or book passages to reinforce reading as students follow along with the text. As students become more comfortable with English, the teacher can place students in small groups or with partners as well as providing time for independent reading. Through small-group and partner configurations, English language learners can receive support and experience the freedom to take the necessary risks in the reading and language learning process.

Traditionally, however, much of the focus during beginning reading instruction is on oral reading and building oral fluency. We commonly observe this in the form of oral reading or round-robin reading in small groups in the early grades. Even with older students, we witness down-the-row or around-the-room oral reading. While it is especially important to give English language learners practice in oral reading, some caution is in order. First, they need time to practice before reading orally since they are struggling with a new language and some new sounds in that language. On the other hand, some English language learners become great "sounders," with little comprehension taking place. Thus, while oral fluency is an appropriate goal, teachers should carefully select the purposes and the methods for oral reading. The chief disadvantage of oral reading is lack of student engagement. Students tune in and out frequently during this type of activity, so teachers should use oral reading sparingly, incorporating various formats for engaging students beyond traditional oral reading. Since guided reading and shared reading were thoroughly discussed in Chapter 3, we highlight here just a few suggestions for oral and silent reading with the whole class, small groups, partners, and individual students.

With the **page and paragraph** method, there is a shared responsibility. The teacher reads one page aloud, then the students read the following paragraph orally or silently. This method helps focus students and keep them moving through the text. Breaking this up with discussion between sections also helps English language learners clear up any misunderstandings. Students can also use this method in pairs when matched with fluent readers.

Just as the name implies, in the **equal portions** method, students work as partners and divide up the reading equally. Each partner orally reads the same amount (usually a page at a time), taking turns. With this technique, students can choose the length of the reading to tackle, an important consideration for beginning and early intermediate English language learners. For instance, students might choose three paragraphs from a selection and, after practicing reading the paragraphs, take turns with a partner alternating reading paragraphs and listening to the partner read.

For **page, paragraph, or pass,** better readers are paired with average readers, and average readers with below-average readers. The better reader reads a page while the partner reads a shorter section or has the option to pass. Teachers would need to monitor this technique to ensure that struggling readers do not pass on all their turns.

Silent with support is a great technique to provide a sense of comfort for English language learners. Basically, students sit together as partners or in small groups. Each reads the selection silently, but turns to others to get help with words or portions of text they do not understand.

To support independent reading behavior and foster self-directed learning, students might try the **self-assisted technique,** which teaches self-monitoring strategies. Students read silently and list or mark difficult words or portions of text with a small self-adhesive note. They basically flag portions of the text they do not understand or jot down key words that need explanation. They then seek assistance (from their partner or the teacher) for the marked parts.

While **choral reading** is a fun option, it also creates a sense of comfort, especially for beginning English language learners. When reading in unison, no one is singled out. To script choral reading, a selection is divided into parts and read orally by entire groups or in assigned groups, according to the spoken lines of characters or some repeating refrain. Chapter 4 on oral language development and Chapter 9 on poetry have more ideas on choral reading.

Drama provides countless opportunities to reinforce reading skills, and **readers theater** is just one option. Readers theater is a variation of choral reading adapted to prose with assigned parts and a simple reading performance of some segment of text (Young, 1990, 1991). See Chapter 4 for more information on readers theater.

Radio reading offers a less monotonous option to round-robin reading. We have found this technique especially helpful with content textbook material. During the reading of a portion of text, students close their books and listen to the "broadcast" by the reader. The emphasis is placed on meaning, not on wordperfect reading. Following radio reading, the reader questions each student about what was read. If any part is unclear, the text can be checked for clarification.

Repeated reading relies on repeated exposure to the same text. This can occur in students' independent and silent rereading of books they choose themselves, or it can come from the teacher's reading aloud of often-requested children's books. In fact, we have been surprised at how students usually want to read silently on their own the book that the teacher has just read out loud to the whole class. Their familiarity with the story and language helps students feel more confident in tackling the decoding and comprehending necessary in independent reading.

Teachers can look for natural opportunities for students to participate through **interactive read alouds.** Students can join in spontaneously on a repeated phrase, take parts with the dialogue, complete a predictable sentence, or simply conclude "The End." The key is to invite student participation in the teacher-led read aloud.

For **echo reading,** teachers need to choose books with short sentences or rhyming or rhythmic text. As they read the line or sentence out loud, students echo or repeat the line, continuing this method with each line. Nancy Shaw's delightful "Sheep" series (e.g., *Sheep in a Jeep*, 1986) is particularly enjoyable to read echo style.

A variation on the written cloze technique, in **cloze reading** the teacher covers key words in the text with self-adhesive notes when reading aloud. Students must figure out what word should be used in the context. The teacher can model the process, trying different alternatives to show which ones make sense. With big books, or enlarged texts, the cloze approach is easy to model for small-group or whole-class reading. Students can also try this with partners, using smaller self-adhesive notes and individual trade books.

Nonprint media, including books in audio, video, and CD-ROM form, can also have a place in developing fluency in your English language learners. They can provide the repeated exposure so crucial to building automaticity in reading. Students can read the book and listen to it on tape, thus maximizing the reinforcement of two learning modalities. Books on tape can assist students with visual impairments as well. Books made into videos or movies can be viewed before reading to provide the prior knowledge framework that enables struggling readers to focus on word-level reading—much like hearing a book read aloud and then tackling it alone in silent reading.

Independent reading is a fundamental approach to providing reading practice. It is so crucial to developing fluency and independence that it should occur every day. Students should be choosing their own reading material whenever possible for independent reading. This may include trade books relevant to particular units of study, but there should also be ample opportunities for students to choose recreational reading like magazines, series books, or whatever else meets their individual interests and levels.

Teacher **read-alouds** can entice students to read an upcoming assignment or to lay the groundwork for a unit or topic of instruction. Even as you demonstrate for students the essential prereading, during-reading, and postreading techniques so helpful in becoming a fluent reader and as you provide a variety of student reading options, you should continue to read good books out loud to provide a model of confident and enthusiastic reading. Indeed, in reading aloud, you can present more challenging books than the students are able to tackle on their own. As Peregoy and Boyle (1997, p. 167) note, "when you read aloud to your students, you involve them in the pleasure function of print, you model the reading process." Jim Trelease, a national read aloud advocate, has two excellent resources available for teachers: *Hey! Listen to This: Stories to Read Aloud* (1992) for elementary-age students, and *Read All about It! Great Read-Aloud Stories, Poems, and Newspaper Pieces for Preteens and Teens* (1993). To assist teachers in locating relevant materials, there are numerous bibliographies, such as *A to Zoo: Subject Access to Children's Picture Books* (Lima & Lima, 1989) and *Best Books for Children* (Gillespie, 1998), that reference children's book by topic or theme. Another bibliography, *Worth a Thousand Words* (Ammon & Sherman, 1996), highlights more mature themes tackled in the increasing number of picture books designed for older readers. More ideas for read-aloud options in the content areas are explored in Chapter 10 on nonfiction literature.

One adaptation of a teacher read aloud we've found particularly effective is the discussion technique known as **Yes, because . . . No, because . . .** or **Both Sides** (Alvermann, 1991; Rothstein & Goldberg, 1993). This strategy gives students an organized way to examine both sides of an issue before reaching a conclusion. Nancy uses the picture book *An Ellis Island Christmas* (Leighton, 1992) for this activity. Students work in pairs, using a paper folded in half. The title of the story and the question to be discussed (e.g., Is immigrating to America worth the hardships?) appear at the top of the page. The teacher reads the story aloud, pausing periodically to allow students to discuss and record reasons from the story that would support both a yes response and a no response to the question. Students' lists should be balanced with reasons on each side. To accomplish this, the teacher encourages students to read between the lines of the selection and not just stick with the literal information. On completing the entire story or a portion of it, students share their reasons for both sides of the question. When Nancy uses *An Ellis Island Christmas*, she likes to stop prior to the end of the story as a means of enticing students to read the book on their own.

In summary, during-reading is a critical phase for teachers to monitor student progress. Supporting English language learners in this phase of the process helps them persist with text material despite the difficulties presented by their new language. Once students have completed the reading assignment, final decisions need to be made for the next phase—postreading.

Postreading

Traditionally, postreading is the phase on which the most emphasis is placed, but often the techniques for following up on reading are less than innovative. Students answer questions at the end of the chapter, or teachers simply ask a series of questions. Frequently, the questions asked after reading focus on low-level or literal concerns of the text. To truly extend student comprehension, other techniques must be considered to push students beyond simple regurgitation of information to higher levels of thinking. For instance, it is critical for students to retain information from an assignment and link it to future reading and learning (transfer). In addition, teachers will want to use strategies that tap into students' affective responses and deeper cognitive understanding of the material—making inferences, detecting flawed logic, noting biases, defending opinions, and so on. Simply giving back the literal information from the reading is not adequate. In the postreading phase, readers should be able to reflect on what has been read and to determine if the purposes for reading were met.

Teachers can assist students by reinforcing their effective use of strategies (Vogt, 1998). We present just a few ideas for extending understanding in the postreading phase. Teachers need to select appropriate postreading activities and organize their postreading plans to reflect the needs of students and the goals of the assignment.

Reading Journals.   Writing in journals in response to reading may be called reading journals, reading logs, response journals, or literature logs. No matter what the name, writing supports literacy development for English language learners, and journals furnish a means of assisting students to actively participate in reading, to record personal reactions and preferences, and to develop writing skills (Gillespie, 1993; Rosenblatt, 1978; Villaume, Worden, Williams, Hopkins, & Rosenblatt, 1994; Wollman-Bonilla, 1991; Wollman-Bonilla & Werchadlo, 1995).

Teachers may choose to have students write or draw in their journals before reading as a means of gathering ideas for later reflection after reading. This technique might be especially appropriate with English language learners who struggle with new vocabulary and syntax in oral communication situations. Along with decisions about when students respond, journal formats may range from free writing to responding to prompts (Martin, 1993). Additionally, students may write for the teacher as sole audience or may pair with classmates, cross-age partners, or adult volunteers via buddy journals (Gillespie, 1993). Whatever the format and whenever the writing takes place, journals provide a "unique opportunity for students to express their ideas and for the teacher to recognize each one's thinking" (Wollman-Bonilla & Werchadlo, 1995, p. 565).

Analysis of student responses in literature journals also replaces the need for traditional comprehension questions because teachers can read journals to ascertain whether students are understanding the reading. This is a natural assessment tool, albeit one that should focus more on comprehension than composition. A crucial point to remember, however, is that an infinite range of responses is possible. "Readers, influenced by past experiences and current circumstances, regional origins and upbringing, gender, age, past and present readings, will vary in their responses" (Karolides, 1992, p. 23). For English language learners, diverse cultures and language backgrounds affect the meaning they construct as they interact with literature.

Questioning. Traditionally, questioning has been viewed as a postreading activity. However, questions can be interspersed at any point in the lesson and in any phase of the reading process. Indeed, teachers should utilize questions at each phase for different purposes. Just and Carpenter (1987) found that questions have different effects depending on when they are asked in the reading and learning process. Furthermore, Wood (1986) found questions to be more effective when delivered closer in time to the text being read.

Before reading, questions help activate background knowledge and focus students on important ideas, acting as cues of what to look for and what to ignore. Moreover, to avoid communicating that the teacher is the only one who questions, students should be allowed to become questioners as well, generating their own questions about what they think the reading assignment will cover. Alvermann and Phelps (1994) suggest that questions before reading are most important and helpful with struggling readers and/or when the assignment is relatively long and difficult.

During-reading, questions can help students self-monitor their own comprehension. Teaching readers to ask questions during reading fosters understanding of difficult material and leads them to become independent learners (Hammond, 1983). Teachers can also effectively intersperse questions, or **slice the text** and discuss each part to reduce the amount of material students must read and understand at the same time (Wood, 1986). Before moving too far along in the reading assignment, teachers can also break the text into more manageable units through the technique of **think-pair-share** (McTighe &

Lyman, 1987). Teachers stop and allow two minutes of individual thinking time, followed by two minutes of discussion with a partner, and then begin a class discussion. Techniques such as this prevent beginning English language learners from becoming overwhelmed with the demands of too much text or new vocabulary. They also furnish teachers with a view of student understanding before proceeding too far into the text or lesson.

Finally, after reading, questions help clarify and extend student comprehension. Answering questions after reading has been found to enhance learning more than reading only (Tierney & Cunningham, 1984). However, teachers should move beyond literal-level questioning about the text. Instead, teachers might ask: Did you find the answers to your questions? What questions do you have that are still unanswered? What evidence did you find to support that interpretation? Alvermann and Phelps (1994) note that if the reading assignment is more manageable and the teacher is focused on broad, general understanding, after-reading questioning, rather than questioning before or during reading, may be the best approach.

Sequencing.   Helping students focus on the sequence of events can be easily accomplished using elements from literature. As an example, during a unit on stories of immigration with high school students at the intermediate proficiency level, Nancy had students build a **human timeline** by placing events into categories along a timeline. Prior to the unit, she located a great reference resource, *Ellis Island: An Illustrated History of the Immigrant Experience* (Chermayeff, Wasserman, & Shapiro, 1991), an outstanding oversized trade book on immigration to the United States bringing together photos, historical information, and fascinating quotes from immigrants. She also used various children's picture books from the unit, including *I Was Dreaming to Come to America: Memories from the Ellis Island Oral History Project* (Lawlor, 1995), which combines artwork with quotes from immigrants. Browsing through these books, she selected numerous quotes that addressed distinct stages or events in the immigration process: reasons for immigrating, leaving the homeland, the journey to America, arriving in America, processing through Ellis Island, life in America, prejudice and discrimination in America, and closing the door to immigration. She created individual cards for each stage. In class, Nancy randomly distributed the cards to volunteers, who moved to the front of the class holding the cards for all to see. The class decided on the correct sequence of immigration events and placed the students in that order, discussing the rationale. At that point, the volunteers taped their cards to a wall in the classroom in the agreed-upon sequence. Next, strips of paper with the various quotations related to events in the immigration process were distributed to groups of three or four students. The students read and discussed the quotes, deciding where their examples belonged in the timeline of immigration. Once students made that determination, a member taped the quotations under the correct category. To conclude the activity, the class took a walking tour of the timeline, reading and talking about the various quotes. This activity tapped into the diverse learning styles present in the classroom and furnished a motivating culminating experience for the unit, which proved to be a relevant one for English language learners in its connection to their personal lives.

Book Reporting.   There are many ways of having students share their understanding of the books they've read. In the past, we have often relied on the oral book report. The opportunity for oral presentation is important for developing oral language skills and helping students become more comfortable in front of an audience. Unfortunately, the results in the past have often been anxiety-provoking for the presenter and boring at best for the audience. One alternative is to combine the oral retelling or summarizing of a book with show and tell about story artifacts, or objects that relate to the book in some way. Often called the brown bag book report, this is a simple and inexpensive comprehension-checking strategy that helps readers build their oral skills and confidence while you assess their comprehension. To top it off, it motivates other children to read the book being reported about. It is a strategy generally used with fiction, picture books, or novels. Creative teachers might even adapt this technique to nonfiction or poetry.

The brown bag book report process begins when students read a book (preferably one they have chosen themselves) and think about the book, the characters, and the main events. They then gather objects or book artifacts that relate to the story, characters, and main events. They can draw items and color them if they can't find the actual items. Discourage students from buying the items. Students then gather the book and all the book artifacts in a bag. (If you want to get fancy, decorate the bag so it fits the book.) In class, they orally retell the book, pulling each book artifact out of the bag as it is relevant to that part of the story. The one question for the teacher to decide ahead of time is whether students should reveal the ending or leave the audience hanging, eager to read the book themselves. Box 5.2 is a brown bag book report for *Shiloh.*

B O X 5.2

Brown Bag Book Report

Here's one example for the Newbery award-winning novel, *Shiloh* (1991), by Phyllis Reynolds Naylor, using story objects Sylvia gathered to share with a class of fifth graders:

Shiloh is a novel about an eleven-year-old boy named Marty Preston who lives in West Virginia (**show bag with rural scene**). One day he finds a dog (**show beagle puppet**) who seems to be very neglected. He falls in love with the dog, names it Shiloh after the bridge where he finds it, and decides it must belong to mean Judd Travers. Judd is so mean that he hunts deer out of season (**show hunting magazine**) and neglects his dogs so they'll be meaner. Marty can't stand this, so he decides to hide Shiloh from Judd and from his family.

This sets up some serious deception, however, that makes Marty very uncomfortable. His mother becomes suspicious and reminds Marty of the time he ate his sister's chocolate bunny (**show chocolate bunny**) and then lied about it. Marty even begs for old, expired groceries (**show fake food and empty sour cream container**) at the local market, arousing sympathy for his family. He keeps his younger sisters away from Shiloh's hidden pen by reminding them there are snakes (**show rubber snakes**) on the hill.

It all comes to a crisis point, however, when Shiloh is attacked by a vicious neighbor dog and has to be taken to the vet. Everyone finds out what Marty has been up to (**show dog collar).**

Does Marty get to keep Shiloh? Does Shiloh go back to live with Judd? You'll have to read the book to find out!

Creative Dramatics.   Drama offers more motivational options to set the stage for responding to reading. For example, the Chinese folktale *Two of Everything* by Lily Toy Hong (1993) is ideal for spontaneous dramatic retelling. With a few props (two hats, two scarves, two hairpins, and two bags of coins), it becomes even more lively. Students of all ages enjoy acting out this story because there is a great deal of action and humor in this classic tale of a man who finds a magic pot that duplicates everything he drops in it.

To respond to a text, Wilhelm (1997) provides several excellent ideas. The first, called **dramatic play,** works especially well with narrative pieces. In this activity, students receive a prompt or situation, generally from the story or work to be read. They then flesh out this story event, taking on the roles of the characters and predicting their actions and responses. This technique uses discussion, problem-solving, and prediction skills and, hopefully, enables students to enter into a character's motivation. Teachers can also use these dramas to assess English language learners' background knowledge (Was the student's dramatic play logical given the specific prompt?) and thus their potential ability to fully understand the selected text. In fact, follow-up class discussions can focus on and attempt to clear up any misconceptions that might eventually interfere with comprehension. After students present their dramatic play, they read to confirm their predicted dramas or present the play to others following the reading.

A second possible use of creative dramatics is the **snapshot or tableaux drama,** which could be utilized with narrative or expository material. For this activity, students "physically or artistically depict the freezing of moments in time that showed physical or emotional relationships, and displayed character gestures, expressions, and activities" (Wilhelm, 1997, p. 101). For instance, in the immigration unit noted earlier, we could have portrayed individuals as they left the homeland, crossed the ocean to their new home, arrived at Ellis Island, and so on. Karen Hesse's book *Letters from Rifka* (1992) also suggests many powerful moments in the immigration experience. Wilhelm suggests that the class create headlines or captions for their snapshots. At the elementary or intermediate level, *Through My Eyes* (1999) by Ruby Bridges provides abundant vignettes and photographs that students can vividly portray in tableaux moments. Beyond motivating and involving students, the visual nature of the snapshots also provides a foundation for future reading for English language learners or helps to review the major events from reading.

We encountered **readers theater** in our discussion of oral language development in Chapter 4, but this technique is an outstanding one to enhance reading ability as well. Readers theater involves students in reading a whole poem, book, or story or a self-contained episode from a story. It is a group method of reading aloud a story that is informal, but still dramatic. Basically, a story or excerpt with plenty of dialogue is transformed into a kind of script with parts. No props or costumes are needed; no lines are memorized. Students volunteer to read aloud characters' lines. Exposition or narration can be assigned to one or more narrators. Purists stick as closely to the original text as possible; others adapt the text or interpret the text in their own words. A readers theater script related to a unit or topic can be used to motivate students and encourage discussion leading up to a separate reading assignment.For example, Nancy used a readers theater script based on Russell Freedman's nonfiction children's book *Immigrant Kids* (1980) as an overview and motivational lead-in to a textbook discussion of immigration.

Picture books are often effective for readers theater scripts since they are often written to be read aloud. Moreover, these may be texts that are more comprehensible to

English language learners because of the illustrations. Some examples of picture books that make good readers theater scripts are *Strega Nona* by Tomie de Paola (1975), *Hattie and the Fox* by Mem Fox (1987), *Why Mosquitoes Buzz in People's Ears* by Verna Aardema (1975), *Arthur Goes to Camp* by Marc Brown (1982), *Alexander and the Terrible, Horrible, No Good, Very Bad Day* by Judith Viorst (1972), and *Lon Po Po* by Ed Young (1989).

In addition, there are countless **creative activities** that teachers might design to help students think about what they have read and respond to the text at a deeper level. Many of these activities are excellent examples of the integration of the language arts—reading, writing, speaking, and listening. Keep in mind that, whenever possible, students should be allowed to choose their preferred response activity, even if from among only two or three options. Also, many students will stay more focused when working with a partner or in a small group, although some students are more effective when working alone.

Parent Activities.   Involving the home and family in promoting the reading development of English language learners is also very important. Often we wrongly assume that parents are too busy or too apathetic to be involved in their children's literacy development. Sometimes language or culture differences do create barriers. There are no excuses, however, for not extending the invitation. A child feels ten feet tall when his/her parent visits school to read aloud to the class. In turn, the parent gets a different perspective on how his/her child interacts in the school environment.

Even if parents and other caregivers are not able to visit the school, they may be able to provide support at home. Many teachers have claimed success with sending home a traveling bookbag—a timely and interesting trade book and journal in a backpack or suitcase. The bookbag goes home with each child on a rotating basis. The family is to read the book and write their responses to it in the journal. They can read other families' entries, as well. This kind of effort pays off in providing additional reading practice for the children, reinforcing connections between home and school and between child and family, and building a sense of community among all the classroom constituents—the teacher, the children, and their families.

In conclusion, there are many options beyond traditional postreading questioning to follow up on reading and extend student thinking. Many of the techniques we described in the prereading, during reading, and postreading sections actually overlap and can be used at two or even all three stages of the reading process. Two excellent professional references that provide techniques for all three phases of the reading process are *Scaffolding Reading Experiences: Designs for Student Success* (Graves & Graves, 1994) and *A Handbook of Content Literacy Strategies* (Stephens & Brown, 2000).

Checking It Out:
Assessing Reading and Vocabulary Development

How do we measure success with a reading experience? Graves and Graves (1994) cite three possible means: comprehension of the material, interest and engagement with the text, and ability to complete the tasks following reading. Since so much of the academic focus of school is on reading, we must ensure that students are able to read well, comprehend at a higher level of understanding, and gain an enjoyment for reading.

There are various **informal assessment** techniques that teachers may use in their classrooms to determine students' reading development and word knowledge. Informal assessment generally focuses on student process. It is a type of monitoring used daily to keep track of students' progress. These informal measures of assessment may be graded, or they may merely serve to provide input for instructional purposes. Following is a brief overview of just a few means of informal assessment through which teachers can determine how students are progressing. In addition to giving teachers necessary information about reading development, many of these techniques can also be used to assess writing, speaking, and listening.

Observation

Teachers might look at students' attitudes toward reading in general, or they could focus on the reading strategies used. For instance, teachers might want to determine which skills students demonstrate for each phase of the reading process. An observation checklist for assessing prereading, during-reading, and postreading skills is provided in Table 5.7.

TABLE 5.7   Checklist to Assess Students' Reading Process Skills

Instructions: Check the skills that the student is able to use in each phase of the reading process. Update this checklist regularly.

Before Reading

- Predicts story topic or content using titles, pictures, captions
- Uses background knowledge to make predictions about the topic

During-Reading

- Is aware when text doesn't make sense
- Uses strategies to "fix up" the difficulty (e.g., rereading a section)
- Able to form questions about the text using title, subheadings, etc.
- Reads to answer own questions about text
- Able to use access features (e.g., table of contents, glossary, index)
- Chooses an appropriate rate for reading different text types
- Able to skim a selection to determine main focus
- Able to scan a selection for specific information

After Reading

- Recalls sufficient and important information
- Can summarize main points

Conferences

Most often, we think of conferencing with students about their writing. However, reading conferences can also be beneficial. Teachers may set up special times to talk to students about what they are reading and how they are processing text. For instance, teachers might ask students questions such as the following: What parts were confusing to you? Why do you think they were confusing? Is the title appropriate? Which characters did you like best? Why? What character reminds you of someone you already know? How?

This one-on-one interaction with students can be very powerful. However, building that time in is very difficult. Many teachers do not take the time for more formal conferences; but they may incorporate on-the-spot conferences at students' desks, or they may pull a student aside for instructional mini-lessons, providing special instruction on one or two specific skills.

Anecdotal Records

Teachers may choose to keep anecdotal records about students' progress. Often, anecdotal records are used to record student misbehavior rather than student growth, but written records and teacher reflections about students' reading development can be helpful in individualizing instruction for students who need special attention. Many teachers keep small self-adhesive notes handy to record observations in the moment. These can later be filed in individual portfolios.

Checklists

Various checklists are available to note student activity and progress in the classroom. Both teachers and students can make use of checklists. For instance, students and teachers could use a checklist to monitor the various genres of literature read during SSR. Many of the lists provided in this chapter can be converted into checklists to monitor student growth.

Assessing Storybook Reading

Teachers can assess reading by conducting individual or small-group assessments of reading comprehension. Using a read aloud, the teacher can stop periodically and have a student predict what comes next. Or the teacher can read a short selection and have a student retell it in his/her own words. Teachers need to determine what specific points must be included for a retelling of a story to be satisfactory.

Assessing Print Concepts

Many schools now require some type of early assessment of students' knowledge of print concepts. This is particularly helpful with preliterate students or students at beginning proficiency levels. Table 5.8 highlights one such option based on the work of Marie Clay (1987).

TABLE 5.8   Assessing Print Orientation Concepts

Hand a children's book upside down to the child.

1. Show me the front of the book.

2. Show me where I begin reading.

3. Show me with your finger where I go next. / Where do I go from here?

4. Point to the beginning of the story on this page. Point to the end of the story on this page.

5. Show me the bottom of the page. Show me the top of the page. Show me the top of the picture. Show me the bottom of the picture.

6. Put these cards on the page so that just one word shows between them. Now move them so that just two words show between them. Now move them again so that just one letter shows between them. Now move them so that just two letters show between them.

7. Show me a little letter that is the same as this one. Now point to a capital letter that is the same as this one.

8. What is this? What is it for? (period, exclamation point, question mark, comma, quotation marks)

Summary

Literature pulls students into the reading process. While textbooks are designed so that one size fits all, literature provides the breadth and depth that more closely reflects the variety and individuality of students in our classrooms. Unlike drills and isolated language practice, literature presents a whole story or text for students to process and respond to. However, English language learners often struggle with reading assignments due to their level of language proficiency and their lack of background knowledge. Teachers, even those not trained to provide special language support, can assist all their students toward successful reading experiences.

English language learners' reading ability develops in stages like those of native English speakers. However, the process of developing literacy while learning English becomes very complex with older students who are not literate in their native language. Two important determinants of successful reading experience are background knowledge and vocabulary. While both of these are important for all students, they are even more critical for English language learners. There are numerous strategies for developing both background language and word knowledge. Prereading strategies can be used to build anticipation and background for reading selections. During-reading strategies promote student involvement and monitoring while reading. Finally, postreading strategies help students extend and deepen their understanding and response to what they have read.

Teachers have many options to consider for students' oral and silent reading. These options provide students with opportunities to work in large groups, in small groups, with partners, and individually. They include guided reading; shared reading; page and paragraph reading method; equal portions reading; page, paragraph, or pass reading; silent reading with support, choral reading; self-assisted reading; readers theater; radio reading; repeated reading; interactive read aloud; echo reading; cloze reading; nonprint media; independent reading; and reading aloud. Such options provide students with wide ranges of support. Moreover, students find a variety of reading options exciting.

Numerous assessment options exist to help teachers in planning and teaching their students. Teachers use information gained from informal assessment measures to determine the amount and degree of teacher support the students need to successfully read the text.

6 Writing with Literature as a Model

"I must write, I must write at all costs. For writing is more than living, it is being conscious of living."

—Anne Morrow Lindbergh

English language learners need to be included in our emphasis on writing, yet a quick look inside the classroom suggests that something quite different may occur. An overview of instructional practices with English language learners reflects an avoidance or over-simplification of the writing process. Teachers routinely defer writing instruction until children have mastered the spoken language (Hadaway, 1990). When writing is incorporated into the classroom, students rarely have a chance for authentic communicative writing experiences designed to foster understanding of the complexities of the composing process (Heath, 1983). Instead, they encounter workbook exercises, grammatically based practice, error correction, and imitation of various styles and organizational patterns (Allen, 1986; Diaz, 1986; Franklin, 1986; Zamel, 1982). Regardless of language background and ability, all children can be writers; therefore, in this chapter, we explore the development of writing for English language learners and how to foster this critical literacy area through the use of literature-based instruction. In our discussion of writing development, we address the following questions.

- **What is the importance of writing to academic success?**
- **How do teachers create a productive writing environment for English language learners?**
- **What are the stages of writing development for English language learners?**
- **What instructional strategies assist English language learners' writing development?**

Let's begin our discussion of writing development by considering the critical role of writing in the schools.

What Is the Importance of Writing to Academic Success?

Schools emphasize reading and writing skills throughout the grades and across the curriculum; indeed, reading and writing are the processes viewed as most critical to academic success. In Chapter 5, we observed that reading is a means to independence in learning. Writing has the potential to take us even farther down the road to self-directed learning. Tompkins (1994, pp. 6–7) describes the three roles of writing as learning to write, learning about written language, and learning through writing. First, students learn to write at the word, phrase, and sentence level and eventually apply the multistep writing process. As students learn to write, they are also examining written language and how writing and speaking differ. Finally, students discover the very valuable tool that writing becomes for the learning process.

Beyond providing another way to communicate, writing offers a means of exploring our own thinking, a way to examine what we know about a subject. Without writing, teachers would have a narrow picture of the comprehension level of students. We cannot look into the mind of someone who is reading to examine his/her understanding of the text, but we can view his/her comprehension and appreciation of text through writing. In reading a student's response to a piece of literature, we can see if that student has learned "to read thoughtfully, to extract meaning from language . . . , to understand characterization, and to appreciate that literature teaches us about life" (Spandel & Stiggins, 1997, p. 3). Plus, with writing we keep a permanent record of what we have learned. The permanence of writing allows us to communicate with others across distance and across time. Yet, at the same time writing allows us to reach beyond ourselves, it also furnishes a means of looking inward. Writing is an expressive outlet for self-communication, a way to chronicle our personal reactions and journeys. Finally, writing is truly the most complex of the communicative arts, incorporating reading as well as oral language.

How Do Teachers Create a Productive Writing Environment for English Language Learners?

Writing is perhaps the most difficult area of the language arts to teach because it is such a highly personal and private act. It is also where we often feel weakest as teachers because we ourselves received little to no instruction in the *process* of writing. Thus, teachers may perceive that it is safer to teach writing in a lockstep manner through the more traditional focus on learning skills and mechanics. Yet, this tactic shortchanges students; eventually they need to learn how to master the process of writing independently. Writing ability grows more critical with each grade level.

Current research and theory offer suggestions for classroom teachers to broaden their vision of writing to emphasize communication and accommodate students' competencies and backgrounds (Strickland & Feeley, 1991). Recognizing that "child ESL learners, early in their development of English can write English and can do so for various purposes" (Hudelson, 1984, p. 221) prompts us to employ writing as the "gateway to literacy" in a second or other language (Jensen, 1993, p. 291). Knowing that "second language acquisition is facilitated when the target language is used in a natural communicative context" (Diaz, 1986, p. 169) encourages us to design authentic instructional activities focusing on "connectedness to the world beyond the classroom" (Newmann & Wehlage, 1993, p. 8). How do teachers create a productive and challenging focus on writing that fosters academic language proficiency and enhanced personal expression? A review of research indicates some key elements that provide the safety net English language learners need to take the risks that writing presents.

To begin, learners need **time and opportunity to write**—regular and substantial practice in writing, aimed at developing fluency (Jochum, 1989). This practice should include using writing as a tool of learning in all subjects in the curriculum, not just in the language arts class. The tendency to wait for fluency in speaking or reading prior to introducing writing is not the answer. "Written products reflect language development at a given point in time" (Hudelson, 1984, p. 231) and provide teachers with valuable information about emerging literacy. Remember the scribbles and invented spellings of first language learners; those are signposts to the stages of development in writing. We can learn the same valuable information when we examine English language learners' attempts at writing.

Providing time alone is not sufficient, however. Students need a **real reason for writing**—the opportunity to write for real, personally significant purposes. Writing proficiency is a "consequence of not only the time spent on the task, but also on the significance of the task" (Farnan, Lapp, & Flood, 1992, p. 551). Calkins (1986, p. 4) concurs, noting that "After detouring around the authentic, human reasons for writing, we bury the students' urge to write all the more with boxes, kits, and manuals full of synthetic writing stimulants." Children learn by being actively engaged in what people do with language rather than by merely being exposed to the form and structure of language (Allen, 1986; Cooper, 1993). We see much more writing produced when children are involved in tasks where they have some choice in what they are writing. In a letter-exchange project that Nancy initiated, she discovered that this format spurred communication. Some students who had never written for teacher-assigned tasks suddenly produced mountains of text. One young English language learner found a new voice and illustrated and composed a poem, "Don't You Be Sad," to send to her pen pal.

Given an authentic reason for composing, writers next deserve a **genuine audience.** Experience in writing for a wide range of audiences, both inside and outside of school, exerts a powerful influence, shaping what we say and how we say it (Crowhurst, 1992) and helping students "understand that written language like oral, is a transactional process" (Dolly, 1990, p. 361). In the majority of instances across classrooms, the teacher is the sole audience for student writing. Peer editing groups can provide some variety, but even more is needed. Arranging for pen-pal exchanges, cross-grade journaling, and/or letters to authors or government officials furnishes a realistic audience for student writing and reflects the purpose of much writing that students will do in the future after they leave school. When students know they will be sharing their work with their classmates (on a voluntary basis), posting it in the hall, or including it in the school newspaper, their level of motivation and investment increases greatly. They have a real reason to write and to care about what their final product looks like.

Observing and emulating is a natural part of any process; thus, the fourth require-ment is **role models.** "Developmental learning cannot begin until the learner has observed the important people in his environment using the desired skill to fulfill their own genuine life purposes" (Holdaway, 1984, p. 16). Modeling can be provided via rich and continuous reading experience, including both published literature of acknowledged merit and the work of peers and instructors. We can learn much from reading diverse texts—variety in word choice and sentence patterns, for starters. In addition, exposure to models of writing in process and writers at work, including both teachers and classmates, offers a glimpse of the work that goes into writing and helps us compare and contrast the many drafts that may be generated during the process of composing versus the finished product of pub-lished work. There is nothing more eye-opening to students than to see their teacher's first draft of a piece and to see how she/he "messes it up" in order to make it better.

Fifth on our list is a **safe environment** "where the errors that all learners must make can be made" (Diaz, 1986, p. 173). As we learned in Chapter 2, learning a language re-quires making mistakes and taking chances. Thus, a positive and supportive atmosphere encourages writers to verbalize their ideas fully and to take the risks needed to progress (Hayes & Bahruth, 1985; Staton, Shuy, Peyton, & Reed, 1988). Teachers are instrumental in setting the tone for a low-risk environment by understanding and appreciating the basic linguistic competence that English language learners bring with them to school and by having positive expectations for students' achievements in writing. To set a positive atmo-sphere, teachers can assist students through the following instructional techniques.

- One-on-one writing conferences, allowing for an understanding of each individual child's strengths and weaknesses.
- Instruction and modeling in the process of writing, learning to work at a task in ap-propriate phases, including prewriting, drafting, and revising.
- Reduced instruction in grammatical terminology and related drills, and a focus on mechanics and grammar in the context of students' actual work.
- Focused mini-lessons for groups of students who need direct instruction in specific strategies and techniques for writing, such as sentence combining.
- Voluntary sharing with peers or partners throughout the writing process, and par-ticularly of the final product.

The next requirement for writers is **feedback.** Teachers have drawn considerable criticism for the lack of specific, helpful feedback provided on students' papers. Students need flexible and cumulative evaluation of writing efforts that stresses revision and is sen-sitive to variations in subject, audience, and purpose. Teachers should avoid vague, ab-stract responses focused on lower-level form and structure, concentrating instead on moderate marking of surface structure errors accompanied by a thoughtful response to composing efforts and attention to sets or patterns of related errors and larger meaning-related issues (Nystrand, 1990). In addition, the teacher ought not to be the only source of feedback. Students can be taught to provide constructive input for each other, too.

With all the elements noted above in place, we are able to meet the final need of English language learners as writers, a **sense of community.** This "sense of community sustains complex learning" (Holdaway, 1984, p. 19). Collaborative activities provide ideas for writing and guidance for revising works in progress. When the entire class is engaged in the process of composing for real purposes, a community of writers evolves. Together, students work, listen, provide feedback, and validate each other's efforts. The emphasis becomes communication and collaboration rather than writing in isolation or competition.

To create a productive writing environment, teachers must have a better understanding of the characteristics English language learners may demonstrate and their abilities as they progress with writing. Therefore, we will consider the phases of writing development in the next section.

What Are the Stages of Writing Development for English Language Learners?

As we examine the characteristics of English language learners with regard to writing, an important question emerges: Is the writing process similar in a first and second or other language? Current research indicates that the processes for both first and second language writers are similar (Edelsky, 1981). For instance, with young English language learners and emergent writing, we see many of the same developmental stages of first language learning, from scribbling and random marks to one letter standing for an entire word or thought and on to phonetic spelling and eventually more traditional spelling. Generally, we all go through these developmental stages in prekindergarten through the primary grades. However, older English language learners without previous school experience and without literacy models in the home environment must progress through these stages as well, despite their age. On the other hand, English language learners who have previous schooling in their home language and have begun the process of writing will probably reflect the later developmental stages in their attempts at English writing. Let's look briefly at the stages of writing behaviors for both first and second language learners. Then we will link these stages to the English language proficiency levels.

Development of Writing Behaviors

Writing behavior reflects a series of developmental stages, as reported by Temple, Nathan, Burris, & Temple (1988). First, emergent writers use **scribbling and drawing.** These scribbles are very random, but often the writer tries to emulate adult cursive writing (Clay, 1987). Drawings may be used in combination with scribbles to help convey meaning. Next, writers move to the **prephonemic stage.** At this point, writers use real letters, usually uppercase, to represent their meaning. These letters reflect no phonemic linking of the letter to the actual sound; the strings of letters are placeholders that may represent whole ideas. Third, writers enter the **early phonemic stage** where they use letters, generally uppercase consonants, to represent entire words. The incomplete nature of their writing reflects some issues surrounding language learning. For instance, they may still be learning the letters of the alphabet and focusing on the initial or final sounds in a word. These factors may lead to this practice of incomplete spelling. In the **letter-naming stage,** children add vowels to one or two consonants in their attempts to spell words. This phase of writing demonstrates children's understanding about language: words are made up of phonemes that occur in a sequence, and these phonemes are represented in writing from left to right in English. In addition, they realize that every word in English contains a vowel, one of the most complex and versatile of phonemes. And, although children may often guess the wrong vowel in their early writing, the presence of vowels signals a major turning point in their writing development. Eventually, writers move to the **transitional stage** where their writing looks more like English. They still use a mix of conventional and phonetic spellings. Common errors include omitting the final silent *e,* substituting familiar phonic elements for less familiar ones, and neglecting double consonants (Reutzel & Cooter, 2000).

With beginning English language learners, there may be considerable mixing of languages at the letter-naming and transitional stages. Therefore, it can be particularly difficult for teachers to determine if the student is writing in English, phonetic English, the home language, a phonetic version of the home language, or a combination of these. Although this can be daunting for the teacher, it should be encouraged as students attempt to get their ideas down on paper. We know that when children are limited to writing only words they are *sure* they know how to spell, they write far less. Encouraging their "invented" spelling is a necessary part of their growing up as writers. **Conventional spelling** represents the last stage of writing development. At this stage students' writing generally reflects consistent, conventional spellings for most words.

Beyond the similarities in the stages of writing behavior, English language learners and first language writers use similar strategies to move forward with writing even when they are uncertain. They place a question mark or blank to hold that place open and come back later, or they use illustrations and even their first language (Hudelson, 1986). These techniques mirror a strategic use of language; once ideas are on paper, they can always go back and fine-tune their writing. Getting the ideas down is the hard part—at least half the process. As one second-grade teacher, Barbara Hairston, told her students, "Anyone can look up how to spell a word, but no one can have the ideas that only you have."

While the writing process has many similarities for both first and second language learners, there are differences. Obviously, proficiency in English will affect student writing. For instance, English language learners may make more syntax and vocabulary errors than first language learners. Some of these errors are developmental, resembling first language learning; others indicate incomplete English language acquisition and a return to first language competence. In the initial stages of second language acquisition, students may revert back to knowledge of the first language to help them in uncertain situations in English (Brown, 1994). However, with increasing proficiency, this happens less and less. Furthermore, if students already know how to write in their home language, they bring an additional source of information about print conventions to the task of writing in English. Finally, the more similar their home language alphabet is to the English alphabet, the more easily their writing skills will transfer to English (Odlin, 1989).

In terms of the levels of language proficiency (beginning, intermediate, and advanced) that we have been highlighting, English language learners will proceed at different rates based on the many factors that affect language acquisition; there is no set timetable for progression from stage to stage. Most importantly, teachers should not avoid the use of writing in the classroom with English language learners. In our classroom visits, we have found that teachers hesitate to have students write in the beginning stages of language acquisition. However, students may use illustrations combined with their home language or English labeling, or simply use home language writing alone. The idea is to involve students in writing activities from the beginning of their language learning process. After all, when learning our first language, we illustrated and made random scribbles on the page. We were writing long before we were proficient in the language; consequently, we can use that same flexibility with English language learners. Indeed, research indicates that students benefit from opportunities to read and write well before they have mastered oral proficiency in English (Goodman, Goodman, & Flores, 1979; Hudelson, 1984; Peregoy & Boyle, 1991). Practice with writing helps students exercise their evolving knowledge of letters, sounds, words, and sentences in English. Indeed, Carol Chomsky proposed that perhaps we ought to consider teaching writing before reading (1971).

Basically, beginning level English language learners, no matter what their age, who have never learned to write in their home language will begin with scribbling and drawing, just like native English speakers. On the other hand, English language learners who have already learned to write in a home language with a Roman alphabet will probably begin at the letter-naming or transitional stage of writing development; those who are writing in a non-Roman alphabet may have to move through the prephonemic or early phonemic stage of English. To consider how best to help students at all phases of development, let's move to an examination of the levels of proficiency and writing.

Beginning Proficiency Level

Emergent writers demonstrate minimal writing skills because of their unfamiliarity with the writing process as well as the language. Other beginning English language learners may understand the writing process but lack the needed vocabulary in English and an awareness of sentence patterns. To provide a written record of learning, they may illustrate and label drawings or write random and unrelated words or phrases. Students with some proficiency in their home language may use their first language to write.

One of the English language learner's first needs is to become acquainted with the English alphabet and language. Trade books with survival English, such as alphabet books and concept books, provide English language learners with simple language and acquaint them with spelling and vocabulary. In addition, labeling the room, constructing word walls, posting real world print, brainstorming and posting vocabulary, and recording students' dictated stories all offer students a glimpse of written English. At the beginning level of proficiency, teachers should focus on frequently used words as drawn from the Dolch list of the 220 most frequently occurring words, along with vocabulary associated with immediate needs: basic classroom objects, colors, numbers, clothing, names, dates, nationality, biographical information, weather, seasons, and family members.

From students' encounters with English at home and at school, they gain an awareness of sound–symbol relationships. Rather than waiting for students to master oral language and to be launched into print, teachers need to allow students to scribble, draw, and write from their first entry into the English speaking classroom. Indeed, classroom encouragement of phonetic spellings is a promising approach toward the development of phonemic awareness and knowledge of spelling patterns (Adams, 1990). Children who write use phonics actively as they figure out each word they want to use and put it in print. If we encourage them to guess how a word may be spelled, they are applying the phonic knowledge they have at that point. Although they may be incorrect, their phonetic spellings are temporary and reflect how much they already know about what letters make which sounds. This information can be very helpful to the teacher, who can offer mini-lessons to children as needed based on their writing stage.

Much of the writing students produce at the beginning proficiency level is speech written down. Because oral competency affects writing, teachers should continue to work on oral language development. One instructional technique that makes writing as similar to speaking as possible is the Language Experience Approach (LEA). In the LEA, teachers provide a concrete experience to the class that becomes the basis for a writing activity. The steps for the LEA are as follows: (1) look at student needs and interests; (2) choose a participatory activity; (3) discuss the activity prior to beginning; (4) participate in the activity; (5) lead the class in an oral reconstruction of the activity; and (6) have students write or dictate stories and record them. The stories become reading material for the class since the students are familiar and comfortable with the language they have used.

Trade books offer the same opportunity for acting out a situation and then writing about it. For instance, as the teacher reads aloud Mem Fox's (1985) *Wilfrid Gordon McDonald Partridge,* students can role play each of Wilfrid's actions to collect a box of memories for Miss Nancy, his friend at the retirement home who has "lost her memory." As a response activity, students can write their own journal entry or story beginning with "I remember."

In Chapter 5 we highlighted problem-solving activities or hypothetical situations. Our example dealt with Phyllis Naylor's *Shiloh* (1991). We were asked to consider what Marty might do about protecting the beagle, Shiloh, from his abusive owner. Instead of discussing options, students might act out various alternatives and then write about the one they like best. After reading the story, students can compare and contrast their choice with the actual conclusion. Using books and dramatic activities helps students generate ideas and think aloud about story elements before they have to write them down. The writing seems to come much more quickly and easily when students have the opportunity to rehearse their thoughts beforehand.

With practice and support, English language learners at this proficiency level copy short, simple statements that they produce orally, and they correctly spell vocabulary that has been previously introduced. For more practice, teachers can involve students in basic writing tasks such as copying and transcribing simple material, listing, identifying, labeling, filling out biographical information on forms, and constructing very simple paragraphs using memorized or familiar text (frame sentences or paragraphs). To increase students' ability to produce longer written products, teachers need to furnish more comprehensible input in the lessons through read alouds, provide personal writing experiences (journals, etc.), and engage the class in prewriting techniques such as talking, brainstorming, and webbing. For instance, the class could brainstorm completions for any of the following frame sentences.

- I like _____ but I don't like _____.
- I like _____ because _____.
- I _____ and then I _____.

For beginning English language learners, "frame" sentences provide a syntax structure to plug new vocabulary into. One pattern that works well is the frame "I like . . . but I don't like. . . ." In a first-grade ESL class, the students came up with the completions shown in Box 6.1. Be sure to note their phonetic spellings.

Intermediate Proficiency Level

At the intermediate level, writers are more aware of their new language and some of the rules associated with its use. They correctly use uppercase and lowercase letters and Arabic numerals and come closer to using punctuation more appropriately. With their new understanding, they begin to employ strategies to avoid errors. Many times, these strategies are negative and work to stifle writing growth. For instance, they limit the amount of writing and use structures and vocabulary they know and feel certain about. They focus on avoiding errors, not on risking and experimenting with language. Students can even become trapped here if the emphasis in the classroom is focused more on correct language production than on content and if they see the teacher's role as giving rules and correcting errors, stressing correctness over content.

To move students along in their writing development, teachers need to read quality literature aloud to serve as a model of written language. At this phase, students begin to understand that writing and speaking are separate; they recognize the difference between speech (informal/casual) and writing (formal). Teacher read alouds help students in this journey as the class discusses the differences between oral and written language. In addition, teachers need to focus student attention on the variety of syntax patterns that are possible. Any quality literature will serve to provide models of literary language and engaging style.

Oral language development assists writing, and prewriting discussion enables intermediate level students to write more complex sentences. Branching out from the familiar and self-related topics to more academic ones, students at this stage write for varied purposes, from responding to content textbooks to writing their own short stories. With practice, students utilize increased vocabulary and demonstrate more variety of sentence patterns; they even begin to manipulate content to meet the needs of different audiences.

BOX 6.1

Frame Sentence Completions from First-Grade Class

we all like pizza but we do not like speng.
we all like brown bins but we do not like green bins.
and we all like turckies and we do not like pig feet.
and we like souer pickles but not dill pickles
and we all like tomallies but we do not like piches.
and we all like tocos but we do not like berryes
but we like halupena but we do not like toco bell.

For instance, they might try their hand at expressive writing, utilizing different styles of language from formal to informal. Some trade books that present different voices within the same book can assist in this process. For instance, *Crossing the Delaware: A History in Many Voices* (Peacock, 1998) presents a historical event in multiple voices ranging from informative to narrative.

To spur student growth, teachers can read aloud books that present students as writers and talk about the process of writing for the protagonists in the stories. For instance, Mark Teague presents a humorous account of a young boy's exaggerated school essay in *How I Spent My Summer Vacation* (1995). This tale even presents a format that students might try—the fib or the exaggeration. If students don't have a true story to tell, they can tell a fib. In read alouds, we can draw students' attention to the use of language, encouraging them to make choices in their own language use in relation to purpose, audience, and context. Beyond opportunities for creative writing, teachers can vary writing through tasks such as short messages, paragraphs, notes and letters, short compositions, and simple note-taking. In Chapter 11, we explore a variety of structured writing formats to begin the research process. Techniques such as data retrieval charts and K-W-L charts help students focus and collect information for eventual writing assignments. While academic writing will become an increasing part of the students' writing tasks, we still need to consider individual needs and interests and allow opportunities for students to cultivate their knowledge and skill with topics of personal importance.

Advanced Proficiency Level

At this level, students will be writing about a wide variety of topics, including familiar and everyday topics, academic content, current events, the factual and concrete as well as the imaginative. Teachers should provide practice in writing cohesive summaries, writing description and narration, taking notes, explaining point of view, and paraphrasing. Exposing students to quality literature is critical for advanced level students since a variety of writing styles can be surveyed. Advanced level students need time and the opportunity to engage in some original writing. For instance, the class might read various fractured fairy tales with different points of view, such those noted in Table 6.1, comparing and contrasting them with the original version of these stories.

With appropriate guidance, students might try their own version of a fractured fairy tale in order to help develop the expressive quality of their writing. Teachers might need to

---

TABLE 6.1   Examples of Published Fractured Fairy Tales

- *Cinder-elly* by Frances Minters
- *Little Red Riding Hood: A Newfangled Prairie Tale* by Lisa Campbell Ernst
- *Somebody and the Three Blairs* by Marilyn Tolhurst
- *The Frog Prince Continued* by Jon Scieszka
- *The Three Little Wolves and the Big Bad Pig* by Eugene Trivizas and Helen Oxenbury
- *The True Story of the Three Little Pigs* by Jon Scieszka

provide some structured support via a technique Golub (1994) calls "twisted fairy tales," using the following steps:

- Brainstorm titles of fairy tales. For English language learners, teachers may need to supply various books for students to look through for this task.
- List the key elements of fairy tales (e.g., prince or princess, a forest).
- Select one particular story, and circle items on the list of key elements that appear in this story.
- Change two of those items (e.g., In "Snow White and the Seven Dwarves," Snow White is given refuge by a rock band).
- Rewrite the story. Discuss items in the stories that had to change.

Each proficiency level provides specific challenges in the process of writing development for the English language learner. Becoming aware of the stages and the behaviors that learners demonstrate at each phase of this process provides a basis for more effective decision making in the instructional process. In the next section, we address the instructional strategies teachers may use to assist English language learners in their journey to become proficient writers.

What Instructional Strategies Assist English Language Learners' Writing Development?

Before we begin a discussion of specific instructional strategies that teachers might use to assist their English language learners, let's quickly review some general considerations drawn from the research on writing instruction (Hillocks, 1986; Noguchi, 1991; Weaver, 1996). Our first important finding advocates a **wider range of reading experiences** for students. This includes reading aloud to students because the experience of hearing good books helps students acquire a broader vocabulary as well as an understanding of syntax and grammar. Linked closely to the first finding is a recommendation to **present good pieces of writing as models for students.** Indeed, research indicates that models of strong writing are more effective than studying grammar as a means to improve writing.

Next, students must **spend a considerable amount of time writing.** In addition to the time spent writing, students need the guided input of teachers in terms of sentence combining and manipulating syntax and mechanics. These concepts are taught most efficiently within the context of the students' own writing, using their own words. To help students self-monitor their progress, teachers need to **supply students with specific questions or criteria for evaluating writing.** Specifying the criteria in advance—even having students help build those criteria for various assignments—and systematically applying the criteria to their own work help students internalize the mechanics of writing more effectively.

Finally, **engaging students in inquiry-based activities** has been shown to be an effective strategy. Inquiry writing, with its questioning process and research techniques to find answers to those questions, helps activate students' critical thinking skills and helps students engage more actively in the writing process. In addition, inquiry writing hones strategies to deal with complex sets of data and enables students to transfer their oral language skills to their writing. As we move through the upcoming writing techniques, teachers should be sure to keep these findings in mind.

The Writing Process

In Chapter 5, we examined the phases of the reading process, considering how readers process text and what readers think about before, during, and after reading. In this section, we explore the writing process, its stages, and instructional activities to incorporate at each stage. Tompkins (1994, p. 7) defines the writing process "as a way of looking at writing instruction in which the emphasis is shifted from students' finished products to what students think and do as they write." The shift away from a product and toward a process provides a framework for teachers to assist students at each step: prewriting, drafting, revising, editing, and publishing.

It is important to keep in mind that the writing process is not a linear sequence of events, but that instead it is cyclical. As needed, writers return to prewriting to generate ideas and plans to continue, and so on. Various researchers have studied the writing process and have documented the fact that individuals use a variety of processes as they write and choose different strategies for different types of writing (Britton, 1970; Emig, 1971; Graves, 1983). Let's begin our examination of the writing process with the first phase, prewriting, a phase that is very critical to the success of English language learners.

Prewriting

According to Tompkins (1994), "prewriting is the getting-ready-to-write stage." Just as with prereading, prewriting has been a neglected phase of instruction. However, it is a critical part of the process, and a significant amount of time should be spent in the prewriting phase. Exactly how much of the writing time should be spent in prewriting? Donald Murray (1982) advocates that 70 percent or more of the time should be devoted to prewriting. This is when students think and plan for upcoming writing. In fact, there is substantial evidence that planning separates effective writers from ineffective ones (Dale, 1997). For English language learners, the lack of vocabulary and knowledge of syntax patterns complicates the process. Therefore, prewriting is important to their success in composing. Prewriting might be divided into two phases: first a focus on content and idea building, and second a focus on development and ordering (Tompkins, 1994).

Content and Idea Building.   The intimidating blank-page syndrome is a real problem for many writers. Before students begin to write, they need to gather ideas, content, and vocabulary. Without content, the writing process is meaningless. Students often have a hard time coming up with ideas, so it is crucial for the teacher to model ways to produce ideas. Whenever possible, however, it is important for students to choose their own topics to maintain a sense of ownership throughout the writing process. Writing is hard enough for motivated, professional writers, but when topics are constantly externally imposed, it is difficult for students to feel that their writing is real or their own. This requires a fine balance between helping students generate ideas and guiding them in choosing and sticking with a variety of topics. Here are some methods of generating content for writing:

■ **Brainstorming/listing.** Generating vocabulary or ideas via brainstorming can be a helpful prewriting technique that provides a data bank to use for writing. This technique works with the whole class, small groups, or individuals. Teachers can brainstorm with the class and write responses on the board, leaving those ideas up as students begin to work on their initial drafts.

■ **Clustering.** This prewriting technique involves a web of brainstormed ideas. Beginning with main topic in the center, the teacher or students can add spokes radiating from the center and record related information. This planning technique serves as an outline to work with during writing.

■ **Observing.** Good observers note details that can enhance the quality of writing. To help students become better observers, have them spend some time observing in the school cafeteria, on the playground, and in other places. Then encourage them to share their observations, noting how we view things with some similarities and differences.

■ **Dramatizing.** Creative dramatics can spur student talk that can later be used as a prewriting idea bank. For example, if students are to write about how they felt on the first day at a new school, an easy entry is to have them role play such a situation and then debrief them to generate ideas for the writing assignment.

■ **Imagining.** To write a description of a memorable event, it would be helpful for students to recall that time. One way to do this is to have students close their eyes and to lead them through a visualization or imagining exercise. (Close your eyes. Remember the first day of school this year. What time did you come to school? What was the weather like? How did you get to school? Do you remember what you were wearing? What class did you go to first?)

■ **Detailing.** One problem in student writing is a lack of details. For a book report, students may write that the book was good. Yet, the teacher needs a bit more information to assess understanding and appreciation for the book. To focus students on providing details, ask students for characteristics of a good book. (What makes a book good? Characters? What kind of characters? Cite some memorable characters in a book you have read. Plot? What makes for an exciting plot? What are examples of books you would label as great? Why? Cite specific reasons.)

■ **Experiencing.** A direct experience such as a simulation or field trip can help students generate ideas. Hands-on experiences are powerful prewriting techniques and help students include more elaboration and specific detail.

■ **Watching films or listening to other media.** Just as with reading, watching films or listening to other media can help build content background. This technique is especially valuable for learners who need concrete images to help in the idea-generation phase. Sonya Blackwell, a middle school teacher, shares a technique she uses in Box 6.2.

BOX **6.2**

Voices from the Field: Promoting Fluency through Music

I use a lesson called Mood Music to increase fluency with detailed descriptions. I bring in a variety of music styles: blues, jazz, classical, country, hard rock, rap, Scottish moors, and so on. We discuss how each style of music evokes its own mood, and then students visualize a scene or event suitable to the style of music. While the song is playing, they write a detailed description of their visualizations. I complete one of these on the overhead for them first, so they can see how rich the details of sight, sound, smell, and even taste can be. Between each song, volunteers share what they wrote. In this way students hear other models of good descriptions and thereby improve their own writing. The students love this activity so much that they groan when the bell rings and beg to do it again in another class. If done before a creative writing unit, the subsequent assignments will contain more depth and rich details.

Development and Ordering.   Once students have generated enough ideas and established a firm foundation of content, they still are not ready to begin writing. They must make some tentative decisions about order and emphasis. They must consider how to develop their paper. It is not enough to have good ideas. Writing must be developed and ordered so that the reader can follow the ideas. Some helpful considerations for this part of prewriting include asking what form the writing will take; how students will develop their papers, and what details, reasons, examples, and incidents they will include; and, if the paper is a description, whether it should reflect a chronology (things happened in this sequence), a space (describing the spatial arrangement of a room beginning at a specific point and moving from one side to the next), or a level of importance (with the most critical points offered first). Students can talk through these questions with a writing partner after the teacher has modeled this decision-making stage with her/his own topic ideas as examples.

Alternative Forms of Writing.   In Table 6.2, we offer numerous alternative forms of writing that teachers might consider (Brozo & Simpson, 1995; Moore, Moore, Cunningham, & Cunningham, 1998; Tchudi & Yates, 1983). Many of these, such as posters, can combine illustrations with writing and are ideally suited to the beginning English language learner. Whatever form teachers encourage or students choose to adopt, it is critical that students examine examples of the format. For instance, if the students decide to use a travel brochure format, the teacher can collect various types of travel brochures and have students compare and contrast these, noting the key features that all the brochures have in common and the specific elements they might like to include in their writing.

Drafting

In the drafting stage, students are engaged in continuous revising and monitoring through a variety of drafts. They read, reread, and revise, cycling through these steps again and

TABLE 6.2   Alternative Formats for Writing

advertisements	film reviews	photo essays
All About ____ books	greeting cards	plays
alphabet books	how-to books	poetry
applications	interviews	pop-up books
autobiographies	journals	posters
biographical sketches	letters	propaganda
book reviews	magazines	raps
cartoons	maps	research
catalogs	memos	songs
children's stories	myths and legends	stories
collaborative reports	newspaper stories	story problems
commercials	oral histories	telegrams
dialogues	pamphlets	timelines
diaries	persuasive essays	travel brochures
dictionaries	petitions	TV scripts
editorials		

again. This repetition of reading and writing is excellent practice for English language learners. In addition to reading and revising, students may participate in any or all of the following drafting behaviors: using references, asking for help, considering word choice, and organizing ideas (introduction, order, transitions, conclusion). The drafting phase might be divided into a focus on rhetorical stance and linguistic choices. Some consideration of the rhetorical stance (voice, audience, purpose, form) begins in the prewriting phase, but a focus on these issues continues throughout drafting and revising.

Rhetorical Stance.   A brief discussion of the issues with relation to rhetorical stance serves to bring them to the forefront and focuses student attention on them. Even with younger learners, discussions about why the author chose to write as he/she did are valuable in bringing student attention to the issues of voice and the like. Table 6.3 provides some ideas that teachers can use to spark student discussion about their writing.

Linguistic Choices.   In addition to considering voice, audience, purpose, and form, students must make many linguistic choices in their writing. These linguistic choices may be tied to rhetorical stance issues such as voice and audience. For instance, if students are writing a play for an elementary class, they will need to use language that is appropriate for that grade level. For English language learners, a large part of the struggle with writing in their new language is a lack of knowledge of vocabulary or a lack of complete understanding of all the shades of meaning involved in word choice. Writers need to choose specific, concrete words that show the reader what they are writing about and use figurative language (e.g., the house was as cold as a tomb) to help add color and detail. They should consider such syntax issues as length of sentences, type of sentence patterns used (e.g., simple, compound, complex), and types of connections and transition elements

TABLE 6.3   Questions Related to Rhetorical Stance

Voice: Who is writing? (e.g., Are you writing as yourself? A contemporary? A voice from the past?) What voice are you using for your paper? Example: If you are writing a journal entry for a pioneer traveling west, you need to know who you are and how you feel about making this journey.	■ Who am I? ■ How do I feel? ■ What do I know? ■ How sure am I?
Audience: In general, most students write for their teachers. We need to expand the possibilities and have students write for real-world audiences. Writing for someone outside of school can be a powerful experience. Example: Write for informational brochures to stock the class library. To assist students with the idea of audience, draw a parallel to television or the movies. Certain advertisements are shown during television shows aimed at a younger audience and others during shows that have an older audience. You must tailor your advertising to the audience for the show. Writing is the same way. Who is listening to what you are writing?	■ Who is listening? ■ What are they ready for? ■ What help do they need? ■ How are they feeling?
Purpose: Why are you writing? If you are writing a letter of complaint, what is your end goal? What words and strategies can you use to accomplish your result? You vary your style of writing based on the purpose of the writing task.	■ What do I want to happen? ■ What is likely to result? ■ What effect do I seek? ■ What am I willing to accept?
Form: Not all writing must look like an essay or a short story. There are various formats for writing. For instance, a complaint to a company should probably take the form of a memo or letter.	■ What form fits this message? (e.g., essay, memo, poster, advertisement, etc.)

needed. Teachers need to help students to express initial thoughts and encourage them to use prewriting notes and experiences

As students are involved in drafting, it is difficult to assess what is going on in their minds. However, teachers obtain some clues by observing and analyzing how students learn in general, and how they deal with the writing process in particular. Using a checklist to keep track of the types of strategies students use while writing can help teachers highlight areas of weakness so that more direct instruction can be provided in those areas.

Revising

Writing takes a great deal of work. If getting the words down on the page was not difficult enough, writers must go back to reread and revise their work. Revising is a critical phase of the writing process. This is the point where students refine their writing. Unlike editing or proofreading, revising involves more substantial changes in text at a meaning level. All too often, students see revision as simply fine-tuning their paper, focusing on superficial concerns such as spelling and some low-level word changes. However, revision is much more work than that. It is not a mechanical process but rather a powerful writing tool.

Revising includes planning, reading, and rereading the text—going back to get an idea of the whole text and revising at all levels. If students are able and willing to revise at a meaningful level, it is less complicated to teach them to cycle back and edit the final draft. Helping students see a need for deeper text changes is difficult, and students are more resistant to changing their work at this level. For English language learners who have struggled to put words on paper, revising may seem overwhelming. On the other hand, revising gives them more time to fine-tune their language.

We are fortunate in this age of technology because the computer makes revising an easier task. Using the cut and paste commands, we can move large portions of text around and try them out, then move them again without having to copy over the whole paper. This may encourage more substantial revision from students. We can model this process for students with our own writing if projection equipment is available, or by simply using sentence strips and physically manipulating them and changing their order. In addition, holding planned as well as informal conferences with students, either individually or in small groups, helps students talk through their writing in a way that fosters the revision process. We can also teach students to meet with each other as they write, revise, and edit their work.

Editing

Editing does not occur until the final stages of the writing process. Indeed, getting caught up too early in editing can hamper the writing process. Editing involves the external and surface-level changes that students normally think of when we mention revision. Editing involves proofreading and polishing—changing text at an external level (punctuation, capitalization, etc.).

For English language learners, spelling and some of the rules of mechanics may present difficulties. However, teaching students about spelling and mechanics is best done in the context of their own writing. We have found that students are most motivated to concentrate on polishing the mechanical correctness of their writing when they have the opportunity to publish or display their work in some formal way. This provides the pressure of an audience and a real purpose for communicating their thoughts in the most correct form possible. Again, we can model the use of technology, showing how spell-checking and other editing tools work. We should also guide students in knowing when to overrule the software's suggestion for word replacement or spelling.

Publishing

Publishing involves the opportunity for students to share their work with others and to showcase students' efforts at the writing process. Especially with English language learners, this positive affirmation of their efforts in a new language can be a powerful motivating force. Students can share their work by having a read around with a peer group or making the work available in a learning center or station. Publishing can involve creating a class book that is bound and available in a classroom library. The work can be posted on a bulletin board in the classroom or in the school hallways. A letter can be mailed to a real audience.

Writing Activities

As we have already discovered, there are countless strategies to make student writing meaningful. Teachers should use a variety of options for student writing assignments and balance this with opportunities for unassigned writing on topics of their own choosing.

In the writing workshop approach, the climate and process of writing are set into place, and students are given a regular block of time for writing of all kinds. They keep writing folders or portfolios of all their writing on an ongoing basis. When time allows, they can continue working on a variety of pieces outside of the more structured writer's workshop time. Regular opportunities for modeling and conferencing are also provided. Mini-lessons are integrated as needed. Within such a context, the teacher can introduce a variety of writing modes, strategies, and techniques, including preparation for writing on demand under the pressure of a test. We provide information and examples of just a few ways teachers can engage students in the act of writing.

Collaborative Writing.   Generally, when we think of writing in classrooms, we imagine students working individually on their own compositions—a solo task. But, is that the only way to write? In *Co-Authoring in the Classroom: Creating an Environment for Effective Collaboration* (1997), Helen Dale makes a solid case for collaborative writing. Fitzgerald (1993, p. 287) concurs, noting that "The elements of writing are best learned in the context of communities of authors and readers who are writing and reading in natural ways."

One of the most powerful benefits of collaborative writing, particularly for English language learners, is that "even less able writers can contribute through verbal input in brainstorming and planning sessions" (Dale, 1997) and "good talk helps to encourage good writing." (Britton, Burgess, Martin, McLeod, & Rosen, 1975, p. 29). Many of the trade books that we suggest as frameworks for writing lend themselves to collaborative or class writing projects. For instance, one fifth-grade ESL class developed an alphabet book entitled *Hola Means Hello.*

Letters.   Letter-writing lowers the anxiety associated with writing because the normal format of a letter eases the blank-page syndrome (Schwartz, 1984). Writers automatically have the opening (greeting) and sometimes more if formulaic or ritualized phrases (e.g., How are you? I'm fine) are utilized. Plus, letter exchanges are versatile; they can be arranged within the same school, age group, or grade level as well as across school districts or geographical locations. Letters provide an opportunity to develop control of writing in a realistic, functional manner (Cambourne, 1988).

Working in collaboration with teachers in the field, we have been able to observe how eagerly students anticipate writing when they know there will be a personal response to their composing efforts. Perhaps because topics are self-selected and deal with relevant concerns, interests, experiences, and questions, the quantity and quality of writing on interactive tasks such as letters often exceeds writing on other assigned tasks (Peyton, Staton, Richardson, & Wolfram, 1990; Staton, 1987). Some students who had never written for teacher-assigned tasks suddenly produced mountains of text. In answer to letters, correspondents read and try to answer important questions so they can get to know one another. Students use feedback to modify their language output, to clarify and elaborate for comprehension, and to prevent and repair communication breakdowns (Dolly, 1990). Responses need to encourage and stimulate a continued dialogue, as we see in Box 6.3.

In addition to actual letter exchanges, there are many trade books that feature letters and letter writing, such as the ones highlighted in Table 6.4. Sharing these in the classroom and participating in a letter exchange lead to rich language opportunities. Teachers might ask students to write a real letter to their favorite author, poet, or illustrator; write a letter to a favorite book character or from a character's point of view; try different kinds of letters (friendly, business, consumer) and mail them; try different formats for correspondence (postcards, flyers, invitations, greeting cards, thank-you notes); try corresponding by computer network or by sending videos; or try to hook up with an international pen pal.

Dialogue Journals.   Journals can also promote students' writing development by combining both of the previous strategies: collaboration and letter writing. Two-way interaction, collaboration, and transaction are the "doing" tasks of language through which children gain linguistic proficiency and functional expertise (Long, 1983; Long & Porter, 1985; Rosenblatt, 1985). Dialogue journals exemplify the process of collaboration or negotiating meaning so crucial to the development of language proficiency (Dolly, 1990).

While there are numerous formats for journal writing, one of the more popular forms is a dialogue journal. Dialogue journals are, in effect, a written conversation between two individuals—teacher and student or fellow students (e.g., peers or cross-age partners). Uncomplicated in structure, dialogue journals provide a purposeful writing task.

B O X **6.3**

Examples of Elaboration in a Letter Exchange

In answer to initial questions from his penfriend, Mario (fifth grade) furnished the following information:

I like to come to school because I want to learn how to speak more English. I enjoy playing baseball. I also like my bike and being with my friends. I have a big family. When I am out of school, I would like to go to Mexico and visit my cousins.

Because Mario's ideas were not fully developed, Mario's pal replied with elaborative responses to encourage him to relate more about his baseball interests. His reply showed the effect of such prompts.

You asked me if I played baseball on a team, but I don't. I just play it for fun. I play baseball with my friends and my cousins, too. When they come to my house we always go to the baseball field and play baseball. I would like to be in a baseball team when I am in high school.

TABLE 6.4   Books Written in Letter Format

- *Dear Alexandra: A Story of Switzerland* by Helen Gudel
- *Dear Levi: Letters from the Overland Trail* by Elvira Woodruff
- *Dear Mr. Henshaw* by Beverly Cleary
- *Letters from Rifka* by Karen Hesse

Yet despite their less structured nature, journal entries are a rich source of teaching material and a compact means of charting the development of student writing over time (Schwartz, 1983). In addition, journals can provide an outlet for self-expression, for sharing students' lives outside the walls of the school, and even for exchanging thoughts about school, if the climate is open. Journal writing can help provide the personal outlet, in which we discover ourselves through writing.

Dialogue journals underscore the idea that composing is a purposeful activity used to communicate thoughts and ideas. Through dialogue journals, students privately share their reactions, questions, and concerns about school and personal matters with teachers. With dialogue journals, students are free to initiate their own topics, change topics as often as they wish, and utilize original formats (e.g., poetry, text with illustrations) to enhance an entry. In short, there is no correct way to write. This freedom helps students grow as writers.

Just as with letter writing, there are countless books that use journals or diaries as the format for the text, including those listed in Table 6.5. Teachers can share these books as examples of the kinds of writing found in journals. An excellent point is the historical nature of many books written in journal or diary format. While many of the examples we share fall into the category of fiction, we draw much of our historical knowledge from primary source documents such as journals. Some instructional ideas for books which feature journals and diaries include the following.

- Keep a journal of daily reflections and share it periodically.
- Try a buddy journal, responding from class to class or across the grades.
- Keep a notebook of observations of people and surroundings.

TABLE 6.5   Books Written in Diary or Journal Format

- *Amazon Diary: Property of Alex Winters* by Hudson Talbot and Mark Greenberg
- *Rachel's Journal: The Story of a Pioneer Girl* by Marissa Moss
- *The Journal of Ben Uchida: Citizen 12559, Mirror Lake Internment Camp, California, 1942* by Barry Denenberg
- *The Journal of Joshua Loper, A Black Cowboy, The Chisholm Trail, 1871* by Walter Dean Myers
- *The Ledgerbook of Thomas Blue Eagle* by Gay Matthaei, Jewel Grutman and Adam Crijanovic
- The "Dear America" and "The Royal Diary" series from Scholastic
- The "Dear Mr. President" series from Winslow Press

- Try typing on a typewriter and using a computer; keep a journal on a disk.
- Seek out primary source journals and diaries for studying history.

Other formats for journals such as academic journals, content journals, learning logs, double-entry journals, and the like. will be explored in Chapter 11 on nonfiction literature. These formats lend themselves to use with nonfiction text and content-related material. Whatever the format, journals are generally the most personal form of writing and should be shared only on a voluntary basis. They should seldom be graded and then only for effort or participation. To do otherwise is to shut down the honest exchange of thoughts and feelings in the journal venue.

Poetic Formats.   Writing poetry and using poetic formats such as biopoems, list poems, diamantes, and so on provide a possible structure to students' writing attempts. In addition, poetry can be a welcome alternative to simply answering questions about content-related reading. Students often think of poetry as the most difficult and challenging form of writing, and indeed it can be. However, in Chapter 10, we also provide models of formulaic poetry such as diamantes or biopoems that can help jump-start students in poetry writing as well as infuse writing into the learning of content.

Using Literature as a Model for Writing.   Donald Graves (1983) claims that all children need to be exposed to good literature, but that children who are "authors" need it even more. One of the best activities for developing writers is to expose students to a wealth of rich, beautiful, descriptive, informative language through good books. Literature provides an outstanding framework for student writing. Sonya Blackwell, a middle school language arts teacher, shared her use of picture books in Box 3.5 in Chapter 3 and discussed their potential to help students with literary devices. In her use of the book, *My Life with the Wave* (Cowan, 1997), she was acquainting students with the technique of personification, but she didn't stop there. Listen as she moves this reading experience into a writing activity in Box 6.4.

BOX **6.4**

Voices from the Field:
Writing Extensions from Trade Books

The students were intrigued by the idea of sharing their room with a wave companion, and their imaginations were further heightened by the vibrant, detailed illustrations. The students had no problem grasping the concept of personification because they were so drawn to the story, drawn to the idea of a wave with human qualities. In fact, the students were upset when the book ended after the boy decides he will bring home a cloud next time. The last page shows a cloud grinning wickedly, with lightning coming from underneath the cloud. They wanted to know what happened when he brought the cloud home. I used this as a creative writing extension, letting students write the cloud sequel and share it with the class—a huge success.

In particular, photo essays, alphabet books, wordless picture books, and question-and-answer books serve as powerful models of writing. The key to having the class use any format is to bring models of that style of writing to class and to discuss them prior to assigning the project. After exposure to various examples of books in these formats, students can attempt to write their own or can work collaboratively and create a class book in one of the formats. Let's consider just a few of the most popular of these examples.

An **alphabet book** doesn't have to be just for young children. Science students could develop an alphabet book for a biology or chemistry unit. Not only will students develop writing potential, but this activity would assist them in becoming actively involved in vocabulary study as well.

Another great writing model can be found in **question-and-answer books.** Franklin Watts Publishing has the "How Would You Survive" series, and Scholastic has several series of question-and-answer books as well. These formats lend themselves to class-developed book projects and are a tremendous starting point for class research because the tables of contents are often listings of questions that can be used for student brainstorming.

A final format, books written in the form of newspapers, is also available as a model of writing to share with classes. Students can compare and contrast broadcast news with the vast variety of print newspapers and then turn to the trade book news format examples. Most **newspaper format trade books** are ideal links to the content areas—social studies and science in particular—because they furnish information about historical eras and so on using a news layout. This demonstrates yet one more method of having students report on their content knowledge. In addition, with the advent of desktop publishing, writing in formats such as the divided column of newspapers is easy to incorporate in the classroom. The class may even decide to develop their own newspaper.

As we can see, there are a variety of ways to assist English language learners in their development of writing in their new language. Beginning with instruction in the phases of the writing process from prewriting through publishing, teachers can assist English language learners to become actively involved in each stage of writing. A variety of writing activities offers options to motivate students no matter what their English language proficiency level.

Once students are actively engaged in writing, we must continue to support them through the assessment process. Determining where English language learners are in their development and offering input designed to assist their growth as writers are critical. Thus, we turn to our assessment section.

Checking It Out: Assessing Writing

Assessing writing is always an area of great debate. First, evaluating student writing is a time-consuming process. Second, we must provide feedback to students on their efforts, but we need to do so with a focus on content and organization, not a preoccupation with form and mechanics. How do we evaluate student writing in an efficient manner but still provide the input that students need in order to grow? Following are some basic considerations (Atwell, 1987; Bratcher, 1994; Calkins, 1986; Spandel & Stiggins, 1997; Tompkins, 1994).

Teachers should consider the purpose of each writing assignment. For instance, the purpose of journals (e.g., dialogue journals, buddy journals, etc.) is to help students practice writing. In general, journal writing is not to be graded. Instead, the focus is on response by the teacher or peer, not mechanics and spelling. In the content areas, the aim is on reporting content, so the teacher can check whether students have grasped the concepts.

In terms of marking students' papers, teachers might consider using another color for grading besides a red pen or not marking the paper at all. Some teachers write notes on adhesive notes and affix these to student papers. Since time efficiency is an issue in grading, teachers may want to develop grading checklists or rubrics with the required elements to be included in the student work and a space for comments.

Every writing assignment is not necessarily for evaluation purposes, and we shouldn't evaluate every assignment in the same way. In fact, only revised and edited work should be graded. Feedback on drafts is appropriate, but grading a draft that is a work in progress is not—especially for English language learners who need time to work through their language issues on a paper.

Providing time for peer editing and revising groups offers support to developing writers. It also means that the papers that come to the teacher will be less time-consuming to grade because students have had a chance to polish their language. When assessing student ability, a wide variety of input is required. Students have strengths and weaknesses, and multiple means of assessment offer a fuller picture of student ability.

Informal Assessment

As we have noted, informal monitoring is used daily to keep track of students' progress. The information provided by various means of informal assessment is critical to effective instructional planning. We highlight just a few methods of informal assessment of writing.

Observation.   Observing students in our classrooms yields a rich source of data about their language development and their growth as writers. For instance, we may take note of any or all of the following:

- What attitude does a student have toward writing?
- What writing strategies is a student using?
- What classmates do students turn to for assistance during writing?
- What types of interactions do students have with their peers during writing?

Conferences.   One of the most powerful forms of assessment is the individual writing conference because teachers have a chance to work with students one-on-one, discussing their writing and encouraging them. However, finding the time to meet in the busy instructional day is often very difficult. Therefore, other alternatives are an option. Teachers may conduct on-the-spot conferences at students' desks. In addition, once English language learners have advanced to the intermediate proficiency level, they may participate in peer conferences about their writing.

Whatever the format—individual or more spontaneous, teacher–student or student–student—conferencing can be utilized at various stages of the writing process or for a variety of purposes. Prewriting conferences help students discuss their plans for writing, generating vocabulary and ideas and considering organizational issues. In drafting conferences, students present their rough drafts, talk about problem areas, and reflect on the next steps to move the writing along. Revising conferences provide an opportunity to discuss specific suggestions about how to improve a student's writing in terms of content and organization. Editing conferences allow a close look at mechanics, syntax, and word choice. Instructional conferences or mini-lessons are used by the teacher to provide focused help on one or two skills for an individual or a small group of students who need some direct instruction. Assessment conferences address a student's overall growth as a writer, establishing a picture of the progress made and the next steps needed.

Anecdotal Records.   Teachers may make written comments about students' writing progress, behavior, or choices. For instance, they may record examples of student behavior during writing workshops or keep a list of writing formats or topics that students are using. In addition, for English language learners, teachers may consider keeping a file folder for each student, noting his/her proficiency level, any pattern of errors that seems developmental, and any that persist over time despite direct instruction.

Writing-Process Checklist.   To document where students are in the writing process for any piece they are working on, teachers may use a checklist noting the activities for each stage of writing process. For instance, a writing-process checklist might have some of the following categories:

Prewriting
- Worked with a group to brainstorm ideas.
- Recorded these ideas in a work folder.

Drafting
- Produced a rough draft from brainstorming session.

Peer Editing
- Shared rough draft with a peer group and made note of their input.

Such a checklist can be filed in a folder for each student. However, some teachers use a white board or laminated poster with a checklist, and students use a dry erase marker to record where they are in the process. This helps teachers monitor the class and specific student needs during a writing workshop.

Portfolios.   Assessing student writing development via portfolios has drawn a tremendous amount of attention in recent years. A simple folder or a more complex portfolio can include student work over the course of a semester or year. This display of work is a tremendous record of development over time and is available both for the student and the teacher to visit periodically. According to Valencia (1992), portfolios can be defined as a collection of work and records collected over time. They are formative and ongoing with an emphasis on performance-based assessment rather than standardized results. Additionally, Valencia stresses that portfolios should not be considered a grab bag because they then become too large.

Grading and Providing Feedback for Student Writing

Informal assessment is generally focused on the process of writing as students move through the stages of prewriting, drafting, editing, and so on. Once students submit their final written products, teachers have new decisions to make. What type of assessment will be used to grade and provide feedback to the students? Following are several formats to consider (Tompkins, 1994).

Checklist.   A checklist contains general criteria that guide the grading of students' papers. Checklists help teachers focus attention on those points and also provide a place to make comments to students about their work. Teachers might even agree with students that they will focus only on certain points, such as the introduction of a paper and capitalization. Global marking of papers can be very time-consuming for the teacher and overwhelming for the student. Chances are that too much feedback will not be internalized by the student, so teachers should concentrate on only a few points at a time.

Primary Trait Evaluation.   Similar to a checklist, a primary trait evaluation notes the essential traits or points that teachers want students to include in their papers. Once the teacher decides what essential points students must include in their work, the teacher then determines the weight in terms of points given to each item. Again, comments to students about their work can be made on the form. The primary trait evaluation is a type of contract teachers develop and provide to students in advance of making the assignment. For example, if a class is to develop a travel brochure, before assigning the task, the teacher should determine what is to be included in the brochure. Possible required items might include a map of the destination, travel facts, climate, and terrain. Once items are brainstormed for required and optional items, the teacher can order them and assign points to the items. Then the grading checklist is distributed to the students, and the class goes over the assignment with teacher guidance.

Rubrics.   Rubrics provide a more structured approach to grading. They generally include essential characteristics of a paper as well as what constitutes a high-quality and a low-quality paper.

Any of these techniques for assessing the process and product of writing is worth the effort. The more teachers monitor and support the writing process through informal assessments, the greater the student's development as a writer. In addition, the more teachers consider assignments beforehand and develop well-thought-out grading criteria, the less time will be spent grading, since students know what is expected.

Summary

In this chapter, we examined the important role that writing plays in developing both literacy and English language development. Moreover, we discussed how writing is a valuable tool for the content areas, helping all students explore what they have learned.

In terms of writing and English language learners, their writing develops in much the same manner as that of their native English speaking peers. Creating productive writing environments for English language learners takes concerted effort and planning as well as a knowledge of the developmental stages of writing and the writing characteristics that nonnative English speakers might display at each language proficiency level. For instance, early writing depends heavily on oral language competence. Indeed, early writing is much like speech written down, so teachers need to continue to work on students' oral language development. Techniques such as the Language Experience Approach, in which students engage in an activity and then dictate their stories to teachers, can provide a model for early writing attempts.

In addition, English language learners best understand and utilize the writing process when their teachers model the process and make each stage clear through carefully developed activities. When teachers assign writing about what is known and is of interest to English language learners, the students feel more comfortable with the language used and risk more in their writing. Teachers might consider free writing or journal activities, where emphasis is on meaning without correction.

English language learners, in particular, need to explore the process of writing—learning to work at a given writing task in appropriate phases, including prewriting, drafting, and revising. One specific prerequisite for English language learners is the need to discuss topics prior to writing since these students display a greater anxiety about topics not previously discussed. In general, teachers should spend more time on prewriting strategies, helping students generate ideas through discussion, illustrating, and brainstorming.

Furthermore, teachers can scaffold students' writing through student–teacher conferencing and asking content-related questions about their writing. We know that writing improves most when teachers provide feedback during the writing process rather than only on final papers.

The need to vary writing assignments is also a critical element of writing instruction. Students enjoy and benefit from a variety of writing forms and structures. Many of these forms can be effectively modeled with literature examples, such as the ones shared in this chapter. Teachers also need to encourage writing as a tool of learning in all subjects across the curriculum.

Finally, assessment and evaluation can support student writing development. Although time-consuming, teachers can choose from a number of assessment procedures. For instance, portfolios provide a glimpse of students' writing development over time, while checklists, rubrics, and primary trait evaluations are excellent for looking at students' final written products.

SECTION THREE

Responding to Culture and Language

Literature is my utopia. Here, I am not disenfranchised. No barrier of the senses shuts me out from the sweet, gracious discourse of my bookfriends.

—Helen Keller

This section provides an overview of three major areas of literature that offer rich opportunities for the literacy development of English language learners. Although all types of literature are worthwhile and useful for teaching, we have chosen three in particular—multicultural literature, folklore, and poetry—because of their unique instructional potential for English language learners. Multicultural literature offers both linguistic and cultural context for students. Folklore is closely linked to the oral tradition of cultures around the world. Poetry, because of its oral delivery, is an outstanding resource for oral language development. There are three chapters in this section.

- **Literacy Learning through Multicultural Literature**
- **Literacy Learning through Folklore**
- **Literacy Learning through Poetry**

7 Literacy Learning through Multicultural Literature

We have no borders when we read.

—Naomi Shihab Nye

In this chapter we look closely at a particular segment of children's literature focused on representing the experiences of authors and peoples of many of the microcultures of the United States. We attempt to identify what multicultural literature is, how to judge the authenticity of multicultural books, and how to use multicultural literature with English language learners, and we provide a brief introduction to the current titles, authors, themes, and trends in publishing multicultural books for young people. In our discussion of multicultural literature in this chapter, we will address the following questions.

- **Why use multicultural literature in the classroom?**
- **What is multicultural literature?**
- **How do we judge cultural authenticity in literature?**
- **How are the cultures of America represented in literature for young people?**
- **How do we incorporate multicultural literature into our teaching of English language learners?**

Let's begin our discussion by considering the many reasons for using multicultural literature in our classrooms, especially with English language learners.

Why Use Multicultural Literature in the Classroom?

When we think about sharing literature with English language learners, the most perfect choice may indeed be what is called multicultural literature. Multicultural literature refers to literature that reflects the experiences, values, and beliefs of a particular culture of people, including European cultures as well as minority cultures. For our purposes, we will be focusing on the four major microcultures dominating American society: African American, Hispanic American, Native American, and Asian American. Books that feature the experiences of these cultures often present issues with which students learning English are very familiar. Themes of identity, family, acceptance, and cultural heritage are prominent in contemporary multicultural literature. There is a natural relevance for immigrant students and for children who are second-generation Americans.

However, multicultural literature is not just a tool for teaching so-called minority students. This new category simply represents an evolution in publishing that recognizes the voices of new authors, sometimes referred to as authors of color, who have stories to tell. Their stories speak to all readers and listeners with their beautiful language, memorable characters, and powerful themes. In the very near future, the multicultural label will become irrelevant, and we will simply seek the best books by any author for every student. For the moment, however, it is helpful to invest time in learning about the new authors, illustrators, and poets who speak from their own cultural perspectives in order to be sure these voices are heard.

All students need to hear these voices. African American authors, for example, do not write only for an African American audience, any more than German Americans write only for German Americans. The range of cultural perspectives in today's literature for children and young adults is quite amazing, and this is not simply an exercise in matching minority literature with the right minority student population. We challenge you to read broadly in multicultural literature, then choose favorite books across all cultural groups to share with students. The point is simply to choose multicultural books, and to choose well. To do this, one must first become aware of the authors and titles available. In Box 7.1, as a case in point, Sonya Blackwell reflects on her plans to increase her own awareness as well as that of her middle school English language learners in terms of multicultural literature.

According to Rudine Sims Bishop (1997) in "Selecting Literature for a Multicultural Curriculum," multicultural literature can serve at least five broad functions.

B O X **7.1**

Voices from the Field: Increasing Student and Teacher
Awareness of Multicultural Literature

My success during the past year encourages a broader use of picture books next year. I plan on having a multicultural featured author every month, complete with a display and a collection of works. I will share some of the picture book selections each month as a way to hook the students into reading more by that author. I also plan to use picture books during my unit on stereotypes. We will explore stereotypes of gender, race, and class in multicultural picture books as a lead in to my unit on *Roll of Thunder, Hear My Cry* (Taylor, 1976).

- ■ It can provide knowledge or information.
- ■ It can change the way students look at their world by offering varying perspectives.
- ■ It can promote or develop an appreciation for diversity.
- ■ It can give rise to critical inquiry.
- ■ It can provide enjoyment and illumine the human experience, in both its unity and its variety.

"Multicultural literature can have a beneficial effect on the school achievement of children who have historically been denied realistic images of themselves and their families, community, and culture" (Bishop, 1997, p. 4).

Clearly an argument can be made for selecting multicultural books for classroom use when we think about how students challenge the status quo, how we promote democratic ideals in our classrooms, and how literature helps with both these tasks. In addition, when one considers the unique challenges to cultural assimilation that many English language learners face, the benefits of sharing books that reflect diverse experiences and points of view are even greater. Dan Hade challenges us to confront our students' and our own assumptions about race, class, and gender critically and openly. He asks us to avoid the "tourist view" of multiculturalism, reading books because they're "cute" or "different." His goal is to promote critical thinking and open discussion and to challenge the status quo: "Silence is the oxygen of racism and bigotry" (1997, p. 237).

What Is Multicultural Literature?

How does one appropriately refer to this kind of literature? *Multicultural* is the generally preferred term because it focuses on the element of many cultures. In this chapter, we focus on the many cultures within the United States. *International Literature,* which refers to books for young people published outside the United States was briefly addressed in Chapter 3. There is a difference between Japanese American literature (multicultural) and Japanese literature (international), for example. Be careful of the cultural conglomerate notion, however, and be sensitive to differences within cultural groups, too (Yokota, 1993). There are significant differences between Chinese and Japanese cultures, for example, within the category of Asian American. By the way, European American literature (German American, Italian American, etc.) is also part of the world of multicultural literature because multicultural technically means many cultures. While many native English speakers receive some introduction elsewhere to the fairy tales collected by the Brothers Grimm, Milne's classic stories of Winnie the Pooh, and *Strega Nona* (de Paola, 1975), our knowledge base of African American children's literature, among others, may be currently less strong. Thus, a separate chapter on multicultural literature is still helpful. In the future, our grandchildren will grow up just as familiar with *Uncle Jed's Barber Shop* (Mitchell, 1993) or the Logan family (Taylor, 1976) as they are with *Little House on the Prairie* (Wilder, 1935) or *Ramona Quimby, Age 8* (Cleary, 1981), and this distinction will become obsolete.

How Do We Judge Cultural
Authenticity in Literature?

The Insider or Outsider Perspective

The question of an author's own culture or background is a significant one in the field of multicultural literature. Much debate has occurred over whether a book can be considered culturally authentic if the author is writing outside of his/her culture. Can a white author write an authentic book about a nonwhite experience? Some would say no and would be able to cite countless examples from the past of books full of error and stereotypes. A few exceptions, however, withstand the close scrutiny of readers and critics from within the culture.

No author should be held accountable for speaking on behalf of her/his *entire* culture with any single book. Let us be careful about making judgments about the entire Muslim world based on reading one novel, like *Shabanu* (Staples, 1989), for example. Though it is a powerful, well-written story, it still represents only one author, one perspective, and one story—just like any book.

It seems logical to acknowledge that having lived in a certain culture provides helpful background for telling an accurate story about that culture. Important details and even subtle nuances of character, setting, or style emerge when an author is very familiar with the culture. Some very gifted authors, however, have managed to use careful research, fact-checking, and even close observation and personal experience to get it right.

How do you know? How can you tell whether a book authentically represents the culture depicted? Interestingly enough, if it is your culture in the story, the authenticity (or lack thereof) usually seems obvious to you. Cultural markers flag the story as representative or typical. However, reading outside our own cultures can present some very real challenges. We are not necessarily well-versed in the particulars of other cultures. That's where book discussion is essential. Collectively, we can share our cultural knowledge base and help each other understand each other's cultures. English language learners, in particular, can benefit from this collaborative process of reading and talking about books. They can share their own cultural backgrounds in a way that honors and celebrates them, and they can engage in a meaningful discussion that helps provide language practice. In the process, we all gain valuable insight and help each other develop awareness and understanding.

Looking for Cultural Markers

What are some of the usual variables one considers when looking closely for cultural authenticity in literature? Rudine Sims Bishop, in "Making Informed Choices" (1992), provides step-by-step guidelines for the close examination of cultural authenticity in children's literature. She also reminds us to include a careful consideration of the traditional literary elements in our analysis of each book. Is it a good story, well written, with strong characters? Cultural accuracy may be rather mechanical if the book's plot does not interest children. Yokota (1993) includes these specific criteria for consideration: cultural accuracy both in detail and with larger issues, richness in cultural detail, authentic dialogue and relationships, in-depth treatment of cultural issues, and inclusion of members of a minority group for a purpose. Slapin, Seale, and Gonzales share their perspectives in relation to Native American children's books in *How to Tell the Difference: A Guide to Evaluating Children's Books for Anti-Indian Bias* (1998). In combination, these authors and scholars offer helpful criteria to guide the novice critic in the careful consideration of multicultural literature for young people. Teachers can model this process of evaluation for students in guiding their own developing critical analysis. The Bulletin of the Center for Children's Books is also an excellent resource for locating the best multicultural literature for classroom use. Bookmark their Web site for the latest updates on new good books: http://www.lis.uiuc.edu/puboff/bccb/.

When using picture books with students, it is important to pay close attention to the illustrations as well as to the text, as noted in Table 7.1. The pictures are an important source of cultural information, especially in the depiction of skin color. Is the skin tone of the characters a believable shade? Most human skin is various tones of brown. Skin colors such as bright red or lemon yellow are not real. In addition, are the skin tones of various characters slightly variable? In real life, a single African American family, for example, may have members of light and dark shades of brown. Are facial features of the characters true to their culture, or are they simply white faces colored in? Is there diversity within the diversity? Is variety within the culture depicted or suggested?

The culture also comes through in the words and the story, especially in novels with few or no illustrations. Here one must read carefully and critically for many of the same kinds of variables. Look closely at the description of physical attributes, especially skin color. Are the language and speech patterns in the dialogue appropriate to the culture? If

TABLE 7.1 Cultural Markers

In the illustrations, look for accuracy and variety in these elements:

- Variation in skin tone
- Facial features
- Body type
- Clothing
- Homes
- Hairstyles/hair texture
- Modern vs. traditional representations
- Urban vs. rural contexts
- Homogeneous or varied representations

In the text, look for accuracy and variety in these elements:

- Description of physical attributes, especially skin color
- Identification of specific culture or nation
- Language patterns; dialect or first language
- Names of characters and forms of address
- Foods
- Celebrations and religious practices

not, does the author explain why these may have been standardized? Often, the author's note in a book is extremely helpful in understanding the cultural context of the book. Is the specific culture even identified in the text, or is a generic culture simply suggested or implied? These details give the reader confidence that the story rings true. Rudine Sims Bishop (1992) challenges us to "Put yourself in the place of the child reader. Is there anything in the book that would embarrass or offend you if it were written about you or the group you identify with? . . . Would you be willing to share this book with a group of mixed-race children? An all-black or all-white group?" (p. 51).

Although it may not always be popular to say so, the first criterion in choosing books to share with children should always be whether the book is well written and interesting. From a very practical standpoint, students are generally uninterested in books that are didactic or sentimental or boring. So the traditional literary tools of strong plot, interesting characters, integral setting, worthwhile theme, and captivating style are still useful measures of a book's worth.

How Are the Cultures of America Represented in Literature for Young People?

African American Children's Literature

According to Violet Harris in "Contemporary Griots: African American Writers of Children's Literature" (1992), a major shift occurred in children's literature in the mid-to-late 1960s with a move to create literature categorized as culturally conscious. Virginia Hamilton's book *Zeely* (1967) is viewed by many as the beginning of the ongoing renaissance in African American children's literature (Harris, 1997).

There are many critically acclaimed and popular examples of African American literature for children and young adults in every genre. Many picture books make excellent read alouds. Sylvia often pairs *Uncle Jed's Barber Shop* (Mitchell, 1993) with the famous Langston Hughes poem, "Dreams" (from *The Dreamkeeper and Other Poems*, 1932/ 1994). Mitchell's historical story conveys the power of dreams in the context of the Depression as well as in the face of racial discrimination. In addition, teachers can call up Martin Luther King, Jr.'s "I Have a Dream" speech on the Internet (http://www.pbs.org; also available in book form, 1997) and encourage students to share their hopes and dreams. One outstanding author who has consistently garnered awards for the quality of her writing is Mildred Taylor. She received the Newbery award for *Roll of Thunder, Hear My Cry* (1976), and her writing has been hailed by both critics and children.

Folktales, such as *John Henry* (Lester, 1994) are a must for inclusion in a Tall Tale unit. Lester's version, illustrated by Jerry Pinkney, vividly portrays this heroic character. Other folktales provide insight into African American traditions, such as *Mirandy and Brother Wind* (McKissack, 1988) with its description of a cakewalk; there is also a cakewalk in *Family Pictures* (1990) by Carmen Lomas Garza. (For more outstanding examples by folktale adapter Patricia McKissack, see Chapter 8 on folklore.) These would all be excellent selections for celebrating African American contributions during Black History Month, although the "this is your month" approach can be rather isolating. There are excellent examples of African American literature to fit any topic or theme, not just in February.

Some African American literature is written in black vernacular English, or black dialect. When done well, it can really make a story sing, and flavors the text with the voice of its people. Yet, dialect can be difficult for those outside the culture to follow, especially for English language learners. It may be necessary for the teacher to read the first chapter or crucial passages aloud to help students follow the story. Students can also discuss pronunciation variations and the way an author uses language to create distinctive and authentic characters. Some African American children's books have become controversial because they are about the unique experience of being black in America. Others outside the culture may find this difficult to accept or understand.

There is also a rich tradition of songs and poems in African American literature for children. To share some of these voices with your students, delve into *Pass It On, My Black Me: A Beginning Book of Black Poetry* (Brown, 1993), and *Ashley Bryan's ABC of African American Poetry* (Bryan, 1997), both excellent anthologies of poems by many of the best African American poets.

Finding the very best-quality African American children's books is also made easier by the establishment of the Coretta Scott King award given annually by the American Library Association. This award is given for both writing and illustrating to African American creators of children's books. The list of award winners and honor books is a rich source of high-quality literature for classroom use. See the ALA Web site for the current award winners and honor choices: <http://www.ala.org/ssrt/csking>.

Hispanic American Children's Literature

For a long time, Hispanic American children's literature was confined to Spanish translations of standard English texts, like *Clifford, the Big Red Dog* (Bridwell, 1989). Although these books can be fun and useful for children who read Spanish, they do not attempt to reflect Hispanic cultures in any way. Now the trend is for Hispanic authors to share their own stories and experiences in a combination of English and Spanish. The text is generally in English, but there is an interlingual use of Spanish. Some authors then provide glossaries for the Spanish words; others expect the story's context to help with meaning. This can be a wonderfully natural way to introduce languages into the classroom, but don't be too self-conscious about your own pronunciation—just make an effort. If you are a Spanish speaker or if you have Spanish-speaking students, use this language expertise to share stories using Spanish more fluidly and fluently. Middle school teacher Colleen Schiebolt drew her native Spanish speakers into lessons by sharing Gary Soto's poems and having students chime in with the Spanish words mixed throughout the poems. Talk with the class about the words and language. Also, recognize that you may have other students who are learning English who are not Spanish speakers. They will also need clarification as you share stories in two *new* languages—English and Spanish.

In the 1990s, two landmark books were published in the evolution of Hispanic American children's literature: *Family Pictures/Cuadros de Familia* (1990) by Carmen Lomas Garza and *Baseball in April* (1990) by Gary Soto, which was the first children's book of stories by a Chicano published by a major publisher. These are still very appealing

---

B O X **7.2**

Five Fun Facts about Gary Soto

- Gary Soto was born in Fresno, California, in 1952.
- Gary Soto did not decide to be poet or writer until he was in college.
- Altogether, Gary Soto's books for adults and young people have sold over a million copies.
- Gary Soto produced the film *The Pool Party,* which received the Andrew Carnegie Medal, and he wrote the libretto for an opera entitled *Nerd-landia* for the The Los Angeles Opera.
- When he was a boy, Gary Soto had chores and jobs like mowing lawns, picking grapes, painting house numbers on street curbs, and washing cars.

Web Sites

The Official Gary Soto Web site: http://www.garysoto.com/
Gary Soto: A Teacher Resource File: http://falcon.jmu.edu/~ramseyil/soto.htm

---

books for students of all ages. Teachers can share Garza's memoirs in art and story form and invite students to create their own visual and verbal autobiographies. Gary Soto, our featured author in Box 7.2, has written work for nearly every genre and for nearly every grade level.

Tomas and the Library Lady by Pat Mora (1997) is one of Sylvia's favorites to share with students. She uses a brown-bag book report to introduce the story. As she summarizes what the book will be about, she takes out a map of the United States to represent the migrant family's travels. Plastic oranges represent their livelihood; a twig from a tree represents the storytelling of Papa Grande; a ball made from a discarded teddy bear is the character's only toy, and a mortar board (graduation hat) symbolizes Tomas' eventual success as a professor. Then she reads the book aloud, including the epilogue, which tells the stunning conclusion of Tomas' true story.

Other true stories can be found in the nonfiction books of George Ancona. *The Piñata Maker* (1994) is a popular example that is typical of his style. Ancona photographs and interviews actual people for his books. Thus, students are introduced to the craft as well as to the culture through the example of an individual or family. His books can be linked with a Foxfire approach to capture the stories, crafts, and traditions of the neighborhood through interviews and writing. We will explore this approach a bit more in Chapter 8 on folklore.

Poems, songs, rhymes, and chants are also an important part of Hispanic children's literature. They can be shared orally from family memories, collected and written down by students, and compiled into a class anthology. There are also more and more published collections of Hispanic poetry for children. Soto's collection of poetry called *A Fire in My Hands* (1990) even provides a brief narrative explanation for each poem describing where the idea for the poem came from. These narratives provide helpful insights for aspiring poets. If you are a Spanish speaker or have Spanish-speaking students, share the Spanish poems or try bilingual read alouds.

Several major awards are now given for Hispanic and Latino children's literature, such as the Americas Award (http://www.uwm.edu/Dept/CLA/outreach_americas.html),

Illustrations by Ed Martinez, copyright © 1993 by Ed Martinez, illustrations. Used by permission of G. P. Putnam's Sons, an imprint of Penguin Putnam Books for Young Readers, a division of Penguin Putnam Inc.

As a Mexican American family gathers to celebrate Christmas and Maria helps makes the tamales, her mother's diamond ring is missing. Do they eat all the tamales in their search for the ring?

Soto, G. (1993). *Too Many Tamales*. New York: Putnam.

the Pura Belpre Award (http://www.ala.org/alsc/belpre.html), and the Tomas Rivera Award (http://www.star.so.swt.edu/today/chautauquan/c19960911.html). These can be helpful for seeking out high-quality literature that reflects Hispanic experiences.

Native American Children's Literature

Native stories and poems for children and young adults often reflect a style of writing that is new to non-Native American readers and listeners. Much is implied rather than stated directly. Descriptions and details may be spartan and few. Plots may seem indirect, even boring to the naive reader. Many stories and poems are translations from Native American languages. It may take the leadership of a sensitive and enthusiastic adult to choose well and to share selections orally with dramatic pauses and follow-up explanations, so experiment with several different genres of Native literature. If you are Native American or if you have Native students in your classroom or community, ask them if they would be willing to share stories, songs, or poems orally, perhaps even in their Native language. Audiotapes (such as those recorded by Joseph Bruchac) can also help convey an effective delivery style. In many Native nations, sharing stories orally is still much preferred over the written word. In fact, some stories are not allowed to be written down. They are perceived as private or sacred and not for public consumption. We all have beliefs we hold dear and would not want shared with people who don't know us well.

Digging for details of authenticity in Native American literature requires multiple strategies. Knowing the author's native heritage helps, but it's no guarantee of authenticity. One must read the author's notes, source notes and all other supporting documentation. We should also consider the importance of small presses for finding truly authentic literature. This is where new authors and illustrators often get their start. One organization dedicated to helping teachers sift through the authentic and the stereotyped is Oyate (http://www.oyate.org), a Native organization working to see that Native lives and histories are portrayed honestly. Their publications and workshops are invaluable to culturally conscious classroom teaching.

Joseph Bruchac, with his Abenaki roots, has been very effective in telling and retelling Native American stories. In addition, he has branched out into poetry, legends, and contemporary tales. His anthologies, collections, even audiotapes are effective with children across the grades. *The Great Ball Game* (1994) is a favorite of many students of all ages with its story of a competition between the birds and the animals. It is very effective as a readers theater script, with half the class taking the part of the animals and the other half the part of the birds. *Many Nations: An Alphabet of Native Americans* (1997) is a wonderful introduction to twenty-six different Native nations. It is another excellent example of how the alphabet book can serve as a springboard for organizing all kinds of information.

Three other Native authors worth paying particular attention to are Shonto Begay, Virginia Driving Hawk Sneve, and Michael Dorris. Shonto Begay, a relative newcomer to the field, uses lush paintings to reflect the colors and textures of the landscape. His stories and verses in *Navajo: Visions and Voices across the Mesa* (1995) reflect a strong and powerful voice. An introduction provides additional insight for the novice reader. More proficient language learners will enjoy experimenting with different genres of writing that Begay uses in creating vignettes of memoirs in this collection. Teachers can contrast this with Carmen Lomas Garza's retelling of her family stories in *Family Pictures* (1990) and lead students to see how their bicultural stories parallel each other or differ.

Virginia Sneve (pronounced Snavy) has created poem collections, short novels, and an outstanding nonfiction collection called the First Americans series. *The Cheyennes* (1996), for example, is full of history and detail about their unique tribal structure, social life, arts, and ceremonies. Other nations in the series include the Sioux, Navajo, Seminole, Nez Perce, Iroquois, Hopi, and Cherokee. Third grade teacher Laura Shopp used the First Americans series as reference materials in her class. Each child wrote a short research paper and did an oral presentation on a group of Native Americans of their choice. Meanwhile, Shopp also read *Morning Girl* aloud, and the class discussed the effects of European exploration on the American Indians.

Michael Dorris's short novel *Morning Girl* (1992) weaves a universal story of growing up, sibling rivalry, and family love. The unique twist is that the story is set among the Taino people in the Bahamas in 1492, just prior to the arrival of Columbus. In addition, it uses two points of view to tell the story, the perspectives of a sister and a brother in alternating chapters. Pair this with Jane Yolen's picture book *Encounter* (1992), and students can discuss who is discovering whom in the "new" world.

There is an abundance of folklore about various Native American legends and beliefs, but many of these have been retold by white authors who may lack the background to capture essential cultural details. One of the few exceptions is the work of picture book author and illustrator Paul Goble. Although born and raised in England, Goble immersed himself in the Native cultures of the American West, and his work has been publicly accepted by the people he depicts. Check out *Buffalo Woman* (1984), for example. Goble includes a foreword and afterword that offer additional background, explanation, and references. Touches like these give readers more confidence that they are reading authentic literature.

Don't overlook Native American poetry. This can include a variety of poetic forms including rhymes, free verse, chants, charms, prayers, blessings, lullabies, warnings, eulogies, wishes, prophecies, healings, war chants, night songs, magic songs, medicine songs, and mother/child poems, among others. In many Native American cultures, rituals and traditions are expressed poetically in stories and songs in everyday life. Some can be shared chorally in a variety of ways, inviting audience participation. Allow students to decide how a poem might best be read aloud: by one lone voice, by a call-and-response chorus, by small groups of voices, or perhaps accompanied with drum or flute.

Asian American Children's Literature

The term *Oriental* is no longer accurate or appropriate for the more than fifty different Asian and Asian Pacific American ethnic groups who share no common history, language, religion, or culture. These groups represent a growing proportion of the U.S. population and thus of our classrooms. Literature by Asian American authors includes a growing body of folktales, picture books, novels, poetry, and nonfiction. A variety of sources can provide quality Asian American literature, including Asia for Children, Master Communications, Inc., 4480 Lake Forest Dr., Suite 302, Cincinnati OH 45242-3726; 513-563-3100; http://www.afk.com.

The recurring themes in Asian and Asian Pacific American children's literature include immigrant adjustment to life in the United States, Asian American and Asian Pacific American history, cross-cultural conflict, sharing Asian and Asian Pacific American culture, and the search for and acceptance of an Asian or Asian Pacific American identity (Aoki, 1992). Many stories are also grounded in symbols and creatures from folklore and myth, especially dragons and demons, which some find controversial.

Laurence Yep is one Asian American author whose writing has been hailed by both critics and children. He has authored folktale picture books for younger children like *The Khan's Daughter* (1997), humorous novels for the middle grades like *Later, Gator* (1995), and historical novels for young adults like *Dragon's Gate* (1993). He consistently creates well-written, award-winning stories that present the struggles of children of Asian descent. English language learners can read and discuss these issues of family pride, individual identity, and cultural conflict.

Being Asian and being American is shown to be a source of conflict, struggle, and pride in many Asian American books for young people. This is clearly portrayed in *Grandfather's Journey* (1993), the Caldecott award-winning picture book by Allen Say in which the grandfather is homesick for his homeland when he is in his adopted country, and homesick for his adopted country when he goes home. Any child who has ever moved may have experienced these same feelings. What might this be like if you are crossing *continents*? Look at two of Allen Say's other picture books to see his family's struggle with identity and his mother's point of view as well: *Tree of Cranes* (1991) and *Tea with Milk* (1999).

Literature by Asian American authors may also be translated into English. For example, *The Animals: Selected Poems* (1992) by Michio Mado is a bilingual collection that provides both the English version and the Japanese version of each poem. Again, the issue of what may be lost or gained in the translation comes up. Perhaps more important from a pedagogical point of view is the value of showing students different alphabetic and nonalphabetic language systems. If you or a student is a speaker of Japanese, Chinese, Korean, Vietnamese, or other Asian language, share examples of stories or poems.

Asian American poetry for young people is more than haiku. Although there are many lovely ancient haiku rhymes to share with children, this form of poetry is often abused by the expectation that children can simply fill in the seventeen syllables and create a work of art. There are many other kinds of poetry represented in the works of Asian American poets. Janet Wong is a new author whose early work explores her Korean, Chinese, and American roots in a fresh and direct way that English language learners will find very relevant. Her poem "Speak Up" (from *Good Luck Gold and Other Poems,* 1994) can be read chorally by many voices or by a lone voice for a powerful message about language and identity.

Other Cultures

Of course, the four cultural groups discussed above are not the only cultures represented in this country. The English language learners in our classrooms come from many countries and cultures, so wherever possible we need to seek out literature that tells the stories of their cultures. Their motivation to learn as well as their self-esteem will benefit. Where there is an absence of published books, we may need to rely on oral storytelling, on student-created books, on new books from small presses, and even on suitable adult literature.

It can be challenging to locate children's books that authentically reflect the experiences of immigrants from the Middle East, for example. Even identifying what is meant by the label Middle East can be controversial. It is clear, however, that there are many children in our schools and communities who are of Arab, Lebanese, Palestinian, Egyptian, Pakistani, Israeli, Iranian, and Iraqi descent, among others. What we really need is books for young people about growing up in America with Middle Eastern background. There are some titles that help fill this need: Naomi Shihab Nye's novel *Habibi* (1997) and several others by her are an excellent beginning point. Pair her coming of age novel (*Habibi*) with her picture book *Sitti's Secrets* (1994) for added insight into a girl's relationship with her foreign grandmother. Then, add the poetry of Nye's collection *The Space between Our Footsteps: Poems and Paintings from the Middle East* (1998) to provide insight into what it means to grow up Arab. Additional resources for teaching appropriately about the Middle East can be found through AWAIR, Arab World and Islamic Resources and School Services, 2137 Rose St., Berkeley CA 94709; 510-704-0517; http://www.telegraphave.com/gui/awairproductinfo.html.

How Do We Incorporate Multicultural Literature into Our Teaching with English Language Learners?

Kaser and Short (1998) talk about their experiences teaching and researching a unit in a working-class school in Tucson in which "the students themselves became the curriculum" and open and voluntary discussion in small groups of four to five students became the essential catalyst for growth and learning. They discovered that "students often discussed how a book related to the culture they shared with members of their age group, an identity we came to think of as 'kid culture'" (1998, p. 185). They discovered how important it was for teachers to tune into their students: "We found that ways of listening needed to be planned into the day [for the teacher], or we missed hearing what children were saying because of the hectic nature of classroom life" (p. 191). Their instructional model included three major components (Kaser & Short, 1998):

- They encouraged children to bring their lives and cultural identities into school.
- They encouraged children to choose their own books.
- They encouraged children to share their reading and their responses with each other.

As students grew with each opportunity to read and respond, the researchers were surprised to find that "When students and teachers recognize the cultures that influence their own lives and thinking, each becomes more aware of how and why culture is important to everyone else. These understandings do not devalue culture or promote cultural 'sameness,' rather, they highlight differences across cultures as important and valued in creating community and pushing everyone's learning. In examining children's talk, we also noted that it was important that children choose the aspects of culture they did and did not want to discuss. . . . Disclosure of self through dialogue or writing is not culturally appropriate for some children" (pp. 189, 191). In addition, students didn't just talk about culture. "While ethnicity mattered to them, other aspects of their own cultures, such as gender, religion, family, community, and social class were sometimes of greater importance to them or were interwoven with issues of ethnicity and race" (p. 187). Their final conclusion? "Cultural diversity is a strength for building powerful learning contexts, not a problem to be solved. Difference, not sameness, makes a classroom and society strong" (p. 192).

Once teachers are aware of the many trade books available, they will be able to weave these into their instruction. Let's look at Box 7.3 for just a few examples of how classroom teachers have done this.

Multicultural literature makes instructional models relevant, interesting, and motivating to students, and in combination with all the other books and teaching resources at our disposal, it offers a core of connection that all English language learners deserve. To assist teachers in their instructional efforts, Table 7.2 offers a few final methods of incorporating multicultural literature into today's diverse classrooms.

Checking It Out: Assessing Language Development through Multicultural Literature

Assessment techniques are not different with multicultural literature. Teachers have all the options that have been discussed in previous chapters with oral language, reading, and writing available to them. For instance, as with all genres of literature, story retelling, particularly with children in the primary grades, is an excellent vehicle for both instruction and assessment. That is, children can retell a story they have just heard or read as a fun and natural way of enjoying the story again and responding to it. As children participate in such an activity, however, the observant teacher can also assess the child's story schema,

---

BOX **7.3**

Voices from the Field:
Weaving Multicultural Literature into Classrooms

June Jacko created a whole poetry unit on the topic of Who Am I? for grades 6 and 7. Students read poems from many different poets of color, discussing the connections in theme between the poems. Another teacher, Peregrina Ramos, integrated multicultural poetry into her total poetry program. When students began writing their own poems, they imitated their favorites across all cultures. Finally, because familiar topics are a good beginning point for getting to know our students and learning language, Nancy and Sylvia collaborated with elementary, middle school, and high school ESL teachers to create a month-long unit on Families connecting all kinds of books related to the topic of families across cultures and across genres.

TABLE 7.2   How to Begin Incorporating Multicultural Literature

- When you read aloud to children, choose books that feature characters from a variety of cultural backgrounds.
- When you feature a particular author, illustrator, or poet of the week, regularly choose a multicultural author.
- When you choose award-winning books for your students, investigate prizes that particularly highlight multicultural contributions, such as the Coretta Scott King Award and the Tomas Rivera Award.
- When you decorate your classroom or library, feature faces, stories, and traditions from a variety of cultural backgrounds.
- Remember the rich literature that is oral, and use storytelling and community folklore to add depth to your students' experiences. (See Chapter 4 for more ideas in this area.)
- Use multicultural literature to enrich the content areas or to supplement the traditional reading program to add other perspectives.

grasp of story structure, and familiarity with story language. Some experts are even suggesting using this method as a routine and gentle means of testing the developing literacy of emergent readers. In addition, this technique can be used with almost any good children's book with a strong, sequential story line.

Props or simple story manipulatives can also be easily created to assist children as they use their language and speaking skills. Story retelling props should correspond closely with the book. In the multicultural classroom and with multicultural literature, the possibilities are endless. Using *Too Many Tamales* (1993) by Gary Soto, the teacher might cut out the main characters, the tamales, and the ring from a second paperback copy, and attach a magnet to the back of each piece. Each story element can be arranged on a painted cookie sheet to assess children's understanding of the story. These same story retelling props can also be dramatic and playful, allowing children to create new stories using the same props. In addition, students can gather or create their own story props and place them in a story center for others to manipulate and enjoy.

One technique that Nancy has found very useful in getting to know students is the microcultures scrapbook. Gollnick and Chinn (1998) note that each person has a combination of microcultures that make him/her unique. Each microculture (e.g., family, language, nationality/ethnicity, gender, age, religion) exerts varying degrees of influence on us at different points in our lives. In order to have students reflect on their membership in various microcultures, Nancy has an assignment that allows students to create a scrapbook to highlight each microculture. Students may include actual photos of family and experiences to depict a microculture (e.g., photos of a quinceñera, bar mitzvah, etc.), or they may illustrate, clip photos from magazines, or include actual memorabilia. The idea is to provide an overview of the student and his/her microculture affiliations and to share these with the class as a means of getting to know one another.

Once students have created their own scrapbooks, they might branch out and create a scrapbook for a character in a book as a means of comparing and contrasting their scrapbook with a fictionalized one. If students present these, this provides an assessment of oral language. The actual scrapbook with its labels and descriptive narrative functions as an assessment of reading and writing.

Summary

Multicultural literature enables all students to see themselves, since it crosses the mainstream and reflects the microcultures of the United States. Multicultural literature is found across the genres and covers a broad spectrum of themes and topics.

There are many benefits accrued from using multicultural literature with English language learners. These benefits range from natural relevance and identification with characters to rich experiences with wonderful literature. Moreover, this literature offers information, opportunities to see the world through new lenses, and even improvement in academic achievement.

Multicultural literature includes the literature of many cultures found in the United States. In this chapter, we highlighted the literature reflecting the cultures and experiences of African Americans, Arab Americans, Asian Americans, Hispanic Americans, and Native Americans.

The cultural authenticity of multicultural literature is very important when selecting books for students. Presence of cultural markers and insider perspectives are two important considerations. However, first and foremost, multicultural literature needs to be well written and to provide a good story or accurate and important information.

Multicultural literature plays an important role in the literacy learning of English language learners. Effective teachers encourage their students to bring their cultural identities to school, to choose their own books, and to share their reading and responses with their classmates. Such instruction enables students to see the strength found in diversity. Isn't it about time that this valuable literature is incorporated into all classrooms?

8 Literacy Learning through Folklore

If you don't know where you want to go, any road will take you there.
—African American proverb

In this chapter, we will explore folklore—a broad genre of literature. Beyond the written tales of a people, folklore also encompasses the traditional stories, customs, beliefs, and sayings preserved orally among a group. Teachers are often unaware of the broadness of the genre of folklore, but it is exactly this scope that offers such a rich source of language learning possibilities as well as an added cultural dimension, particularly for English language learners. We will address the following questions in this chapter.

- **What is folklore, and how does it reflect culture?**
- **What are the benefits of using folklore in the classroom?**
- **What does the study of folklore include?**
- **How can teachers use folklore with English language learners?**

Let's begin our discussion of folklore by defining this genre and noting the breadth of opportunities within it.

What Is Folklore, and How Does It Reflect Culture?

Folklore is essentially defined as the tales or stories of a people, hence its name. The knowledge and stories of our ancestors were passed by word of mouth from generation to generation long before this information was recorded in written form. With its roots deep in the oral traditions of a group, folklore reflects at least two levels of a culture. First, folklore emerges from the folk, or grassroots, culture. The stories, traditions, customs, and sayings of the folk culture are of such long duration—some of them over a thousand years old—that they cannot be traced to one single person. Who was the originator of *Little Red*

Riding Hood? Who first used the saying "Every cloud has a silver lining"? No one knows. At this level of entry, folklore is spread by word of mouth, or through action and observation in the case of nonverbal behaviors or customs. With each link in the chain of transmission, the story, saying, or custom may be altered somewhat. Each folk performer leaves a faint imprint by crafting the story or saying to fit the audience and the setting.

This verbal and nonverbal level of folklore is ideally suited for the English language learner. All cultures participate in this type of folklore through storytelling, children's chants, gestures, rhymes, riddles, and proverbs. Indeed, folklore in this form served as means of literacy development for preliterate societies in the past and still functions this way in the present in many developing nations. So, all English language learners bring a wealth of background knowledge of this type of language and activity into the classroom despite their level of reading, writing, or general education. Some English language learners may even possess a greater understanding and appreciation of this genre than native English speakers, so folklore at this level can be a great equalizer in the classroom. Unfortunately, most teachers plan lessons with folklore derived from the next level of culture—the popular culture—and bypass this wonderful oral language development opportunity.

One difficulty with folklore as it enters the popular culture is the issue of authenticity. After undergoing the many translations and revisions that are a part of crafting stories for the general public, individuals from the culture of origin may not recognize the traditional lore they grew up with. Teachers need to consider this as they choose from the many published versions of folklore linked to various ethnic groups. English language learners may even provide valuable assistance to the teacher by adding their input in the matter of authenticity. Don't assume, for example, that all Mexican American children will be familiar with La Llorona or with a published folktale about this legendary character.

Whether the stories we use in the classroom have made their way to the popular culture or simply have their roots in the folk culture, folklore offers many valuable instructional possibilities. We consider the benefits of this genre next.

What Are the Benefits of
Using Folklore in the Classroom?

Because folklore is such a powerful and personal genre, it has the capability of involving students at any language proficiency level and drawing on the rich diversity of student backgrounds in any classroom. Through folklore, students become personally involved in thought, culture, and expression (Renner & Carter, 1991). According to Krogness (1987) and Wilson (1988), the benefits of folklore study are many including its potential to deal with our universal experience and recurring human problems, to examine the artistic and creative efforts of all human beings, not just the elite, and to cross disciplinary lines (e.g., by looking at folk beliefs relating to illness in science class or researching the historic roots of folk sayings).

Given a population of linguistically and culturally diverse students, the benefits of folklore simply multiply (Tchudi & Mitchell, 1999). Through folklore, all students come to a greater appreciation of their own cultural heritage and that of others (Gonzalez, 1982;

Lutz, 1986). For instance, a project to collect and share family folklore fosters students' pride and helps them see their uniqueness and understand the uniqueness of others (Renner & Carter, 1991). When teachers begin their instructional efforts with personally relevant and familiar topics, students feel more comfortable and are encouraged to speak and write more freely (Gonzalez, 1982). The language and activities of family and neighborhood offer an important comfort zone in the language learning process (Hadaway, 1990; Hadaway & Cukor-Avila, 1987).

Many types of traditional literature are available to today's students; they can read and listen to the entire range of folklore from riddles and rhymes to fables, fairytales, folktales, myths, and legends. Most anthologies and readers include selections of traditional literature. Yet without the powerful illustrations found in the trade book versions, English language learners may still struggle with the text. Published traditional literature can generally be found in picture book format with rich illustrations to cue the reader to important story elements, as well as to provide visual cultural details for the story. In addition, students might check out the Web site, www.falcon.junu.edu/~ramsevil/tradlit, which offers information on folktales, mythology, and other forms of traditional literature.

This genre provides engaging reading material, since folktales are generally short stories that can be read quickly. This brief format is ideal for English language learners who may lack the English proficiency to tackle more lengthy and complex reading assignments. Plus, young students delight in the oral qualities captured in print, such as Verna Aardema's use of onomatopoeia in *Traveling to Tondo* (1991), and they readily join in as the teacher reads the sounds made by the various animal characters.

Given the many instructional benefits of folklore, teachers need to consider using this genre more frequently. Therefore, in the next section we examine what types of folklore can be included in the classroom.

What Does the Study of Folklore Include?

Folklore is easily integrated into any language arts program and across the curriculum at any grade level; yet, it is not a strong component of ESL programs according to a survey we recently conducted of 120 ESL and grade-level teachers working with English language learners in grades K–12. One-third of these teachers noted that they never included folklore with their ESL classes; the other two-thirds used folklore sometimes. When asked what type of folklore they included in the classroom, they all gave only trade book examples of folktales (e.g., *John Henry, Three Little Pigs, Johnny Appleseed,* Aesop's fables, etc.), and in general, they used the selections within the basal reader or anthology. These data highlight the tendency of teachers to overlook the verbal and nonverbal categories of folklore, moving right to the many published works of traditional literature. However, beginning with the folk culture level provides a foundation for later discussion of how the printed tales came into being.

There are numerous categories of folklore from verbal to nonverbal varieties as well as folk culture and popular culture examples, as highlighted in Table 8.1 (Gonzalez, 1982; Lutz, 1986; Renner & Carter, 1991). Not only are these rich categories for language study, but their interdisciplinary potential is obvious. For the geography class, a survey of any

U.S. map yields countless place names highlighting the influence of various ethnic groups on our history. In science, a survey of folk medicine demonstrates that many traditional herbal cures are valid medicine in today's world. Working collaboratively, history and science classes can collect the personal stories surrounding historical events such as floods, hurricanes, or tornadoes. Furthermore, family recipes can be used in math to teach measurement along with the differences in measuring systems among different countries.

To get to know students and to engage students with familiar topics, teachers often include a unit on the family. Nancy used the Kotkin and Baker (1977) guide as the impetus for her work with a high school ESL teacher (Hadaway & Mundy, 1992). They planned a family folklore unit beginning with an emphasis on oral folklore and personal experience stories and moved to trade books later. First, students engaged in a study of names and naming practices. To introduce this segment of the unit, they read aloud the section "My Name" from Sandra Cisneros' *The House on Mango Street* (1984). In this touching vignette, Esperanza relates how she received her name and how she feels about it: "In English my name means hope. In Spanish it means too many letters. At school they say my name funny as if the syllables were made out of tin and hurt the roof of your mouth. But in Spanish my name is made out of a softer something like silver, not quite as thick as sister's name Magdalena which is uglier than mine" (pp. 12–13). Afterward,

TABLE 8.1   Categories of Folklore

- Cumulative tales
- Pourquoi tales
- Fairy tales
- Animal and beast tales
- Horror and ghost stories
- Noodlehead and trickster tales
- Realistic tales
- Fables and myths
- Epics and legends
- Religious stories
- Chants and jump rope rhymes
- Tongue twisters, finger plays, hand-clapping games
- Autograph sayings
- Fractured fairy tales
- Jokes, riddles, proverbs, puzzles, games, and rhymes
- Jingles, folk songs, and ballads
- Traditional or folk medicine
- Beliefs and superstitions
- Customs concerning pregnancy, birth, and baptism
- Personal experience narratives
- Gestures
- Architecture, handicraft, and art
- Stories behind place names
- Oral history
- Folkways regarding courtship, betrothal, and weddings
- Traditional festivals and celebrations

students created illustrations using the letters of their names, then shared these with a partner, discussed whether they liked their names, and noted any stories behind their names.

Continuing with the theme of family stories, the trade books *They Were Strong and Good* (Lawson, 1968) and *How Many Days to America* (Bunting, 1992) were shared to assist students with writing personal experience narratives on the topics of how their parents met and about their journey to America. The students enjoyed this unit, and their stories about family experiences came more easily than previously assigned topics. A thematic unit could easily evolve from any section of the Katkin and Baker questionnaire (1977), including those noted in Table 8.2.

Traditional literature includes a wide range of published variations, too. Folklore is a type of traditional literature, but this literary genre also includes myths, legends, and fables. Indeed, even the category of folktale includes fairy tales, tall tales, pourquoi tales, trickster tales, fractured tales, and created folktales. This is a very popular niche in the publishing market, and many well-written and beautifully illustrated versions can be found that have immense appeal across the grade levels. The best examples reflect careful study of the root culture so that the language and illustrations accurately reflect the story's culture for the reader. *Mufaro's Beautiful Daughters* (Steptoe, 1987), for example, is an outstanding example of a cinderella tale rooted in the flora and fauna of Zimbabwe. Yet it reflects a universality in character and theme that appeals to even secondary-level students.

Folklore is a rich genre that provides many language growth opportunities for English language learners and the potential for increasing cultural awareness. When teachers do use folklore, however, it is generally focused on the study of published traditional literature trade books and not the full range of written, verbal, and nonverbal folklore options. However, the breadth of folklore provides so much more potential for teaching and learning. In the next section, we highlight the many instructional possibilities with folklore.

TABLE 8.2   Collecting Family Folklore: Some Themes

- Family names
- Traditions and customs
- Stories of childhood, adolescence, school, marriage, work, religion, and politics
- Recreation and games
- Tales of the black sheep of the family
- Courtship, betrothal, weddings, and marriage
- Historical events associated with weather or nature
- War or immigration experiences
- Financial sagas ("rags to riches")
- Family expressions and phrases
- Holidays and celebrations
- Reunions and family gatherings
- Recipes, cooking, and food taboos
- Extended family
- Funeral and burial customs
- Stories behind family heirlooms, photos, or memorabilia

How Can Teachers Use Folklore with English Language Learners?

As we stated initially, folklore includes the knowledge and stories of a people. This lore is just what Wigginton and his students from Appalachia collected in the several volumes of the Foxfire project (1991/1992). They set out to record how the local folk performed certain tasks, used language, entertained themselves, and so on. Classroom teachers can use this same idea by shaping class activities around several folklore themes, including how to make or do something, how to teach something, and how to entertain. We will explore each of these themes along with ideas for classroom activities and suggested literature links.

How to Make or Do Something

Students can talk to their families to collect information, such as cures for common maladies (e.g., hiccups or folk maladies such as mal de ojo), traditions and preparations for family celebrations and holidays, ways to predict the weather or fortune, or recipes for traditional dishes (e.g., menudo, latkes, etc.). These themes are touched on in many trade books. For instance, Carmen Lomas Garza's bilingual books *In My Family/En Mi Familia* (1996) and *Family Pictures/Cuadros de Familia* (1990) provide illustrations and text in both English and Spanish that describe traditional holidays and family celebrations as well as folk illnesses and cures. Bernhard provides a wonderful overview of the many ways and times of year that the new year is celebrated around the world in *Happy New Year!* (1996), while Janet Wong focuses on the lunar new year in *This Next New Year* (2000). For a more factual approach, Diane Hoyt-Goldsmith details the traditions of real-life families from various cultures in *Apache Rodeo* (1995), *Arctic Hunter* (1992), *Pueblo Storyteller* (1991), *Celebrating Hanukkah* (1996), *Celebrating Kwanzaa* (1993), *Day of the Dead* (1994), and many more.

How to Educate

One of the functions of folklore is to educate—to teach manners and social behaviors (Simmons, 1990). For instance, eating customs vary across cultures and make an interesting study. We don't all eat the same things, use the same types of utensils, or even eat at the same time. How do we learn the correct way to eat in our culture, and how easy is it to adapt to a different eating style? Friedman's (1984) *How My Parents Learned to Eat* provides an inside view of the cultural differences that come into play as an American sailor courts a Japanese girl and they adjust to each other's way of eating. After reading the book, students can share their families' typical foods and the customs surrounding their preparation and serving.

There are many books that provide a foundation of basic proverbs and folk sayings to begin a class discussion, including *Dichos: Proverbs and Sayings from the Spanish* (Aranda, 1977) and *The Green Grass Grew All Around: Folk Poetry from Everyone* (Schwartz, 1992). *First Things First* (Fraser, 1990) and *A Word to the Wise and Other Proverbs* (Rayevsky, 1994) are interesting visual depictions of many proverbs.

Logic, wisdom, and problem solving all come together in the short story collections *Stories to Solve* (1985), *More Stories to Solve* (1990), and *Still More Stories to Solve* (1994), all by George Shannon, who has taken folktales and brainteasers from around the world and retold them in a short story–puzzle format. When read aloud, they encourage students to figure out the ending for themselves.

Folklore has also served to educate the listener and reader about the creation of the world, the history of its people, and the moral values the culture holds dear. Myths, legends, and fables evolved as distinct literary vehicles with these specific purposes. For example, creation stories from around the world can be shared in Virginia Hamilton's *In the Beginning* (1988) and Ann Pilling's *Creation* (1997). Erik Jendresen and Joshua Greene combine their talents in the retelling of *Hanuman* (1998), based on one of India's most sacred texts, the *Ramayana*. Through these works, teachers can set the stage for encouraging their English language learners to share creation stories from their own cultures.

Greek, Norse, and Roman mythology also fascinate young people. These myths are often hero myths that do not seek to explain anything, but are instead the grand adventures of the gods. Greek and Roman myths can be found in Aliki's *The Gods and Goddesses of Olympus* (1994), Rockwell's *The One-Eyed Giant and Other Monsters from the Greek Myths* (1996), and Hutton's *Persephone* (1994). Current collections of Norse myths are found in Osborne's *Favorite Norse Myths* (1996) and Philip's *Odin's Family* (1996). Greek, Roman, Norse, and other myths from around the world are available in general collections such as Philip's *The Illustrated Book of Myths* (1995) and Hoffman's *A First Book of Myths* (1999). Students are also intrigued by the parallels between the supernatural powers of the gods of mythology and the superhuman abilities of the cartoon and television heroes of popular culture, such as Superman, Batman, the X-Men, and the like.

Legends share stories of heroic deeds of historical figures. The people in legends really existed, but their lives and deeds may be embellished in the story. Robert San Souci's retelling of *Fa Mulan* (1998) is a notable example of a legend based on a historical figure. Mulan's glorious fictional deeds continue to inspire people, though little is known about the real-life model. Disney's movie version *Mulan* increases the accessibility of the book for English language learners and young readers and is generally regarded as culturally authentic.

In fact, many legends and folktales have been made into films and videos that are popular with children (often with little care for cultural specificity or authenticity). Cinderella, Snow White, Robin Hood, King Arthur, and others appear in movies that often become the "real" version to students. It can thus be an interesting learning experience to watch a video version of Cinderella, for example, and then compare it with picture book versions such as those illustrated by Marcia Brown, Susan Jeffers, or Nonny Hogrogian, even with older students.

Fables are often short stories with animal characters that teach lessons also intended to educate the young, often with mixed results. Both Russell (1997) and Savage (2000) point out that children frequently miss the intended message of the morals presented in stories. Yet, students enjoy the fables for their clever animal characters and conflicts, even though their parents often wish their children would internalize the morals. *The Ant and the Grasshopper* (Poole, 2000) is an example of the many Aesop's fables available in picture book formats. Bierhorst (1988) retold Aztec fables in *Doctor Coyote*. The Jataka tales are Indian fables dealing with Buddha's animal rebirths before he became the Enlightened One. Jataka tales can be found in Martin's *The Hungry Tigress* (1999) and Demi's *Buddha Stories* (1997). Many fables still remain in oral form, and students could be invited to share those that are not yet in books.

How to Entertain

Beyond teaching people the do's and don'ts of a culture, one of the main functions of folklore is to entertain. Jokes, riddles, games, songs, and storytelling all have this purpose. Mexican American students may be familiar with the *corridos* or ballads often sung to report actual events. In his book *With a Pistol in His Hand: A Border Ballad and Its Hero* (1958), Americo Paredes researched the history behind a popular ballad (*corrido*) about a border hero from the Mexican American community. This ballad was the impetus for the 1980s movie, *The Corrido of Gregorio Cortez*.

Many books teach games of all kinds from countries all around the world. *Hopscotch around the World* (1992) by Mary Lankford and *Simon Says . . . Let's Play* (1990) by Sally Foster are two helpful examples. In addition, Joanna Cole and Stephanie Calmenson have created an extensive series of books ideal for the beginning English language learner, including *Crazy Eights and Other Card Games* (1994), *Marbles: 101 Ways to Play* (1998), *Pin the Tail on the Donkey and Other Party Games* (1993), *Miss Mary Mack and Other Street Rhymes* (1990), and many more. If the students know some American playground lore, they may enjoy *Juba This and Juba That* (Hopson, 1996), in which even second and third verses to "Cinderella dressed in yellow" are available. Students usually enjoy putting their own hand-clapping, jump-roping, and game-playing rhymes into print. The class can publish a collection using any simple desktop publishing program.

Many young people are familiar with the endless storytelling sessions as family members gather for the holidays, or they may have experienced parties or gatherings where ghost stories were the expected fare. Many of the ghost or horror stories shared in these settings are actually urban legends (e.g., the Kentucky Fried rat or the vanishing hitchhiker) offered as true stories. Brunvand (1989a, 1989b) has a series of books that provide different versions of the most popular urban legends, and these would be excellent resources to use when planning a unit such as this with secondary-age English language learners. Check out the latest on the Tales of the Wooden Spoon Web site at http://snopes.simplenet.com/spoons/legends/legends.htm. It is full of information and examples of urban legends.

The range in length and reading levels found in published folktales make them a good choice for the most diverse classes. Children learning English benefit from the repetition and predictable language patterns found in many trade book folktales. For instance, *The Bossy Gallito* (Gonzalez, 1994) is a cumulative tale in which language and actions are repeated over and over. This repetition and predictable text support young readers' early English reading attempts. For example, the teacher can take each phrase within the cumulative pattern and record these on cards that are distributed to groups of students. As the phrase comes up in the story, students can read along and even act out the meaning. Since the phrases are repeated over and over, the opportunities for building oral proficiency as well as word recognition and comprehension increase. Folktales can also be used with older students. One fifth-grade teacher reads from Virginia Hamiltion's *The People Could Fly* (1985) so that her students better understand how the slaves expressed their fears and hopes to one another through story. For older students, combine this book with an examination of the From Remus to Rap: A History in Theory and Practice of the African American Storytelling Tradition Web site at http://falcom.jnu.edu/~ramseyil/drama.htm, which provides exposure for secondary-level students to African American traditional culture, for even richer study.

Many pourquoi folk tales intrigue students with their odd explanations of how things came about. It may be animal appearance or behavior such as *How Turtle's Back Was Cracked* (Ross, 1995), *How the Camel Got Its Hump* (Kipling, 1991), and *How Rooster Got His Crown* (Poole, 1999). Others shed light on human behavior and customs, as does *How the Ox Star Fell from Heaven* (Hong, 1991), which illustrates why people eat three meals a day, and *The Birds' Gift* (Kimmel, 1999), which explains how the tradition of pysanky eggs began in the Ukraine. English language learners might write their own pourquoi tales explaining contemporary cultural phenomena. One fifth-grade teacher reads pourquoi tales when her English language learners study animal camouflage and adaptation in science, for example.

The perfect complement to geography or social studies are tall tales, often set in specific regions; they are exaggerated narratives containing oversized boisterous characters, humorous actions, and picturesque language. Children can sit spellbound as they listen to stories of Paul Bunyan, Mike Fink, John Henry, Febold Feboldson, and Pecos Bill. Their stories are available in many excellent tall tale collections (see Osborne, 1991; San Souci, 1991; Walker, 1993) or delightful picture books such as Julius Lester's *John Henry* (1994). Writing their own hyperbolic stories comes more readily with these outrageous story models.

A very popular international folk story motif is the trickster tale, which humorously portrays protagonists who use wit, pranks, deceit, and mischief to triumph over their often more powerful foes. Yet, tricksters do not always prevail; they are often victims of another's trickery. Sample trickster tales from around the world include *Tops and Bottoms* (Stevens, 1995), *Maui and the Sun* (Bishop, 1996), *Mr. Pak Buys a Story* (Farley, 1997), and *Jump on Over! The Adventures of Brer Rabbit and His Family* (Parks, 1989). English language learners may well know trickster tales that have not yet been written down.

Finally, older students really enjoy fractured fairy tales in which authors have altered or mixed up the characters, settings, or plots of more traditional well-known tales. These books are best for intermediate and advanced language learners since they can handle the language twists in these parodies. Jon Scieszka's *The True Story of the Three Little Pigs* (1989) remains one of the most popular examples of this subgenre. Students also enjoy his story collections, like *The Stinky Cheese Man and Other Fairly Stupid Tales* (1992), and his parodies of Aesop's fables in *Squids Will Be Squids* (1998). Other popular examples are Michael Emberley's *Ruby* (1992), Fiona French's *Snow White in New York* (1986), Paul Rosenthal's *Yo, Aesop!: Get a Load of These Fables* (1997), Diane Stanley's *Rumpelstiltskin's Daughter* (1997), and Audrey Wood's *The Bunyans* (1996). Teachers find it valuable to compare the fractured versions with the traditional European antecedents and to discuss the differences. As we note in Chapter 6, advanced students may later create their own fractured fairy tales while teachers working with intermediate proficiency students might talk about the effects that changing the setting has on a tale.

Showcasing a featured author who has an extensive repertoire of folk stories available for young people is one more tool for engaging students in reading and sharing folklore. One outstanding example, highlighted in Box 8.1, is Patricia McKissack, a reteller and adapter of a variety of tales, including African American narratives, Cajun tall tales, and Bible stories. Gather some of her books, read them aloud, post a few "fun facts," and lead the students in making connections and extensions based on her work. As students read several books collected or adapted by a single author, they can consider how the author tries to capture the oral flavor of the storyteller's version.

Students enjoy hearing and reading folklore, and various extension activities enable students to respond to stories through art, drama, movement, and games. These

---

B O X **8.1**

Five Fun Facts about Patricia McKissack

- One of Pat's fondest memories is of her third grade teacher displaying a poem she wrote on the class bulletin board.
- Pat's grandfather was a storyteller who greatly influenced her.
- Pat and her husband Fred met when they were teenagers; he proposed on their second date, and they were married four months later, after they both graduated from Tennessee State University.
- Most often, Pat coauthors with her husband Fred. As a team they have written more than seventy-five books.
- Pat decided to write books with an African American focus for children because she was frustrated with the lack of such selections available for her students.

Video Interview

"Good Conversation: A Talk with the McKissacks" (1997). Tim Podell Productions. P.O. Box 244, Scarborough, NY 10510; 1-800-642-4181: This video shares an interview with both Patricia and Fred McKissack set in their home in a suburb of St. Louis, Missouri.

Web Sites

http://teacher.scholastic.com/authorsandbooks: Biographical information is available about Patricia and Fred McKissack.
http://teacher.scholastic.com/writewit/biograph/index/htm: The McKissacks provide an online workshop on how to research and write a biographical sketch. Students who complete the challenge receive a personalized certificate of achievement signed by the McKissacks.

Author Quotes

"I grew up not seeing myself in a book. When you don't see yourself in a book, you're not so prone to want to read it. And, if you don't read often, you don't read well. If you don't read well, then you're doomed, almost, for failure."

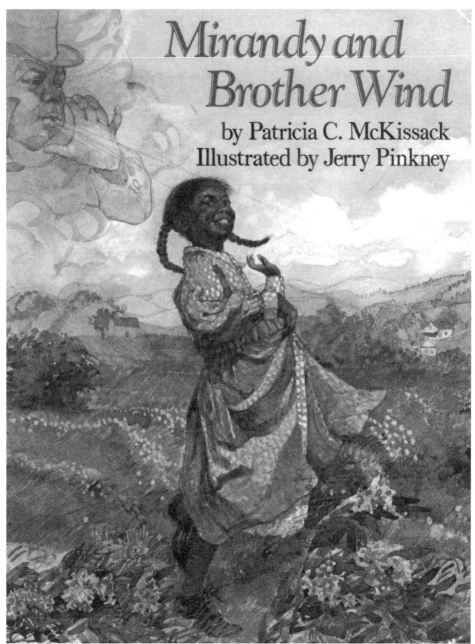

Illustration © 1988 by Jerry Pinkney. Used by permission of Alfred A. Knopf Children's Books, a division of Random House, Inc.

Students can share folk traditions (like the cakewalk) from their own cultures and communities.

McKissack, Patricia. (1988). *Mirandy and Brother Wind*. New York: Scholastic.

instructional activities are fun, but more importantly, they facilitate understanding and promote student responses (Rosenblatt, 1978). Activities can be modified according to students' language proficiency.

Of course, it would be a special treat to invite a professional storyteller into the classroom to perform if the budget allows. There is nothing quite like hearing a story told by a real storyteller. Often the school's parent–teacher organization is open to hosting a storyteller on campus. Sometimes librarians or even parents have a knack for storytelling and are willing to share their gifts. If nothing else, there are excellent audiotapes of stories told by professional storytellers that can be very effective in the listening center.

Creative dramatics supplies many language building options when linked to folklore. As teachers read stories with repetitive lines, children often chime in. Teachers can foster this type of participation through story drama. Young and Ferguson (1995) recommend using story drama with Eric Kimmel's *Anansi and the Moss Covered Rock* (1988). Students join the teacher as they hear the repeated line "Isn't this a strange moss covered rock!" After the students have heard the story once, they are ready participate in story drama. The teacher reads Anansi's parts, while a student acts out the action, and other children play the variety of animal roles by reading the text or simply improvising the lines. Such improvisation and interaction are important to all children, but they are especially important for English language learners who need opportunities to use their new language in meaningful, low-risk settings (Ferguson & Young, 1996). Drama offers more than fun for students; Montone and Short (1994) found drama particularly helpful with English language learners. Creative dramatics enhanced comprehension for these students because what they didn't grasp while reading they could later see acted out before them.

Finally, Cianciolo (1993) recommends comparing variant tales, suggesting that the comparison will result in understanding "the similarities and differences among the stories by highlighting story elements, or motifs, that were repeated" (p. 82). More importantly, by finding variants related to students' ethnic, racial, or geographical background, teachers can help students take pride in their heritage and unify the classes while focusing on individuals within the group.

As we can see, folklore offers teachers many instructional options for English language learners. Indeed, teachers who utilize folk literature in their classrooms report a high level of student engagement and enthusiasm. However, our data indicate that teachers do not make frequent use of folklore. Our purpose in writing this chapter is to acquaint teachers with the many excellent titles of folklore as well as to encourage them to provide some guidance in incorporating folklore into the classroom literacy experience.

Checking It Out: Assessment Options for Folklore

Folklore provides many options for assessment. Retellings, according to Browne and Cambourne (1990), provide an excellent means of assessing students' comprehension, knowledge of text forms and conventions, and control of vocabulary and grammar. Either oral or written retellings help teachers assess students' comprehension, but Brown and Cambourne recommend oral retellings for English language learners. A possible advantage of the oral retelling may lie in the fact that students' writing ability or attitude toward writing often influences how much and how well they write. Thus, the oral retelling is often perceived as being less stressful for some students. Whether retellings are oral or written, however, teachers should develop a rubric, or grading checklist, in advance to determine the critical elements they want students to include in their retelling (e.g., a sense of story structure, names of characters, theme, plot episodes).

Glazer recommends providing students with opportunities to practice retelling stories before using retellings as an assessment tool (1992). Schulz (1998) developed a retelling guide; a sample guide for Simms Tabback's *Joseph Had A Little Overcoat* (1999) appears in Box 8.2.

Such a guide scaffolds the student's retelling in many ways. First, students learn what type of information is expected in story retellings. Second, they can utilize the story and author information to introduce their retelling. Third, a skeleton of the story is provided to cue student retelling. Fourth, the story event cues are in the proper order. Students find such support helpful and comforting as they attempt to retell stories.

B O X **8.2**

Sample Retelling Guide

Joseph Had a Little Overcoat by Simms Taback

Retold by _____

◆ Joseph had a _____. It was old and worn.

little overcoat
jacket
vest
scarf
necktie
handkerchief
button

◆ So he made a _____ out of it and . . .

jacket
vest
scarf
tie
handkerchief
button
book

you can always make something from nothing.

TABLE 8.3   Response Guide for *Moss Gown*

Response Guide for *Moss Gown*

Directions: Listed down the page are six events or statements from *Moss Gown* (Hooks, 1987). Listed across are the names of characters involved in the story. Using the symbols in the key, indicate whether that character would agree or disagree with the statement. Be prepared to support your answers with examples from the book.

Key: A = Agree with D = Disagree X = Doesn't apply ? = Not enough info	Candace Moss Gown	Retha	Grenadine	Gris-Gris Woman	First Cook	Young Master	Candace's Father	Mistress of the House
Beauty is in the eye of the beholder.								
Children should waste all of their parents wealth and property.								
Money is more important than love.								
Helped people realize their dreams.								
They were turned out to sleep in the fields.								
I love you more than meat loves salt.								

Student response guides are also helpful to focus students on important information. In addition, they may encourage students to return to the text to assess their understanding. In Table 8.3, we provide a sample response guide contributed by Jennifer Zocher.

Summary

Folklore—the stories of a people—is particularly well suited for English language learners. Indeed, some English language learners possess a greater familiarity and appreciation of this genre than their English-speaking peers.

Teachers find many reasons to include folklore in the curriculum. The study of folklore often leads to a greater appreciation of students' own cultural heritage and that of others. Moreover, English language learners read, write, and discuss familiar tales more freely. Finally, folklore lends itself to literature study, dramatic interpretation, and discussion of cultural values and attributes.

Folklore's many types and subgenres are a treasure trove of opportunities for teachers and students. Many teachers begin with the oral folklore before moving into the more frequently used folk literature. Oral folklore includes jokes, riddles, rhymes, proverbs, folk songs, folk medicine, courting and wedding customs, oral histories, and many others. Meanwhile, written folklore, or folk literature, includes the subgenres of fable, folktale, myth, and legend. Within each subgenre, teachers can offer a variety of types. For instance, folktales include trickster tales, fairy tales, pourquoi tales, and others.

Folk literature lends itself to many types of response that benefit English language learners. Drama, writing, storytelling, and comparing various versions contribute to students' enjoyment and understanding of this powerful genre. Students have much to gain when their teachers encourage the study of folklore and folk literature. Oral and written retellings are effective methods of assessing both comprehension and story understanding.

9 Literacy Learning through Poetry

Don't just make poetry available, make it unavoidable.
—from Cullinan, Scala, and Schroeder (1995, p. 116)

In this chapter, we will take a look at an often neglected genre of literature—poetry. While poetry offers tremendous benefits in terms of language development, especially for English language learners, teachers tend to avoid the study of poetry because of their own negative associations from school. The mere mention of the word *poetry* puts many people off, conjuring up recollections of forced memorization, searches for hidden symbolism, or counting meter. Moreover, teachers working with English language learners tend to assume that this genre will be too difficult for students struggling with a new language. In order to encourage teachers to stretch their instructional repertoire to include poetry and integrate this genre into the classroom routine in meaningful ways that consider the linguistic development of English language learners, we will address the following questions.

- **Why use poetry with English language learners?**
- **How do teachers create an appropriate environment for poetry?**
- **What are some strategies for sharing poetry?**
- **How can teachers follow up after poetry has been shared?**

First, let's examine why poetry offers some unique language growth opportunities for the English language learner.

Why Use Poetry with English Language Learners?

Various genres of literature furnish teachers and English language learners with opportunities to explore language. Yet among the many genres available to teachers in a literature-based curriculum, poetry continues to be neglected. Many teachers have had negative experiences that keep them from sharing poetry. Students then grow into a similar dislike of or apathy about poetry. It's a shame, since poetry can really grab students of any age and language proficiency level. Poetry can be musical, memorable, and fun. It can also be spartan, emotional, and moving. Today's selection of poetry for young people has varied styles, topics, and themes. Poets range from Shel Silverstein to Valerie Worth, and poems can be about girl bullies (in "The New Kid on the Block" by Jack Prelutsky from *The New Kid on the Block,* 1984) or racism ("The Incident" by Countee Cullen from *Pass It On: African American Poetry for Children,* 1993). Readers can surely find poems that speak to them, given the proper introduction. That is the key: providing open access to poetry without the roadblocks of formal analysis. Opportunity for in-depth responding and understanding can follow when teachers create an environment for spontaneous pleasure in poetry. Poet and teacher Georgia Heard puts it this way: "Kids need to become friends with poetry. . . . They need to know that poems can comfort them, make them laugh, help them remember, nurture them to know and understand themselves more completely" (Heard, 1999, p. 20).

Poetry, however, is especially effective for language learning (Cullinan, Scala, & Schroder, 1995). Indeed, we would advocate that poetry is an ideal entry point into a literature-based curriculum and literacy development. In particular, poetry provides many instructional advantages for English language learners. The reading and rereading of poetry through read aloud and choral reading activities promotes fluency (Gasparro & Falleta, 1994). Poetry's brevity and short lines appear manageable and therefore are not so intimidating to the reluctant or struggling reader (Christison & Bassano, 1995; Cullinan, Scala, & Schroder, 1995). Beginning readers more easily decipher the meaning of poetry because of the rhythm, repetition, and rhyme, and the fact that the accent falls on meaningful words (Christison & Bassano, 1995; Richard-Amato, 1996). Poetry serves as a brief but powerful anticipatory set for other literature as well as for the introduction of concepts and content across the curriculum (Chatton, 1993; Cullinan, Scala, & Schroder, 1995). It provides a source of brief character sketches, scenes, and stories that can prompt writing from students (Vogel & Tilley, 1993). The variety of poetry formats—such as formula, concrete (shape), found, and model poetry—offer wonderful beginning writing opportunities (Tompkins, 1994; Fagin, 1991).

Brevity of form is one of the most obvious benefits of poetry. For teaching English language learners, poetry has the advantage of coming packaged in very few words, relatively speaking. Poems can be read and reread in very little time. Each rereading can be approached in a slightly different way, too, through choral reading or poetry performance. The length is less intimidating to English language learners overwhelmed by longer prose and streams of new vocabulary. Although poetry may also present new words and concepts, this shorter appearance provides a motivating advantage.

The strong oral quality of poetry is another powerful pedagogical plus. Poetry is meant to be read aloud. The poem's meaning is more clearly communicated when both read and heard. As poet Brod Bagert has indicated, just as songs are not just sheet music, poetry is not just text (1992). It helps language learners acquire correct word pronunciations and incorporates listening vocabulary to aid their overall comprehension. In addition, the rhythm and/or rhyme of poetry can help English language learners begin to get a sense of the sound of English words and phrases in artful, yet natural language. When

English language learners participate in choral reading, they have the opportunity to develop their own oral fluency. Experimenting with various arrangements also helps with expression and builds student confidence. As English language learners gain practice in reading poems aloud using various formats, they become more fluent in their delivery, and that boosts their confidence in their performance. This all-important oral language foundation is a natural in the world of poetry, in which one is expected to hear the language before truly understanding it. For an example of what these practices look like in the classroom, check out Box 9.1 and listen to Nicole Blake, a third grade teacher. Plus, look back to Chapter 4 on oral language for more ideas about developing these skills in English language learners.

An additional benefit of poems is that they tend to be about one thing. This crystallized focus of poetry can aid English language learners as they use their word knowledge to make sense of new content. The poems' context can help the reader or listener incorporate new vocabulary. Even wordplay, puns, colloquialisms, and double meanings can be experienced and explained through poetry. For example, a poem like "Leftovers" (*It's Thanksgiving*, 1982) by Jack Prelutsky is very clearly about one subject. Although words like *bisque* or *fritters* may be unfamiliar, the poem's context helps provide a broader context and clarification. This kind of wordplay can be particularly challenging for English language learners who may interpret words and phrases literally. Poetry provides a playful example of the creative ways language can be used. When English language learners read the poem, hear the poem read aloud, and participate in a choral reading of the poem, they've had multiple modes of reinforcement for meaningful language learning. As Sharon Gill found in her classroom use of poetry, "Poetry is written to be read again and again. . . . Repeated readings allow children to gain fluency and build sight vocabulary while having successful reading experiences. Poetry also contains elements of predictability such as rhyme, rhythm and repetition which make reading easier" (Gill, 1996, p. 28).

Finally, poetry also offers affective benefits. Poetry embodies emotion, imagination, and often both. It can help us see old things in new ways. It can make us laugh out loud, or stop and think. It is this element that often grabs readers and listeners first. The humor of

---

B O X **9.1**

Voices from the Field: Literacy Learning through Poetry

"Every morning, we do something different with a poem: I introduce the poem, read it once through, then the students echo-read with me; we talk about meaning, we arrange the poem into some kind of choral reading, we notice contractions, rhyming words, word patterns, 'words in words'; students talk about ideas for illustrating the poem and can take them home to share with their families."

Nicole's emphasis on reading poetry aloud and on talking openly about poetry every day in her third grade classroom provides the kind of practice with words and language so essential to the continuing oral language development of elementary-age students, especially those learning English.

Silverstein's "Sarah Cynthia Sylvia Stout" (*Where the Sidewalk Ends*, 1974), or the power of Langston Hughes' "Dreams" (*The Dreamkeeper and Other Poems,* 1932/1994), or the pathos of "But I Have Mr. Cratzbarg" by Kalli Dakos (*Don't Read This Book, Whatever You Do!* 1993) are all qualities that speak to students today. It's a rich literary heritage children ought to experience. Moreover, English language learners naturally connect with contemporary poems when led to them by an enthusiastic teacher without a hidden agenda. That's where we must begin; enthusiastically sharing poems out loud with English language learners for the pleasure of the words, sounds, rhymes, and meaning is our first poetic responsibility.

How Do Teachers Create an Appropriate Environment for Poetry?

Creating an environment that promotes poetry is similar to creating a classroom that welcomes literature in general. An open-minded and enthusiastic teacher is the first essential ingredient. Books of poetry must become part of the classroom library, prominently displayed, accessible to young readers, and read aloud enthusiastically by the teacher. Gathering poetry books for a classroom collection for English language learners is not always an easy task since less poetry is published than other genres. When a new poetry book comes out that we like, we buy it. Poetry books seem to go out of print too quickly, and they are not as frequently reprinted in paperback form as other genres. Luckily, more and more variety is present in poetry for young people today. Any good classroom collection should strive to reflect this and should include the classics, humorous poems, multicultural poetry, haikus.

In addition to a set of poetry books, Steinbergh (1994) recommends that classrooms contain a listening center to highlight poetry. Poems on tape, along with the corresponding books of poems, make an excellent addition to the listening center. They provide additional practice in listening and reading, models of effective read alouds, and, especially, assistance with pronunciation and expression. Multiple repetitions help the learner process the new sounds and meanings of the language. Taped poetry also serves as an additional model of writing. Because poems are short, the visit to the listening center can also be brief. Many poets have recorded their own poems, and there is nothing quite like hearing poems recited by the poets themselves. Shel Silverstein's gravelly voice, Jack Prelutsky's outrageous singing, and Ashley Bryan's mellifluous performance are all perfect for a listening center. When English language learners become comfortable with reading aloud a favorite poem, they may want to tape-record themselves reading it aloud, copy it in their best handwriting, illustrate it themselves, and place the tape and text in the listening center for other English language learners to enjoy. This can be a source of pride as well as language practice.

An additional asset to a poetry collection is the inclusion of bilingual poetry. There are many collections of poetry in both English and Spanish, for example, including *Laughing Out Loud, I Fly: Poems in English in Spanish* by Juan Herrera (1998), *My Mexico/Mexico Mio* by Tony Johnston (1996), and for intermediate students *That Tree Is Older Than You Are* (1995) collected by Naomi Shihab Nye, or poems that have examples of code switching—using Spanish words and phrases within the English text—such as *Confetti* by Pat Mora (1999) or *Canto Familiar* by Gary Soto (1995). Other bilingual collections include Michio Mado's Japanese/English anthologies, *The Animals* (1992) and *The Magic Pocket* (1998). English language learners or their parents could read poems in their native language and provide a written version as well. Such a focus on promoting other languages can foster a positive learning environment.

Several Internet sites also offer audio versions of poems, including new kinds of experimental poetry. Check out the following resources: Poets and Writers, Inc. offers audio files of some poems at www.pw.org, and *Poetry Magazine* supplies audio clips of poems at www.poetrymagazine.com.

There are also many different forms of poetry for children. This includes narrative, lyric, and free verse, as well as limericks, ballads, concrete, and haiku, among others. We know from studies of children's preferences (Kutiper & Wilson, 1993) that most children enjoy narrative storytelling poems that have a regular, distinctive rhythm, strong sound patterns, plenty of humor, and not too much abstract and figurative language. At least we know that's what they like at first. It is our contention that children develop a taste for many different kinds of poems once they are introduced to them.

Anthologies

The format of the poetry anthology has been around since publishing began. It's a practical way to collect a multitude of poems on a variety of subjects by many different poets. For example, a recent anthology edited by poet Jack Prelutsky is a single-topic collection of animal poems called *The Beauty of the Beast* (1997). It is visually appealing and includes many excellent poems without being overwhelming. In addition, the more narrow topic of animals makes it easier for a teacher or librarian to conceive of how to connect it with the current curriculum. This more teacher-friendly thematic collection approach is becoming very popular. Practically speaking, it makes it even easier to open a science or social studies lesson with a poem when a book of poems on that very topic is available. For English language learners, this content connection provides enormous help for comprehension when poems of related subject matter are shared (Krashen & Terrell, 1983). Multicultural poetry is also often first published in cultural anthologies, such as in *Pass It On: African American Poetry for Children* (Hudson, 1993), *That Tree Is Older Than You Are* (Nye, 1995), or *On the Road of Stars: Native American Night Poems and Sleep Charms* (Bierhorst, 1994). These provide an excellent introduction to poetry from cultural perspectives that may be unfamiliar to teachers or English language learners. Moreover, they provide relief from the rather impersonal presentations within textbooks. "Harriet Tubman" (Greenfield, *Honey I Love*, 1978), for example, is a spirited poem about the Underground Railroad to share in social studies.

Poetry anthologies can provide a similar connection in the reading or language arts class. Lee Bennett Hopkins has several collections of poems ideal for English language learners with beginning language proficiency. For example, his books of poems such as *Blast Off! Poems about Space* (1995), *Dino-Roars* (1999), and *Sports! Sports! Sports!* (1999) all include simple poems with strong rhyme and imagery ideal for the English language learner. Collections of poems gathered because of their similar form can help the teacher provide multiple models of one kind of poem. *Splish Splash* (Graham, 1994), for example, is a poetry book of only concrete (or shape) poems. Each poem is another example of the same concept—that a poem can look on the page like the object it describes. Other examples of concrete poetry include *Concrete Is Not Always Hard* (Pilon, 1972), *Seeing Things* (Froman, 1974), and *Walking Talking Words* (Sherman, 1980). In addition, collections of haiku (*Haiku: The Mood of the Earth*, Atwood, 1971) or limericks (*The Book of Pigericks,* Lobel, 1983) or free verse (*All the Small Poems*, Worth, 1987) help the English language learner look at several examples of the same form of poem in one place.

Individual Poets

Poetry also comes in the form of works by individual poets. *Where the Sidewalk Ends* (Silverstein, 1974) is probably the best-known example of this. Shel Silverstein's first collection of his own wacky verse and drawings has been a huge hit with native speakers and English language learners alike. Such "standards" by Shel Silverstein, Jack Prelutsky, and Judith Viorst are readily available, and these are the poets often voted on by children as their favorites (Kutiper and Wilson, 1993). However, "new" writers are gaining in popularity, too, such as Kalli Dakos, Douglas Florian, and Naomi Shihab Nye. So incorporating new voices into the classroom library is an ongoing endeavor. Poets such as Janet Wong, Gary Soto, and Nikki Giovanni give voice to many experiences.

Which poets should one choose for the classroom? A good place to begin is with *A Jar of Tiny Stars* (Cullinan, 1996), a collection of poetry by recipients of the National Council of Teachers of English (NCTE) Poetry Award, given to a poet for the body of her/his work. This collection provides a sampling of children's favorite poems by the first ten award recipients. It also includes quotes and autobiographical information about each poet—perfect for creating a small poetry corner with a rotating featured poet. For updates on NCTE Poetry Award news, see http://www.ncte.org/poetry. Copeland and Copeland (1993, 1994) also developed poet profiles helpful for classroom use in promoting poetry. Plus, the Internet offers an excellent resource for finding out more about individual poets; some even have their own Web pages.

Including a featured poet center is a physical way of showcasing the works of an individual poet. By gathering a selection of books by one poet, reading aloud his/her poems, and sharing a few biographical details, we can help students see the writer behind the words. With Douglas Florian, our featured author in Box 9.2, students will discover he is both a poet and an artist who enjoys wordplay and formula poems. Many of his works provide opportunities for talking about the English language and the borrowing and coining of words. As English language learners learn a little about the background of poets, they can better understand how life experiences influenced a writer's work.

Sharing a variety of poems by differing authors, English language learners can become acquainted with the vast array of possibilities within the genre of poetry. In addition, they are hearing their new language modeled in an understandable and meaningful format. The next section examines the many techniques for involving students more actively in poetry through choral reading and poetry performance.

BOX **9.2**

Five Fun Facts about Douglas Florian

- He is both an artist and a poet.
- He has illustrated many nonfiction books for other writers.
- A flea market purchase inspired his first poetry writing.
- He grew up in and still lives in New York.
- He wears a yarmulke (look it up).

Web Site

The following Web site provides biographical information and a photo of Douglas Florian: http://www.eyeontomorrow.com/embracingthechild/aflorian.htm.

What Are Some Strategies for Sharing Poetry?

The first step in inviting children into the oral world of poetry is very simply by reading poems aloud to the class. Modeling is always the best place to start. In fact, Cullinan, Scala, and Schroder (1995) recommend that we read a poem aloud at least twice, although children may often ask for even more readings. Poet and teacher Georgia Heard says, "make sure there's a lot of silence around this first reading" (1999, p. 31).

Reading poems out loud to English language learners helps them attend both to the sounds of the words and lines as well as to their meaning. It sets the stage for student participation in the read aloud process. For English language learners, this modeling step cannot be skipped. It familiarizes them with what the words of the poem should sound like and engages their listening comprehension in making sense of the poem's meaning. In addition, there is an affective benefit as teachers communicate to their students pleasure in the sounds of the words and the rhythm of the lines. By their willingness to share poems out loud, teachers subtly extend an invitation to English language learners to follow their lead in trying poetry.

Keep in mind, however, that cultural factors affect how English language learners present themselves in social situations and which behaviors they believe are acceptable for formal presentation. As McClure reminds us, "Organized choral reading is a rather formal teacher-directed process. . . . Often, when the teachers read a familiar selection or one that rhymed, the children would spontaneously join in, essentially creating a choral reading of the poem. They would frequently do the same thing when sharing poetry with each other. . . . It seems that the teachers provided a model for responding to poetry through choral reading, and the children shaped the activity to fit their own needs" (1990, p. 52). Once invited to participate, English language learners can be creative in inventing their own methods of choral presentation. Experimenting with this idea, Cynthia Loesch, a middle school teacher, notes, "The appreciation for choral reading was a complete surprise. I thought that sixth grade boys would not want to read poetry together in a group, but I was mistaken. They thoroughly enjoyed it and experienced a great deal of success. I will continue to offer this . . . to my ESL students."

If you have to choose just one title by our featured poet, this might be the best buy. Although it doesn't have the lush, colorful illustrations of his shorter picture book anthologies, it is packed full of rhythmic, humorous, appealing poetry that works well with nearly all proficiency and grade levels.

Florian, Douglas. (1994). *Bing Bang Boing.* Harcourt Brace.

To start the process off, we will be presenting a sampling of choral reading formats including teacher modeling, having everyone read the poem in unison, having students join in on a repeated line or refrain, having two student groups do call and response, having multiple groups do multiple stanzas, having individuals read solo lines, using two voices, and singing poems (Swartz, 1993). These techniques are presented in sequence by level of difficulty for English language learners with the most simple and easy to follow strategies first, followed by the more complex ones that require more oral language proficiency and reading comprehension.

Teacher Modeling

As the model, the teacher begins by choosing poems he/she enjoys and sharing them with expression and enthusiasm. Beware of the tendency to read lines, especially rhyming lines, in a singsong voice. Moreover, Chatton (1993) recommends studying the line breaks to determine how the poem should be read. Don't rush the lines. Look around the room, if you can, as you read the poem. If possible, display the words of the poem on the chalkboard or with an overhead. This is especially essential for English language learners at the beginning or intermediate level of language proficiency. Seeing the words while hearing them is additional reinforcement for children who are learning to read and/or learning English.

A good first poem to share is "Three Wishes" by Karla Kuskin (*Near the Window Tree*, 1975). Every child has made wishes. In this poem, the poet wishes for a good book. Older English language learners may enjoy Gary Soto's "Ode to Family Photographs" (*Neighborhood Odes*, 1992). This celebration of cockeyed family pictures is even more fun if students bring their own crazy photographs to share, along with the stories behind them. A second grade teacher, Laura Turner, shared the poem "What the Wind Swept Away Today" by Douglas Florian from *Bing Bang Boing* (1994). In order to help her ESL students comprehend the poem more fully, she had each student create a picture for one line of the poem—to help them visualize the poem's list of objects that the wind blew away. After reading the poem and sharing the illustrations, the class also discussed the humor in the improbable event noted in the last line of the poem.

Sharing a poem out loud should be a regular part of the daily routine, for as poet Brod Bagert says, "A child's first encounter with poetry happens only once" (1992, p. 21). Jennifer Gillard, an elementary teacher, concurs, noting that while she has been using one poem per day for choral response, she plans to include more since the children really look forward to it and always ask for more!

Everyone Reads the Poem in Unison

Now that you have set the stage for hearing poems out loud, invite English language learners to join in for unison read alouds—if they haven't already jumped in. Choose shorter poems with a strong rhythm, and read the poem out loud first as a model. Even nonreaders can participate in reading aloud poems when their voices needn't carry the whole poem. Sylvia found one poem that has been irresistible to first graders through fourth graders: "My Monster" by Douglas Florian (*Bing Bang Boing,* 1994). Beware! You must have a sense of humor about the last lines: "That's no monster, that's my teacher!" On a more serious note, Langston Hughes' classic poem "Dreams" from *The Dreamkeeper and Other Poems* (1932/1994) has a powerful message in eight short, straightforward lines. Again, reading the poem aloud may prompt a rich discussion afterward.

Students Join in on a Repeated Line or Refrain

This third strategy for choral reading requires students to learn about timing and jump in only when their lines come up. However, they still participate as a whole class, with no pressure to perform individually. As always, the teacher reads the entire poem out loud first. Then, in repeated readings, students join in on a line or refrain that pops up repeatedly in the poem. Many poems are particularly effective for this performance strategy, including "Louder" by Jack Prelutsky from *The New Kid on the Block* (1984), in which students say the word *louder* whenever it appears, and "Things" by Eloise Greenfield *(Honey, I Love,* 1978), in which students say the line "ain't got it no more" each time it occurs. For English language learners, this is a way to participate as a group with all the other students in a low-pressure setting because all voices blend together. It can be helpful to write the word or phrase on a strip of paper and lift it high, as a visual cue, when students have their turn.

Two Student Groups: Call and Response

Once students are familiar with poems read aloud in parts, teachers can divide the class in half to read poems using the call-and-response method. The best poems for this performance strategy have lines structured in a kind of back-and-forth way. In "Copycat," from *Which Way to the Dragon* (1997) by Sara Holbrook, for example, the lines of the poem sound just like two groups of children mimicking each other by repeating what the other says. It's the perfect poem to read out loud antiphonally. Other examples for two groups to read aloud in this back-and-forth manner are "Clock-Watching" by Carol Diggory Shields *(Lunch Money and Other Poems about School,* 1995) and "Twins" by Douglas Florian from *Bing Bang Boing* (1994).

Multiple Groups, Multiple Stanzas

If you've tried each of these strategies, the students are probably ready for even more challenging choral reading methods. Using multiple small groups is the next step in bringing poems to life with oral presentation. Obviously this puts the focus on fewer students; thus, it may take more practice. However, when English language learners have participated in unison and large-group read alouds, this is not usually a problem. Try, Janet Wong's "Face It" *(A Suitcase of Seaweed,* 1996) with three stanzas that reflect the writer's musings on her nose, her eyes, and her mouth and how each represents a different part of her identity. Three groups could each read a different stanza, using motions to point to each body part in turn. If English language learners can participate with a small group or a partner for their given lines, they generally feel more secure in participating in this oral exercise.

Individual Solo Lines

Some poems are list-like in their structure, and these work well for what is sometimes called "linearound" choral reading in which individual voices read individual lines. After English language learners have participated in group variations, most are usually eager to volunteer to read a line solo. However, be sure the poem is familiar before students volunteer for individual lines. Always begin by reading the poem aloud to them. Language learners feel especially vulnerable about mispronouncing words or messing up the timing. With practice, this interplay of group and individual voices can be very powerful for bringing the poem to life. Brod Bagert advises students to ask themselves "What face should I make when I say these words?" to help them create appropriate facial expressions, voice inflection, and even body movement (Bagert, 1992, p. 19).

Students might try "What if?" by Shel Silverstein (*A Light in the Attic*, 1981) with each what-if worry read by a different voice. "Pledge" by Carol Diggory Shields (*Lunch Money and Other Poems about School*, 1995) is also ideal for individual voices alternating with the whole class in this mock recitation of the Pledge of Allegiance. (Before using the poem "Pledge," teachers should clarify what the correct Pledge of Allegiance really sounds like.) One kindergarten teacher used Douglas Florian's "Delicious Wishes" (*Bing, Bang, Boing,* 1994) with each child taking a different wish (e.g., "I wish I could whistle") to read and act out. For an informal evaluation, she watched to see if the students were able to act out the new vocabulary as they recited their lines. This poem also allowed her Hispanic ESL students to practice the difficult *sh* sound that can prove so problematic to Spanish speakers.

Two Voices

Probably the most difficult form of choral reading is reading aloud poetry for two voices. This requires synchronization of reading as well as getting used to two completely different lines sometimes being read at the same time. Paul Fleischman's poems may be the best-known examples of poems written for two voices, including the Newbery award-winning *Joyful Noise* (1988) poems about insects and the *I Am Phoenix* (1985) bird poems. *Math Talk* by Theoni Pappas (1991) is another excellent resource for poems for two voices, and the content is a natural for connecting with lessons in mathematics. These are excellent beginning points for English language learners in the middle grades.

Singing Poems

Another strategy for performing poetry is to sing poems. While not a particularly complex method, it is irresistible fun, works at every grade level, and takes a brave teacher (or other volunteer) to lead the way. Students of all ages and language backgrounds love the connection of music and poetry. Basically, you match poems to song tunes that contain the same meter. It seems to be most effective with tunes that have a strong, rhythmic beat, such as "Row, Row, Row Your Boat" or "Mary Had a Little Lamb," and poems that are very rhythmic. One of the students' all-time favorites has been "School Cafeteria" by Douglas Florian (*Bing Bang Boing,* 1994), a hilarious poem about cafeteria food that can be sung to the tune *"Ninety-Nine Bottles of Beer (or Pop) on the Wall."*

Other Creative Alternatives

Once the invitation to share poems chorally has been extended, teachers and students can generate their own creative alternatives. For instance, in Box 9.3, Sonya Blackwell describes her use of "jump-in" reading and "popcorn" reading with middle school English language learners.

Beyond reading the poem, the class can add actions for the words. "One first grade class performed a poem using silent movements, and the rest of the class guessed which poem they were performing" (Heard, 1999, p.13). Barbara Chatton challenges us to consider adding pantomime, sound effects, and background music and to consider inviting English language learners to translate their favorite poems from English into their native languages or into American Sign Language of the deaf (Chatton, 1993). English language learners may want to adapt their favorite poems to rap, chants, or cheerleading yells and use puppets, props, gestures, or clapping. For beginning English language learners, frame sentences provide a syntax structure to plug new vocabulary into. These frame sentences

---

B O X **9.3**

Voices from the Field: Creative Alternatives for Poetry

I have had more success with poetry than any other genre. When I bring a poem out during class, the students look at each other with huge smiles on their faces, as if we are all about to share in some hidden secret. The smiles grow as we read the poem aloud, the words seeming to tickle our tongues with their rhythms and repetitions. Some read aloud activities I've used are "popcorn reading" and "jump-in" reading.

With "popcorn reading," we have usually already read the poem at least twice aloud, straight through. Next, the students are able to pick favorite lines or phrases from the poem and then call them out, in random order around the room. The same lines can be repeated, too, which gives the class a sense of unity because they know someone liked the same line that they did. When a poem is read this way, the class is creating new rhythms and new meanings from the original words. The activity flows more smoothly if you give clear instructions:

- Students should read no more than one line aloud at a time.
- They should not start saying their line until they hear a pause from the last reader.
- It is acceptable to read the same line several times.

With "jump-in" reading, a student is called on to read the first two lines, but before they finish the second line, another student will join voices with the first. When the second line is completed, the first reader will stop reading, and the second reader will read, until a third joins in, and so on. The mixture of voices, some soft and low, others high and bold, bring a beautiful music to the words, allowing the students to revel in oral language.

Sometimes, when introducing a new poem, I read it aloud once, then use "jump-in" and "popcorn" readings so that we have read it three times. I think this repetition and rereading helps students become better readers and definitely helps new language learners with language acquisition.

can then be used to create a list poem that can be read as a chant. In Chapter 6, we shared one frame pattern that works well: "I like _____ but I don't like _____.

Alma Flor Ada, Violet Harris, and Lee Bennett Hopkins, in their anthology *A Chorus of Cultures* (1993), suggest that "physical involvement puts children at ease and encourages listening comprehension" (p. 32) and that "representing the actions of a poem, the feelings in the poem, allowing even for silent participation, especially for children acquiring English" is essential to their language learning. Indeed, this linking of language and action is the foundation of the very popular ESL instructional method, Total Physical Response (Asher, 1982). Many poems lend themselves to acting out or highlighting vocabulary. Shel Silverstein's "Boa Constrictor" from *Where the Sidewalk Ends* (1974) focuses on body parts, and Douglas Florian's "The Bully" from *Bing Bang Boing* (1994) provides numerous action phrases. A kindergarten teacher, Amelia Harden, had students make monster masks out of paper plates to wear as they acted out monster motions to accompany the oral reading of "A Monster's Day," a poem by Douglas Florian from *Monster Motel* (1993). An excellent resource for more creative presentation ideas is Caroline Feller Bauer's *The Poetry Break* (1995).

As we discovered, there are countless methods of engaging students with poetry and with its rhythmic language. Through teacher modeling and choral reading formats, students have an opportunity to jump in when they feel more comfortable with the language. The interactive potential of choral reading and poetry performance are ideal ways to build oral language with English language learners. Next, we consider how to move students more deeply into poems and consider the meaning of the words.

How Can Teachers Follow Up after Poetry Has Been Shared?

"Even experienced teachers who seem to have no problem dealing with other genres often ask, 'What do I do with a poem besides read it?'" (Tchudi & Mitchell, 1989, p. 215). Clearly, teachers need training in the reading and responding process as well as updates on children's and young adult literature and new methods of assessment to add to their repertoire.

"Passive listening isn't enough. . . . Understanding can deepen enjoyment . . . show them how to uncover the subtle nuances of meaning and what poets do to forge an emotional connection with the reader" (McClure, 1990, p. 68). So states Amy McClure in her year-long study of actual poetry sharing in elementary classrooms. As teachers, we lay the foundation for understanding poetry by first providing enjoyment. It is our contention that enjoyment comes from emphasizing the oral presentation of poetry. Poetry is a genre intended to be shared orally, and sharing is an important ingredient for providing access to poetry for the English language learner. This emphasis on the oral aspects of poetry acknowledges their students' unique need to incorporate the heard and spoken word into their vocabularies before attempting to read and write these words. The same could be said for the follow-up response to poetry. As we invite English language learners to dig deeper into this genre and examine the craft of the poet, we need to begin with oral discussion and small-group sharing to help students articulate what they see before urging them to write their analyses or create original poetry.

How do we proceed without butchering the poem? Poet and teacher Georgia Heard is often a poet-in-residence in the schools: "Rather than standing up in the front of the room and asking questions about a poem I already know the answers to, I want to put my students in the position of learning about the poem for themselves. The key to learning how to enter the door of a difficult poem is to teach our students how to unlock the door themselves, and for them to find pleasure in this process" (1999, p. 43). Be open to students' differing responses, but urge them to support their observations in some way. Remember that responses can vary based on cultural differences, too. Heard helps children through what she calls the three "layers" of poetry: inviting them into poetry, helping them connect with poetry, and guiding them toward analyzing the craft of poetry (1999). McClure (1990, p. 47) suggests using one or two of these facilitating questions:

- "What did you think?
- "What did you like about this poem?"
- "Does this remind you of anything you know about?"

Furthermore, Lockward (1994) offers advice to teachers on what not to do with poetry: do not explain the poem to students; do not give tests on poetry; and do not impose the critics on students. Instead, he urges teachers to expose students to beautiful, powerful language; allow time for multiple oral readings of a poem; and lead a discussion that encourages a personal relationship with a poem.

For English language learners who are anxious about contributing to class discussions because their language skills may not yet be fluent, alternative grouping may be more helpful than asking the right questions. Ask the English language learner to turn to a partner and talk with her/him about "what the poet is saying here." English language learners are often more comfortable sharing their opinions with one classmate, rather than with the class as a whole. Small groups or poetry circles also function well for digging deeper into a poem's meaning.

One teacher, June Jacko, used art projects in small groups to help children explore multicultural poetry. Each group had a different poem, and after all the poems had been introduced, read by the teacher, and performed by the class, each group created a small mural to illustrate its poem. Groups then explained their murals to the class as a whole. This kind of response activity helped students think deeply about a poem, talk critically with classmates about the words and ideas, and express themselves creatively about their own interpretations of the poem's meaning. After read aloud and choral response activities, Sonya Blackwell follows up with alternatives such as those highlighted in Box 9.4 with her middle school students.

Checking It Out: Assessment Issues with Poetry

Oral Fluency

As students participate in choral reading in the classroom, teachers can observe their level of participation. As students move toward individual participation in choral reading, teachers can assess oral fluency with the assigned lines. Plus, as students work in

B O X **9.4**

Voices from the Field: Responding to Poetry

After read aloud and choral response activities, I like to have students reflect on the poem through written response using techniques such as the following.

1. Journal about what the author or a character from the poem looks like; describe character traits, clothing styles, region, etc.
2. Choose a line from the poem, copy it onto the paper, then use it as a jumping-off point into a personal connection. (This works best when I prepare one of my own examples on an overhead transparency and show it to the class prior to the assignment. Students see my reflections as a fellow writer, and they tend to delve deeper into their own experiences when they see the depth of mine.)
3. Write a poem or a reflection on the poem's theme. For example, if the poem is titled "My Best Friend," students describe their own special person. (That poem and activity brought one of my classes to tears this year because of the depth of the responses. Since then, those students have been more willing to take risks in their writing, projects, and discussions.)

collaborative groups to script their own choral reading of poems, teachers can check out their oral skills as they negotiate the meaning of the poem and how it should be performed.

After the teacher has spent ample time reading poetry aloud and leading students in choral reading of poetry, students can perform poems on their own. Students can work in pairs or small groups to decide how to perform a poem. With practice, English language learners can even choose their own poem, arrange it, perform it for an audience, and evaluate their performance. If possible, teachers can audiotape or videotape presentations so they can critique students or have students conduct a self-assessment. In Table 9.1, we present a checklist for a student self-assessment.

TABLE 9.1   Rubric for Reviewing Oral Poetry Performance

- Good choice of poem(s)
- "Scripting" the chosen poem into a kind of play
- "Scoring" the motion and emotion of the poem with gesture or pantomime
- Having a confident stance
- Facing the audience
- Using an "outside" voice
- Filling the space with big gestures
- Final performance of the poem overall

Reading Comprehension

As students interact in collaborative groups to respond to poems, their reading comprehension can be monitored. Through their comments in the group, teachers can assess students' level of understanding. In addition, students' written responses to poetry, through class activities or a response log, provide a tremendous source of information about their level of understanding of the poems they are encountering in class.

Summary

Teachers often neglect poetry in their classrooms and across the curriculum. In part, they feel intimidated by this genre; in addition, they feel poetry is too difficult for students who are struggling to learn a new language. Yet, poetry has many benefits for students in general and English language learners in particular. Today's poetry utilizes a variety of styles, topics, and themes that speak to young people. Moreover, poetry is an ideal portal to literacy development and the literature-based curriculum. Its repetition, rhythm, and rhyme make it easily readable for beginning readers. Plus, it serves as a wonderful tool for introducing concepts and content across the curriculum. Finally, poetry offers students many exciting writing models.

Teachers create an inviting, poetry-friendly environment by selecting an inviting classroom poetry collection that includes anthologies, collections on single topics or by individual authors, and picture book versions of single poems. This collection is most effective when it is accompanied by a listening center where students not only listen to poetry, but also record their own classroom anthologies.

Poetry can be shared through numerous read aloud and poetry performance/choral reading techniques and singing. As teachers model their favorites, students also enjoy sharing theirs. Once a poem has been shared, however, many teachers are uncertain about what to do next. It is important for teachers to help students see the many ways to respond to and interpret poetry.

Finally, poetry's value extends beyond the language arts to the entire curriculum. This motivational genre introduces and presents content across the curriculum in a refreshing manner. Poetry can be easily paired with other genres for all kinds of lessons.

Exploring Content

Truth is eternal, knowledge is changeable.
It is disastrous to confuse them.

—Madeleine L'Engle

As children progress through school, the content of the curriculum broadens and the focus of instruction changes from helping children learn to read to helping them read to learn. Less time is devoted to reading instruction and far more time is devoted to reading science, social studies, and math texts. A typical school day for an English language learner mirrors these same issues. This final section of the book looks closely at the benefits of using nonfiction literature in developing content knowledge and literacy. Many instructional strategies and literature connections are provided, including a sample unit in Chapter 12 on the topic of weather. This section contains three chapters.

- **Literacy Learning through Nonfiction Literature**
- **Strategic Use of Nonfiction Literature with English Language Learners**
- **Interdisciplinary Literacy Learning through Literature-Based Instruction**

10 Literacy Learning through Nonfiction Literature

My alma mater was books, a good library.
—Malcolm X

While basic communication skills help move children along the road to fluency in English and aid in informal situations, the most crucial steps in the pathway to English proficiency and school success are focused on fluency as it relates to academic language (Cummins, 1980). The considerable gap between English language learners' ability to communicate and their ability to function effectively in content area classes means that content literacy, or the ability to use reading and writing to acquire new knowledge in a given area, poses a problem. Thus, in this chapter we explore the powerful genre of nonfiction literature, discovering how it is a natural complement to expository material from textbooks and reference materials generally used in the content areas. We will address the following questions in this chapter.

- **Why use nonfiction literature with English language learners?**
- **What types of nonfiction literature link language and content development?**
- **Where do biographies fit?**
- **What makes nonfiction literature unique and ideal for content study?**

First we examine the rationale for linking language learning with academic content via nonfiction literature.

Why Use Nonfiction Literature with English Language Learners?

Within the sheltered environment of the English as a second language class, the goal is literacy learning. Outside the ESL setting, whether in secondary content classes or grade-level elementary classrooms, English language learners struggle with new concepts presented in a new language. Even after a semester or so in an ESL class, students may still have only basic conversational skills. Success in school, however, is related to the formal listening, speaking, reading, and writing skills of the content areas (Cummins, 1980). It may take the English language learner five years or more to reach that level of proficiency (Thomas & Collier, 1995). Therefore, teachers need to support language development by linking literacy lessons to the content curriculum and textbooks.

Many students comment that their textbooks are both confusing and boring (Hynd, McNish, Guzzetti, Lay, & Fowler, 1994). If native English speaking students find their books confusing, imagine the difficulty nonnative English speakers must be having. For English language learners, the expository writing of textbooks offers a special challenge in terms of the more difficult readability level, unfamiliar text structure, and vocabulary (Chamot & O'Malley, 1987). Several criticisms are leveled at content textbooks (Vacca & Vacca, 1999). Their comprehensive and encyclopedic nature overwhelms students, in particular English language learners. In their overview of a huge body of content, they generally lack an extensive study of specific topics. To appeal to a larger audience, they may sidestep controversial topics in favor of a more general stance. Textbooks are not considerate texts. They are sometimes written above the grade level intended and tend to use abstract, technical vocabulary and unfamiliar text structure and styles.

These limitations of textbooks make it imperative for teachers to use other sources of information in the classroom with all students, in particular with English language learners. As a means of supplementing textbooks and helping students master the many new concepts to be learned, a variety of print materials must be available.

Nonfiction literature offers a rich source of meaningful text to spur literacy development with countless choices that approach students' varied levels of optimal input. A growing body of nonfiction picture books provides the supportive structure, coverage of new concepts, and visual cues to assist with comprehension for the student learning English (Greenlaw, Shepperson, & Nistler 1992: Neal & Moore, 1991/1992). Fortunately, the variety of nonfiction books being published today includes an incredible array of topics, formats, and styles to interest all readers, including English language learners. A wide range of nonfiction has emerged in the last twenty years, and the publishing world continues to deliver a good variety of nonfiction for children, as reflected in the growing list of outstanding recipients of the Orbis Pictus Award for Outstanding Nonfiction for Children (see the Web site at www.ncte.org/elem/pictus/). In addition, current printing and production technology have resulted in nonfiction books that are colorful and appealing. This range of nonfiction books adds to their appeal as scaffolds for literacy and concept development for English language learners.

Perhaps teachers still believe that children want to hear only stories. Certainly, fiction selections far outnumber nonfiction choices in basals and anthologies used in schools. According to a survey we conducted of 120 ESL and grade-level teachers working with English language learners in grades K–12, the use of fiction is at least double that of nonfiction. Moreover, the teachers questioned were uncertain what nonfiction really was. Most of their reported use of nonfiction revolved around textbooks for science and social studies, with a few well-known authors of nonfiction trade books such as Seymour Simon mentioned occasionally. Yet, we have only to look at standardized test passages to see that nonfiction passages far outnumber fiction passages.

Our focus on fiction may actually work to students' disadvantage—particularly English language learners, who need the academic language that nonfiction literature selections provide. Although quality may vary greatly, the interest in information is as high for children as for the general adult population. Booksellers' statistics regularly show that nonfiction is the most popular genre (how-to books, self-help books, celebrity biographies, etc.). Choosing appropriately is based partly on student interest in the subject and partly on literary criteria relevant to nonfiction such as accuracy, organization, and style (Vardell, 1991, 1996).

The intent behind nonfiction literature is to provide readers with information about the world around them. Thus, nonfiction books are an outstanding literacy tool for English language learning, presenting new vocabulary and concepts in a very concrete manner. Beginning with familiar images, lower-level books offer an opportunity for children to see literature as a vehicle for understanding their surroundings and finding answers to their questions. Much of the literature we first share with children before they come to school is nonfiction, such as simple board books showing photographs or information about items in the everyday life of the child like a dog, toy, bed, or cup. This visual–symbol link between familiar and unfamiliar concepts is a rich literacy opportunity for students learning English. Generally, these books are organized along topical lines, such as items of clothing, means of transportation, kinds of animals, and the like. Krashen and Terrell (1983) support the topical or thematic presentation of vocabulary for English language learners, arguing that such a strategy offers the student an immediate network of relationships linking new words and concepts.

The fascination with facts found in the best nonfiction literature appeals to readers of all ages and language proficiency levels. In fact, nonfiction is a genre ideally suited to sharing across the grade levels since the books offer new information not necessarily linked to particular grade levels. A simple nonfiction picture book such as *Black Whiteness, Admiral Byrd Alone in the Antarctic* by Robert Burleigh (1998) can be successful with older students who are unfamiliar with this particular topic. Even adults enjoy new information presented in this straightforward and visual way. Such books provide authentic language but present that language in a manageable yet enticing form. They are very different than the many published series often designed for English language learners in which skills and grammar activities accompany staid dialogues and narrative stories that have been "dumbed down" through readability formulas. In Box 10.1, we hear Vera Csorvasi describe how she has incorporated nonfiction books in her high school ESL classroom.

Once teachers are convinced about the appeal and the effectiveness of nonfiction literature for English language learners, they begin to think about implementing this genre into the classroom. In planning for instruction, teachers ask the questions such as the following: What books should they incorporate? Which books link to topics in the various content areas? In the next section, we provide an overview of the many types of nonfiction books that are available.

What Types of Nonfiction Literature Link Language and Content Development?

Teachers may choose from many types of nonfiction as they begin to link the literacy focus of their classroom with the content curriculum. All learners need experiences with different text types. As students and teachers explore the many fine nonfiction works

B O X   **10.1**

Voices from the Field:
Using Nonfiction Tradebooks with High School ESL Students

So far I have tried a variation of the individual reading approach. For example, I wanted to give students the chance to talk about their countries of origin and to give other students a chance to learn about different countries of the world. Therefore, I conducted a prereading activity where we listed the countries the students came from. Then, the students *not* from that country brainstormed things they knew about that particular country and listed things they would like to find out. Using nonfiction trade books during the silent reading period, students had to look for particular information about the countries we were talking about as well as seek out additional interesting information. I remember the students just loved the books and would engage in sustained reading for long stretches of time. Toward the end of class, we would answer the questions that students had posed at the beginning of the lesson.

available today, they will readily recognize the many ways these works support the content areas, providing a repetition and extension of key concepts and ideas. To further strengthen the connection between language and content concepts, teachers can scan content textbooks to familiarize themselves with the important topics and themes and to help plan interdisciplinary units such as the one described in Chapter 12.

Many people think of nonfiction as simply collections of facts, but a close investigation of the genre reveals several different kinds of factual books within the general category of nonfiction. In addition, many believe that nonfiction books are fine for research papers and not much else. Again, a creative consideration of the many different types of nonfiction books will lead to a variety of instructional applications in the classroom, such as for oral reading, recreational reading, modeling writing, and other language activities. In the next chapter, we will be examining in more detail the many instructional techniques for using nonfiction across the curriculum with English language learners. For now, let's consider the many possibilities within the genre of nonfiction (Hepler, 1998).

Concept Books

Concept books present basic information about a single topic in a simple and interesting manner. For instance, Tana Hoban uses photographs illustrating groupings of objects in larger and smaller numbers to help young readers understand quantity concepts in *More, Fewer, Less* (1998). While these books are often thought of as books for young children, teachers working with English language learners will find them a source of wonderful visuals for helping students learn English labels for concepts they are familiar with in their own languages. Students can imitate the format by bringing a Polaroid camera into the classroom, photographing objects arranged in purposeful ways (such as behind the desk, under the table, next to the chair), and creating their own concept books (for spatial orientation, for example).

Photo Essays

Much like a documentary film or an issue of *National Geographic,* photo essays document and validate the text with photographs on nearly every page. As noted in Chapter 1, these junior coffee-table books are definitely designed for a wide audience of readers from the early grades through high school. Thus, we can readily see how this subgenre is emotionally involving for readers. For instance, *In the Forest with Elephants* (1998) combines Roland Smith's illuminating prose with Michael Schmidt's lavish photographs to offer a rare and intimate look at the training and care of elephants in Myanmar, where one-third of Asia's elephant population resides. *Lacrosse: The National Game of the Iroquois* (1998) by Diane Hoyt-Goldsmith describes the game of lacrosse, its origins, and both historical and contemporary connections to the Iroquois peoples.

Most of us use books like these to gain an overview of a topic without focusing on every single idea presented. For this reason, photo essays transcend grade levels as long as the topic is appropriate to the age level. Once students have thumbed through one of these books, they can log on to http://www.nationalgeographic.com for the latest photos and stories of the National Geographic Society. This excellent Web site even includes educational links for teachers and students.

Life-Cycle Books

Extending on information from the science textbook, life-cycle books present the life of an animal in more detail and with more appeal than is possible in the textbook format. Laurence Pringle received the 1998 Orbis Pictus Award for *An Extraordinary Life: The Story of a Monarch Butterfly* (1997). Pringle introduces readers to the life-cycle, feeding habits, migration, predators, and mating of the monarch butterfly through the observation of one particular female monarch he calls Danaus. The illustrator illuminates and enhances the text with sidebars, maps, and colorful paintings that are sure to engage English language learners. Another exceptional life-cycle book to assist with academic language is *Box Turtle at Long Pond* (George, 1989). Once students have read books about a life-cycle, they can practice using graphic organizers to map the content from the book or role play the various stages of development.

Activity, Craft, Experiment, and How-to Books

Activity, craft, experiment, and how-to books invite readers to engage in activities beyond reading. The hands-on approach of these books directly involves English language learners, a technique supported by such methods as Total Physical Response (Asher, 1982) discussed in Chapter 2. For instance, after reading aloud *Creepy Crawlies A to Z* (Ainsworth, 2000), Pat Bach, a fourth-grade teacher, had students refer to the book to construct models of insects with marshmallows and toothpicks. Barbara Valenta's *Pop-O-Mania: How to Create Your Own Pop-Ups* (1997) offers simple directions to take readers through the fundamentals of paper engineering. This enticing, reader-friendly guide to making pop-up cards and books is cleverly and colorfully constructed with several moving pieces, flaps, and pop-ups illustrating each technique described. In addition, teachers might want to send students to the Web where they can learn "the fast and easy way . . . to do just about anything" at www.ehow.com.

Journals and Diaries

Journals and diaries provide the basis for either the content or organizational structure of many recent information books. In the case of diaries, the format may already be familiar to English language learners which helps in their transition to the specific examples used in the classroom. For instance, in *Children of Topaz* (1996), Michael Tunnell and George Chilcoat utilize twenty excerpts from the diary Japanese American teacher Lillian "Anne" Yamauchi Hori kept with her third graders while in an internment camp during World War II. The authors provide detailed commentary to put each diary entry in the context of what was happening in the camp and in the country.

As noted in Chapter 6, journals and diaries can provide a framework or model of writing. In response to readings, students can compose their own journal and diary entries, or they can take the persona of a famous person from history and create journal entries from his/her point of view. As a means of practicing reading and speaking while strengthening content comprehension, students might read aloud selected journal entries and audiotape them. Students can record a handful of their favorite entries from *I, Columbus* (Roop, 1990) or *My Season with Penguins* (Webb, 2000). Other students can then listen to these student-made tapes while they follow along with the book. Hearing the entries read aloud makes them come alive in a very personal way (and provides authentic motivation for English language learners to practice pronunciation and expression). The tapes also furnish another source of documentation of language growth.

Survey Books

Survey books acquaint readers with a topic. Either as a prereading tool to introduce a topic or a postreading follow-up, these books furnish a scaffold for English language learners as they encounter text or reference material on the same topics. One first grade teacher we worked with used the K-W-L chart (Ogle, 1986) with the survey book *Baby Animals* (Royston, 1992), as noted in Box 10.2.

Trade books can also be excellent preparation for tackling content textbooks. For example, biologist Nicola Davies acquaints young readers with the world's largest mammal the *Big Blue Whale* (1998). Her lively, conversational text and Nick Maland's cross-hatched pen-and-ink illustrations lure readers to learn about this huge creature. Bold watercolor and ink illustrations attract children to Martin Jenkins's *Chameleons Are Cool* (1998), in which they learn amazing facts about these reptiles: their features, their behaviors, and their ability to change colors. The prolific nonfiction author Gail Gibbons offers basic survey books with colorful cartoon-style illustrations, helpful captions, and exposition on nearly two hundred different subjects. *The Reasons for Seasons* (1995) and *Exploring the Deep Dark Sea* (1999) are just two books by Gibbons.

The school librarian can be an invaluable resource person for gathering a set of books on a particular topic for classroom use, such as whales or reptiles. Many librarians are willing to pull mini-collections in advance or order books based on teacher requests

---

B O X **10.2**

Voices from the Field: Using Nonfiction Survey Books

Since the students had just read a story about a baby raccoon, they listed that information in the first column. Then, the teacher asked the class if they wanted to know about any other baby animals, and she recorded their responses in the second column. At this point, the teacher read the book to the class and filled in the final column with information the class had discovered. The teacher noted that "some animals that they wanted to know about were not in the book, so we used encyclopedias to look up the animals and then filled in the information and reviewed the chart." The positive effect of this technique is highlighted by the teacher's reflections on the lesson: the students "were amazed at what they knew already and excited about what they learned." In order to assist the English language learners in her class, she placed pictures of animals next to their names on the K-W-L chart.

---

and frequently taught units. Nancy and Sylvia put together their own collection of animal books for use in lessons with four third-grade classes with English language learners. Once students had a chance to browse through the survey books on different kinds of animals, they worked together in small groups to record information on a chart and then created list poems to report what they had learned. We spotlight a couple of these poems in Box 10.3.

As students express interest in particular subjects within the unit topics, the teacher can seek out more books for further reading. Beverly Kobrin's *Eyeopeners II* (1995) is a helpful guide to choosing quality nonfiction by subject. Nonfiction can help teachers discover the hidden, unexpressed reading interests of the reluctant reader.

Informational Storybooks

Informational storybooks contain information embedded in a story form. This hybrid subgenre utilizes a story line to carry the information in a lively fashion. Joanne Ryder's *Lizard in the Sun* (1994) and *Shark in the Sea* (1997) from her Just for a Day informational storybook series are excellent for beginners. With full-color illustrations, each book asks the reader to become the creature just for a day, and integrates story and factual information in a very appealing way.

Contributions to this subgenre by Joanna Cole and Bruce Degen have been amazing. In the Magic School Bus series, Cole deftly weaves three strands to make these books so appealing to children: narration, dialogue bubbles, and children's reports. The innovative writing style allows each book to function as both fantasy and information, and the books can be used to help English language learners differentiate between the two. The *Magic School Bus Explores the Senses* (1999) and *The Magic School Bus and the Electric Field Trip* (1997) are two examples of the exciting field trips Ms. Frizzle and her students undertake on their school bus. See also the Magic School Bus Web site at http://place.scholastic.com/magicschoolbus for helpful teaching ideas.

BOX **10.3**

Students' List Poems Based on Nonfiction Survey Books

The Bat

I have sharp teeth I am furry I fly and I have sharp nails.
I live in a big cave.
I am the size of your hand.
I eat moths and butterflys.
I am furry and I come out at night.

The Leopard

I have sharp teeth.
My tail moves furiously.
I have black spots.
I live in grassy plains.
I eat all kinds of large mammals.
What am I
I'm a leopard!!

Browsing Books

Many works of nonfiction include such breadth of information that simply sampling information here and there can be an effective introduction to a topic; thus, the term *browsing books.* As adult readers, we typically browse through magazines and newspapers digesting all kinds of new and unconnected information. This same technique is very effective for English language learners, and browsing books are motivational lures, enticing students into engaged scanning of a text with pauses at points of particular interest. For instance, browse through the pages of the Orbis Pictus Award-winning *Safari Beneath the Sea, the Wonder World of the North Pacific Coast* by Diane Swanson (1994). Stop at any point and enjoy the photographs provided by the Royal British Columbia Museum. There are many fascinating tidbits in captions, sidebars, and boxes, such as the section on the living night light on page 17. The class might also leaf through Bruce McMillan's *Going on a Whale Watch* (1992) and note the new whaling terms he introduces alongside the color photos and scenes. For English language learners, this kind of "browsing" approach is most effective when the topic is somewhat familiar or related to a unit of study currently under investigation. Teachers can invite learners to browse through nonfiction books in pairs to lead each other in discovering and sharing their findings.

Trivia Books, Almanacs, Accounts of Strange and Bizarre Occurrences

Though literary critics would discount these as having any literary value at all, books of trivia, almanacs of facts, and accounts of strange and bizarre occurrences are popular forms of nonfiction with children and young adults. Students enjoy poring over the latest edition of *The Guinness Book of World Records* (2000), *The World Almanac for Kids* (Israel, 2000), and *The Kids' World Almanac of Baseball* (Aylesworth, 1996). Because the passages are rarely very long, this makes an excellent "sponge" activity for those few unplanned moments in the day. The teacher can read aloud selected examples until students become confident enough to volunteer to share their own findings with the class. Moreover, the brief length and tidbit format are ideal for English language learners. These books have incredible appeal to students of all ages and language proficiency levels. They may not win any literary prizes, but they often lure struggling readers into a book for the first time.

Where Do Biographies Fit?

Biography, a literary work describing the life of a person, is sometimes categorized within the genre of nonfiction, though not always. Through biographies, readers gain a wonderful overview of the historical era during which an individual lived and also gain insight into how a key figure might shape a culture. Biographies make excellent choices for English language learners because when reading about American historical figures, they receive a lesson in the culture of the United States. The professional resource *Learning about Biographies* (Zarnowski, 1990) is an excellent tool for any teacher planning to use this type of nonfiction. For instance, Zarnowski suggests several meaningful activities focused on biographies, including creating life-timelines and dressing up and dramatizing a biographical subject.

Authors can write biographies using a variety of approaches, formats, and types. For example, in looking at three biographies about Charles Lindbergh we can readily see the different approaches and types. Both Louise Borden's *Good-bye, Charles Lindbergh* (1998) and Robert Burleigh's *Flight* (1991) are picture book biographies that make great use of illustration to help carry the events and provide clues to meaning for English language learners. Moreover, each accounts for a certain portion or aspect of Lindbergh's life. *Flight* is the story of Lindbergh's historic nonstop Trans-Atlantic flight from New York to Paris, while *Good-bye, Charles Lindbergh* presents the story of a young boy who meets Lindbergh when he lands his small biplane in a Mississippi field. A difference in the two picture book biographies is the approach. Burleigh's *Flight* is authentic biography, intertwining powerful full-page color illustrations by Mike Wimmer with details of this true story that are sure to capture the reader. For example, did you know Charles Lindbergh flew with no radio or parachute (so he could accommodate extra fuel) and brought five chicken sandwiches with him, which he didn't eat (so he wouldn't get sleepy)? Meanwhile, Borden takes a true story and weaves it into biographical fiction in which reconstructed action and imagined conversations are utilized. The third Lindbergh biography, James Cross Giblin's *Charles A. Lindbergh: A Human Hero* (1997), is authentic biography in a chapter book format. Giblin covers Lindbergh's controversial and tragic life along with his achievements. Using all three of the Lindbergh biographies would be a powerful instructional approach for English language learners. *Flight* and *Good-bye, Charles Lindbergh* provide the prereading foundation for the eventual chapter book format of Giblin's work. Focusing on one topic and exploring it from multiple perspectives using several sources of information provides the literacy workout that English language learners need in order to master language and content.

Picture Book Biographies

Many authors use a picture book biography format to make it possible for young children to experience biography. However, this is not to say that picture book biographies are only for young children. In picture book biographies, the illustrations often convey as much information as the text, and that makes them a perfect literacy tool for English language learners and a great lesson overview even for older learners.

Many notable picture book biographies are now available. The picture book biographies by Diane Stanley are wonderful examples. *Good Queen Bess, the Story of Elizabeth I of England* by Diane Stanley and Peter Vennema (1990) is illustrated with paintings and portraiture reminiscent of the Elizabethan era. The narrative of Elizabeth's life unfolds with as much drama as any contemporary novel.

Collective Biographies

Collective biographies contain chapter-length sketches of a number of figures related to a given topic or theme. These lend themselves to interdisciplinary or thematic units in that the subjects have a common connection. For instance, Russell Freedman's *Indian Chiefs* (1987) presents the stories of six notable western chiefs who led their people in a historic time of crisis: Quanah Parker, Washakie, Red Cloud, Chief Joseph, Satanta, and Sitting Bull. Freedman's effective use of quotes, picture captions, and engaging text arouse readers' curiosity about the time period, the effects of western expansion on the Indians, and each chief's personal life. Students who are intrigued by this genre may enjoy www. Biography.com, an excellent site for short biographies about all kinds of people.

Complete Biographies

A complete biography spans the subject's entire life and is perhaps the most ambitious to read and write. Two noteworthy authors of complete biographies are Russell Freedman and Jean Fritz. These authors have set a standard for others to follow by writing lively, engaging biographies without fictionalizing their subjects' lives. Subjects of Freedman's biographies include Abraham Lincoln, Martha Graham, Louis Braille, Franklin and Eleanor Roosevelt, the Wright brothers, and Chief Crazy Horse. Jean Fritz has written about many historical figures, including James Madison, Theodore Roosevelt, Harriet Beecher Stowe, and Elizabeth Cady Stanton. To assist students in getting started with these more lengthy and complicated works, a visual such as a timeline might be used as a prereading organizer. To focus on the information provided in complete biographies, students may continue to use the same timeline as a summary or note-taking organizer.

To follow up, students who read or research a historical personage may consider summarizing their subject's life in a biopoem (Gere, 1985). Using this highly structured poem formula, English language learners can report the facts they've learned without the anxiety of necessarily creating a lengthy narrative. The biopoem can also serve as a form of natural assessment of their reading and understanding. Box 10.4 shows one biopoem format.

Autobiographies and Memoirs

Autobiographies and memoirs are biographies written by the subjects themselves. Thus, these books can be biased or more subjective than those written by impartial authors, but can also provide interesting insights into character and personality.

Dealing with prejudice and discrimination is a recurring challenge for many minority authors (and many language-minority students), and several poignant examples are present in recent autobiographies and memoirs. For instance, Yoshiko Uchida tells of her experiences as a second-generation Japanese American and her family's internment in a Nevada concentration camp during World War II in her autobiography, *The Invisible Thread* (1991). In *The Lost Garden* (1991), Laurence Yep describes how he grew up as a Chinese American in San Francisco and how he came to use his writing to celebrate his family and come to terms with his ethnic heritage. Nicholasa Mohr's *Growing Up inside the Sanctuary of My Imagination* (1994) details her struggle as someone who felt neither Puerto Rican nor American while going back and forth between both countries. These books would be an ideal connection for English language learners who experience a great deal of cultural conflict in adjusting to a new language and a new country.

As we can see, there are many types of nonfiction literature that teachers can use to link language learning to the content areas. The resourceful teacher will find that using a sampling of nonfiction books will better prepare English language learners for content learning as well as extend their language development.

B O X **10.4**

Biopoem Format

Line 1. First name
Line 2. Four traits that describe the character
Line 3. Relative ("brother," "sister," "daughter," etc.) of _____
Line 4. Lover of _____ (list three things or people)
Line 5. Who feels _____ (three items)
Line 6. Who needs _____ (three items)
Line 7. Who fears _____ (three items)
Line 8. Who gives _____ (three items)
Line 9. Who would like to see _____ (three items)
Line 10. Resident of _____
Line 11. Last name

What Makes Nonfiction Literature
Unique and Ideal for Content Study?

The literary criteria usually used for evaluating and selecting fiction (character, plot, set-ting, theme) do not generally apply when choosing quality nonfiction. It is important, therefore, to look for other distinctive features when choosing good examples of nonfic-tion. The most important criterion is accuracy, because readers go to nonfiction literature for facts. See how Patricia Lauber handles the changing information about dinosaurs in *The News about Dinosaurs* (1989). (There's no longer such a thing as the brontosaurus.) Other features such as organization, style, and the look of the book are also important. Bamford and Kristo (2000) provide a helpful checklist for anyone searching out the best nonfiction books for children and young adults.

Access features (Bamford and Kristo, 2000) are also distinctive in nonfiction litera-ture. Elements such as the table of contents, index, author notes, and glossary provide tools that enable readers to dip into nonfiction texts. During read aloud, browsing, and sharing times, the teacher can model how one uses these access features to find particular things in a book. In Jerry Stanley's *Children of the Dust Bowl* (1992), for example, high school students can see how Steinbeck's novel *The Grapes of Wrath* (1939/1993) affected the westward migration. Students of all ages may find it interesting to look up what the educational curriculum of these outcast children included. For instance, they made their own makeup in chemistry.

Nonfiction literature is also special in its incorporation of graphic organizers, charts, tables, maps, timelines, and the like. These, too, need to be introduced to students in a contextualized fashion that models how to read them for meaning. For example, Jim Murphy's Orbis Pictus Award-winning book *The Great Fire* (1995) is a fascinating ac-count of the famous Chicago fire that nearly destroyed the city. Not only does Murphy debunk the myth that a cow started the fire by kicking over a lantern, but he also discusses the role of nineteenth-century newspapers in spreading that rumor. In addition, the maps that appear at regular intervals throughout the book show, even better than words might, just how the fire began, spread, and consumed the city; the shaded area grows in each successive map. These kinds of extra features have gradually become standard in the best nonfiction writing, as authors and publishers have come to respect the curiosity and intelli-gence of child and young adult readers. For the student learning English, these access fea-tures can be explained and modeled "a la carte" in trade books before they're encountered en masse in content textbooks.

A useful exercise for all students, but in particular for English language learners, is to compare and contrast the various types of books encountered in the classroom. A hands-on inspection of the writing style and text features of narrative fiction, nonfiction literature, and textbooks helps students grasp how these different text types vary in terms of their purpose and internal structure. For instance, nonfiction literature has characteris-tics of both narrative fiction and expository textbooks and as such provides a powerful transition into the more difficult features of the content textbook.

One additional way to model the special aspects of nonfiction writing is to highlight a featured author known for writing high-quality nonfiction books. Teachers can set up a display with Seymour Simon's books and personal facts, for example, just as we have done in Box 10.5. Then they can read a few of his books aloud and encourage students to

B O X **10.5**

Five Fun Facts about Seymour Simon

- Seymour Simon has written more than two hundred books.
- Seymour Simon was born August 9, 1931, in New York.
- Seymour Simon was a science teacher in New York public schools for twenty-three years.
- Seymour Simon is a proud father and grandfather (see his Web site for photos).
- Seymour Simon Day was declared in Houston, Texas, on June 29, 1999.

Professional Resource

- Bourne, B., and Saul, W. (1994). *Using Seymour Simon's Astronomy Books in the Classroom.* New York: Morrow.

See the Seymour Simon Web Site

- http://www.users.nyc.pipeline.com:80/~simonsi/

This book continues to be one of Simon's most popular with its irresistible subject, striking photographs, and fascinating facts.

Simon, S. (1992). *Snakes.* New York: HarperCollins.

browse through others. If possible, students might post a bit of biographical information and a photograph of the author or surf the Web for interesting information about him/her. Once students have read two or more books by the same author, teachers can engage them in a critical discussion of the author's style, choice of subject matter, presentation of information, and so on. For example, a close examination of Seymour Simon's books will lead students to discover his consistent use of primary source photographs, along with his knack for describing things in ways the average reader can understand and visualize.

In summary, content area textbooks pose problems for many readers, and these difficulties are magnified for English language learners. In addition to encountering subjects about which they have no prior knowledge, students find textbooks difficult to read and filled with technical terms. While often better written, newer textbooks still pose many challenges to beginning and struggling readers. In addition, textbooks provide only one perspective; thus, teachers need to search for supplemental materials that extend the concepts, provide different explanations, or utilize simpler terms. Nonfiction literature offers one powerful alternative. Nonfiction books provide the most current information on an incredible variety of subject matter, in several different innovative formats, and using appealing illustrations and language. Moreover, they provide excellent support for content textbooks and instruction.

Beyond instruction, teachers must also consider the issues surrounding assessment of English language learners in the content areas. In the next section, we provide an introduction to some of the issues related to assessing English language learners in the content areas. We continue with this discussion of assessment in the content areas in the next two chapters of this section.

Checking It Out:
Assessment Issues in the Content Areas

Assessment in the content areas is as critical and controversial as literacy assessment, particularly when considering English language learners. Yet, schools need baseline data about not only literacy development but also the content knowledge of English language learners. O'Malley and Pierce (1996) note that schools use content area assessment with English language learners for three purposes: to monitor student progress toward instructional objectives, to reclassify the students (e.g., move them to a different special language program or to the grade-level classroom), and to serve as a measure of accountability as in benchmark exams for various grade levels and state-mandated exit exams.

Because the public believes that content knowledge is as crucial as literacy development, many states require students to pass a high school exit exam in order to graduate. Currently, seventeen states require English language learners to pass such content area tests (Rivera & Vincent, 1997). How do English language learners handle the demands of testing in a new language? The states exercise several alternatives when testing English language learners, including the following (O'Malley & Pierce, 1996; Rivera & Vincent, 1997):

- Exempting them from testing for one to three years.
- Allowing test accommodations.
- Providing tests in students' home languages.
- Using alternative assessment procedures.

While schools would lobby for these alternatives because they decrease the likelihood that low average test scores will be reported to the public, O'Malley and Pierce (1996) question the practice for two reasons. First, excluding students from testing prevents the school from gathering data about their English language learners' progress. Second, these altered scores may prevent schools from receiving the support to assist English language learners.

In light of the assessment dilemma, we propose that integrated language and content area instruction is the most effective route for English-language learners since effective content instruction has been shown to facilitate language learning (Kessler & Quinn, 1980) and because the academic language needed for school success takes longer to develop (Collier, 1989). Assessment in the content classrooms, however, presents some difficulties, since most of these measures are more language dependent; hence, it is difficult to determine whether a student is experiencing language or content problems (Short, 1993). In order to more closely meet the needs of English language learners who are struggling with language and assessment, O'Malley and Pierce suggest three adaptations that teachers may utilize in their classrooms (1996, p. 166): scaffolding assessment techniques, differentiated scoring, and visible criteria.

The first adaptation, scaffolding assessment techniques, reduces the language demands on the English language learner by providing contextual support for meaning. As we discovered in Chapter 2, context embedded language (with visual cues to meaning) is easier to understand. Just as teachers support their instruction with manipulatives and visuals, so can we scaffold assessment. O'Malley and Pierce suggest the following techniques to reduce the language demands in assessment (1996, p. 166): exhibits or projects, visual displays, organized lists, tables or graphs, short answers. Each of these alternatives provides visual cues to meaning or less-elaborate language requirements.

Next, teachers may consider differentiated scoring, or separating scores on written work for language and content. Teachers must determine what the objective of the assignment is—mastery of content, ability with language, or both. While we would argue that both language and content are necessary for school success, academic fluency takes a long time to develop. As students gain control of their new language, they are also learning new concepts. Therefore, teachers must determine what criteria to use in assessing students on assignments.

Finally, the use of visible criteria involves providing students with specific information on how their work will be graded prior to beginning an assignment. This has long been one of our recommendations for assessment with all students. However, with English language learners in particular, knowing what is expected of them serves to lower the anxiety level about both their language ability and their work requirements. Check out the example of visible criteria from a fourth-grade teacher in Box 10.6.

In the next two chapters, we examine strategies for using nonfiction literature across the curriculum and provide an interdisciplinary literature-based unit. We will provide even more ideas for content area assessment in these chapters.

B O X **10.6**

Voices from the Field: Using Visible Criteria for Assessment

As a case in point of the idea of visible criteria for assessment, one fourth-grade teacher shared this example at a recent workshop. In order to acquaint her English language learners with the United States, she had her students develop brochures for each of the states. To provide visible criteria, she developed a grading checklist that she distributed to them prior to the assignment. She spent time discussing the project in class and linking her comments back to the grading checklist. In addition, she displayed previous student work and linked elements of these examples back to the checklist. Students felt much more secure about the assignment with specific guidelines and examples to follow.

Summary

Textbooks offer many challenges to students in general, and such challenges are magnified for English language learners. Nonfiction literature can mitigate many difficulties presented by textbooks, assisting English language learners in developing the crucial academic language necessary for success. Consequently, teachers can link literacy learning and content learning by utilizing more nonfiction literature in the classroom.

Nonfiction books for children and young adults come in many types. Informational books include concept books, photo essays, survey books, life-cycle books, diaries and journals, browsing books, how-to books, informational storybooks, and biographies of all kinds. Many students prefer these books to fiction, and, as teachers, we must give children many opportunities with this rich genre of literature. Just as there are many types of nonfiction, there are multitudes of classroom applications for these wonderful resources that help English language learners develop both literacy strategies and content knowledge.

11

Strategic Use of Nonfiction Literature with English Language Learners

The possession of facts is knowledge, the use of them is wisdom.
—Thomas Jefferson

In the previous chapter, we discussed the fact that English language learners need assistance with the heavier conceptual loads of content texts and instructional matter. One method we recommended to emphasize both language and content was linking nonfiction trade books with units of study. We highlighted various subcategories of nonfiction literature to enrich students' academic language. In this chapter, we explore various research-based techniques to link nonfiction literature with textbooks and content instruction. We will answer the following questions.

- **How do teachers link nonfiction literature with the content areas?**
- **How do teachers introduce students to nonfiction literature?**
- **What strategies engage English language learners with nonfiction literature and the expository writing in textbooks?**

Let's examine how teachers can include nonfiction literature with content in any classroom.

How Do Teachers Link Nonfiction Literature with the Content Areas?

Linking nonfiction literature with content study serves to heighten students' interest and provides the scaffolding necessary for English language learners to process and understand new concepts and information. As an example, students are often keenly interested in the solar system. However, in spite of their interest, English language learners often find the vocabulary and concepts of science, especially as presented in textbooks, overly challenging. In response to the complexity of the material, teachers can introduce new topics with informational picture books. Teachers may read such books aloud to students, assign books for independent reading, or have students read a book together in small groups.

Putting such an idea into action might look like this. Students might be given any of the following books to read in small groups: Franklyn M. Branley's *Comets* (1987), *The Planets in Our Solar System* (1987), *Rockets and Satellites* (1987), or *The Sun: Our Nearest Star* (1988) or Seymour Simon's *The Long View into Space* (1979), *The Moon* (1984), *Stars* (1986), or *The Sun* (1986). Following the reading, students can talk about the books in groups, share what they learned with the class, and then compare viewpoints and construct semantic maps as a scaffold to the textbook reading. After reading and discussing the science textbook and conducting science experiments and activities, teachers may further extend the topic with additional nonfiction literature. For example, *To Space and Back* (1986) by Sally Ride with Susan Okie, *101 Questions and Answers about the Universe* (1984) by Roy Gallant, *Journey to the Planets* (1993) by Patricia Lauber, or Seymour Simon's planet books, such as *Saturn* (1985), are all appropriate extension books. Teachers often find this approach successful because it helps insure a high level of motivation and comprehension.

In Box 11.1, we present another example of this technique. Look at how Rina Ramos, an elementary teacher at both third and fifth grade levels, has integrated nonfiction literature into her teaching.

Chapter 12 furnishes a more detailed example of this approach, linking literature from various genres with an interdisciplinary unit of study highlighting weather, seasons, and natural disasters. This unit can be used in grades K through 12, and we provide some

---

B O X **11.1**

Voices from the Field: Example of Nonfiction Integration

During a unit on the solar system, we integrate language and content by using many nonfiction trade books. Because one of the hardest reading skills for all children to comprehend is the use of graphic information, I like to focus on this with my bilingual students. (Those who speak very little English can often feel sucessful with the language if they can understand the concepts by using just a few English words to help cue them as they decipher the graphic information.)

After studying some of the factual information about the sun and working with diagrams and the like, I use just the text portion of Seymour Simon's book *The Sun* (1986). I then assign two students to each page of text and ask them to make a diagram to illustrate the information. It's amazing to see how much they learn as they interpret the text into visual information. It is also a wonderful assessment to evaluate how well they understand what is being said. Finally, we put together our class version of Simon's *The Sun*, illustrated by us! All year long, they continually reinforce their language and the information taught as they revisit and reread their book with pride.

vignettes of its use with a high school ESL class. Following are suggestions for helping teachers introduce nonfiction books into their classrooms.

How Do Teachers Introduce Students to Nonfiction Literature?

Because nonfiction literature is not necessarily the genre of choice in classrooms, teachers and students may be unaware of the possibilities that exist. As a beginning, Chapter 10 provided an overview of various types of nonfiction literature with examples of trade books in each category. In this section, we explore ways teachers can use those trade books to introduce English language learners to this fascinating genre.

Author Studies

An excellent way of promoting students' awareness of quality nonfiction literature is by featuring nonfiction authors with a display of books and information in the classroom. In recent years, several high-quality children's authors have built up a body of work of nonfiction that children enjoy. These include Seymour Simon, Gail Gibbons, Lois Ehlert, and Joanna Cole for the younger grades, and Russell Freedman, Patricia Lauber, James Cross Giblin, and Rhoda Blumberg for the upper grades. Creating an awareness of authors and their works is important when working with English language learners since these students often come from another country and a different curriculum. While students within the American K–12 environment might be familiar with some of these authors and their works, it is unlikely that children new to this country would be.

Not only does the featured author approach promote reading, but it also enables students to begin to notice the distinctive style of each author. In examining a half-dozen books by the popular Seymour Simon, students quickly discover his penchant for science and scientific topics, his use of authentic photographs for the books' illustrations, his use of metaphorical language in describing animals and objects, and more. For English language learners in particular, reading more than one book by the same author promotes confidence in their ability to comprehend an author whose style they have come to understand and enjoy. Krashen and Terrell (1983) recommend focusing on one author or topic because narrow reading takes advantage of natural repetition of vocabulary as well as similar syntax, familiar context, and authorial voice.

Use of a Core Book

As we incorporate more and more trade books in our teaching, teachers are experimenting with replacing or supplementing one-size-fits-all basal readers and content textbooks with alternative reading material more suited to the needs and interests of their students. In the upper grades, this is often in the form of class sets of novels. What is not often considered is using class sets of nonfiction books in the same way—for whole-class reading, discussion, and response and comprehension-building activities. There are many excellent nonfiction titles that bear close study, including *People* (1988) by Peter Spier, a picture book full of details celebrating cultural diversity across the globe; *Leonardo da Vinci* (1996) by Diane Stanley, a richly illustrated biography that brings this great mind and talent vividly to life for the older grades; and *Children of the Dust Bowl* (1992) by Jerry Stanley, a fascinating account of children who deserve a chance at education and success despite the prejudice of the time, which is a parable for modern times as well. With each student reading the same title, teachers can feel confident in planning learning activities based on a common knowledge base, and students, particularly English language learners, can feel more confident in their reading.

Read Alouds

Reading aloud develops oral language proficiency, which has a tremendous effect on eventual success in reading and writing. Reading aloud nonfiction, however, rarely seems to occur. There seems to be a widespread but unspoken understanding that fiction is for read aloud time, and nonfiction is for library-research time. In reality, reading aloud nonfiction at any age level can be spontaneous and interactive.

The first step to successfully sharing nonfiction in read aloud sessions is to recognize that there are many ways to share books (Vardell, 1998). The traditional approach of choosing a book and reading the entire text out loud from cover to cover (in one session or across several sessions) is only one way. With nonfiction, this is probably not the most typical approach. Quite honestly, most nonfiction books do not lend themselves to a cover-to-cover read aloud. The concept density is simply too intense for one sitting. Students (especially English language learners) may well be overwhelmed by the amount of new information and terminology in one book when presented with it all at once. However, just as children enjoy hearing favorite selections of fiction read aloud over and over again, so will they make repeated requests for favorite nonfiction titles to be shared again during read aloud time. Each read aloud session deepens the understanding and comprehension students have of the text. With some nonfiction books, multiple readings may be essential to absorb all the layers of information. Therefore, we will provide examples of both traditional and nontraditional ways to read nonfiction aloud.

Cover-to-Cover Read Alouds.   There are probably two practical ways to share a nonfiction book in its entirety during read aloud sessions: as a stand-alone high-quality work of literature that is ideally suited for the oral language development of English language learners, or in conjunction with a particular unit of study that couples content with language learning.

Look to the winners and honor books of the Orbis Pictus Award, given each year by the National Council of Teachers of English for outstanding nonfiction for children. Steve Jenkin's Orbis Pictus honor book, *Hottest, Coldest, Highest, Deepest* (1998), is an excellent example of a cover-to-cover read aloud that is ideal for any age. This nonfiction trade book offers a read aloud opportunity geared for two reading levels. The main line of text is very basic and focuses on geographic facts (e.g., what is the highest/coldest place in the world, etc.). A short paragraph with more data about each geographic location is also provided. Thus, teachers can read only the main line of text for a quick overview, or they can add the additional information to furnish more elaboration and spark discussion. If students respond to this book, Jenkins has written another work with a very similar format highlighting facts from the animal kingdom—*Biggest, Strongest, Fastest* (1995).

The Newbery, Caldecott, and Coretta Scott King award winners and honor books also include some titles of nonfiction that lend themselves to being read aloud. An excellent example of lyrical language for oral sharing is found in *Winter* by Ron Hirschi (1990), with phrases like "winter is weasel white" and "winter is a time for robins and sparrows to search for the last summer berries" (unpaged). Nature photographs add to the beauty of the whole. *Winter across America* (1994) and *Autumn across America* (1993) by Seymour Simon are two other examples of strong read aloud books that match beautiful nature photographs with eloquent prose.

Longer nonfiction works can also be shared during read aloud time, much as a novel is read aloud one chapter at a time over several days or weeks. This is especially useful for the upper grades, where the sustained study of a topic can be linked with a particular nonfiction title. For example, many of the works of Russell Freedman lend themselves to a chapter-by-chapter read aloud. *Children of the Wild West* (1983), *Buffalo Hunt* (1988), *The Wright Brothers* (1991), and *Kids at Work* (1994) are just a few. Each of these books begins with a chapter that summarizes the total work. This initial chapter would be a wonderful overview, providing the big picture before all the details are shared in succeeding chapters. Indeed, such an introduction fosters eventual independent reading by English language learners of the subsequent chapters, in which they would learn, for example, that the Wright Brothers were dapper single men who repaired bicycles and on the side developed an airplane based on brochures they got in the mail from the Smithsonian (*The Wright Brothers*, 1991). Each section of Freedman's books has a title that provides the main idea for the text. For example, "From the Brains to the Tail" gives the listener a pretty good idea of what to expect from this chapter in *Buffalo Hunt* (1988). Freedman's use of primary source data for both text and illustration is also an excellent example for middle-grade researchers.

The act of reading aloud helps give biographies a voice by bringing the subject to life. Kathryn Lasky's *The Librarian Who Measured the Earth* (1994), illustrated by Kevin Hawkes, is a picture book biography that is a perfect read aloud. The large, colorful illustrations are effective for group sharing, and the story of the resourceful and inquisitive Eratosthenes captivates all ages. Pat Cummings' collected interviews, *Talking with Artists* (1992) and *Talking with Artists,* Volume II (1995), can be linked with works by the subjects. Those autobiographical interviews could, in fact, be read aloud by two readers, in a kind of press conference format similar to readers theater.

Each of these works is typical of many others that can captivate audiences in a read aloud session. They can be read in one sitting with mature listeners and with English language learners with more advanced proficiency levels, or the text can be spread over several sessions.

Participatory Read Alouds.   Many nonfiction works lend themselves to participatory or interactive read aloud modes. For example, *Come Back, Salmon: How a Group of Dedicated Kids Adopted Pigeon Creek and Brought It Back to Life* (1993) by Molly Cone contains several sections built on a dialogue between a teacher and students. Chapter 3, "The

Fish That Went to School," and Chapter 6, "Come Back, Salmon," both lend themselves to a read aloud in parts, with the teacher and students sharing aloud respective lines from the book. With practice, this may even lead to the adaptation of nonfiction texts for readers theater (Young & Vardell, 1993).

Other nonfiction texts, such as Patricia McMahon's *Chi-Hoon: A Korean Girl* (1993), feature the voice of one character throughout. This individual's lines or parts could be read aloud by a student while the teacher reads the remaining text. In this example, Chi-Hoon's diary entries are interspersed in the narrative, including this one for Wednesday: "We went on a school picnic. We went to Kyongbuk-kung. After lunch, it rained. First the boys had their pictures taken together. Then the girls. Because of the rain, we couldn't play games. Instead, we sang and told riddles on the bus. It was fun" (p. 37). Some nonfiction texts do not involve student perspectives, but they still lend themselves to effective participatory read alouds. Whether students are reading aloud dialogue or diary-like entries or responding with practical activities while listening, students who participate actively in the read aloud session will find that their direct involvement insures a higher level of motivation and comprehension.

Chapter or Excerpt Read Alouds.   Many more informational books are perfect for sharing orally in bits and pieces. They are often organized in parts or subcategories that lend themselves to sharing. Particularly for English language learners, this sharing in small doses serves as an adaptation for varying levels of listening proficiency. An example of an excellent work of nonfiction, any chapter of which makes interesting sharing, is *From Hand to Mouth, or, How We Invented Knives, Forks, Spoons, and Chopsticks and the Table Manners to Go with Them* (1987) by James Cross Giblin. The chapter entitled "The Rise and Fall of Table Manners" is a fascinating story about how forks came to America, among other things.

Even some biographies work effectively in excerpts or section read alouds. Share the chapters "How Yani Paints" and "Yani and Her Father" from *A Young Painter: The Life and Paintings of Wang Yani—China's Extraordinary Young Artist* (1991) by Zheng Zhensun and Alice Low. These two chapters give students a feeling for how the young artist works as well as for how her gift affects her family. The excellent biographical work, *Sojourner Truth, "Ain't I a Woman?"* (1992), by Patricia and Fredrick McKissack is a fascinating study. Reading aloud the chapter "Free Belle" or "Ain't I a Woman" might be enough to lure English language learners in the secondary grades to read the rest of her story on their own. Each chapter functions as a story in itself about this fascinating woman and the times she lived in, first as a slave, then as a free woman. In addition, the short biographies in the section "More about the People Sojourner Truth Knew" stand alone as interesting read aloud material. Many collective biographies also include pieces short enough for reading aloud, such as those in *Inspirations: Stories about Women Artists* (1989) by Leslie Sills or *Afro-Bets Book of Black Heroes from A to Z* (1988) by Wade Hudson and Valerie Wilson Wesley.

Caption Read Alouds.   Much of the nonfiction literature published today is packed with illustrations and photographs, often in full color. Skimming through only the pictures and captions may provide a bird's-eye view of the overall content of such a book. It helps fine-tune students' visual literacy skills, guiding them in using illustrations as informational cues in the reading process. Showing pictures and sharing captions in the read aloud session can be a kind of sneak preview of the book as a whole, which would assist English language learners before they tackle an entire text or a unit of study on that topic. Consider, for example, the following caption for a gripping photograph in Charlotte Wilcox's *Mummies and Their Mysteries* (1993): "When farmers found this body in a Danish bog in 1950, they immediately called the police. The 2000-year-old body was so well preserved, the farmers thought the man had been recently murdered. The rope used to hang him was still around his neck" (p. 51).

Dorothy Hinshaw Patent uses captions and photographs very effectively throughout her nonfiction works. See, for example, the photographs that accompany these captions (from *Yellowstone Fires: Flames and Rebirth*, 1990): "Smoke from the fires often blocked out the sun" (p. 21); "Most of the fires created a mosaic of burned places, killed trees, and unburned areas. As time passes, these varied patches will result in a greater variety of habitats for the park plants and animals" (p. 34). Even without pictures, the vivid descriptions found in the captions provide excellent material for the read aloud and discussion.

Other outstanding sources for good captions and exciting illustrations include *To Space and Back* by Sally Ride with Susan Okie (1986), which includes full-color NASA photographs; *The Great Fire* by Jim Murphy (1995), with sepia tone illustrations and photos; and *Children of the Dust Bowl: The True Story of the School at Weedpatch Camp* by Jerry Stanley (1992), with actual photographs from the period. Sharing captions and illustrations during read alouds is an excellent way to incorporate nonfiction into the curriculum and can lead to identifying main ideas.

Browsing. Many nonfiction titles employ a multilayered format, with information presented in narrative, sidebars, illustrations, and captions. These more chaotic formats can be made to seem less formidable by a read aloud experience that guides students in processing all the multiple sources of information. For example, Richard Platt's *Incredible Cross-Sections*, illustrated by Steven Biesty (1992), is a favorite among students. As pages are unfolded and spread out, students may point out their favorite scenes or details to the class.

Browsing may be an excellent strategy for students' first introduction to the Magic School Bus series of books. Author Joanna Cole and illustrator Bruce Degen have created a nonfiction book format that includes story narrative, dialogue, expository passages, captions, and illustrations full of details. A first read aloud might simply share the story narrative. For example, in *The Magic School Bus Lost in the Solar System* (1992), listeners can follow Ms. Frizzle and her class on their magical tour of the solar system as they lose Ms. Frizzle in space, solve the problem with the help of her lesson plans, and are reunited and return to earth. Successive read alouds can then highlight expository passages, share captions, and point out additional details. Students can join in on each layer of read aloud.

As students become more and more familiar with nonfiction as a genre and with its peculiarities of form and format, the read aloud sessions can expand into demonstration and explication from both a reader's and a writer's point of view. Just as we point out how fiction writers use setting to create a mood, we can direct students to notice how and why nonfiction writers use a great variety of tools and devices to organize their ideas and to make that organization more reader-friendly.

Introducing Reference Aids and Expository Text Structures.   As we build students' exposure to nonfiction, many possibilities for extension present themselves. For instance, it is possible to introduce or highlight the technical aspects of nonfiction text. This includes the internal structure for how the author has organized the information—for example, using chronological sequence, comparing and contrasting, or presenting ideas from the general to the specific. In addition, teachers can model how nonfiction authors use reference aids such as maps, a table of contents, the index, and a glossary as well as how the text format is organized with headings and subheadings, boxes and sidebars, and the placement of illustrations and graphic aids including charts, graphs, and timelines. Such modeling reinforces needed skills for English language learners and lays the groundwork for academic study skills.

To the novice reader, all these elements can be intimidating and confusing. The teacher can explain what each of these text elements is, providing the labels ("This is called a glossary"), authentic examples ("Here is the glossary from Wilcox's *Mummies and Their Mysteries*"), and explanations on the spot ("The glossary is a list of words and meanings that helps us with this subject. Here is the word *bog*. Let's read what a bog is"). In the give and take, teachers can help students clarify their understanding of all these pieces of text. Using high-quality nonfiction trade books helps provide an interesting and meaningful context for identifying these elements and building vocabulary for English language learners. As students become more familiar with how these work in books they enjoy, they may be better equipped to recognize and use these tools in textbooks.

These reference tools can also be presented quite naturally in the read aloud experience. Deciding which excerpt to read requires referring to a table of contents. Penny Colman's comprehensive work *Rosie the Riveter, Women Working on the Home Front in World War II* (1995) offers many choices for read alouds. Reading aloud the table of contents can involve the students in choosing a starting chapter. Afterwards, a discussion of how the author chooses titles for each chapter and why the chapters are organized the way they are is a rich opportunity for developing the thinking behind the writing and organizing of expository text.

The same kind of practice can be used to demonstrate the value of an index. This time, begin at the end with an overhead transparency of the index pages. Again, students can choose intriguing topics. The read aloud leader looks for the reference within the text. Show students how to read only the relevant material. So often, less-able readers, especially English language learners, need permission not to read the entire page, not realizing that skimming and scanning is appropriate and necessary. Try Patricia Lauber's excellent nonfiction work *Seeing Earth from Space* (1990). Look up *drought* on page 48 or *oil spill* on page 72, and find the references to read aloud. Be sure to share the incredible photographs from space showing actual droughts and oil spills.

These are just a few methods for bringing nonfiction to the attention of students and linking it to units of study. The next section provides strategies for engaging students with nonfiction literature while helping them past the more difficult language of textbooks.

What Strategies Engage English Language Learners with Nonfiction Literature and the Expository Writing in Textbooks?

Many of the techniques we presented in Chapter 5 to pique student interest and build background knowledge prior to reading, to sustain comprehension during reading, and to follow up after reading are excellent techniques for expository and nonfiction text. Prediction, anticipation guides, option guides, problem-solving activities, hypothetical situations, and attitude inventories are just as applicable to nonfiction and exposition as to fiction. In addition, vocabulary techniques such as semantic mapping and the semantic feature analysis from Chapter 5 are essential methods to build student word knowledge in the content areas. However, we want to highlight a variety of additional options for teachers to use. All of these techniques can be used to link nonfiction trade books with the content textbook. Most importantly, these strategies reflect principles believed to be effective with English language learners: integrating language with content instruction (Snow & Brinton, 1988); using cooperative problem-solving activities (Moll & Diaz, 1987); and providing activities to build background knowledge (Reyes & Molner, 1993).

Lesson Frameworks

As we have noted, the academic language and new content concepts in expository and nonfiction materials present challenges to English language learners. As a result, students may need additional assistance with these texts. Lesson frameworks such as the directed reading thinking activity (DRTA) (Stauffer, 1969, 1976) and the K-W-L chart (Ogle, 1986) provide support, leading students through the entire reading process and allowing teachers to assess student background and monitor their progress. These frameworks can be used with the whole class or small groups.

The **directed reading thinking activity** offers a structured process for approaching reading assignments. It is not designed for every reading assignment, but rather for those that present more difficulty, particularly textbook reading. Teachers may begin by modeling the DRTA with a nonfiction book that may be more engaging to students. In this lesson framework, the teacher follows a process emphasizing the prereading phase to prepare students to handle text independently. In Box 11.2, we have provided the steps to the DRTA, along with an example of possible questions and instructional moves using the *Environmental Atlas of the United States* (Mattson, 1993).

The **K-W-L chart** (Ogle, 1986) devotes two columns to the prereading phase, activating students' background knowledge (K = What Do I Know?) and encouraging them to make predictions about the upcoming reading (W = What Do I Want to Know?). In the last column (L = What Did I Learn?), students note what they learned as they read, and this can tap into both during-reading and postreading. An additional extension includes making a K-W-L Plus chart and having students construct a semantic map to synthesize the information in their chart (Carr & Ogle, 1987). One excellent method for building student background knowledge prior to a reading assignment or the beginning of an instructional unit is to use a browsing technique with the K-W-L chart, as noted in Box 11.3.

B O X **11.2**

Directed Reading Thinking Activity Example

1. The class examines the title, subtitle, and graphic aids and makes predictions. The teacher uses the title, cover, and table of contents to begin the prediction process by asking questions. (What topics do you think the author will address? Why? Looking at the table of contents, we see on page 46 that the author addresses the topic "Where We Put Trash." What information will be presented here?)

2. The teacher questions students about predictions. (Why do you think the author will discuss the topic of recycling in the section on garbage?)

3. Students learn strategies to deal with unknown words and phrases that may come up in the reading (e.g., reading to the end of the sentence, using picture clues, sounding out the word, etc.). (On page 9, we see several terms in bold print. What are these terms? [landform, erosion, glaciers, moraines] Why is bold print used for some words in a book? How can you determine the meaning of these terms? One way authors define a new term is to describe the word with examples. For instance, the author states: "The special features of the earth, like mountains, river valleys, or canyons, are called landforms" [p. 9]. We can almost create a one-to-one relationship for this new word then [mountains, river valleys, canyons = landforms].)

4. The teacher works with students to help them adjust their reading rate to the purposes and the material. (Each page contains brief description as well as illustrations, captions, and graphic organizers. At what rate should you read text that switches format like this? Why? How might you decide to read these pages—the short chunks of information first or the longer descriptive passages? Why?)

5. During silent reading, the teacher observes students and notes any difficulties.

6. After students are finished, they close their books, and the teacher leads the class in a quick check on comprehension. (What types of pollution were mentioned in the book? What types of solutions did the author present? Can you think of any more possibilities?)

7. Students return to the text to continue the prediction, reading, proving cycle.

8. Follow-up activities may include discussion, mapping the selection, illustrating the selection, writing a response, and so on. (Depending on proficiency levels, the teacher might assign students to work in groups to create semantic maps depicting the facts about air and water pollution, or students could design a persuasive poster about litter and garbage.)

Text-Preview Techniques

Expository and nonfiction texts have a different look and sound than the typical narrative pattern found in many basals or anthologies. Therefore, teachers may choose to review texts with students prior to assigning independent reading. For instance, the teacher can demonstrate a quick inspection of a chapter using the **survey technique** (Aukerman, 1972). The following focus points and questions might be asked for the first chapter of any nonfiction book. Then students could independently utilize this strategy in subsequent chapters.

BOX **11.3**

Fact Fest:
Browsing through Nonfiction to Build Background Knowledge

Instead of presenting a prereading explanation to build and activate background knowledge, teachers can create a more interactive atmosphere with these steps.

- With the help of the school or public library, locate numerous picture books related to a reading selection, theme, or topic.
- Bring these resources into the classroom and divide the books among several groups of students.
- Each group utilizes a K-W-L chart.
- Using the topic, title, or table of contents of a selection, the students brainstorm what they already know and jot this down in the first column.
- Then the group considers questions they would like to know more about and topics they hope will be addressed in the resource books. They write those points in the middle column.
- Finally, the students open the books and browse through the pages and illustrations, discussing the information and noting what they learned in the third column of the chart.
- Taking the information from the chart and group discussion, students create a graphic representation of what they learned and post this for the class to view. In addition, students select their favorite book from this activity and read aloud a fascinating fact they learned.

As the class walks through the top picks and interesting information gained through the process, a foundation of background knowledge has been established that will help students process the reading assignment later.

- Based on the title of the chapter, what information do you think the author will present? If you convert the title to a question, what would that question be?
- Read the introduction, summary, and questions. What seem to be the author's main points? What topics will be addressed?
- Read the headings and subheadings. Convert them to questions.
- Notice the print in special type. Why are certain words or phrases highlighted?
- Study visual materials such as pictures, maps, and diagrams. What do the graphics tell you about the chapter's content?

Similar to the survey technique, an **organizational walk-through** (Holbrook, 1984) involves surveying the chapter or reading and focusing student attention on the organizational writing pattern or text structure (time order, comparison and contrast, cause and effect, problem and solution, listing). Students then create their own graphic organizers or grids reflecting that organizational pattern in the during-reading stage. For example, Patricia Lauber (1989) sets up a dichotomy in *The News about Dinosaurs*. She presents what we have previously known to be true about various kinds of dinosaurs and contrasts this with what recent discoveries have uncovered. Each time, the contrasting point of view begins "The news is." Students could create a simple chart by folding paper in half lengthwise and writing "old facts" on one side and "the news is" on the other, listing examples of each.

In the **visual reading guide** (Stein, 1978), the focus is the graphic material—the charts, diagrams, and so on. After deciding which graphic aids are key to the reading, the teacher highlights these and notes all the elements, first drawing attention to why such aids occur in expository writing and why these examples are important to this chapter. If the graphic aids are presented in a similar fashion throughout the text, the teacher can make a transparency and demonstrate the graphic aid pattern, stressing features such as font differences (italics, boldface), subheadings, figure and table captions, marginal glosses, labeled diagrams, and the like. Any of the books in the Magic School Bus Series written by Joanna Cole and illustrated by Bruce Degen will reveal examples of a variety of graphic tools, including charts, tables, pictures and captions, and diagrams.

Introducing students to a book via a **text overview** (Vacca & Vacca, 1989) lessens the intimidation factor. As an example of the information that students might find helpful, Mora Butterfield provides a one page introduction to *1,000 Facts about the Earth* (1992) and its features, noting that key words are in bold type, each two-page spread has a "Strange but True" box with fascinating facts, there is an index on pages 46–48, a listing of facts is presented with bullets, and mini-facts are noted at the top of each page. Teachers can extend the text overview by creating a scavenger hunt that provides hands-on experience for students as they search to find the information requested by the teacher. Some basic points to consider in a text overview are presented in Table 11.1, but teachers can adapt this to specific texts.

Each of the text preview strategies we have highlighted is appropriate for students in grades K–12. Once students feel comfortable with the organization of the text, it is time to engage them with the actual information presented in the book through discussion and hands-on activities.

Discussion and Response Strategies

Given the emerging oral language development of English language learners, teachers may wish to consider controlled discussion techniques such as the Four Level Reflection Guide (Lazear, 1991), Save the Last Word for Me (Buehl, 1995) or Yes, Because . . . No,

TABLE 11.1   Some Questions for a Text Overview

- According to the table of contents, what are the major divisions of the book?
- How many chapters/divisions are in the book?
- What common sections occur in each chapter of the text (objectives, summary, etc.)? What is the purpose of these sections?
- Is there a glossary? Check out the definition of a term, and then find that term in the text using the index.
- Are there appendices? What is their purpose?

Because . . . (Rothstein & Goldberg, 1993) or Both Sides (Alvermann, 1991). These techniques allow students to read, reflect, and respond in a written format first, which gives them ideas to draw from for the verbal discussion to follow.

In the **Four Level Reflection Guide** (Lazear, 1991), students respond at four levels that address both the cognitive and the affective domains. They first use a worksheet with the following levels and react to each level as they read.

- Level 1: How am I involved?
- Level 2: What are the pluses and minuses, and what do I find interesting?
- Level 3: What do I think could/should be done?
- Level 4: What can I do now?

Students' reactions at each level become the fuel for the discussion. For instance, ecology and the environment is a popular topic with K–12 students, so Nancy worked with several secondary school colleagues to create an Earth Day lesson. English language learners used books such as *Garbage: Where It Comes from, Where It Goes* (Hadingham & Hadingham, 1990) and *Trash* (Charlotte Wilcox, 1988), then responded to the Four Level Reflection Guide prior to the class discussion.

In **Save the Last Word for Me** (Buehl, 1995)**,** students read a selection and then choose five statements they either agree with, disagree with, or wish to respond to. They write each statement on an index card and write a personal response on the back of each card. In groups, each person reads his/her cards but may not share the personal response on the back of the card until each member responds to the front statement. To put this technique into action, all students might read the same book or portions of the same text— for instance, Jerry Stanley's *I Am an American* (1994) about the internment of Japanese Americans during World War II—and then choose five statements that evoke a powerful reaction for discussion. An adaptation is to have students read different books on the same topic (e.g., the Holocaust) and share personal responses from several sources. Some excellent nonfiction resources for the Holocaust include *We Remember the Holocaust* (Adler, 1989), *I Have Lived a Thousand Years: Growing Up in the Holocaust* (Britton-Jackson, 1997), *Five Diaries of Teenagers Who Died in the Holocaust* (Boas, 1995), *Memories of Anne Frank: Reflections of a Childhood Friend* (Gold, 1997), *No Pretty Pictures: A Child of War*, (Lobel, 1998), *Bearing Witness: Stories of the Holocaust* (Rochman & McCampbell, 1995), and *Hiding to Survive: Stories of Jewish Children Rescued from the Holocaust* (Rosenberg, 1994).

The **Yes, Because . . . No, Because . . .** (Rothstein & Goldberg, 1993) or **Both Sides** (Alvermann, 1991) discussion technique provides an opportunity for students to examine two sides of an issue. To implement this technique, students work in pairs or small groups to reflect on a question related to a reading assignment. For instance, with the nonfiction book *If Your Name Was Changed at Ellis Island* (Levine, 1993), students might consider the following question: Was immigration worth the hardships? After sharing the title of the selection and the question, the teacher begins to read. The teacher stops several times while reading, and each time students talk about the reasons that support both a yes and a no response. The idea is to listen, read between the lines, and offer points not explicitly stated in the text.

Graphic Organizers

There are a host of formats for graphic organizers that can be used at any point throughout the reading process. In the prereading phase, graphic organizers provide an overview of the reading to come with the major points and the relationship among them clearly delineated. Alvermann and Phelps (1994) note that teachers can create the graphic organizer in advance of a reading assignment, but that organizers are more effective when students participate in their construction.

Using the tree-diagram technique, the **structured overview** or **hierarchy** (Barron, 1979) represents the hierarchical relationships among facts and concepts in reading material and how this information is organized. Basically, this strategy provides a visual outline noting the level of importance of the ideas. To create a structured overview, decide which concept is the most important idea (superordinate concept) for students. This concept or phrase is placed at the top of your hierarchy and serves as the umbrella concept under which all the other information falls. Then examine the text for supporting facts and concepts. (Hint: Look at headings and subheadings throughout the chapter.) Text headings or coordinate concepts fall below your superordinate concept. Subheadings are placed below the coordinate concepts. Once it is created, teachers walk students through the overview as an advanced organizer prior to reading or beginning an entire unit of study.

One method nonfiction writers use to organize expository text is to rely on chronological order to guide the sequencing of information. **Timelines** are the logical graphic organizer to represent this chronological structure. For instance, in the Orbis Pictus Award-winning *Across America on an Emigrant Train* by Jim Murphy (1993), students in the upper grades can identify each year or period of years covered in the chapter. They can then work together to create a timeline to accompany the book.

Examples of timelines in nonfiction literature serve as models, a type of reading guide, and they spur discussion and student activities. The chronological timeline, for example, is incredibly helpful in David Adler's *We Remember the Holocaust* (1989). This device provides a helpful mechanism for relating and connecting the events that unfold throughout the text. Also consider Zack Rogow's *Oranges* (1988), with its methodical chronology and colorful drawings showing the production of oranges from clearing the fields to planting, grafting, irrigating, picking, hauling, selling, and so on. Students can read the text and write out important events on index cards. Then they can order the cards, constructing a timeline from the data. They may transfer the timeline to the board or overhead for class discussion or keep it with their own papers.

Similar to timelines, **flowcharts** help students grasp the sequence of activities. However, their branching structure allows students to depict more options than the simple linear sequence of a timeline. Passages that describe or provide directions may be ideal as material for developing flowcharts. For example, students can participate as they listen when the teacher reads aloud the step-by-step guidelines for figuring out "On which day of the week were you born?" from Marilyn Burns' *Math for Smarty Pants* (1982, p. 29). Many other nonfiction titles detail the how-to's of experiments, games, and other activities. Teachers should model the construction of a flowchart first, using a common activity like the steps involved in getting ready for school each morning. Then, with subsequent sequential instructions or tasks, students may work together to note the steps in the process on index cards and construct the flowchart. *Make Me a Peanut Butter Sandwich and a Glass of Milk* by Ken Robbins (1992) provides the data for several flowcharts on how to make peanut butter, make bread—from growing wheat to transporting the packaged bread to the store—and manufacture milk.

Assisting students to recognize text structure can positively affect reading achievement. Moreover, there are many **text structure maps** that can be developed to highlight the predominant pattern of text. At first, teachers may need to define the text structure of a reading passage (e.g., cause and effect) and provide the map format. As noted earlier, *The News about Dinosaurs* by Patricia Lauber (1989) has a clearly defined structure for the presentation of information. Lauber presents a brief summary of previously held beliefs about dinosaurs, then breaks the text with "The news is," after which the most current and often contradictory findings are shared. This use of generalization and example is one way a nonfiction author may choose to lay out a book. In *A River Ran Wild* (1992), Lynne Cherry employs a problem-solution-result structure to describe the evolution of the Nashua River from a clean and clear river to a polluted area clogged by industrial waste.

One text structure, comparison and contrast, is easy to map using formats such as Venn diagrams or H-maps (Devine, 1989). As a during-reading technique, compare and contrast maps serve to focus English language learners on the text structure of a selection, and the maps can be utilized as a prewriting tool for a comparison and contrast paper. For example, *Talking Walls* (Knight, 1992) and *Talking Walls: The Stories Continue* (Knight, 1996) make powerful statements about the similarities and differences among the world's peoples. Margy Burns Knight's nonfiction picture books introduce famous wall landmarks from around the world with fascinating details and insights into what the walls tell us about each culture. From the Great Wall of China to the Berlin Wall, brief passages and colorful illustrations lend themselves to a comparison and contrast discussion. Comparison and contrast can also be illustrated for students by examining the Coretta Scott King Award-winning book *Christmas in the Big House, Christmas in the Quarters* by Patricia and Fredrick McKissack (1994). Having two oral readers (one reader for chapters about the Big House, and the other for those about the Quarters) helps students clearly hear the two distinctive points of view. Teachers can follow up by mapping the information in a Venn diagram or H-map and discussing why the authors chose comparison and contrast for their organizational structure.

Recently, Nancy used the H-map format with the book *Families: A Celebration of Diversity, Commitment, and Love* by Aylette Jenness (1990). The format of this book is such that any of the family profiles could be read aloud and discussed. Real children and their families are pictured and detailed in first-person narratives, including the adoptive family of Tam, the blended family of Jody, Jennifer's family on a commune, and Nhor's foster family, among others. The entire book is excellent, but need not be read from cover to cover in order to discover the variety of families representative of our society today. In a unit on families in a high school ESL class, students read one story of a more traditional nuclear family, Brian's, and then in groups heard another story of Nhor's nontraditional family. Using an H-map (see Figure 11.1), students noted similarities and differences between Brian's and Nhor's families. As a final step, they compared and contrasted their own families to Brian's and Nhor's and then wrote their family stories, patterned after the examples. Using this organizational aid meant that these English language learners were

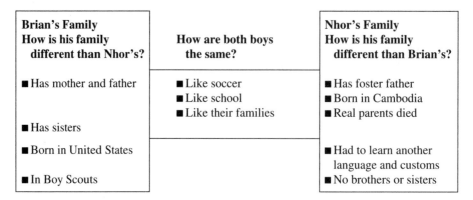

FIGURE 11.1   H-Map (Comparison-and-Contrast Map) for Families Unit

able to write well-developed papers in spite of their limited proficiency (Hadaway & Mundy, 1992).

Writing

As we discussed in Chapter 6, writing is an excellent process for developing literacy and exploring content. Several writing formats are ideally suited to exploring concepts and reporting new knowledge in the content areas, including academic journals, content journals, learning logs, double-entry journals, jot charts, and data-retrieval charts.

Students may use a journal in a notebook or other type of folder to keep a personal written record of their content area learning, including their predictions, expectations, and understanding of new concepts. Such a journal is known as an **academic journal, content journal,** or **learning log.** The content of the journal may be student selected, or the teacher may provide prompts to guide student reflection (e.g., What difficulties did you encounter with the text reading or lesson today? What questions did you have as you were reading your assignment?). Teachers may ask students to clarify, articulate, and confirm their own learning and state the concepts learned in writing. As an example, after reading *A River Ran Wild* (Cherry, 1992), the teacher might ask students to write a few sentences about the following: Explain how the people of the Nashua River managed to clean up their river valley. What could you do to bring about change if you saw a polluted or littered area? In a **double-entry journal,** students divide the page of their journal into two sections: What the Text Says/What I Say. Then, they take notes and consider personal reactions to the information (what they agree or disagree with, points that are particularly interesting or disturbing, etc.) or summarize and consolidate the information for study purposes.

An additional format, the **jot chart or data-retrieval chart,** is used to collect and record data in a simple and convenient form so that it can be used later for analysis and interpretation. The chart provides a matrix, with key concepts to be analyzed or described across the top and questions to answer down the side. This is a great format to organize note-taking from research and reading. Because the chart allows students to gather the same kinds of information across two or more samples, it makes comparison and contrast easy. When the data-retrieval chart is filled in, students can summarize the information in written form and ask a series of questions about the data that will help establish relationships, inferences, and meaning. Nancy used this technique in a unit on immigration with a high school ESL class (see Table 11.2).

Reference Aids

Expository text is full of all kinds of reference aids that can be systematically introduced. One at a time, through instruction and in the context of quality trade books, these tools can be demonstrated as the informative devices they are. For instance, **graphs and charts,** while common in textbooks, may be difficult to comprehend. As a personalized introduction to data reported in chart or graph form, the class can collect and synthesize information from students (e.g., number of family members, kinds of pets, favorite foods, recreational activities, etc.) to construct the display Our Class in Graphs. From this project, students can compare and contrast the graphs and charts in their textbooks and even construct examples from readings. The class may utilize a two-way process, either developing graphic aids from data in written form or translating written text into a graph or chart display.

Nonfiction books provide a wealth of material to synthesize for graphic aids. For example, the class might construct a comparison of students' home countries or regions to begin the year as a get-acquainted activity. The alphabet book *Children from Australia to Zimbabwe: A Photographic Journey around the World* (Ajmera & Versola, 1996) is an

TABLE 11.2 Comparison of Immigrant Groups

	Group #1	**Group #2**	**Group #3**
Immigrant Group: Where did they come from?			
Reasons for Immigration: Why did they leave?			
Time Frame of Immigration: How did they get here?			
Where They Settled: What did they find?			
Way of Life: What did they do?			
Contribution to Area: What lasting impact did they make?			

ideal source of information for a class graphing activity. This book highlights countries and children around the world, providing both descriptive text and bulleted facts that students can convert to graphs.

As another type of a reference aid, Jim Murphy's Orbis Pictus Award-winning book, *The Great Fire* (1995), is an excellent example of how helpful **maps** can be in telling a story. The scale and magnitude of the Great Fire of Chicago is vividly conveyed by the expanding gray area on the maps provided throughout the book. As the details of the fire unfold, transparencies of the maps can reveal the extent of the fire in a very concrete and visual way.

In conclusion, we have provided just a few examples linking content literacy activities with nonfiction books. While these techniques are of particular use to students learning English, these same teaching strategies benefit all students by building and expanding their background knowledge and more actively involving them in the reading and writing demands of their academic subjects. In the next section, we continue our discussion of assessing English language learners in the content areas.

Checking It Out:
Assessment Issues and Content Learning

Because research documents a strong relationship between comprehension and vocabulary knowledge, prior knowledge, active engagement with text, and metacognitive awareness, those elements of content area instruction serve as excellent starting points for beginning assessment (McNeil, 1992). In addition, O'Malley and Pierce (1996) note that teachers need to monitor the conceptual knowledge, reading comprehension, vocabulary skills, thinking skills and written response skills of English language learners as content instruction is provided. We dealt with the assessment of reading comprehension and metacognitive awareness in Chapter 5, while writing assessment was covered in Chapter 6. Here we turn our attention to assessment issues with regard to vocabulary and concept knowledge and prior knowledge.

Vocabulary and Concept Knowledge

One of the greatest needs in content area learning is word and concept knowledge. Teachers must constantly assess where students are in their understanding of the terms and ideas of the various academic subjects. One measure of an individual's vocabulary knowledge is the **cloze** test. To construct a cloze test, the teacher selects an unfamiliar passage of 250 to 300 words from the students' textbook or required reading. After the first sentence is left intact, the teacher deletes every fifth word for intermediate grades and above. For the primary grades, teachers should remove every seventh or tenth word (Mariotti & Homan, 1997). Then students fill in the blanks left by the deleted words. Students will not come up with perfect scores, but their scores indicate whether they are able to handle material independently, require some assistance, or need considerable assistance.

Another method for assessing vocabulary as well as conceptual knowledge is the **semantic map** (Johnson & Pearson, 1984). We discussed semantic maps in Chapter 5 as a method of building word knowledge. However, semantic maps demonstrate more than students' ability to define a term; they reflect an understanding of the hierarchies and connections between concepts. A semantic map is one type of graphic organizer. Other graphic organizers presented in this chapter can also be used as assessment techniques.

Additionally, the **semantic feature analysis** (Anders & Bos, 1986; Anders, Bos, & Wilde, 1986; Toms-Boronowski, 1983) introduced in Chapter 5 is an excellent informal assessment technique. Teachers can simply create a grid of rows and columns, listing the members of a concept or topic studied down the side (e.g., geometric shapes) and the features or attributes of those concepts across the top (e.g., three sides, four sides, etc.). Then students can check the characteristics belonging to each member of the concept.

Finally, teachers might observe students engaged in the **list-group-label method** (Taba, 1967) as a means of assessing vocabulary and concept knowledge. This variation on brainstorming can be used with whole-class, group, or individual study. Using the vocabulary from any nonfiction trade book, teachers simply follow these steps.

- List all the words associated with a topic or concept (e.g., pollution).
- Group the words into categories (e.g., air pollution, water pollution, waste pollution). Some words may belong in multiple categories.
- Label the groups of words, and discuss why the terms listed fit into each category.

Most importantly, teachers need to move away from the more traditional assessments of vocabulary and conceptual knowledge that simply measure definitions or associations. Instead, we need to utilize assessments that encourage students to recognize and generate attributes, examples, and nonexamples as is the case with the the semantic feature analysis or to sense and infer relationships as reflected in the list-group-label method (Simpson, 1987).

Prior Knowledge

Background knowledge is critical to learning in the content areas, since we learn more effectively when we build on our previous understandings (Gagne, Yekovich, & Yekovich, 1993). As we noted in Chapter 2, English language learners often dismiss prior knowledge they have in their home language because they assume that it does not apply in English. Yet, this prior knowledge—whether in the home language or in English—is the foundation upon which we build for instruction of new concepts. In order to effectively instruct English language learners, O'Malley and Pierce (1996, p. 175) recommend that teachers determine what a student knows about new concepts in a lesson, how this information is organized in a student's memory, and how the information can be retrieved for learning.

Determining prior knowledge, however, can be complicated with English language learners due to their limited proficiency. To assist in this process, O'Malley and Pierce (1996) have adapted previous work by Holmes and Roser (1987) suggesting six methods for assessing what students know: nonverbal, recognition, structured questions, unstructured discussions, free recall, and word association. **Nonverbal** assessment might include teacher observation of students during a Total Physical Response lesson. As the teacher gives directions or commands, are students able to respond appropriately? For instance, the teacher asks students to point to the appropriate picture in a book (e.g., Show me the picture of a polluted river.) **Recognition** tasks look much like a multiple-choice test. The teacher raises a question orally and provides specific answer options, and the student must choose the correct answer. **Structured questions** involve teachers' probing questions to determine the depth of student understanding. As an example, in a lesson on the environment teachers might ask: What is pollution? What types of pollution exist? What are some causes of air pollution? Water pollution? What are some solutions to these issues? In an **unstructured discussion,** the teacher asks students about their own personal experiences (e.g., Have you ever seen an example of water pollution? Where? What did it look like?). For **free recall,** the teacher might invite students to write a story about pollution, sharing everything they know about the topic. Finally, **word association** is much like brainstorming. When the teacher throws out a topic, students chime in with everything they know. Each of these methods provides information about students' prior knowledge and helps the teacher fine-tune instruction to more closely meet students' language proficiency levels and to build the foundation of concept knowledge needed for upcoming lessons.

Many other methods are also available to tap into students' prior knowledge. The **K-W-L chart,** mentioned previously, provides the teacher with a glimpse of student background knowledge and their ability to logically predict topics and ideas that might be presented in a book. In addition, the teacher can observe the information that the student retrieves from the reading.

The access features in textbooks and nonfiction trade books provide an opportunity for another type of assessment option, the **Content Reading Inventory** or CRI (Readence, Bean, & Baldwin, 1995), to determine students' prior knowledge with textbooks. The CRI has three major sections: (1) use of book parts (e.g., table of contents, index, glossary, graphic aids, chapter introduction/summary, appendices) and references (e.g., encyclopedia, atlas, etc.); (2) vocabulary knowledge (e.g., word meanings and use of context); and (3) comprehension (literal and inferential). Generally, the teacher constructs a CRI based on a book in order to determine how well the students can use the text and learn from it. A more creative and active approach might be to design a scavenger hunt activity in which students find tidbits of information from a group of nonfiction books. Then students could discuss the book features characteristic of nonfiction books and compare them to the textbook. The CRI could be used as a follow up to the scavenger hunt and discussion to assess students' ability to transfer this knowledge to their textbook.

In conclusion, content area assessment provides an opportunity to not only examine concept knowledge but also to look at language development. Varied assessment techniques provide a fuller picture of a student's language growth and content knowledge and also allow teachers to select the most appropriate instructional procedures to meet individual needs.

Summary

Nonfiction trade books furnish meaningful input for literacy activities as English language learners develop both language and content literacy. Teachers employ numerous strategies to scaffold their English language learners' content learning with nonfiction literature. These activities range from individual, small-group, and whole-class reading and sharing configurations.

Teachers employ many creative strategies for introducing their students to nonfiction literature. One popular technique is the nonfiction author study, which combines learning about the author as well as his/her works. The core book is another effective technique that involves the entire group in reading and discussing a single book. Reading nonfiction trade books aloud enables teachers to demonstrate a plethora of read aloud strategies and reference-aid skills. While a lack of understanding of English text structure creates many obstacles for English language learners in content classrooms, teachers often use trade books to teach such structures to their students.

Teachers often teach their students a variety of strategies to help them develop prior knowledge before reading, sustain comprehension while reading, and extend understanding after reading. These strategies may be introduced with nonfiction literature. Then students are helped to apply them to textbooks.

Finally, teachers can monitor their English language learners' concept development, vocabulary, and prior knowledge using cloze tests, semantic maps, semantic feature analysis, or the list-group-label method. Other assessment techniques are also explored in the chapter.

12 Interdisciplinary Literacy Learning through Literature-Based Instruction

Books are children of the brain.

—Jonathan Swift

Using the research base on literature-based instruction and effective instructional strategies for English language learners highlighted in the previous chapters, we outline in this chapter an interdisciplinary unit on the topic of weather. Much of the unit was actually taught by Nancy and a public school colleague, JaNae Mundy, in a high school ESL setting (Hadaway & Mundy, 1999), but units like this are applicable at any level from K through grade 12. Here, we chronicle the steps from the planning through the implementation of a unit using a variety of trade books and learning activities. We will address the following questions.

- **How do teachers plan for literature-based instruction?**
- **How do teachers introduce the unit to English language learners?**
- **What steps do teachers use in implementing a literature-based unit?**
- **What can we learn from our instructional efforts with literature-based instruction?**

Let's begin with a discussion of the rationale and planning that goes into literature-based instruction.

How Do Teachers Plan for Literature-Based Instruction?

We know that informational texts provide an excellent literacy vehicle for English language learners, reinforcing language through content concepts that students encounter outside the sheltered environment of the ESL classroom. Indeed, Chamot and O'Malley (1994, p. 102) argue "that ESL instruction is moving in the direction of greater integration of language and content and that the development of academic-language proficiency will become the major objective of ESL instruction in schools." Clearly, continued progress in academic language proficiency is crucial to the success of English language learners as they deal with more content curriculum and standardized tests.

Using a topic or theme to connect learning activities across the curricular subjects, we can maximize the opportunity for transfer of knowledge from one lesson to another. In particular, for elementary classrooms, this approach can be utilized to reintroduce the science, social studies, and other curricular subjects that have been eliminated from the instructional day because of high-stakes testing and the reemphasis on reading, language arts, and math.

Which topics or themes we use depends on several variables, including the teacher's interest and expertise, the books and resources available, and the fit of the topic to the curricular objectives as well as to state and national standards (Vardell, 1995). Thematic strands can connect lessons in one subject area or across multiple subjects. However, it is also possible to link a topic in science, math, or social studies to the language arts strategies and activities that are the instructional focus, as well as to use fiction to add a personal dimension to the content. We will show how the topic of weather can be used to integrate all curricular areas using all major genres of literature along with other resources.

Planning Collaboratively

We have found that the planning process is especially engaging and motivating when done collaboratively. It is much easier when we share resources and generate ideas together. After discussing a topic idea at length, we use our own libraries of childrens' books, the local public library, and Internet resources like Amazon.com in planning, brainstorming, and investigating all available resources related to the topic at hand. When available, school libraries can also be invaluable in assessing the availability of books on certain topics. Library personnel are usually eager to help with this stage of the planning process.

When Nancy and her colleague from the high school originally planned this unit, they used the public library shelves as a resource file of ideas and spent time reflecting about possible topics as well as about the students, their language backgrounds, and their potential interest in various topics. After brainstorming options, they finally decided to focus on weather, integrating the related areas of seasons, weather phenomena, and weather disasters. While student choice certainly can drive unit selection, they based their decision for this unit on the link to the curriculum and the familiarity of concepts, knowing that the more background knowledge students bring to the page, the easier the process of comprehension (Allen, 1994). So, even if the English labels for weather concepts were not familiar, all English language learners would have experienced the concepts—some degree of seasonal change along with various weather phenomena and perhaps some weather disasters—wherever they had lived. The interplay of the culturally diverse students' geographic backgrounds would add another element of interest. Finally, linking literature with real world print resources, like current magazine and newspaper accounts of local weather-related happenings, can pique student interest further. Some possible areas of weather study that emerged from the brainstorming process included daily weather statistics, weather words, weather predictions, and weather concepts.

Using the multitude of children's books available, Nancy and JaNae considered instructional objectives, selected titles to tie to those planned literature-based activities for whole-class instruction, cooperative ?s, and individual reading (Chamot & O'Malley, 1994). Based on th ed a daily calendar of the unit—ideas, topics to be covered, re uage and content activities. The length of units varie de and language proficiency, anywhere from ? a month or two with secondary-level stud

Considering

A crucial part grounds, includi nds, and previous school experi entation of this unit was a self-con The eighteen students in the class n fourteen to nineteen. While the uage proficiency, the students re d listening. The class was compos grade reports sometimes reflected another anguage proficiency for the content classrooms. The unds reflected diverse geographic origins—Vietnam, Mexic opia—which offered great comparison-and-contrast opportunities duri uscussions. Additional variety was supplied by the amount of time the students had been in the United States. Some were newly arrived, such as a young Polish student whose father worked at the university; others had been in the country for several years, often with sporadic school attendance. All of these factors are important as you launch into any unit, particularly in terms of building background knowledge, filling in the gaps between students' experiences and the knowledge base needed.

How Do Teachers Introduce the Unit to English Language Learners?

To introduce the unit, teachers need to highlight various activities for the upcoming weeks. Students respond best when they can anticipate what is coming up and have some ownership in the progress of the unit. To begin with, students can emphasize concrete language and vocabulary by recording weather statistics (temperature, sun, clouds, precipitation, etc.) daily on a class chart. Several books can be used to lead into this activity, including Lee Bennett Hopkins' poem "A Week of Weather" from *Weather: Poems for All Seasons* (1994); poems for each month and each season in Marilyn Singer's *Turtle in July* (1989); and John Updike's poem collection, *A Child's Calendar* (1999), with a poem for each month of the year.

Students can incorporate their new vocabulary into a weather journal, more closely linking ESL with content instruction. The chart and the students' journals serve as sources of data for many interdisciplinary activities, such as graphing the temperature fluctuation from day to day, again connecting language learning and content exploration. Moreover, real world print resources from daily weather reports in newspapers, national weather maps and statistics, and weather-related Web sites combine the concepts from books students are reading with everyday text they encounter outside the classroom. It is also important to set up a classroom library that includes a display of weather books along with relevant objects like an umbrella, mittens, and sunglasses, and a featured author center, such as the one highlighted in Box 12.1, with the many weather books written by Gail Gibbons, for example.

What Steps Do Teachers Use in Implementing a Literature-Based Unit?

Introducing Vocabulary

The first instructional activities should furnish an overview of the topic. To accomplish this, Nancy and JaNae used two informational picture books, *Weather Words* (Gibbons, 1990) and *What Will the Weather Be?* (DeWitt, 1991), for read aloud and response. Prereading activities might include brainstorming for background knowledge (What words associated with weather do you know? Who is responsible for the weather predictions we read in newspapers and see on television?) and prediction strategies (How do we know what the weather will be each day? Based on the title, what do you think this book will be about?). Then the class can move through the books together, discussing new ideas and working on vocabulary through the visual–verbal connection—guessing the meaning of new terms from illustrations in the text and developing graphic aids to remember meanings (Moe, 1989; Neal & Moore, 1991/1992).

B O X 12.1

Five Fun Facts about Gail Gibbons

1. As a small child growing up in Oak Park, Illinois, Gail wrote stories, drew pictures to fit the words, and then put her books together using yarn to bind the pages.
2. Gail had a job creating television graphics, which led her to working on a children's show called *Take a Giant Step*, and later *Talk with a Giant*, which led to writing books for children.
3. Gail has written and illustrated more than a hundred nonfiction books for children.
4. Gail lives in a home that uses passive solar energy that she and her husband built themselves in Corinth, Vermont.
5. Gail makes maple syrup each spring with family and friends and markets it through the Goose Green Maple Syrup Company. All proceeds go to local Vermont charities.

Gail Gibbons' Home Page

http://www.gailgibbons.com/

Gibbons' use of clear and colorful cartoon illustrations combined with simple labeling and captioning helps English language learners learn basic weather terminology.

Gibbons, G. (1996). *Weather Words and What They Mean.* New York: Holiday House.

An especially useful visual–verbal technique that Nancy and JaNae tested is a graphic organizer, the continuum. Using this technique, the high school students discussed each weather word and its meaning and placed new vocabulary items for various kinds of rain (drizzle, shower, rain, rainstorm, flood), snow (flurry, sleet, snow, blizzard), and wind (breeze, wind, gale, tornado, hurricane) along continuums to denote increasing intensity. English language learners often find this graphic organizer activity useful in helping them remember vocabulary words and their meaning. For this exercise, a simple horizontal line is employed with each end reflecting the extremes (i.e., drizzle, flood). However, students can also work with a vertical continuum using font size to differentiate levels of intensity (see Figure 12.1).

Whatever the format chosen, teachers need to stress that there are different kinds of rain or wind, and that while words can be similar in meaning, not all synonyms are interchangeable. Poetry can also be tremendously helpful in introducing synonyms and nuances of meaning. Constance Levy's poem "Drizzle" from *A Tree Place and Other Poems* (1994) is one outstanding example. Later, students will enjoy illustrating their continuum

drizzle

shower

rain

rainstorm

thunderstorm

flood

FIGURE 12.1   Possible Continuum Depicting Intensity of Rain Words

Reprinted with permission from Children's Informational Picture Books Visit a Secondary ESL Classroom by N. L. Hadaway & J. Mundy, 1999, *Journal of Adolescent and Adult Literacy, 42,* 464–475.

or visual display of meaning with bolts of lightning, snowflakes, and cues to meaning. This activity focuses students on word choice and the picture they are painting in the reader's mind. Our results show that students began to incorporate this new vocabulary into their weather journals and class discussions to more precisely describe daily weather conditions.

Introducing Weather Concepts

Next, Nancy and JaNae focused more specifically on concepts related to the topic of weather. Reading aloud *What Will the Weather Be?* provided a rich source of content concepts introducing high- and low-pressure areas along with warm and cold fronts. The clear presentation of these weather concepts accompanied by illustrations offers the opportunity to incorporate a discussion of similarities and differences, leading to the text structure format of comparison and contrast. To capitalize on this organizational pattern, Nancy and JaNae differentiated the two types of fronts, warm and cold, using H-maps or comparison-and-contrast maps (Figure 12.2) (Hadaway & Mundy, 1999). The H-map works well, helping students recognize a specific text pattern, take notes, and write summary statements (Hadaway & Young, 1994). Consequently, teachers can incorporate this technique into other lessons, and English language learners can carry this strategy to their content classes. It can even be applied to two poems—for instance, "Deciduous" and "Evergreen" by Eve Merriam from her collection *The Singing Green* (1992).

For a unit including the language arts, teachers may want to use the five-novel approach or literature circles for deeper reading of core novels. This reading-workshop

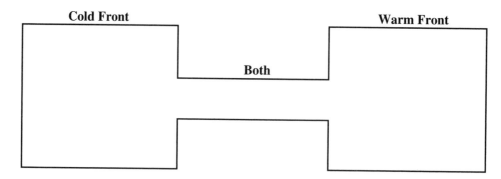

FIGURE 12.2   H-Map Comparing and Contrasting Warm and Cold Fronts

approach uses class sets of five copies of five books (more or less) selected for a variety of reading and proficiency levels. After a brief talk on the books by the teacher, each student chooses the one he/she prefers. Students read their novels, stopping periodically to discuss their books with their literature circle. Of course, the teacher monitors their progress, even assigning page deadlines at regular intervals, and conducts small-group and whole-class activities throughout the reading. Assessment of student comprehension occurs in small group conferences, as well as through a menu of response activities from which students can choose. One fifth grade teacher, Debi Young, had students keep a manila folder for all their work related to their novel. They illustrated the front cover with a book scene (that was not on the published cover) and filled the inside of the folder with a series of six to twelve blocks containing a picture and caption or a paragraph summarizing each book chapter. Her students enjoyed reporting on their reading in this highly visual way, and she felt confident they were doing the reading. In addition, she interspersed their individual work with planned instruction like vocabulary-building activities.

Reviewing Concepts and Vocabulary through Collage Word Art and Concrete Poems

As a review technique at this point in the unit, students can work in groups to make a collage of weather words and pictures cut from magazines and newspapers. The opportunity to browse through magazines and newspapers can reinforce their new weather knowledge and provide evidence that they have mastered the new concepts and vocabulary. As Nancy and JaNae taught the unit they heard students say, "Here's a good example of a rainstorm!" "Look at this tornado and all the damage!" Once the weather-word collage art is completed, the groups can present their product to the class with a short oral explanation, which also serves as an informal assessment of student comprehension of concepts and use of new vocabulary.

Books of concrete poetry can also be used to demonstrate how words and images work together to explain a concept. With concrete poems, the words are arranged on the page to suggest the visual image they describe. For example, "Winter" with its "spectacle of unexpected snow" and "First burst of spring" are two examples by J. Patrick Lewis

(*Doodle Dandies: Poems That Take Shape*, 1998) that show as well as tell about weather and weather images and moods. Graham also has a fun concrete poem about hail in her collection *Splish Splash* (1994). Students can use the weather words they are learning to create their own concrete poems, arranging definitions or associations to suggest the shape of a tornado, rainbow, or cloud, for example.

Taking Time for Independent Reading

Creating a specialized classroom library of weather books is an important part of the unit experience. Because there are more books about weather available than can be utilized in the unit, teachers can provide opportunities for students to expand on the information introduced in read aloud time with other resource books. Many of these supplemental books can be displayed as browsing books (e.g., *Storms*, Wood, 1990)—busy pages filled with chunks of text, illustrations with captions, and fascinating trivia—a format ideally suited for English language learners, nonreaders, and reluctant readers. (See Table 12.1 for examples of browsing books about weather.) Teachers know they are making an impact when students take advantage of free time, turning to these books to explore concepts of special interest to them or choosing weather books for their DEAR (drop everything and read) or SSR (Sustained Silent Reading) time. Students can jot their own responses to a book on a small self-adhesive note inside the book. In this way, students can informally share their own recommendations of good parts of good books with each other.

Creating Authentic Extensions

To engage the class in hands-on language activities, teachers and students can turn to informational books filled with easy-to-implement experiments. Using the book *Usborne Science and Experiments: The Power of Nature* (1997), teachers can model how authors prefer the format of the diagram to explain processes that are less clear in exposition or narrative writing. Experiments from *Be an Expert Weather Forecaster* (Taylor-Cork, 1992) and *Earth Science for Every Kid: 101 Easy Experiments That Really Work* (VanCleave, 1991) help show students how thermometers work, how to make raindrops in a jar, and how tiny water droplets grow into raindrops.

While making raindrops in a jar, students can explore precipitation, condensation, and evaporation. Then the class can follow up with Joanna Cole's famous Ms. Frizzle in

TABLE 12.1 Selected Weather Books for Browsing

- *National Audubon Society First Field Guide: Weather* by J. Kahl
- *Questions and Answers about Weather* by M. J. Craig
- *Weather* by Seymour Simon
- *The Weather Sky* by Bruce McMillan
- *What Will the Weather Be Like Today?* by P. Rogers
- *El Nino: Stormy Weather for People and Wildlife* by Caroline Arnold
- *Tornadoes* by Seymour Simon
- *Lightning* by Seymour Simon

The Magic School Bus at the Waterworks (1986) and read about an imaginary field trip through the water cycle. Students will quickly pick this up, excitedly calling out the vocabulary terms and remembering that they have previously explored this territory. In the high school classroom where Nancy taught these activities, students commented, "That's precipitation like we saw in the jar activity!" This response provided evidence that retention and transfer of concepts were occurring.

Extending the Unit: Wind, Rain, and Clouds

For more depth on the topic of weather, the class can move on to wind, rain, and clouds. Such extensions are easy, even if the textbook does not go into depth, because teachers can turn to more informational picture books, novels, storybooks, and poetry.

Wind.   For read aloud, the teacher can share *Feel the Wind* (Dorros, 1989) to lead into a discussion of what makes wind and the force of wind. From the resource, *Be an Expert Weather Forecaster* (Taylor-Cork, 1992), students can explore wind patterns such as the westerlies, doldrums, and trade winds and discover how wind is measured using the Beaufort scale. Afterward, when recording the daily weather statistics as a class, students can add their estimation of the force of the wind with the Beaufort scale. Poetry and picture books add a narrative dimension to the topic with "What Are You, Wind" by Mary O'Neill from *Spectacular Science* (Hopkins, 1999), selections from *Make Things Fly: Poems about Wind* edited by Dorothy Kennedy (1998), or the story of where things go when they blow away found in *Attic of the Wind* by Doris Lund (1966).

Rain.   Moving on, the class can read Using *What Makes It Rain? The Story of a Raindrop* (Brandt, 1982) as a springboard to the graphic organizer of the rain cycle from a science textbook, and students can talk through the process of precipitation, condensation, and evaporation. The cycle graphic organizer of the sequence of events is yet another technique you can utilize with both picture books and content texts, and it is a format that students can transfer to other content classes.

Fiction and poetry on the subject of rain are also abundant. Picture books like *One Monday Morning* (Shulevitz, 1967), *Where Does the Butterfly Go When It Rains?* (Garelick, 1961), *Rain Rain Rivers* (Shulevitz, 1988), Peter Spier's *Rain* (1982) and *Noah's Ark* (1992), *Ben's Dream* (Van Allsburg, 1982), and *Mushroom in the Rain* (Ginsburg, 1974) provide details and descriptions that add information, provide fantasy adventures, or convey a special mood and tone. The words and images of poetry offer yet another perspective on the subject of rain. Look for wordplay and word pictures in "Sidewalk Measles" from *The Sky Is Full of Song* (Hopkins, 1983), *James and the Rain* (Kuskin, 1995), and "Summer Rain" from *Rainy Day Stories and Poems* (Bauer, 1986).

Clouds.   Finally, share Tomie de Paola's *The Cloud Book* (1975), and examine the excellent illustrations from *Weather* (Smith, 1990) to study various types of clouds. After reading and discussing clouds and watching them outside, the class can experiment with the new descriptive vocabulary encountered by writing descriptions or even poems about clouds, first as a class and then in groups. DePaola paints vivid but concrete images of clouds, for instance, comparing cumulus clouds to cauliflower, which can help the students in their artistic renditions.

Beyond introducing specific types of clouds, *The Cloud Book* also uses amusing cartoon-like illustrations to present idioms: "he's in a fog," "she has her head in the clouds," "in the morning, mountains [of clouds], in the evening fountains [of rain]." Because figurative language is particularly confusing for students learning another language, these illustrations and related expressions provide a wonderful link to expressions associated with weather. With the help of the teacher, the class can brainstorm additional expressions—for example, raining cats and dogs—and search through phrase dictionaries such as *A January Fog Will Freeze a Hog* (Davis, 1977) to extend their knowledge. Following the use of nonfiction, stories and poems can add another layer of information and enjoyment on the subtopic of clouds. Simple picture books like *It Looked Like Spilt Milk* (Shaw, 1947), *Cloudy with a Chance of Meatballs* (Barrett & Barrett, 1978), *Sector 7* (Wiesner, 1999), or *Cloud Dance* (Locker, 2000) use the world of clouds to mystical or hilarious effect. A poem like "White Floating Clouds" in *The Earth Is Painted Green* (Brenner, 1994) uses science vocabulary in poetic ways.

Looking at Weather for All Seasons

Linking the topic of weather to the seasons is a natural transition, and several informational picture books, fiction, and poetry can be used. First, *Weather Forecasting* (Gibbons, 1987) presents each season and its associated vocabulary along with weather forecasting and weather maps. From previous study of warm and cold fronts, students can incorporate this information and apply it directly to reading and interpreting the weather maps in local newspapers. When Nancy led this activity with secondary English language learners, students found the demystification of weather maps and their many symbols exciting. With newspapers available in the class each day, these high school students began to pore over the weather maps and share their forecast predictions. Follow this discussion with poems selected from Arnold Adoff's *In for Winter, Out for Spring* (1991), and compare how news reports of weather and poems about weather differ in their use of language.

Exploring the seasons further, you can incorporate resources such as *Autumn Weather* (Mason, 1991), *The Reason for the Seasons* (Gibbbons, 1995), *Winter across America* (Simon, 1994), and *Autumn across America* (Simon, 1993) for facts and impressions of the seasons. Then the class can brainstorm a semantic map, noting representative weather patterns, colors, activities, clothing, and holidays connected with the seasons. Students can reproduce this map on their own paper to use as a vocabulary bank for future activities related to the seasons. This exercise may generate some lively discussion and sharing as you talk about the typical American presentation of the seasons. For instance, when Nancy led a brainstorming session about winter with the high school ESL class, students offered terms such as *snow, sledding, skiing.* Nancy asked if those were really typical of their new home, Texas, or even of their previous homes. This led to a sharing of personal examples from their home countries and a discussion of how books, movies, and the media shape our images and expectations of the seasons. For example, Seymour Simon's books *Autumn across America* and *Winter across America* use visual images that are typical northeastern U.S. representations of the seasons (i.e., snow and ice for winter), but the text notes the wide range of climatic conditions for the seasons according to the different geographic regions.

Using the semantic map as a vocabulary builder and prewriting technique, Nancy and JaNae next had the class paste up poetry. In groups, students clipped words and phrases from magazines and newspapers about the season of their choice. They arranged their words and phrases into a poem, placing the words and phrases anywhere on the page. Class members shared their pasted-up poems, and everyone guessed which season was being described. This proved to be a good oral language workout. This activity can then be linked to a discussion of seasonal holidays—for example, Groundhog Day and its tradition of predicting the end of winter. The riddle poems of *Where Do Fish Go in Winter and Answers to Other Great Mysteries* (Koss, 1987) prompt student questions and discussion. Poetry from Leland Jacobs' collection *Just around the Corner: Poems about the Seasons* (1993), David Booth's anthology *Voices on the Wind: Poems for All Seasons* (1990), Myra Cohn Livingston's *A Circle of Seasons* (1982), or Jane Yolen's collection *Snow, Snow: Winter Poems for Children* (1998) can be compared to their paste up poetry creations.

Writing about Weather

With all this scaffolding, English language learners are eventually ready to try their hands at some creative writing. They may enjoy sharing family weather stories, such as the time the family sat in the bathtub during a tornado warning, or writing personal experience narratives about weather-related adventures they have had (camping, playing in the rain, building snow creatures, etc.). For more poetry writing, you can introduce the format of diamante poems and generate an example as a class. Students can work individually or with a partner to write a diamante on one season or to create one comparing and contrasting two seasons. See Table 12.2 for instructions on writing a diamante.

When Nancy worked with JaNae to teach the weather unit with high school ESL students, most students created bilingual diamantes that they posted around the classroom. Students enjoyed circulating to view the bilingual versions and compare English and native language versions. Box 12.2, offers one example of a Spanish-English diamante by a high school ESL student that compares and contrasts fall and spring (Hadaway & Mundy, 1999).

Researching Weather Disasters

As a culminating activity or to take the unit even farther and incorporate an extended research project for intermediate and advanced proficiency students, students can research weather-related disasters—floods, hurricanes, and tornadoes—or other weather topics of interest to them. For any student, but particularly for middle and high school English language learners, picture books can be a less intimidating—and often a more interesting—introduction into research and can serve as a prereading introduction to the typical reference book in the school library. Informational picture books such as *Storms* (Wood, 1990), *Natural Wonders and Disasters* (Goodman, 1991), *Flood* (Waters, 1991), *Hurricane* (Archer, 1991), *Hurricanes: Earth's Mightiest Storms* (Lauber, 1996), *Tornado!*

TABLE 12.2   Writing a Diamante Poem

Definition of a Diamante: A seven-line contrast poem written in shape of a diamond; applies knowledge of opposites and parts of speech.

Line 1: one noun as subject
Line 2: two adjectives describing subject
Line 3: three participles (ending in *-ing*) telling about subject
Line 4: four nouns (first two related to subject, second two related to the opposite)
Line 5: three participles telling about the opposite
Line 6: two adjectives describing the opposite
Line 7: one noun that is the opposite of the subject

(Graf, 1999), and *Tornado Alert* (Branley, 1988) along with real world print sources can be put to use to discover more about topics. The class can work in cooperative groups using the jigsaw method.

First, however, it is important to think aloud about the research process students will be using and to create a master rubric. Since tornadoes are common in Texas, Nancy started with that weather disaster in leading high school ESL students in this activity. The

B O X   12.2

Student-Generated Bilingual Diamante Comparing Two Seasons

fall
briskly crisply
cloudy yellow sleepy
falling changing growing raining
sunny new happy
happily warmly
spring

otono
ligero seco
nublado amarillo dormir
callendo cambiando naciendo lloviendo
soliado nuevo feliz
feliz caloroso
verano

Student Generated Bilingual Diamante Comparing Two Seasons reprinted with permission from Children's Informational Picture Books Visit a Secondary ESL Classroom by N. L. Hadaway & J. Mundy, 1999, *Journal of Adolescent and Adult Literacy, 42,* 464–475.

students generated questions to focus their search for information. These general questions were extended to all weather disasters under examination as students devised a jot chart to guide their note-taking. Table 12.3 shows the format the class finally devised to help with the research efforts. With this structured format, students are able to define the disaster; record specific seasons associated with it; cite causes and effects (to property, people, and weather); and note famous disasters in each category, interesting facts, specific geographic zones where each disaster might occur, and any prevention or precautionary measures.

Proceeding through three steps, the groups implement the jigsaw. First, the group chooses one member to become an expert on a weather disaster. Next, the experts meet and complete the jot chart. Finally, once experts amass the necessary information, they return to their original groups to debrief and teach others about their specific weather disaster.

Once this activity is completed, the students move to the library for more detailed research. By this point, the informational children's books have provided a prereading

TABLE 12.3   Jot Chart for Research Activity

	Floods	**Hurricanes**	**Tornadoes**
Define this weather disaster.			
What specific seasons (if any) are associated with this weather disaster?			
What are the causes of this weather disaster?			
What are the effects of this weather disaster on property? On people? On weather?			
Note some famous disasters for each type of weather disaster (year, location, name, if applicable).			
Cite at least three interesting facts associated with each disaster.			
Note specific geographic regions where each disaster might occur.			
Note any prevention or precautionary measures that might be taken for each disaster.			

Reprinted with permission from Children's Informational Picture Books Visit a Secondary ESL Classroom by N. L. Hadaway & J. Mundy, 1999, *Journal of Adolescent and Adult Literacy, 42,* 464–475.

framework to help English language learners conduct independent research using standard reference materials. For this phase of the study, students research a famous flood, tornado, or hurricane. They note when and where (using a map) it occurred, the extent of damage (physical property costs, loss of life, real world damage), any reconstruction or rebuilding costs, and preventive measures for future occurrences. In the high school ESL class Nancy worked with, one student was intrigued by Patricia Lauber's description of Hurricane Andrew in *Hurricanes: Earth's Mightiest Storms* (1996) and chose that storm and its destructive path across south Florida to highlight.

In reporting their research results, students create a poster session or a Power Point® presentation about their specific weather disaster. During this culminating activity, students tackle the regular library materials well after the informational picture books have laid the foundation, so they feel more confident using academically challenging texts. Students who particularly enjoy this area of study may want to continue with the topic in their recreational reading, choosing survival stories for their free time. Once a topic like this has been explored in such depth, it is amazing what a long life it will have in students' conversations, connections, and ongoing reading and writing choices.

What Can We Learn from Our Instructional Efforts with Literature-Based Instruction?

Nancy conducted much of this unit in a high school ESL classroom over a period of two months. In collaboration with the regular teacher, the focus was primarily on using nonfiction, especially informational picture books. While very pleased with the student involvement in the unit and with the learning that occurred, Nancy and JaNae also spent time reflecting afterward on how the unit could be improved. This is an important part of thematic or interdisciplinary teaching that helps us improve.

First, the use of informational picture books provides a natural connection to the often-dreaded content textbook since both generally use an expository style of writing. Students struggle with the difficult format of textbooks, and informational books serve as an instructional bridge to textbooks (Allen, 1994). One suggestion for using informational picture books is to make specific reference to the external aids as well as to the internal structure of the text (Law & Eckes, 1990). Nancy and JaNae made some initial jaunts into internal text structure when they worked with the comparison-and-contrast structure of warm and cold fronts and when they read about the rain cycle and examined a textbook graph. Yet, while they drew student attention to language patterns, concepts, and vocabulary from the books, they failed to directly walk students through the external aids to comprehension—pictures, maps, italics, boldface print, size and shapes of words to signal relative importance—and then, to compare these aids to the ones used in content textbooks.

Second, the informational picture books Nancy and JaNae selected were a success with the students, especially the browsing books. The class enjoyed the books' colorful, reader-friendly instructive format. Nevertheless, age appropriateness is a key issue in materials selection (Allen, 1994). We believe that teachers are pivotal to the success of the process, first in the selection of materials and next in their presentation. As we examine literature options, we always place ourselves in the position of the audience. If we are engaged by a text and its information and not put off by the illustrations or formatting, then the material has passed our first test. We would advocate, for instance, that any of Seymour Simon's books has universal appeal to children and adults. On closer examination, we consider the author's writing style, accuracy of content, and interest level of the text.

Just as crucial as selection is instructional presentation. Nancy and JaNae approached the weather unit confident about the materials, and they communicated their enthusiasm about the selected books to the students, likening these informational picture books to a preparation phase for later reading and writing activities. Indeed, students stepped up to the challenge of library research after the foundation was laid through informational picture books. In fact, Nancy and JaNae shared their own fascination with specific text examples and commented on the new material they were learning through the use of these resources. As students spent free time browsing through the classroom library of weather books, Nancy and JaNae modeled engaged reading, excitedly looking through books and sharing fascinating bits of trivia with each other. For instance, did you know that "the most snow to fall in a year was at Paradise, Mount Rainier, in the winter of 1971. About 1,224 inches fell, enough to reach a third of the way up the Statue of Liberty!" (Wood, 1990, p. 11).

Finally, while Nancy and JaNae made good use of real world print from newspapers and magazines, they neglected other familiar visual mediums. A motivational prelude to the unit with video clips of radar screens and weather maps from televised weather reports can pique interest and fold naturally into brainstorming for students' background knowledge and prereading predictions about the specific informational picture books. Moreover, with the increasing availability of Internet in schools and individual classrooms, students can access a host of Web sites with weather radar updates and forecasts. They could have confirmed their information by tuning into the Weather Channel or accessing a weather Web site via the Internet. Another forgotten visual connection was video; the Weather Channel, for example, offers various affordable videos about weather phenomena, any one of which would have worked well with the books selected for the jigsaw activity during the final research prior to the library phase. For our many visual learners and for English language learners who need the added visual context to support the comprehension of print concepts, connecting print with media makes sense. Obviously, there are countless ways to fine-tune an instructional unit. These three points represent just a few of the more important considerations that emerged from reflections as Nancy and JaNae moved through the process of implementing the unit.

Checking It Out: Assessing the Weather Unit

Various forms of assessment were used throughout the actual implementation of this weather unit, and many more were possible. To track student progress throughout the unit, teachers can use a grid similar to the one in Table 12.4 to indicate the assignments in a unit and provide space for student self-assessment and teacher assessment.

TABLE 12.4 Weather Unit Tracking Sheet

Name_____ **Date of Completion**_____

Assignment and Points	Student's Check	Teacher's Check
1. Reading log for all weather books read (5)		
2. Weather words continuum (5)		
3. Weather journal (10)		
4. H-map (5)		
5. Novel or literature circle journal (10)		
6. Word collage (5)		
7. Concrete poem (5)		
8. Experiment write-up (5)		
9. Extension activities (10)		
10. Diamante (5)		
11. Paste-up poetry (5)		
12. Family weather story (10)		
13. Jot chart (5)		
14. Research project (15)		
Total Points		

Teacher Comments:

Summary

Research can inform and transform. That is the premise of this chapter as we put to use all the information from the previous chapters. Here we see that literature-based instruction has much to offer students, especially English language learners. This chapter presents the framework for a weather unit based on informational picture books used in conjunction with related fiction and poetry.

The results of the unit were positive; students were actively engaged with text. The short length and visual nature of picture books, in particular, helped English language learners comprehend the concepts presented, and through class discussions and written work related to the unit, we saw an increase in their vocabulary. Also, the students benefited from the cooperative nature of the lessons, practicing listening and speaking skills and learning new concepts and labels for familiar physical phenomena from each other. To demonstrate their comprehension, they wrote about the weather and seasons in journals, and poetry, and research presentations. Plus, due to the interdisciplinary nature of the unit, links to other areas of the curriculum were made. Even after the unit ended, students were inclined to begin class with a weather report noting the temperature, cloud conditions, and so on. Using informational picture books provided the necessary scaffolding for acquiring new knowledge. So, it seems that many of us are already aware that "one way to get an overview of a topic is to consult a picture book" (Freeman 1991, p. 471).

PROFESSIONAL REFERENCES

Ada, A. F., Harris, V., & Hopkins, L. B. (1993). *A chorus of cultures: Developing literacy through multicultural poetry.* Carmel, CA: Hampton-Brown Books.

Adams, M. J. (1990). *Beginning to read: Thinking and learning about print.* Cambridge, MA: MIT Press.

Allen, V. G. (1986). Developing contexts to support second language acquisition. *Language Arts, 63,* 61–66.

Allen, V. G. (1989). Literature as a support to language acquisition. In P. Rigg & V. G. Allen (Eds.), *When they don't all speak English: Integrating the ESL student into the regular classroom* (pp. 55–64). Urbana, IL: National Council of Teachers of English.

Allen, V. G. (1994). Selecting materials for the reading instruction of ESL children. In K. Spangenberg-Urbschat & R. Pritchard (Eds.), *Kids come in all languages: Reading instruction for ESL students* (pp. 108–131). Newark, DE: International Reading Association.

Allington, R. L., & Cunningham, P. M. (1996). *Schools that work: Where all children read and write.* New York: HarperCollins.

Alvermann, D. E. (1991). The discussion web: A graphic aid for learning across the curriculum. *The Reading Teacher, 45,* 92–99.

Alvermann, D. E., & Phelps, S. E. (1994). *Content reading and literacy: Succeeding in today's diverse classrooms.* Boston: Allyn & Bacon.

Ammon, B. D., & Sherman, G. W. (1996). *Worth a thousand words: An annotated guide to picture books for older readers.* Englewood, CO: Libraries Unlimited.

Anders, P. L., & Bos, C. (1986). Semantic feature analysis: An interactive strategy for vocabulary development and text comprehension. *Journal of Reading, 29,* 610–616.

Anders, P. L., Bos, C. S., & Wilde, S. (1986). *The effects of vocabulary strategies on the reading comprehension and vocabulary learning of junior high students.* Paper presented at the Thirty-Sixth National Reading Conference, Austin, TX.

Anderson, R. C., Hiebert, E. H., Scott, J. A., & Wilkinson, I. A. G. (1985). *Becoming a nation of readers: The report of the commission on reading.* Washington, DC: The National Institute for Education.

Andrews, L. (1998). *Language exploration and awareness: A resource book for teachers* (2nd ed.). New York: Longman.

Aoki, E. (1992). Turning the page: Asian Pacific American Children's literature. In V. J. Harris (Ed.), *Teaching multicultural literature in grades K–8* (pp.

109–135). Norwood, MA: Christopher-Gordon.

Asher, J. (1982). *Learning another language through actions: The complete teachers' guidebook.* Los Gatos, CA: Sky Oaks.

Atwell, N. (1987). *In the middle: Writing, reading, and learning with adolescents.* Portsmouth, NH: Boynton/Cook.

Au, K. (1993). *Literacy instruction in multicultural settings.* Ft. Worth, TX: Harcourt Brace Jovanovich.

Aukerman, R. C. (1972). *Reading in the secondary school.* New York: McGraw Hill.

Ausubel, D. P. (1968). *Educational psychology: A cognitive view.* New York: Holt, Rinehart and Winston.

Bagert, B. (1992). Act it out: Making poetry come alive. In B. Cullinan (Ed.), *Invitation to read: More children's literature in the reading program* (pp. 14–23). Newark, DE: International Reading Association.

Bailey, K. M. (1983). Competitiveness and anxiety in adult second language learning: Looking at and through the diary studies. In H. W. Seliger & M. H. Long (Eds.), *Classroom oriented research in second language acquisition.* Rowley, MA: Newbury House.

Bamford, R. A., & Kristo, J. V. (2000). *Checking it out nonfiction K–8: Good choices for best learning.* Norwood, MA: Christopher-Gordon.

Barron, R. (1979). Research for the classroom teacher: Recent developments on the structured overview as an advance organizer. In H. Herber & J. Riley (Eds.), *Research in reading in the content areas: The fourth report.* Syracuse, NY: Syracuse University Reading and Language Arts Center.

Bauer, C. F. (1995). *The poetry break: An annotated anthology with ideas for introducing children to poetry.* New York: H. W. Wilson.

Bean, T., Sorter, J., Singer, H., & Frazee, C. (1986). Teaching students how to make predictions about events in history with a graphic organizer plus options guide. *Journal of Reading, 29,* 739–745.

Beebe, L. M. (1983). Risk-taking and the language learner. In H. W. Seliger & M. H. Long (Eds.), *Classroom oriented research in second language acquisition.* Rowley, MA: Newbury House.

Berko-Gleason, J. (1982). Insights from child acquisition for second language loss. In R. D. Lambert & B. F. Freed (Eds.), *The loss of language skills.* Rowley, MA: Newbury House.

Bernhardt, E. B. (2000). Second-language reading as a case study of reading scholarship in the 20th century. In M. L. Kamil, P. B. Mosenthal, P. D. Pearson, & Barr, R. (Eds.), *Handbook of reading research* (pp. 791–811). Mahwah, NJ: Lawrence Erlbaum.

Bishop, R. S. (1992). Multicultural literature for children: Making informed choices. In V. J. Harris (Ed.), *Teaching multicultural literature in grades K–8* (pp. 37–53). Norwood, MA: Christopher-Gordon.

Bishop, R. S. (1997). Selecting literature for a multicultural curriculum. In V. J. Harris (Ed), *Using multiethnic literature in the K–8 classroom* (pp. 1–19). Norwood, MA: Christopher-Gordon.

Bourne, B., & Saul, W. (1994). *Using Seymour Simon's astronomy books in the classroom.* New York: Morrow.

Bradley, J., & Thalgott, M. (1987). Reducing reading anxiety. *Academic Therapy, 22,* 349–358.

Bratcher, S. (1994). *Evaluating children's writing: A handbook of communication choices for classroom teachers.* New York: St. Martin's Press.

Britton, J. (1970). *Language and learning.* London: Allen Lane.

Britton, J., Burgess, T., Martin, N., McLeod, A., & Rosen, H. (1975). *The development of writing abilities: 11–18.* London: Macmillan.

Brodkey, D., & Shore, H. (1976). Student personality and success in an English language program. *Language Learning, 26,* 153–159.

Brown, H. D. (1994). *Principles of language learning and teaching* (3rd ed.). Englewood Cliffs, NJ: Prentice Hall.

Browne, H., & Cambourne, B. (1990). *Read and retell.* Portsmouth, NH: Heinemann.

Brozo, W. G., & Simpson, M. L. (1995). *Readers, teachers, learners: Expanding literacy in secondary schools.* Englewood Cliffs, NJ: Prentice-Hall.

Brunvand, J. H. (1989a). *Curses! Broiled again! The hottest urban legends going.* New York: W. W. Norton.

Brunvand, J. H. (1989b). *The vanishing hitchhiker: American urban legends and their meanings.* New York: W. W. Norton.

Buchoff, R. (1995). Family stories. *The Reading Teacher, 49,* 230–233.

Buehl, D. (1995). *Classroom strategies for interactive learning.* Madison, WI: Wisconsin State Reading Association.

Calkins, L. M. (1986). *The art of teaching writing.* Portsmouth, NH: Heineman.

Cambourne, B. (1988). *The whole story: Natural learning and acquisition of literacy in the classroom.* Auckland, NZ: Ashton Scholastic.

Carr, E., & Ogle, D. (1987). K-W-L Plus: A strategy for comprehension and summarization. *Journal of Reading, 30,* 626–631.

Carrell, P., Devine, J., & Eskey, D. (1988). *Interactive approaches to second language reading.* Cambridge: Cambridge University Press.

Cary, S. (1997). *Second language learners.* York, ME: Stenhouse Publishers.

Chambers, A. (1996). *The reading environment: How adults help children enjoy books.* York, ME: Stenhouse Publishers.

Chamot, A. U., & O'Malley, J. M. (1989). The cognitive academic language learning approach. In P. Rigg & V. G. Allen (Eds.), *When they all don't speak English: Integrating the English as a second language student into the regular classroom* (pp. 108–125). Urbana, IL: National Council of Teachers of English.

Chamot, A. U., & O'Malley, J. M. (1987). The cognitive academic language learning approach: A bridge to the mainstream. *TESOL Quarterly, 21,* 238.

Chamot, A. U., & O'Malley, J. M. (1994). Instructional approaches and teaching procedures. In K. Spangenberg-Urbschat & R. Pritchard (Eds.), *Kids come in all languages: Reading instruction for ESL students* (pp. 82–107). Newark, DE: International Reading Association.

Chatton, Barbara. (1993). *Using poetry across the curriculum: A whole language approach.* Phoenix, AZ: Oryx.

Chermayeff, I., Wasserman, F., & Shapiro, M. J. (1991). *Ellis Island: An Illustrated history of the immigrant experience.* New York: Macmillan.

Chomsky, C. (1971). Write first, read later. *Childhood Education, 47*(6), 296–299.

Christenbury, L. (1992). "The guy who wrote this poem seems to have the same feelings as you have": Reader-response methodology. In N. J. Karolides (Ed.), *Reader response in the classroom: Evoking and interpreting meaning in literature* (pp. 33–44). New York: Longman.

Christison, M. A., & Bassano, S. (1995). Expanding student learning styles through poetry. In J. M. Reid (Ed.), *Learning styles in the ESL/EFL classroom* (pp. 96–107). Boston: Heinle & Heinle.

Cianciolo, P. (1993). Folktale variants: Links to the never-ending chain. In G. T. Blatt (Ed.), *Once upon a folktale* (pp. 80–93). New York: Teachers College Press.

CIERA. (2000). *Improving the reading achievement of America's children* [On-line]. Available: www.ciera.org/ciera/information/principles/.

Clay, M. M. (1987). *Writing begins at home: Preparing children for writing before they go to school.* Portsmouth, NH: Heinemann.

Coles, G. (1998). *Reading lessons: The debate over literacy.* New York: Hill and Wang.

Collier, V. P. (1989). How long? A synthesis of research on academic achievement in a second language. *TESOL Quarterly, 23,* 509–531.

Collier, V. P., & Thomas, W. P. (1989). How quickly can immigrants become proficient in school English? *Journal of Educational Issues of Language Minority Students, 16,* 187–212.

Cooper, J. D. (1993, Winter). Helping children construct meaning: A changing view of literacy learning.

Educators' Forum, 1–2.

Cooper, J. D. (2000). *Literacy: Helping children construct meaning.* Boston: Houghton Mifflin.

Copeland, J., & Copeland, V. (1993). *Speaking of poets.* Urbana, IL: National Council of Teachers of English.

Copeland, J., & Copeland, V. (1994). *Speaking of poets 2.* Urbana, IL: National Council of Teachers of English.

Cortes, C. E. (1994). Multiculturation: An educational model for a culturally and linguistically diverse society. In K. Spangenberg-Urbschat & R. Pritchard (Eds.), *Kids come in all languages: Reading instruction for ESL students* (pp. 22–35). Newark, DE: International Reading Association.

Crafton, L. (1983). Learning from reading: What happens when students generate their own background information? *Journal of Reading, 26*, 586–593.

Crawford, J. (1992). *Hold your tongue: Bilingualism and the politics of "English only."* Reading, MA: Addison-Wesley.

Crawford, J. (1995). *Bilingual education: History, politics, theory, and practice* (3rd ed.). Los Angeles: Bilingual Educational Services.

Crowhurst, M. (1992). Some effects of corresponding with an older audience. *Language Arts, 69*, 268–273.

Cullinan, B. E. (1987). *Children's literature in the reading program.* Newark, DE: International Reading Association.

Cullinan, B., Scala, M., & Schroder, V. (1995). *Three voices: An invitation to poetry across the curriculum.* York, ME: Stenhouse Publishers.

Cummins, J. E. (1980). The construct of language proficiency in bilingual education. In J. E. Alatis (Ed.), *Georgetown University roundtable on language and linguistics* (pp. 76–93). Washington, DC: University Press.

Cummins, J. (1981). The role of primary language development in promoting educational success for language minority students. In California State Department of Education (Ed.), *Schooling of language minority students: A theoretical framework* (pp. 3–49). Los Angeles: Evaluation, Dissemination, and Assessment Center, California State University.

Cunningham, P. M., & Allington, R. L. (1999). *Classrooms that work: They can all read and write.* New York: Longman.

Dale, H. (1997). *Co-authoring in the classroom: Creating an environment for effective collaboration.* Urbana, IL: National Council of Teachers of English.

Delahunty, G. P., & Garvey, J. J. (1994). *Language, grammar and communication: A course for teachers of English.* New York: McGraw-Hill.

Delpit, L. (1995). *Other people's children: Cultural conflict in the classroom.* New York: The New Press.

Devine, T. G. (1989). *Teaching reading in the elementary school: From theory to practice.* Boston: Allyn & Bacon.

Diaz, D. M. (1986). The writing process and the ESL writer: Reinforcement from second language research. *The Writing Instructor, 5*, 167–175.

Diaz-Rico, L. T., & Weed, K. Z. (1995). *The cross-cultural, language and academic development handbook: A complete K–12 reference guide.* Boston: Allyn & Bacon.

Dolly, M. R. (1990). Integrating ESL reading and writing through authentic discourse. *Journal of Reading, 33*, 360–365.

Dufflemeyer, F., Baum, D., & Merkley, D. (1987). Maximizing reader-text confrontation with an extended anticipation guide. *Journal of Reading, 31,* 146–151.

Dulay, H. C., & Burt, M. K. (1974). Errors and strategies in child second language acquisition. *TESOL Quarterly, 8*, 129–136.

Edelsky, C. (1981). From "JIMOSALCO" to "7 naranjas se calleron e el arbol-est-triste en lagrymas": Writing development in a bilingual program. In B. Cronnel (Ed.), *The writing needs of linguistically different students* (pp. 63–98). Los Alamitos, CA: Southwest Regional Laboratory.

Elley, W. (1991). Acquiring literacy in a second language: The effect of book-based programs. *Language Learning, 41*, 375–411.

Elley, W. B., & Mangubhai, F. (1983). The impact of reading on second language learning. *Reading Research Quarterly*, 19, 53–67.

Emig, J. (1971). *The composing processes of twelfth graders.* Champaign, IL: National Council of Teachers of English.

Ervin-Tripp, S. (1974). Is second language learning like the first? *TESOL Quarterly, 8*, 111–127.

Fagin, L. (1991). *The list poem: A guide to teaching and writing catalog verse.* New York: Teachers and Writers Collaborative.

Farnan, N., Lapp, D., & Flood, J. (1992). Changing perspectives in writing instruction. *Journal of Reading, 35*, 550–556.

Ferguson, P. M., & Young, T. A. (1996). Literature talk: Dialogue improvisations and patterned conversations with second language learners. *Language Arts, 73,* 597–600.

Fisher, B. (1989). The environment reflects the program. *Teaching K–8, 20*, 82, 84, 86.

Fitzgerald, J. (1993). Teachers' knowing about knowledge: Its significance for classroom writing instruction. *Language Arts, 70*, 282–289.

Fortson, L., & Reiff, J. (1995). *Early childhood curriculum.* Boston: Allyn & Bacon.

Fountas, I. C., & Pinnell, G. S. (1996). *Guided reading instruction: Good first teaching for all children.* Portsmouth, NH: Heinemann.

Franklin, E. A. (1986). Literacy instruction for LES children. *Language Arts, 63,* 51–60.

Freeman, D. E., & Freeman, Y. S. (1994). *Between worlds: Access to second language acquisition.* Portsmouth, NH: Heinemann.

Freeman E. B. (1991). Informational books: Models for student report writing. *Language Arts, 68,* 470–473.

Friedberg, B., & Strong, E. (1989). "Please don't stop there!": The power of reading aloud. In J. Hickman & B. E. Cullinan (Eds.), *Children's literature in the classroom: Weaving Charlotte's web* (pp. 39–48). Needham Heights, MA: Christopher-Gordon.

Fromkin, V., & Rodman, R. (1993). *An introduction to language* (5th ed.). Ft. Worth, TX: Harcourt Brace.

Gagne, E. D., Yekovich, C. W., & Yekovich, F. R. (1993). *The cognitive psychology of school learning* (2nd ed.). New York: HarperCollins.

Gardner, R. C., & Lambert, W. E. (1972). *Attitudes and motivation in second language learning.* Rowley, MA: Newbury House.

Gasparro, M., & Falletta, B. (1994, April). *Creating drama with poetry: Teaching English as a second language through dramatization and improvisation.* Washington, DC: ERIC Clearinghouse on Languages and Linguistics. (ED 368 214)

Gere, A. R. (1985). *Roots in the sawdust: Writing to learn across the disciplines.* Urbana, IL: National Council of Teachers of English.

Gibbons, P. (1993). *Learning to learn in a second language.* Portsmouth, NH: Heinemann.

Gill, S. (1996). Shared book experience with poetry. *The State of Reading, Journal of the Texas State Reading Association, 3*(1), 27–30.

Gillespie, J. S. (1993). Buddy book journals: Responding to literature. *English Journal, 82,* 64–68.

Gillespie, J. T. (1998). *Best books for children: Preschool through grade 6.* New Providence, NJ: R. R. Bowker.

Glazer, S. M. (1992). *Reading comprehension: Self-monitoring strategies to develop independent readers.* New York: Scholastic.

Gollnick, D. M., & Chinn, P. C. (1998). *Multicultural education in a pluralistic society* (5th ed.). Upper Saddle River, NJ: Merrill.

Golub, J. (1994). *Activities for an interactive classroom.* Urbana, IL: National Council of Teachers of English.

Gonzales, F. (1993). Creating education that works: Building bilingual teacher competences. *Intercultural Development Research Association Newsletter, 20,* 4–8.

Gonzales, F., Alvarado, A., Crow, M. I., Sánchez, M. J. G., Jiménez, M., Menchaca, M. E., & Rives, P. D. (1995). *Starting today. . . . Steps to success for beginning bilingual educators.* San Antonio: Intercultural Development Research Association.

Gonzalez, R. D. (1982). Teaching Mexican American students to write: Capitalizing on culture. *English Journal, 71,* 20–24.

Goodman, K., Goodman, Y., & Flores, B. (1979). *Reading in a bilingual classroom.* Rosslyn, VA: National Clearinghouse for Bilingual Education.

Goodman, K. S., Shannon, P., Freeman, Y. S., & Murphy, S. (1988). *Report card on basal readers.* Katonah, NY: Richard C. Owen Publishers.

Grabe, W. (1991). Current developments in second language reading research. *TESOL Quarterly, 25*(3), 375–400.

Graham, C. (1978a). *Jazz chants.* New York: Oxford University Press.

Graham, C. (1978b). *Jazz chants for children.* New York: Oxford University Press

Graham, C. (1986). *Small talk.* New York: Oxford University Press.

Graham, C. (1988). *Jazz chant fairy tales.* New York: Oxford University Press.

Graves, D. (1983). *Writing: Teachers and children at work.* Portsmouth, NH: Heineman.

Graves, M., & Graves, B. (1994). *Scaffolding reading experiences: Designs for student success.* Norwood, MA: Christopher-Gordon.

Greenlaw, M. J., Shepperson, G. M., & Nistler, R. J. (1992). A literature approach to teaching about the Middle Ages. *Language Arts, 69,* 200–204.

Guiora, A. Z., Beit-Hallami, B., Brannon, R. C., Dull, C. Y., & Scovel, T. (1972). The effects of experimentally induced changes in ego states on pronunciation ability in second language: An exploratory study. *Comprehensive Psychiatry, 13,* 30–42.

Gunning, T. (2000). *Best books for building literacy for elementary school children.* Boston: Allyn & Bacon.

Hadaway, N. L. (1990). Reading and writing for real purposes in the English as a second language classroom. *Reading Education in Texas, 6,* 67–75.

Hadaway, N. L., & Cukor-Avila, P. (1987). Dual language input, dual language output: Writing in an elementary bilingual program. *Papers in Applied Linguistics—Michigan, 3,* 46–63.

Hadaway, N. L., & Mundy, J. (1992). Crossing curricular and cultural boundaries: A study of families and family folklore. *English Journal, 81*(6), 60–64.

Hadaway, N. L., & Mundy, J. (1999). Children's informational picture books visit a secondary ESL classroom. *Journal of Adolescent and Adult Literacy, 42,* 464–475.

Hadaway, N. L., Vardell, S. M., & Young, T. A. (2001). *Content literacy through nonfiction for English language learners.* Manuscript submitted for publication.

Hadaway, N. L., & Young, T. A. (1994). Content literacy and second language learning: Instructional decisions. *The Reading Teacher, 47,* 522–527.

Hade, D. (1997). Reading multiculturally. In V. J. Harris (Ed.), *Using multiethnic literature in the K–8 classroom* (pp. 253–256). Norwood, MA: Christopher-Gordon.

Haggard, H. L. (1982). The vocabulary self-collection

strategy: An active approach to word learning. *Journal of Reading, 26,* 203–207.

Haggard, M. (1989). Instructional strategies for developing student interest in content area subjects. In D. Lapp, J. Flood, & Farnan (Eds.), *Content area reading and learning: Instructional strategies* (pp. 70–80). Englewood Cliffs, NJ: Prentice Hall.

Hall, M. A. (1988). Beyond phonics to language-centered learning. In J. L. Davidson (Ed.), *Counterpoint and beyond: A response to "Becoming a nation of readers"* (pp. 25–50). Urbana, IL: National Council of Teachers of Reading.

Halliday, M. A. K. (1978). Language structure and language function. In J. Lyons (Ed.), *New horizons in linguistics* (pp. 140–165). Hamondsworth, England: Penguin.

Halliday, M. A. (1989). *Spoken and written language.* New York: Oxford University Press.

Hamayan, E., & Pfleger, M. (1987). *Developing literacy in English as a second language: Guidelines for teachers of young children from non-literature backgrounds.* National Clearinghouse for Bilingual Education. Teacher Resource Guide Series, No. 1.

Hammond, D. (1983). How your students can predict their way to reading comprehension. *Learning, 12,* 62–64.

Harris, V. (1992). Contemporary griots: African American writers of children's literature. In V. J. Harris (Ed.), *Teaching multicultural literature in grades K–8* (pp. 55–108). Norwood, MA: Christopher-Gordon.

Harris, V. (1997). Children's literature depicting blacks in *Using multiethnic literature in the K–8 classroom.* In V. J. Harris (Ed.), *Using multiethnic literature in the K–8 classroom* (pp. 21–58). Norwood, MA: Christopher-Gordon.

Harste, J. C., Short, K. G., & Burke, C. (1988). *Creating classrooms for authors: The reading-writing connection.* Portsmouth, NH: Heinemann.

Harwayne, S. (2000). *Lifetime guarantees: Toward ambitious literacy teaching.* Portsmouth, NH: Heinemann.

Hayes, C. W., & Bahruth, R. (1985). Querer es poder. In J. Hansen, T. Newkirk, & D. Graves (Eds.), *Breaking ground: Teachers relate reading and writing in the elementary school* (pp. 97–108). Portsmouth, NH: Heinemann.

Heard, G. (1999). *Awakening the heart: Exploring poetry in elementary and middle school.* Portsmouth, NH: Heinemann.

Heath, S. B. (1983). *Ways with words: Language, life, and work in communities and classrooms.* New York: Cambridge University Press.

Hepler, S. (1998). Nonfiction books for children: New directions, new challenges. In R. Bamford & J. Kristo (Eds.), *Making facts come alive: Choosing quality nonfiction literature K–8* (pp. 3–17). Norwood, MA: Christopher-Gordon.

Herber, H. (1978). *Teaching reading in content areas* (2nd ed.). Englewood Cliffs, NJ: Prentice Hall.

Herman, J. L., Aschbacher, P. R., & Winters, L. (1992). *A practical guide to alternative assessment.* Alexandria, VA: Association for Supervision and Curriculum Development.

Heyde, A. (1979). *The relationship between self-esteem and the oral production of a second language.* Unpublished doctoral dissertation, University of Michigan.

Hillocks, G., Jr. (1986). *Research on written composition: New directions for teaching.* Urbana, IL: ERIC Clearinghouse on Reading and Composition Skills and the National Conference on Research in English.

Hindley, J. (1997). *In the company of children.* York, ME: Stenhouse Publishers.

Hoffman, J., Roser, N., & Battle, J. (1993). Reading aloud in classrooms: From the modal toward a "model." *The Reading Teacher, 46,* 496–503.

Holbrook, H. T. (1984). Prereading in the content areas. *Journal of Reading, 27,* 368–370.

Holdaway, D. (1979). *The foundations of literacy.* Sydney: Ashton-Scholastic.

Holdaway, D. (1984). *Stability and change in literacy learning.* Portsmouth, NH: Heinemann.

Holmes, B. C., & Roser, N. I. (1987). Five ways to assess readers' prior knowledge. *The Reading Teacher, 40,* 646–649.

Hudelson, S. (Ed.). (1981). *Learning to read in different languages.* Washington, DC: Center for Applied Linguistics.

Hudelson, S. (1984). "Kan yu ret an rayt en ingles": Children become literate in English as a second language. *TESOL Quarterly, 18,* 221–238.

Hudelson, S. (1986). ESL children's writing: What we've learned, what we're learning. In P. Rigg & D. S. Enright (Eds.), *Children and ESL: Integrating perspectives* (pp. 23–54). Washington, DC: Teachers of English to Speakers of Other Languages.

Hudelson, S. (1987). The role of native language literacy in the education of language minority children. *Language Arts, 64,* 827–241.

Hymes, D. (1970). On communicative competence. In J. Gumperz & D. Hymes (Eds.), *Directions in sociolinguistics* (pp. 35–71). New York: Holt, Rinehart, & Winston.

Hynd, C. R., McNish, M. E., Guzzetti, B., Lay, K., & Fowler, P. (1994). *What high school students say about their science texts.* Paper presented at the annual meeting of the College Reading Association, New Orleans.

Jensen, J. M. (1993). What do we know about the writing of elementary school children? *Language Arts, 70,* 290–294.

Jobe, R., & Dayton-Sakari, M. D. (1999). *Reluctant readers: Connecting students and books for successful reading experiences.* Markahm, ON: Pembroke

Publishers Limited.

Jochum, J. (1989). Writing: The critical response. *Texas Reading Report, 12*, 1–10.

Johnson, D. D., & Pearson, P. D. (1984). *Teaching reading vocabulary.* New York: Holt, Rinehart, and Winston.

Just, M., & Carpenter, P. (1987). *The psychology of reading and language comprehension.* Boston: Allyn & Bacon.

Karolides, N. J. (1992). The transactional theory of literature. In N. J. Karolides (Ed.), *Reader response in the classroom: Evoking and interpreting meaning in literature* (pp. 21–44). New York: Longman.

Kaser, S., & Short, K. (1998). Exploring culture through children's connections. *Language Arts, 75*(3), 185–192.

Kessler, C., & Quinn, M. F. (1980). Positive effects of bilingualism on science problem-solving ability. In J. E. Alatis (Eds.), *Georgetown University Round Table on Languages and Linguistics* (pp. 295–308).

Kobrin, B. (1995). *Eyeopeners II: Children's books to answer children's questions about the world around them.* New York: Scholastic.

Kotkin, A. J., & Baker, H. C. (1977). *Family folklore interviewing guide and questionnaire.* Baltimore, MD: Maryland Arts Council Folklife Program.

Krashen, S. D. (1981). *Second language acquisition and second language learning.* Oxford: Pergamon.

Krashen, S. (1982). *Principles and practices in second language acquisition.* Oxford: Pergamon.

Krashen, S. D. (1985). *The input hypothesis: Issues and implications.* New York: Longman.

Krashen, S. (1993). *The power of reading: Insights from research.* Englewood, CO: Libraries Unlimited.

Krashen, S. (1997/1998). Bridging inequity with books. *Educational Leadership, 55*(4), 18–22.

Krashen, S. D. (1998). Every person a reader: an alternative to the California Task Force Report on Reading. In C. Weaver (Ed.), *Reconsidering a balanced approach to reading* (pp. 425–452). Urbana, IL: National Council of Teachers of English.

Krashen, S. D., & McQuillan, J. (1998). The case for later intervention: Once a good reader, always a good reader. In C. Weaver (Ed.), *Reconsidering a balanced approach to reading* (pp. 409–422). Urbana, IL: National Council of Teachers of English.

Krashen, S. D., & Terrell, T. D. (1983). *The natural approach.* San Francisco: Alemany Press.

Krogness, M. M. (1987). Folklore: A matter of the heart and the heart of the matter. *Language Arts, 64*(8), 808–817.

Kutiper, K., & Wilson, P. (1993). Updating poetry preferences: A look at the poetry children really like. *The Reading Teacher, 47*(1), 28–34.

Law, B., & Eckes, M. (1990). *The more-than-just-surviving handbook: ESL for every classroom teacher.* Winnipeg, Canada: Peguis.

Lazear, D. (1991). *Seven ways of teaching: The artistry of teaching with multiple intelligences.* Palatine, IL: IRI/Skylight Publishing.

Lima, C. W., & Lima, J. A. (1989). *A to zoo: Subject access to children's picture books.* New York: Bowker.

Lindfors, J. W. (1987). *Children's language and learning* (2nd ed.). Englewood Cliffs, NY: Prentice-Hall.

Lockward, D. (1994). Poets on teaching poetry. *English Journal, 83*(5), 65–70.

Long, M. H. (1983). Native speaker/non-native speaker conversation and the negotiation of comprehensible input. *Applied Linguistics, 4*, 126–141.

Long, M. H., & Porter, P. A. (1985). Group work, interlanguage talk, and second language acquisition. *TESOL Quarterly, 19*, 207–228.

Lutz, E. (1986). Using folk literature in your reading program. *Journal of Reading, 30*, 76–78.

Making a difference means making it different: Honoring children's rights to excellent reading education [Online]. Available: www.reading.org/positions/MADMMID.html.

Mariotti, A. S., & Homan, S. P. (1997). *Linking reading assessment to instruction: An application worktext for elementary classroom teachers.* Mahwah, NJ: Lawrence Erlbaum Associates.

Martin, P. (1993). "Capture silk": Reading aloud together. *English Journal, 82*, 16–24.

Matazano, J. B. (1996). Discussion: Assessing what was said and what was done. In L. B. Gambrell & J. F. Almasi (Eds.), *Lively discussions.: Fostering engaged reading* (pp. 250–264). Newark, DE: International Reading Association.

McCaslin, N. (1987a). *Creative drama in the intermediate grades.* Studio City, CA: Players Press.

McCaslin, N. (1987b). *Creative drama in the primary grades.* Studio City, CA: Players Press.

McCaslin, N. (1990). *Creative drama in the classroom* (5th ed.). Studio City, CA: Players Press.

McClure, A. (1990). *Sunrises and songs: Reading and writing poetry in the classroom.* Portsmouth, NH: Heinemann.

McGowan, T., & Guzzetti, B. (1991, January–February). Promoting social studies understanding through literature-based instruction. *Social Studies,* 16–21.

McKeon, D. (1992). Introduction. In *TESOL resource packet* (p. 1). Alexandria, VA: Teachers of English to Speakers of Other Languages.

McNeil, D. (1966). Developmental psycholinguistics. In F. Smith & G. A. Miller (Eds.), *The genesis of language: A psycholinguistic approach.* Cambridge, MA: MIT Press.

McNeil, J. D. (1992). *Reading comprehension: New directions for classroom practice* (3rd ed.). New York: HarperCollins.

McTighe, J., & Lyman, F. (1988). Cueing thinking in the

classroom: The promise of theory-embedded tools. *Educational Leadership, 45* (April), 18–24.

Milon, J. (1974). The development of negation in English by a second language learner. *TESOL Quarterly, 8,* 137–143.

Moe, A. J. (1989). Using picture books for reading vocabulary development. In J. W. Stewig & S. L. Sebesta (Eds.), *Using literature in the elementary classroom* (pp. 23–34). Urbana, IL: National Council of Teachers of English.

Moll, L. C., & Diaz, S. (1987). Change as the goal of educational research. *Anthropology and Education Quarterly, 18,* 300–311.

Montone, C., & Short, D. (1994). *Bringing a reading passage to life: A creative comprehension activity.* Washington, DC: Center for Applied Linguistics. (ERIC Document Reproduction Service No. ED 424 741)

Mooney, M. E. (1990). *Reading to, with, and by children.* Katonah, NY: Richard C. Owen, Publishers.

Mooney, M. E. (1994). Reading to children: A positive step on the road to literacy. *Teaching PreK–8, 25*(1), 90–92.

Moore, D. W., Moore, S. A., Cunningham, P. M., & Cunningham, J. W. (1998). *Developing readers and writers in the content areas.* New York: Longman.

Moore, D. W., Readence, J. E., & Rickelman, R. J. (1989). *Prereading activities for content area reading and learning.* Newark, DE: International Reading Association.

Moss, B. (1992). Children's nonfiction trade books: A complement to content area texts. *The Reading Teacher, 45,* 26–32.

Murray, D. H. (1982). *Learning by teaching.* Montclair, NJ: Boynton/Cook.

Nagy, W. E., Herman, P. A., & Anderson, R. C. (1985). Learning words from context. *Reading Research Quarterly, 20,* 233–253.

Natalicio, D. S., & Natalicio, L. F. S. (1971). A comparative study of English pluralizaton by native and non-native English speakers. *Child Development, 42,* 1302–1306.

National Association for Bilingual Education. (1992). *Professional standards for the preparation of bilingual/multicultural teachers.* Washington, DC: Author.

Neal, J. C., & Moore, K. (1991/1992). The Very Hungry Caterpillar meets Beowulf in secondary classrooms. *Journal of Reading, 35,* 290–296.

Newmann, F. M., & Wehlage, G. C. (1993). Five standards of authentic instruction. *Educational Leadership, 50,* 8–12.

New Zealand Ministry of Education. (1996). *Reading for life: The learner as a reader.* Wellington, NZ: Learning Media.

Noguchi, R. R. (1991). *Grammar and the teaching of writing: Limits and possibilities.* Urbana, IL: National Council of Teachers of English.

Nystrand, M. (1990). Writing as a verb. In G. Hawisher & A. O. Soter (Eds.), *On literacy and its teaching: Issues in English education* (pp. 144–158). Albany, NY: State University of New York Press.

Odlin, T. (1989). *Language transfer: Cross-linguistic influence in language learning.* Cambridge: Cambridge University Press.

Ogle, D. (1986). K-W-L: A teaching model that develops an active reading of expository text. *The Reading Teacher, 39,* 563–570.

Olmstead, C. (1999). Literacy issues for English language learners in the regular classroom. Presentation made to the Benton-Franklin Council IRA, Richland, WA.

O'Malley, J. M., & Pierce, L. V. (1996). *Authentic assessment for English language learners: Practical approaches for teachers.* New York: Addison-Wesley.

Ovando, C. J., & Collier, V. P. (1998). *Bilingual and ESL classrooms: Teaching in multicultural contexts.* Boston: McGraw Hill.

Paredes, A. (1958). *With a pistol in his hand: A border ballad and its hero.* Austin, TX: University of Texas Press.

Peregoy, S., & Boyle, O. (1991). Second language oral proficiency characteristics of low, intermediate, and high second language readers. *Hispanic Journal of Behavioral Science, 13,* 25–47.

Peregoy, S. F., & Boyle, O. F. (1997). *Reading, writing, and learning in ESL: A resource book for K–12 teachers* (2nd ed.). New York: Longman.

Peregoy, S. F., & Boyle, O. (2001). *Reading, writing, and learning in ESL: A resource book for K–12 teachers* (3rd ed.). New York: Longman.

Peyton, J. K., Staton, J., Richardson, G., & Wolfram, W. (1990). The influence of writing task on ESL students' written production. *Research in the Teaching of English, 24,* 142–171.

Piper, T. (1998). *Language for all our children.* Englewood Cliffs, NJ: Merrill.

Porter, R. P. (1990). *Forked tongue: The politics of bilingual education.* New York: Basic.

Presley, M., Allington, R., Morrow, L. M., Baker, K., Nelson, E., Warton-McDonald, R., Block, C. C., Tracey, D., Brooks, G., Cronin, J., & Woo, D. (1998). The nature of effective first-grade literacy instruction [On-line]. Available: http://cela.albany.edu/1stgradelit/index.html.

Ravem, R. (1968). Language acquisition in a second language environment. *International Review of Applied Linguistics, 6,* 175–185.

Readence, J. E., Bean, T. W., & Baldwin, R. S. (1995). *Content area reading: An integrated approach.* Dubuque, IA: Kendall/Hunt Publishing Company.

Reed, A. J. S. (1994). *Reaching adolescents: The young*

adult book and the school. Englewood Cliffs, NJ: Merrill/Prentice Hall.

Renner, S. M., & Carter, J. M. (1991). Comprehending text—Appreciating diversity through folklore. *Journal of Reading, 34*(8), 602–604.

Reutzel, D. R., & Cooter, R. B., Jr. (2000). *Teaching children to read: Putting the pieces together* (3rd ed.). Upper Saddle River, NJ: Merrill.

Reyes, M. L., & Molner, L. A. (1991). Instructional strategies for second-language learners in the content areas. *Journal of Reading, 35*(2), 96–103.

Richard-Amato, P. A. (1996). *Making it happen: Interaction in the second language classroom* (2nd ed.). New York: Longman.

Rivera, C., & Vincent, C. (1997). High school graduation testing: Policies and practices in the assessment of English language learners. *Education Assessment, 4,* 335–355.

Rochman, H. (1993). *Against borders: Promoting books for a multicultural world.* Chicago, IL: American Library Association.

Rosenblatt, L. (1985). Viewpoints: Transaction versus interaction—A terminological rescue operation. *Research in the Teaching of English, 19,* 96–107.

Rosenblatt, L. M. (1978). *The reader, the text, the poem: The transactional theory of the literary work.* Carbondale, IL: Southern Illinois University Press.

Roser, N. L., Hoffman, J. V. & Farest, C. (1990). Language, literature, and at-risk children. *The Reading Teacher, 43,* 554–559.

Rothstein, V., & Goldberg, R. (1993). *Thinking through stories.* East Moline, IL: LinguiSystems.

Routman, R. (2000). *Conversations: Strategies for teaching, learning, and evaluating.* Portsmouth, NH: Heinemann.

Russell, D. L. (1997). *Literature for children: A short introduction.* New York: Longman.

Salinger, T. S. (1996). *Literacy for young children* (2nd ed.). Englewood Cliffs, NJ: Merrill.

Sampson, M., Allen, R., & Sampson, M. (1990). *Pathways to literacy.* Chicago: Holt, Rinehart & Winston.

Samway, K. D., & Whang, G. (1995). *Literature study circles in a multicultural classroom.* York, ME: Stenhouse Publishers.

Savage, J. F. (1994). *Teaching reading using literature.* Madison, WI: Brown and Benchmark.

Savage, J. F. (2000). *For the love of literature: Children and books in the elementary years.* Boston: McGraw-Hill.

Scarcella, R. C., & Oxford, R. L. (1992). *The tapestry of language learning: The individual in the communicative classroom.* Boston: Heinle & Heinle.

Schulz, A. R. (1998). *Supporting intermediate and secondary readers: Selected interactive approaches for grades 4–12.* Costa Mesa, CA: California Reading Association.

Schwartz, D. (1995). Ready, set, read—20 minutes each day is all you'll need. *Smithsonian, 3,* 83–89.

Schwartz, J. (1983). Using journals to encourage the writing processes of second graders. *The Elementary School Journal, 84,* 15–20.

Schwartz, M. (1984). Defining voice through letter writing. *The English Record, 35,* 10–12.

Short, D. J. (1993). Assessing integrated language and content instruction. *TESOL Quarterly, 27,* 627–656.

Simmons, E. R. (1990). *Student worlds, student words: Teaching writing through folklore.* Portsmouth, NH: Boynton/Cook.

Simpson, M. L. (1987). Alternative formats for evaluating content area vocabulary understanding. *Journal of Reading, 30,* 20–27.

Slapin, B., Seale, D., & Gonzales, R. (1998). *How to tell the difference; A guide to evaluating children's books for anti-Indian bias.* Berkeley, CA: Oyate.

Sloan, S. (1991). *The complete English as a second language/EFL cooperative and communicative activity book.* Burlingame, CA: ALTA Book Center Publishers.

Smith, J. & Elley, W. (1997). *How children learn to read.* Katonah, NY: Richard C. Owen, Publishers.

Snow, M. A., & Brinton, D. M. (1988). Content-based language instruction: Investigating the effectiveness of the adjunct model. *TESOL Quarterly, 22,* 553–574.

Spandel, V., & Stiggins, R. J. (1997). *Creating writers: Linking writing assessment and instruction.* New York: Longman.

Staton, J. (1987). The power of responding in dialogue journals. In T. Fulwiler (Ed.), *The journal book* (pp. 47–63). Portsmouth, NH: Heinemann.

Staton, J., Shuy, R., Peyton, J. K., & Reed, L. (1988). *Dialogue journal communication: Classroom, linguistic, social and cognitive views.* Norwood, NJ: Ablex Publishing Corporation.

Stauffer, R. (1969). *Directing reading maturity as a cognitive process.* New York: Harper & Row.

Stauffer, R. (1976). *Teaching reading as a thinking process.* New York: Harper & Row.

Stein, H. (1978). The Visual Reading Guide (VRG). *Social Education, 42,* 534–535.

Steinbergh, J. (1994). *Reading and writing poetry: A guide for teachers.* New York: Scholastic.

Stephens, E. C., & Brown, J. (2000). *A handbook of content literacy strategies.* Norwood, MA: Christopher-Gordon.

Stewig, J. (1981). Choral speaking: Who has the time? Why take the time? *Childhood Education, 58,* 25–29.

Strickland, D. S., & Feeley, J. T. (1991). Development in the elementary school years. In J. Flood, J. M. Jensen, D. Lapp, and J. R. Squire (Eds.), *Handbook of research on teaching the English language arts* (pp. 286–302). New York: Macmillan.

Swartz, L. (1993). *Classroom events through poetry.* Markham, Ontario: Pembroke.

Taba, H. (1967). *Teacher's handbook for elementary social studies.* Reading, MA: Addison-Wesley.

Tannen, D. (1990). *You just don't understand: Women and men in conversation.* New York: Morrow.

Tchudi, S., & Mitchell, D. (1989). *Explorations in the teaching of English* (3rd ed.). New York: Harper & Row.

Tchudi, S., & Mitchell, D. (1999). *Explorations in the teaching of English* (4th ed.). New York: Longman.

Tchudi, S. N., & Yates, J. (1983). *Teaching writing in the content areas: Senior high school.* Washington, DC: National Education Association.

Temple, C., Martinez, M., Yokota, J., & Naylor, A. (1998). *Children's books in children's hands: An introduction to their literature.* Boston: Allyn & Bacon.

Temple, C., Nathan, R., Burris, N., & Temple, F. (1988). *The beginnings of writing* (2nd ed.). Boston: Allyn & Bacon.

TESOL. (1975). *Guidelines for the certification and preparation of teachers of English to speakers of other languages in the United States.* Alexandria, VA: Author.

Thomas, W., & Collier, V. (1995). Language minority student achievement and program effectiveness. *California Association for Bilingual Education Newsletter, 17*(5), 19, 24.

Tierney, R., & Cunningham, J. (1984). Research on teaching reading comprehension. In P. D. Pearson (Ed.), *Handbook of reading research* (pp. 609–656). New York: Longman.

Tompkins, G. E. (1994). *Teaching writing: Balancing process and product.* New York: Merrill.

Toms-Boronowski, S. (1983). An investigation of the effectiveness of selected vocabulary teaching strategies with intermediate grade level students. *Dissertation Abstracts International, 44,* 1405A (University Microfilms No. 83-16, 238).

Trachtenburg, P. (1990). Using children's literature to enhance phonics instruction. *The Reading Teacher, 43,* 648–654.

Traill, L. (1996). *Little celebrations teacher's resource book.* Glenview, IL: Celebration Press.

Traill, L. (1999). *The Leanna Traill literacy teaching and learning institute.* Auckland, NZ: Literacy Learning (NZ) Ltd.

Tunnell, M. O., & Jacobs, J. S. (2000). *Children's literature, briefly.* Upper Saddle River, NJ: Merrill.

Urzua, C. (1987). "You stopped too soon": Second language children composing and revising. *TESOL Quarterly, 21,* 279–305.

Vacca, R. T., & Vacca, J. A. L. (1989). *Content area reading* (3rd ed.). New York: Scott Foresman & Company.

Vacca, R. T., & Vacca, J. A. L. (1999). *Content area reading* (6th ed.). New York: Longman.

Valencia, S. (1992, January). *Implementing literacy portfolio assessment.* Paper presented at the meeting of the Southwest Regional International Reading Association, Tucson, AZ.

Van Allen, R., & Allen, C. (1967). *Language experience activities.* Boston: Houghton Mifflin.

Vardell, S. M. (1991). A new "picture of the world": The NCTE Orbis Pictus Award for outstanding nonfiction for children. *Language Arts, 68,* 474–479.

Vardell, S. M. (1995). Thematic units: Integrating the curriculum. In M. Sorensen and B. A. Lehman (Eds.), *Teaching with children's books: Paths to literature-based instruction* (pp. 129–136). Urbana, IL: National Council of Teachers of English.

Vardell, S. M. (1996). The language of facts: Using nonfiction books to support language growth. In A. A. McClure & J. V. Kristo (Eds.), *Books that invite talk, wonder, and play.* Urbana, IL: National Council of Teachers of English.

Vardell, S. M. (1998). Using read-aloud to explore the layers of nonfiction. In R. A. Bamford & J. V. Kristo (Eds.), *Making facts come alive: Choosing quality nonfiction literature K–8* (pp. 151–167). Norwood, MA: Christopher-Gordon.

Vardell, S. M., & Copeland, K. A. (1992). Reading aloud and responding to nonfiction: Let's talk about it. In E. B. Freeman & D. Goetz Person (Eds.), *Using nonfiction trade books in the elementary classroom.* Urbana, IL: National Council of Teachers of English.

Villaume, S. K., Worden, T., Williams, S., Hopkins, L., & Rosenblatt, C. (1994). Five teachers in search of a discussion. *The Reading Teacher, 47,* 480–487.

Vogel, M., & Tilley, J. (1993). Story poems and the stories we've been waiting to tell. *English Journal, 82,* 86–89.

Vogt, M. E. (1992, October). *Authentic assessment.* Keynote address at the meeting of the Fall Education Symposium, Arlington, TX.

Vogt, M. E. (1998, May). *Developing strategic readers.* Paper presented at the meeting of the International Reading Association, Orlando, FL.

Waggoner, D., & O'Malley, J. M. (1985). Teachers of limited-English-proficient children in the United States. *Journal of the National Association for Bilingual Education, 9,* 25–42.

Weaver, C. (1996). *Teaching grammar in context.* Portsmouth, NH: Boynton/Cook.

Wells, G. (1986). *The meaning makers: Children learning language and using language to learn.* Portsmouth, NH: Heinemann.

Wigginton, E. (1991/1992). Culture begins at home. *Educational Leadership, 49,* 60–64.

Wilhelm, J. D. (1997). *"You gotta be the book": Teaching engaged and reflective reading with adoles-*

cents. Urbana, IL: National Council of Teachers of English.

Wilkins, D. A. (1976). *Notional syllabuses.* London: Oxford University Press.

Wilkins, D. A. (1979). Grammatical, situational, and notional syllabuses. In C. J. Brumfit & K. Johnson (Eds.), *The communicative approach to language teaching* (pp. 82–90). Oxford: Oxford University Press.

Wilson, W. A. (1988). The deeper necessity: Folklore and the humanities. *Journal of American Folklore, 101*(400), 156–167.

Wollman-Bonilla, J. E. (1991). *Response journals: Inviting students to think and write about literature.* New York: Scholastic.

Wollman-Bonilla, J. E., & Werchadlo, B. (1995). Literature response journals in a first-grade classroom. *Language Arts, 72,* 562–570.

Wood, D., & Nurss, J. (1988). Print rich classrooms support the development of print awareness. *Georgia Journal of Reading, 14,* 21–23.

Wood, K. (1986). The effect of interspersing questions in text: Evidence for "slicing the task." *Reading Research and Instruction, 25,* 295–307.

Yokota, J. (1993). Issues in selecting multicultural children's literature. *Language Arts, 70*(March), 156–167.

Young, T. A., & Ferguson, P. M. (1995). From Anansi to Zomo: Trickster tales in the classroom. *The Reading Teacher, 48,* 490–503.

Young, T. A., & Vardell, S. M. (1993). Weaving readers theatre and nonfiction into the curriculum. *The Reading Teacher, 46,* 396–406.

Zamel, V. (1982). Teaching composition in the ESL classroom: What we can learn from research in the teaching of English. *TESOL Quarterly, 16,* 26–39.

Zarnowski, M. (1990). *Learning about biographies: A reading-and-writing approach for children.* Urbana, IL: National Council of Teachers of English.

CHILDREN'S AND YOUNG ADULT LITERATURE REFERENCES

Coding Scheme for Books in this Bibliography

Proficiency level is indicated by B, I, or A.

> **B**=Beginning (non-English speaking to some).
> **I**=Intermediate (limited to average fluency).
> **A**=Advanced (average fluency to ready to be mainstreamed).

The **type of book** is indicated by PB, CB, NF, or P.

> **PB**=Picture book.
> **CB**=Chapter book.
> **NF**=Nonfiction.
> **P**=Poetry.

> **Coding scheme example:** B/PB (Beginning proficiency/picture book).

Aardema, V. (1975). *Why mosquitoes buzz in people's ears.* New York: Dial Press. **I/PB**

Aardema, V. (1991). *Traveling to Tondo: A tale of the Nkundo of Zaire.* New York: Knopf. **I/PB**

Adler, D. (1989). *We remember the Holocaust.* New York: Henry Holt. **A/NF**

Adoff, A. (1991). *In for winter, out for spring.* San Diego: Harcourt Brace Jovanovich. **I/P**

Ahlberg, J., & Ahlberg, A. (1978). *Each peach pear plum.* New York: Viking Press. **B/PB**

Ainsworth, L. (1996). *Creepy crawlies A to Z.* New York: Scholastic. **B/PB**

Ajmera, M., & Versola, A. R. (1996). *Children from Australia to Zimbabwe: A photographic journey around the world.* Durham, NC: Shakti for Children. **I/NF**

Aliki. (1990). *Manners.* New York: HarperCollins. **I/NF**

Aliki. (1994). *The gods and goddesses of Olympus.* New York: HarperCollins. **I/PB**

Altman, L. J. (1993). *Amelia's road.* New York: Lee & Low. **B/PB**

Ancona, G. (1994). *The piñata maker.* San Diego: Harcourt Brace. **I/NF**

Anholt, C., & Anholt, L. (1998). *Big book of families.* Cambridge, MA: Candlewick. **I/P**

Anno, M. (1977). *Anno's counting book.* New York: Crowell. **B/PB**

Aranda, C. (1977). *Dichos: Proverbs and sayings from the Spanish.* Santa Fe, NM: SunstonePress. **I/NF**

Archer, J. (1991). *Hurricane!* New York: Crestwood House. **I/NF**

Arnold, C. (1998). *El niño: Stormy weather for people and wildlife.* New York: Clarion. **A/NF**

Arnosky, J. (1994). *All about alligators.* New York: Scholastic. **I/NF**

Asch, F. (1998). *Cactus poems.* San Diego: Harcourt Brace. **I/P**

Ashabranner, B. (1986). *Children of the Maya: A Guatemalan Indian odyssey.* New York: Dodd, Mead. **A/NF**

Ashabranner, B. (1987). *The vanishing border: A photographic journey along our frontier with Mexico.* New York: Dodd, Mead. **A/NF**

Ashabranner, B. (1993). *Still a nation of immigrants.* New York: Cobblehill Books. **A/NF**

Ashabranner, B. (1996). *Our beckoning borders: Illegal immigration to America.* New York: Cobblehill. **A/NF**

Ashabranner, B. (1997). *Dark harvest: Migrant farm workers in America.* New Haven, CT: Linnet Books. **A/NF**

Atkin, S. B. (1993). *Voices from the field: Children of migrant farm workers tell their stories.* Boston: Little, Brown. **I/NF**

Atwood, A. (1971). *Haiku: The mood of the Earth.* New York: Scribners. **I/P**

Axtell, D. (2000). *We're going on a lion hunt.* New York: Holt. **B/PB**

Aylesworth, T. G. (1996). *The kids' world almanac of baseball.* Mahwah, NJ: World Almanac Books. **I/NF**

Badt, K. L. (1994). *Greetings!* Chicago, IL: Children's Press. **I/NF**

Baker, J. (1991). *Window.* New York: Greenwillow. **B/PB**

Barrett, J., & Barrett, R. (1978). *Cloudy with a chance of meatballs.* New York: Macmillan. **I/PB**

Barton, B. (1990). *Bones, bones, dinosaur bones.* New York: Trumpet Club. **B/PB**

Base, G. (1987). *Animalia.* New York: Abrams. **I/PB**

Base, G. (1989). *Jabberwocky.* New York: Abrams. **I/PB**

Bash, B. (1993). *Shadows of night: The hidden world of the little brown bat.* San Francisco: Sierra Club. **I/NF**

Bates, K. L. (1994). *O beautiful for spacious skies.* San Francisco: Chronicle Books. **I/PB**

Bauer, C. F. (1986). *Rainy day stories and poems.* New York: HarperCollins. **I/P**

Bauer, M. D. (1986). *On my honor.* Boston: Houghton Mifflin. **I/CB**

Begay, S. (1995). *Navajo: Visions and voices across the mesa.* New York: Scholastic. **I/P**

Bernhard, E. (1996). *Happy new year!* New York: Lodestar Books. **I/PB**

Bierhorst, J. (1988). *Doctor Coyote: A Native American Aesop's fables.* New York: MacMillan. **I/CB**

Bierhorst, J. (Ed.). (1994). *On the road of stars: Native American night poems and sleep charms.* New York: MacMillan. **I/P**

Bierman, C. (1988). *Journey to Ellis Island: How my father came to America.* New York: Hyperion. **I/PB**

Bishop, G. (1996). *Maui and the sun: A Maori tale.* New York: North-South Books. **I/PB**

Bitton-Jackson, L. (1997). *I have lived a thousand years: Growing up in the Holocaust.* New York: Scholastic. **I/NF**

Blume, J. (1970). *Are you there, God? It's me, Margaret.* New York: Bradbury. **I/CB**

Boas, J. (1995). *Five diaries of teenagers who died in the Holocaust.* New York: Scholastic. **I/NF**

Booth, D. (1990). *Voices on the wind: Poems for all seasons.* New York: Morrow. **I/P**

Borden, L. (1998). *Good-bye, Charles Lindbergh.* New York: Margaret K. McElderry Books. **B/PB**

Brandt, K. (1982). *What makes it rain? The story of a raindrop.* Mahwah, NJ: Troll Associates. **I/NF**

Branley, F. M. (1987). *Comets.* New York: HarperCollins. **I/NF**

Branley, F. M. (1987). *Rockets and satellites* (2nd ed.). New York: Crowell. **I/NF**

Branley, F. M. (1987). *The planets in our solar system.* New York: HarperCollins. **I/NF**

Branley, F. M. (1988). *The sun: Our nearest star.* New York: HarperCollins. **I/NF**

Branley, F. M. (1988). *Tornado alert.* New York: Thomas Y. Crowell. **I/NF**

Brenner, B. (1994). *The earth is painted green: A garden of poems about our planet.* New York: Scholastic. **I/P**

Bridges, R. (1999). *Through my eyes: The autobiography of Ruby Bridges.* New York: Scholastic. **I/NF**

Bridwell, N. (1989). *Clifford, the big red dog.* New York: Scholastic. **B/PB**

Briggs, R. (1978). *The snowman.* New York: Trumpet Club. **B/PB**

Brown, H. J., Jr. (1991). *Live and learn and pass it on!* Nashville, TN: Rutledge Hill Press. **I/NF**

Brown, M. T. (1982). *Arthur goes to camp.* Boston: Little, Brown. **I/PB**

Brown, M., & Krensky, S. (1993). *Perfect pigs: An introduction to manners.* New York: Little, Brown. **I/PB**

Bruchac, J. (1992). *Thirteen moons on turtle's back.* New York: Putnam. **I/P**

Bruchac, J. (1994). *The great ball game.* New York: Dial. **I/PB**

Bruchac, J. (1997). *Many nations: An alphabet of Native Americans.* Mahwah, NJ: Bridgewater Books. **I/PB**

Bruchac, J. (1998). *The Earth under Sky Bear's feet: Native American poems of the land.* New York: Philomel. **I/P**

Bryan, A. (Ed.). (1997). *Ashley Bryan's ABC of African American poetry.* New York: Atheneum. **I/P**

Buehner, C. (1995). *It's a spoon, not a shovel.* New York: Penguin Putnam. **I/PB**

Bukiet, S. (1993). *Scripts of the world.* Cincinnati, OH: AIMS International Books. **I/NF**

Bundschuh, R. (1991). *How to survive middle school: A humorous guide to the wonder years.* Grand Rapids, MI: Zondervan. **I/NF**

Bunting, E. (1992). *How many days to America: A Thanksgiving story.* New York: Clarion. **I/PB**

Bunting, E. (1996). *Going home.* San Diego, CA: Harcourt Brace. **I/PB**

Burleigh, R. (1991). *Flight: The journey of Charles Lindbergh.* New York: Philomel. **I/PB**

Burleigh, R. (1998). *Black whiteness: Admiral Byrd alone in the Antarctic.* New York: Atheneum. **I/NF**

Burns, M. (1982). *Math for smarty pants.* Boston: Little, Brown. **I/NF**

Butterfield, M. (1992). *1,000 facts about the Earth.* New York: Scholastic. **I/NF**

Carle, E. (1969). *The very hungry caterpillar.* New York: Philomel. **B/PB**

Carle, E. (1987). *Have you seen my cat?* New York: Scholastic. **B/PB**

Carle, E. (1993). *Today is Monday.* New York: Scholastic. **B/PB**

Carroll, L. (1997). *Through the looking glass.* Los Angeles: LRS. **A/CB**

Cha, D. (1998). *Dia's story cloth.* New York: Lee & Low Books. **I/PB**

Chermayeff, I., Wasserman, F., & Shapiro, M. J. (1991). *Ellis Island: An illustrated history of the immigrant experience.* New York: Macmillan. **A/NF**

Cherry, L. (1992). *A river ran wild.* New York: Scholastic. **I/PB**

Chin-Lee, C. (1997). *A is for Asia.* New York: Orchard Books. **I/PB**

Cisneros, S. (1984). *The house on Mango Street.* Houston, TX: Arte Publico Press. **I/CB**

Cleary, B. (1977). *Ramona and her father.* New York: Morrow. **I/CB**

Cleary, B. (1981). *Ramona Quimby, age 8.* New York: Morrow. **I/CB**

Cleary, B. (1983). *Dear Mr. Henshaw.* New York: Morrow. **I/CB**

Cohn, A. L. (1993). *From sea to shining sea: A treasury of American folklore and folk songs.* New York: Scholastic. **I/CB**

Cole, J. (1986). *The magic school bus at the waterworks.* New York: Scholastic. **I/PB**

Cole, J. (1989). *Anna Banana: 101 jump-rope rhymes.* New York: Morrow Junior Books. **I/P**

Cole, J. (1992). *The magic school bus lost in the solar system.* New York: Scholastic. **I/PB**

Cole, J. (1997). *The magic school bus and the electric field trip.* New York: Scholastic. **I/PB**

Cole, J. (1999). *The magic school bus explores the senses.* New York: Scholastic. **I/PB**

Cole, J., & Calmenson, S. (1990). *Miss Mary Mack and other street rhymes.* New York: Morrow. **I/P**

Cole, J., & Calmenson, S. (1993). *Pin the tail on the donkey and other party games.* New York: Morrow. **I/PB**

Cole, J., & Calmenson, S. (1994). *Crazy eights and other card games.* New York: Morrow. **I/PB**

Cole, J., & Calmenson, S. (1998). *Marbles: 101 ways to play.* New York: Morrow. **I/PB**

Colman, P. (1995). *Rosie the riveter: Women working on the home front in World War II.* New York: Crown. **A/NF**

Cone, M. (1993). *Come back, salmon: How a group of dedicated kids adopted Pigeon Creek and brought it back to life.* San Francisco: Sierra Club. **I/NF**

Cowan, C. (1997). *My life with the wave.* New York: Lothrop, Lee & Shepard. **I/PB**

Craig, M. J. (1969). *Questions and answers about weather.* New York: Four Winds Press. **I/NF**

Crews, D. (1978). *Freight train.* New York: Viking. **B/PB**

Crews, D. (1980). *Truck.* New York: Scholastic. **B/PB**

Crews, D. (1985). *School bus.* New York: Puffin. **B/PB**

Cullinan, B. (Ed.). (1996). *A jar of tiny stars.* Honesdale, PA: Wordsong/Boyds Mills Press. **I/P**

Cummings, P. (Ed.). (1992). *Talking with artists.* New York: Bradbury. **I/NF**

Cummings, P. (Ed.). (1995). *Talking with artists, Volume II.* New York: Simon & Schuster. **I/NF**

Dahl, R. (1995). *The magic finger.* New York: Viking. **I/CB**

Dakos, K. (1990). *If you're not here, please raise your hand.* New York: Simon & Schuster. **I/P**

Dakos, K. (1993). *Don't read this book, whatever you do!* New York: Four Winds Press. **I/P**

Das, P. (1996). *I is for India.* Parsippany, NJ: Silver Press. **I/PB**

Davies, N. (1998). *Big blue whale.* Cambridge, MA: Candlewick Press. **B/PB**

Davis, H. (1977). *A January fog will freeze a hog.* New York: Crown Publishers. **I/NF**

Davis, K. (1996). *Who hops?* San Diego: Harcourt Brace. **B/PB**

Day, A. (1985). *Good dog, Carl.* San Marcos, CA: Green Tiger Press. **B/PB**

Day, A. (1988). *Frank and Ernest.* New York: Scholastic. **I/PB**

Day, A. (1990). *Frank and Ernest play ball.* New York: Scholastic. **I/PB**

Day, A. (1994). *Frank and Ernest on the road.* New York: Scholastic. **I/PB**

Deedy, C. A. (2000). *The yellow star: The legend of King Christian X of Denmark.* Atlanta: Peach Tree. **I/PB**

Demi. (1997). *Buddha stories.* New York: Henry Holt. **A/CB**

Denenberg, B. (1999). *The journal of Ben Uchida: Citizen 12559, Mirror Lake Internment Camp, California 1942.* New York: Scholastic. **I/CB**

de Paola, T. (1975). *The cloud book.* New York: Holiday House. **I/PB**

de Paola, T. (1975). *Strega Nona.* Englewood Cliffs, NJ: Prentice-Hall. **I/PB**

DeWitt, L. (1991). *What will the weather be?* New York: HarperCollins. **I/PB**

Dooley, N. (1991). *Everybody cooks rice.* Minneapolis: Carolrhoda. **I/PB**

Dooley, N. (1996). *Everybody bakes bread.* Minneapolis: Carolrhoda. **I/PB**

Dorris, M. (1992). *Morning girl.* New York: Hyperion. **I/CB**

Dorros, A. (1989). *Feel the wind.* New York: Harper and Row. **I/PB**

Dorros, A. (1992). *Esta es mi casa.* New York: Scholastic. **I/PB**

Dorros, A. (1993). *Radio man.* New York: HarperCollins. **I/PB**

Dunphy, M. (1993). *Here is the arctic winter.* New York: Hyperion. **I/PB**

Dunphy, M. (1994). *Here is the tropical rain forest.* New York: Hyperion. **I/PB**

Dunphy, M. (1999). *Here is the African savannah.* New York: Hyperion. **I/PB**

Ehlert, L. (1989). *Eating the alphabet: Fruit and vegetables from a to z.* New York: Trumpet Club. **B/PB**

Ehlert, L. (1990). *Color farm.* New York: Lippincott. **B/PB**

Emberly, M. (1992). *Ruby.* Boston: Little, Brown. **I/PB**

Emberley, R. (1989). *City sounds.* Boston: Little, Brown. **B/PB**

Emberley, R. (1989). *Jungle sounds.* Boston: Little, Brown. **B/PB**

Ernst, L. C. (1995). *Little Red Riding Hood: A new-fangled prairie tale.* New York: Scholastic. **I/PB**

Ets, M. E. (1978). *Just like me.* New York: Puffin. **B/PB**

Falwell, C. (1993). *Feast for 10.* New York: Scholastic. **B/PB**

Farley, C. (1997). *Mr. Pak buys a story.* Morton Grove, IL: Albert Whitman & Company. **B/PB**

Fisher. L. E. (1995). *Gandhi.* New York: Antheneum. **I/NF**

Fleischman, P. (1985). *I am Phoenix: Poems for two voices.* New York: HarperCollins. **I/P**

Fleischman, P. (1988). *Joyful noise: Poems for two voices.* New York: HarperCollins. **I/P**

Florian, D. (1993). *Monster motel.* San Diego: Harcourt Brace. **I/P**

Florian, D. (1994). *Beast feast: Poems and paintings*. San Diego: Harcourt Brace. **I/P**

Florian, D. (1994). *Bing, bang, boing*. SanDiego: Harcourt Brace. **I/P**

Foster, S. (1990). *Simon says . . . let's play*. New York: Cobblehill. **I/NF**

Fox, M. (1985). *Wilfrid Gordon McDonald Partridge*. Brooklyn, NY: Kane/Miller. **I/PB**

Fox, M. (1987). *Hattie and the fox*. New York: Simon & Schuster. **B/PB**

Fraser, B. (1990). *First things first: An illustrated collection of sayings useful and familiar for children*. New York: HarperCollins. **I/NF**

Freedman, R. (1980). *Immigrant kids*. New York: E. P. Dutton. **I/NF**

Freedman, R. (1983). *Children of the wild west*. New York: Clarion. **I/NF**

Freedman, R. (1987). *Indian chiefs*. New York: Holiday House. **I/NF**

Freedman, R. (1988). *Buffalo hunt*. New York: Holiday House. **I/NF**

Freedman, R. (1991). *The Wright brothers: How they invented the airplane. Original photographs by Wilbur and Orville Wright*. New York: Holiday House. **I/NF**

Freedman, R. (1994). *Kids at work: Lewis Hine and the crusade against child labor*. New York: Clarion. **I/NF**

French, F. (1986). *Snow White in New York*. Oxford: Oxford University Press.

Friedman, I. R. (1984). *How my parents learned to eat*. New York: Houghton Mifflin. **I/PB**

Fritz, J. (1993). *Just a few words, Mr. Lincoln: The story of the Gettysburg Address*. New York: Putnam. **I/PB**

Froman, R. (1974). *Seeing things: A book of poems*. New York: Crowell. **I/P**

Frost, R. (1978). *Stopping by the woods on a snowy evening*. New York: Dutton. **I/P**

Gallant, R. A. (1984). *101 questions and answers about the universe*. New York: Macmillan. **I/NF**

Gallaz, C., & Innocenti, R. (1985). *Rose blanche*. Mankato, MN: Creative Education. **I/PB**

Garelick, M. (1969). *Where does the butterfly go when it rains?* Greenvale, NY: Mondo. **I/NF**

Garza, C. L. (1990). *Family pictures/Cuadros de familia*. San Francisco, CA: Children's Book Press. **I/PB**

Garza, C. L. (1996). *In my family/En mi familia*. San Francisco, CA: Children's Book Press. **I/PB**

George, W. T. (1989). *Box turtle at Long Pond*. New York: Greenwillow. **I/PB**

Gibbons, G. (1990). *Weather words*. New York: Holiday House. **I/PB**

Gibbons, G. (1993). *Weather forecasting*. New York: Aladdin Books. **I/PB**

Gibbons, G. (1996). *The reasons for seasons*. New York: Holiday House. **I/PB**

Gibbons, G. (1996). *Weather words and what they mean*. New York: Holiday House. **I/PB**

Gibbons, G. (1999). *Exploring the deep dark sea*. Boston: Little Brown. **I/PB**

Giblin, J. C. (1987). *From hand to mouth, or, how we invented knives, forks, spoons, and chopsticks and the table manners to go with them*. New York: Crowell. **I/NF**

Giblin, J. C. (1997). *Charles A. Lindbergh: A human hero*. New York: Clarion Books. **A/NF**

Ginsburg, M. (1974). *Mushroom in the rain*. New York: Macmillan. **B/PB**

Goble, P. (1984). *Buffalo woman*. Scarsdale, NY: Bradbury. **I/PB**

Goble, P. (1992). *Love flute*. New York: Bradbury Press. **I/PB**

Gold, A. L. (1997). *Memories of Anne Frank: Reflections of a childhood friend*. New York: Scholastic. **I/NF**

Gonzalez, L. M. (1994). *The bossy gallito/ ell gallo de bodas*. San Diego: Harcourt Brace. **I/PB**

Goodman, B. (1991). *Natural wonders and disasters*. Boston: Little, Brown. **I/NF**

Goor, R., & Goor, N. (1983). *Signs*. New York: Crowell. **B/PB**

Graf, M. (1999). *Tornado! The strongest winds on Earth*. Logan, IA: Perfection Learning, **I/NF**

Graff, N. P. (1993). *Where the river runs*. Boston: Little, Brown & Company. **I/NF**

Graham, J. B. (1994). *Splish splash*. Boston: Houghton Mifflin. **I/P**

Greenfield, E. (1978). *Honey, I love*. New York: HarperCollins. **I/P**

Greenfield, E. (1991). *Night on neighborhood street*. New York: Dial. **I/P**

Gudel, H. (1999). *Dear Alexandra: A story of Switzerland*. Norwalk, CT: Sound Prints. **I/PB**

Guinness book of world records, 2000. (2000). New York: Bantam. **I/NF**

Gwynne, F. (1970). *The king who rained*. New York: Simon & Schuster. **I/PB**

Gwynne, F. (1976). *A chocolate moose for dinner*. New York: Simon & Schuster. **I/PB**

Gwynne, F. (1980). *The sixteen hand horse*. New York: Simon & Schuster. **I/PB**

Gwynne, F. (1988). *A little pigeon toad*. New York: Simon & Schuster. **I/PB**

Hadingham, E., & Hadingham, J. (1990). *Garbage: Where it comes from, where it goes*. New York: Simon & Schuster. **I/NF**

Hamilton, V. (1967). *Zeely*. Orlando: Harcourt Brace. **I/CB**

Hamilton, V. (1985). *The people could fly: American black folktales*. New York: Knopf. **I/CB**

Hamilton, V. (1988). *In the beginning: Creation stories from around the world*. San Diego: Harcourt Brace Jovanovich. **I/CB**

Haskins, J. (1991). *Count your way through the Arab world*. Minneapolis: Carolrhoda Books. **B/PB**

Henkes, K. (1991). *Chrysanthemum*. New York: Greenwillow. **I/PB**

Herrera, J. F. (1998). *Laughing out loud, I fly: Poems in English in Spanish.* New York: HarperCollins. **I/P**

Herrera, J. F. (2000). *The upside down boy/El niño cabeza.* San Francisco, CA: Children's Book Press. **B/PB**

Hesse, K. (1992). *Letters from Rifka.* New York: Puffin. **I/CB**

Hesse, K. (1997). *Out of the dust.* New York: Scholastic. **I/P**

Hirschi, R. (1990). *Winter.* New York: Cobblehill Books. **B/PB**

Hoban, T. (1973). *Over, under, and through and other spatial concepts.* New York: Greenwillow. **B/PB**

Hoban, T. (1983). *I read signs.* New York: Greenwillow. **B/PB**

Hoban, T. (1983). *I read symbols.* New York: Greenwillow. **B/PB**

Hoban, T. (1987). *26 letters and 99 cents.* New York: Greenwillow. **P/PB**

Hoban, T. (1995). *Colors everywhere.* New York: Greenwillow. **P/PB**

Hoban, T. (1998). *More, fewer, less.* New York: Greenwillow Books. **P/PB**

Hoberman, M. (1991). *Fathers, mothers, sisters, brothers: A collection of family poems.* Boston: Joy Street Books. **I/P**

Hoffman, M. (1999). *A first book of myths: Myths and legends for the very young around the world.* New York: DK Publishing. **I/NF**

Holbrook, S. (1997). *Which way to the dragon?* Honesdale, PA: Wordsong/Boyds Mills Press. **I/P**

Hong, L. T. (1991). *How the ox star fell from heaven.* Morton Grove, IL: Albert Whitman & Company. **B/PB**

Hong, L. T. (1993). *Two of everything.* Morton Grove, IL: A. Whitman. **I/PB**

Hooks, W. H. (1987). *Moss gown.* New York: Houghton Mifflin. **I/PB**

Hopkins, L. B. (1983). *The sky is full of song.* New York: Harper & Row. **I/P**

Hopkins, L. B. (1994). *Weather: Poems for all seasons.* New York: HarperCollins. **B/P**

Hopkins, L. B. (Ed.). (1995). *Blast off! Poems about space.* New York: HarperCollins. **B/P**

Hopkins, L. B. (1996). *School supplies.* New York: Simon & Schuster. **I/P**

Hopkins, L. B. (1998). *Families, families.* New York: William H. Sadlier. **B/P**

Hopkins, L. B. (1999). *Spectacular science: A book of poems.* New York: Simon & Schuster. **I/P**

Hopkins, L. B. (Ed.). (1999). *Dino-roars.* New York: Golden Books. **B/P**

Hopkins, L. B. (Ed.). (1999). *Sports! Sports! Sports!* New York: HarperCollins. **B/P**

Hopson, D. P. (1996). *Juba this and juba that: 100 African-American games for children.* New York: Simon & Schuster. **I/P**

Hort, L. (2000). *The seals on the bus.* New York: Henry Holt. **B/PB**

Hoyt-Goldsmith, D. (1991). *Pueblo storyteller.* New York: Holiday House. **I/NF**

Hoyt-Goldsmith, D. (1992). *Arctic hunter.* New York: Holiday House. **I/NF**

Hoyt-Goldsmith, D. (1993). *Celebrating Kwanzaa.* New York: Holiday House. **I/NF**

Hoyt-Goldsmith, D. (1994). *Day of the Dead.* New York: Holiday House. **I/NF**

Hoyt-Goldsmith, D. (1995). *Apache rodeo.* New York: Holiday House. **I/NF**

Hoyt-Goldsmith, D. (1996). *Celebrating Hanukkah.* New York: Holiday House. **I/NF**

Hoyt-Goldsmith, D. (1998). *Lacrosse: The national game of the Iroquois.* New York: Holiday House. **I/NF**

Hudson, W. (1988). *Afro-bets: Book of black heroes from a to z.* New York: Just Us Books. **I/NF**

Hudson, W. (Ed.). (1993). *Pass it on: African American poetry for children.* New York: Scholastic. **I/P**

Hudson, W., & Wesley, V. W. (1998). *Book of black heroes from a to z.* New York: Just Us Books. **I/NF**

Hughes, L. (1932/1994). *The dreamkeeper and other poems.* New York: Knopf. **I/P**

Hunt, J. (1989). *Illuminations.* New York: Bradbury. **I/PB**

Hutton, W. (1994). *Persephone.* New York: McElderry. **I/PB**

Intrater, R. (1995). *Two eyes, a nose, and a mouth.* New York: Scholastic. **B/PB**

Israel, E. (2000). *The world almanac for kids, 2001.* Mahwah, NJ: World Almanac Books. **I/NF**

Jacobs, L. (1993). *Just around the corner: Poems about the seasons.* New York: Henry Holt. **I/P**

Jendresen, E., & Greene, J. M. (1998). *Hanuman: Based on Valmiki's Ramayana.* Berkeley, CA: Tricycle Press. **I/PB**

Jenkins, M. (1998). *Chameleons are cool.* Cambridge, MA: Candlewick Press. **I/NF**

Jenkins, S. (1995). *Biggest, strongest, fastest.* New York: Scholastic. **B/PB**

Jenkins, S. (1998). *Hottest, coldest, highest, deepest.* Boston: Houghton Mifflin. **B/PB**

Jenness, A. (1990). *Families: A celebration of diversity, commitment, and love.* Boston: Houghton Mifflin. **I/NF**

Jiang, J. L. (1997). *Red scarf girl.* New York: HarperCollins. **I/CB**

Johnston, T. (1996). *My Mexico~Mexico Mio.* New York: Penguin Putnam. **I/P**

Joslin, S. (1986). *What do you do, dear?* New York: HarperCollins. **I/PB**

Joslin, S. (1986). *What do you say, dear?* New York: HarperCollins. **I/PB**

Kahl, J. (1998). *National Audubon Society first field guide: Weather.* New York: Scholastic. **I/NF**

Kennedy, D. M. (1998). *Make things fly: Poems about wind.* New York: M. K. McElderry Books. **I/P**

Kimmel, E. A. (1988). *Anansi and the moss covered rock*. New York: Holiday House. **I/PB**

Kimmel, E. A. (1999). *The birds' gift: A Ukrainian Easter story*. New York: Holiday House. **I/PB**

Kindersley, A. (1997). *Children just like me*. New York: DK Publishing. **I/NF**

King, M. L., Jr., & King, C. S. (1997). *I have a dream*. New York: Scholastic. **I/PB**

King-Smith, D. (1985). *Babe the gallant pig*. New York: Crown. **I/CB**

Kipling, R. (1991). *How the camel got its hump*. New York: Simon and Schuster. **I/PB**

Knight, M. B. (1992). *Talking walls*. Gardiner, ME: Tilbury House. **I/PB**

Knight, M. B. (1993). *Who belongs here? An American story*. Gardiner, ME: Tilbury House. **I/PB**

Knight, M. B. (1996). *Talking walls: The stories continue*. Gardiner, ME: Tilbury House. **I/PB**

Koss, A. G. (1987). *Where do fish go in winter and answers to other great mysteries*. Los Angeles: Price Stern Sloan. **I/P**

Krach, M. S. (1997). *D is for doufu: An alphabet book of Chinese culture*. Arcadia, CA: Shen's Books. **I/PB**

Kuskin, K. (1975). *Near the window tree*. New York: Harper & Row. **I/P**

Kuskin, K. (1980). *Dogs and dragons, trees and dreams*. New York: Harper & Row. **I/P**

Kuskin, K. (1995). *James and the rain*. New York: Simon & Schuster. **B/PB**

Lankford, M. D. (1991). *Is it dark? Is it light?* New York: Alfred A. Knopf. **B/PB**

Lankford, M. (1992). *Hopscotch around the world*. New York: Morrow. **I/PB**

Lasky, K. (1994). *The librarian who measured the earth*. Boston: Little, Brown. **I/PB**

Lauber, P. (1989). *The news about dinosaurs*. New York: Bradbury. **I/NF**

Lauber, P. (1990). *Seeing earth from space*. New York: Orchard. **I/NF**

Lauber, P. (1993). *Journey to the planets* (4th ed.). New York: Crown. **I/NF**

Lauber, P. (1996). *Hurricanes: Earth's mightiest storms*. New York: Scholastic. **I/NF**

Lawlor, V. (1995). *I was dreaming to come to America: Memories from the Ellis Island Oral History Project*. New York: Penguin. **I/NF**

Lawson, R. (1968). *They were strong and good*. New York: Viking Press. **I/PB**

Leighton, M. R. (1992). *An Ellis Island Christmas*. New York: Puffin. **I/PB**

L'Engle, M. (1962). *A wrinkle in time*. New York: Farrar, Straus, & Giroux. **I/CB**

Lester, J. (1994). *John Henry*. New York: Dial. **I/PB**

Leventhal, D. (1994). *What is your language?* New York: Dutton Children's Books. **I/PB**

Levine, E. (1993). *If your name was changed at Ellis Island*. New York: Scholastic. **I/NF**

Levine, E. (1995). *I hate English* New York: Scholastic. **I/PB**

Levy, C. (1994). *A tree place and other poems*. New York: M.K. McElderry Books. **I/P**

Lewis, J. P. (1998). *Doodle dandies: Poems that take shape*. New York: Atheneum. **I/P**

Livingston, M. C. (1982). *A circle of seasons*. New York: Holiday House. **I/P**

Lobel, A. (1970). *Frog and toad are friends*. New York: Harper and Row. **I/CB**

Lobel, A. (1972). *Frog and toad together*. New York: Harper and Row. **I/CB**

Lobel, A. (1983). *The book of pigericks*. New York: Random House. **I/PB**

Lobel, A. (1998). *No pretty pictures: A child of war*. New York: Greenwillow. **I/CB**

Locker, T. (2000). *Cloud dance*. San Diego: Silver Whistle/Harcourt. **I/PB**

Lund, D. (1966). *Attic of wind*. New York: Parents' Magazine Press. **I/PB**

Macdonald, F. (1995). *How would you survive in the Middle Ages?* New York: Franklin Watts. **I/NF**

MacLachlan, P. (1985). *Sarah, plain and tall*. New York: Harper & Row. **I/CB**

Mado, M. (1992). *The animals: Selected poems*. New York: Margaret K. McElderry. **I/P**

Mado, M. (1998). *The magic pocket*. New York: McElderry Books. **I/P**

Martin, B., Jr. (1970). *Brown bear, brown bear*. New York: Holt, Rinehart & Winston. **B/PB**

Martin, B., Jr. (1987). *Here are my hands*. New York: Henry Holt. **B/PB**

Martin, R. (1999). *The hungry tigress: Buddhist myths, legends, and Jataka tales*. Oxford, MA: Yellow Moon Press. **I/CB**

Marzollo, J. (1990). *Pretend you're a cat*. New York: Penguin Putnam. **B/PB**

Mason, J. (1991). *Autumn weather*. New York: The Bookwright Press. **I/NF**

Matthaei, G., Grutman, J., & Cvijanovic, A. (1994). *The ledgerbook of Thomas Blue Eagle*. Charlottesville, VA: Thomasson-Grant. **I/PB**

Mattson, M. (1993). *Environmental atlas of the United States*. New York: Scholastic. **I/NF**

McCurdy, M. (1995). *The Gettysburg Address*. New York: Scholastic. **I/PB**

McDonald, F. (1994). *I love animals*. Cambridge, MA: Candlewick. **B/PB**

McDonald, S. (1992). *Alphabatics*. New York: Aladdin. **B/PB**

McGrath, B. B. (1994). *The M&M's brand counting book*. Watertown, MA: Charlesbridge. **B/PB**

McKissack, P. (1988). *Mirandy and Brother Wind*. New York: Scholastic. **I/PB**

McKissack, P., & McKissack, F. (1992). *Sojourner Truth: Ain't I a woman?* New York: Scholastic. **I/NF**

McKissack, P., & McKissack, F. (1994). *Christmas in*

the big house, Christmas in the quarters. New York: Scholastic. **I/NF**

McMahon, P. (1993). *Chi-Hoon: A Korean girl*. Honesdale, PA: Boyds Mills. **I/NF**

McMillan, B. (1988). *Growing colors*. New York: Lothrop, Lee & Shephard. **B/PB**

McMillan, B. (1989). *Time to—*. New York: Lothrop, Lee & Shephard. **B/PB**

McMillan, B. (1990). *Mary had a little lamb*. New York: Scholastic. **B/PB**

McMillan, B. (1991). *Eating fractions*. New York: Scholastic. **B/PB**

McMillan, B. (1992). *Going on a whale watch*. New York: Scholastic. **I/PB**

McMillan, B. (1996). *The weather sky*. New York: Farrar, Straus, Giroux. **I/PB**

Medearis, A. S. (1995). *Skin deep and other teenage reflections*. New York: Macmillan. **I/P**

Medina, J. (1999). *My name is Jorge on both sides of the river: Poems in English and in Spanish*. Honesdale, PA: Boyds Mills. **I/P**

Merriam, E. (1992). *The singing green: New and selected poems for all seasons*. New York: Morrow. **I/P**

Miller, M. (1990). *Who uses this?* New York: Greenwillow. **B/PB**

Minters, F. (1994). *Cinder-elly*. New York: Penguin. **I/PB**

Mitchell, M. K. (1993). *Uncle Jed's barber shop*. New York: Simon and Schuster. **I/PB**

Mohr, N. (1994). *Growing up inside the sanctuary of my imagination*. New York: Messner. **I/CB**

Moore, K. (1997). *If you lived at the time of the American Revolution*. New York: Scholastic. **I/NF**

Mora, P. (1997). *Tomas and the library lady*. New York: Knopf. **I/PB**

Mora, P. (1999). *Confetti: Poems for children*. New York: Lee and Low. **I/P**

Mora, P. (2000). *My own true name: New and selected poems for young adults*. Houston, TX: Arte Publico. **I/P**

Morgan, P. (1989). *The turnip*. New York: Philomel. **I/PB**

Morris, A. (1989). *Bread, bread, bread*. New York: Lothrup, Lee & Shephard. **B/PB**

Morris, A. (1989). *Hats, hats, hats*. New York: Lothrup, Lee & Shephard. **B/PB**

Morris, A. (1992). *Houses and homes*. New York: Lothrup, Lee & Shephard. **B/PB**

Morris, A. (1995). *Shoes, shoes, shoes*. New York: Lothrup, Lee & Shephard. **B/PB**

Moss, M. (1998). *Rachel's journey: The story of a pioneer girl*. San Diego: Harcourt Brace. **I/CB**

Murphy, J. (1993). *Across America on an emigrant train*. New York: Clarion. **I/NF**

Murphy, J. (1995). *The great fire*. New York: Scholastic. **I/NF**

Myers, W. D. (1999). *The journal of Joshua Loper, a black cowboy, the Chisholm Trail, 1871*. New York: Scholastic. **I/CB**

Nayer, J. (1994). *A tree can be. . . .* New York: Scholastic. **B/PB**

Naylor, P. R. (1991). *Shiloh*. New York: Atheneum. **I/CB**

Neitzel, S. (1989). *The jacket I wear in the snow*. New York: Greenwillow. **I/PB**

Neitzel, S. (1992). *The dress I'll wear to the party*. New York: Greenwillow. **I/PB**

Neitzel, S. (1995). *The bag I'm taking to Grandma's*. New York: Greenwillow. **I/PB**

Nye, N. S. (1992). *This same sky: A collection of poems from around the world*. New York: Four Winds. **A/P**

Nye, N. S. (1994). *Sitti's secrets*. New York: Simon and Schuster. **I/PB**

Nye, N. S. (1995). *That tree is older than you are: A biliingual gathering of poems and stories from Mexico with paintings by Mexican artists*. New York: Simon & Schuster. **A/P**

Nye, N. S. (1997). *Habibi*. New York: Simon and Schuster. **I/CB**

Nye, N. S. (1998). *The space between our footsteps: Poems and paintings from the Middle East*. New York: Simon and Schuster. **A/P**

Osborne, M. P. (1991). *American tall tales*. New York: Knopf. **I/CB**

Osborne, M. P. (1996). *Favorite Norse myths*. New York: Scholastic. **I/CB**

Pappas, T. (1991). *Math talk*. San Carlos, CA: Wide World. **I/P**

Park, F., & Park, G. (1998). *My freedom trip: A child's escape from North Korea*. Honesdale, NJ: Boyds Mills Press. **I/PB**

Parks, V. D. (1989). *Jump on over! The adventures of Brer Rabbit and his family*. San Diego: Harcourt Brace Jovanovich. **I/CB**

Patent, D. H. (1990). *Yellowstone fires: Flames and rebirth*. New York: Holiday House. **I/NF**

Paterson, K. (1977). *Bridge to Terabithia*. New York: Crowell. **I/CB**

Paul, A. W. (1991). *Eight hands round: A patchwork alphabet*. New York: HarperCollins. **I/PB**

Peacock, L. (1998). *Crossing the Delaware: A history in many voices*. New York: Scholastic. **I/NF**

Philip, N. (1995). *The illustrated book of myths: Tales and legends of the world*. New York: Dorling Kindersley. **I/CB**

Philip, N. (1996). *Odin's family: Myths of the Vikings*. New York: Orchard. *I/CB*

Pilling, A. (1997). *Creation: Read-aloud stories from many lands*. Cambridge, MA: Candlewick Press. **I/CB**

Pilon, A. B. (1972). *Concrete is not always hard*. Middleton, CN: Xerox Education Publications. **I/P**

Platt, R. (1992). *Incredible cross-sections*. New York: Knopf. **I/NF**

Polacco, P. (1994). *Pink and Say*. New York: Philomel. **I/PB**

Poole, A. L. (1999). *How the rooster got his crown*. New York: Holiday House. **I/PB**

Poole, A. L. (2000). *The ant and the grasshopper*. New York: Holiday House. **I/PB**

Prelutsky, J. (1982). *It's Thanksgiving*. New York: Scholastic. **I/P**

Prelutsky, J. (1984). *The new kid on the block*. New York: Greenwillow. **I/P**

Prelutsky, J. (1997). *The beauty of the beast: Poems from the animal kingdom*. New York: Alfred A. Knopf. **I/P**

Pringle, L. P. (1997). *An extraordinary life: The story of a monarch butterfly*. New York: Orchard. **I/NF**

Raschka, C. (1993). *Yo! Yes?* New York: Scholastic. **B/PB**

Raskin, E. (1966). *Nothing ever happens on my block*. New York: Scholastic. **I/PB**

Rayevsky, R. (1994). *A word to the wise and other proverbs*. New York: Morrow. **I/NF**

Ride, S., & Okie, S. (1986). *To space and back*. New York: Lothrop, Lee & Shepard. **I/NF**

Robbins, K. (1992). *Make me a peanut butter sandwich and a glass of milk*. New York: Scholastic. **I/PB**

Rochman, H., & McCampbell, D. Z. (1995). *Bearing witness: Stories of the Holocaust*. New York: Orchard. **I/NF**

Rockwell, A. (1996). *The one-eyed giant and other monsters from the Greek myths*. New York: Greenwillow. **I/CB**

Rockwell, A. (2000). *Career day*. New York: HarperCollins. **B/PB**

Rogers, P. (1989). *What will the weather be like today?* New York: Orchard. **B/PB**

Rogow, Z. (1988). *Oranges*. New York: Orchard. **B/PB**

Rohman, E. (1994). *Time flies*. New York: Dragonfly. **B/PB**

Roop, P. (1990). *I, Columbus, my journal 1492–1493*. New York: Walker. **I/NF**

Rosen, M. (1989). *We're going on a bear hunt*. New York: Margaret K. McElderry Books. **B/PB**

Rosenberg, M. (1986). *Making a new home in America*. New York: Lothrop, Lee, & Shepard. **I/NF**

Rosenberg, M. B. (1994). *Hiding to survive: Stories of Jewish children rescued from the Holocaust*. New York: Clarion.

Rosenthal, P. (1997). *Yo, Aesop! Get a load of these fables*. New York: Simon & Schuster. **I/B**

Ross, G. (1995). *How turtle's back was cracked: A traditional Cherokee tale*. New York: Dial. **I/PB**

Rowling, J. K. (1988). *Harry Potter and the sorcerer's stone*. New York: Scholastic. **A/CB**

Royston, A. (1992). *Baby animals*. New York: Little Brown. **I/NF**

Ryan, P. (1994). *100 is a family*. New York: Hyperion Books for Children. **I/PB**

Ryder, J. (1994). *Lizard in the sun*. New York: Mulberry Books. **I/PB**

Ryder, J. (1997). *Shark in the sea*. New York: Morrow. **I/PB**

Rylant, C. (1987). *Children of Christmas*. New York: Orchard. **I/CB**

Rylant, C. (1988). *Every living thing*. New York: Aladdin Books. **I/CB**

Sampson, M. (1996). *The football that won. . . .* New York: Trumpet Club. **I/PB**

Sanders, M. (1995). *What's your name? From Ariel to Zoe*. New York: Holliday House. **I/NF**

San Souci, R. D. (1991). *Larger than life: The adventures of American legendary heroes*. New York: Doubleday. **I/CB**

San Souci, R. D. (1998). *Fa Mulan*. New York: Hyperion. **I/PB**

Say, A. (1991). *Tree of cranes*. Boston: Houghton Mifflin. **I/PB**

Say, A. (1993). *Grandfather's journey*. Boston: Houghton Mifflin. **I/PB**

Say, A. (1999). *Tea with milk*. Boston: Houghton Mifflin. **I/PB**

Schwartz, A. (1992). *And the green grass grew all around: Folk poetry from everyone*. New York: HarperCollins. **I/P**

Scieszka, J. (1989). *The true story of the three little pigs*. New York: Viking Kestrel. **I/PB**

Scieszka, J. (1991). *The frog prince continued*. New York: Penguin. **I/PB**

Scieszka, J. (1992). *The stinky cheese man and other fairly stupid tales*. New York: Viking. **I/CB**

Scieszka, J. (1998). *Squids will be squids: Fresh morals, beastly fables*. New York: Viking. **I/CB**

Scott, A. H. (1990). *One good horse: A cowpuncher's counting book*. New York: Greenwillow. **B/PB**

Seuss, Dr. (Geisel, Theodor). (1937). *And to think I saw it on Mulberry Street*. New York: Random House. **I/PB**

Seuss, Dr. (1968). *The foot book*. New York: Random House. **B/PB**

Shannon, G. (1985). *Stories to solve*. New York: Greenwillow. **I/CB**

Shannon, G. (1990). *More stories to solve*. New York: Greenwillow. **I/CB**

Shannon, G. (1990). *Still more stories to solve*. New York: Greewillow. **I/CB**

Shaw, C. (1947). *It looked like spilt milk*. New York: Harper & Row. **B/PB**

Shaw, N. (1986). *Sheep in a jeep*. Boston: Houghton Mifflin. **B/PB**

Shaw, N. (1989). *Sheep on a ship*. Boston: Houghton Mifflin. **B/PB**

Shaw, N. (1991). *Sheep in a shop*. Boston: Houghton Mifflin. **B/PB**

Shaw, N. (1992). *Sheep out to eat*. Boston: Houghton Mifflin. **B/PB**

Shaw, N. (1994). *Sheep take a hike*. Boston: Houghton Mifflin. **B/PB**

Shaw, N. (1997). *Sheep trick or treat*. Boston: Houghton Mifflin. **B/PB**

Shea, P. D. (1995). *The whispering cloth: A refugee's story*. Honesdale, PA: Boyds Mills Press. **I/PB**

Sherman, I. (1980). *Walking talking words.* New York: Harcourt Brace. **I/NF**

Shields, C. D. (1995). *Lunch money and other poems about school.* New York: Dutton. **I/P**

Shulevitz, U. (1967). *One Monday morning.* New York: Macmillan/McGraw Hill. **B/PB**

Shulevitz, U. (1988). *Rain rain rivers.* New York: Farrar, Straus and Giroux. **B/PB**

Siebert, D. (1988). *Mojave.* New York: HarperCollins. **I/PB**

Siebert, D. (1989). *Heartland.* New York: Crowell. **I/PB**

Sills, L. (1989). *Inspirations: Stories about women artists.* Morton Grove, IL: Albert Whitman. **I/NF**

Silverstein, S. (1974). *Where the sidewalk ends.* New York: HarperCollins. **I/P**

Silverstein, S. (1981). *A light in the attic.* New York: HarperCollins. **I/P**

Simon, S. (1979). *The long view into space.* New York: Crown. **I/NF**

Simon, S. (1984). *The moon.* New York: Four Winds Press. **I/NF**

Simon, S. (1985). *Saturn.* New York: Morrow. **I/NF**

Simon, S. (1986). *Stars.* New York: Morrow. **I/NF**

Simon, S. (1986). *The sun.* New York: Morrow. **I/NF**

Simon, S. (1992). *Snakes.* New York: HarperCollins. **I/NF**

Simon, S. (1993). *Autumn across America.* New York: Hyperion. **I/NF**

Simon, S. (1993). *Weather.* New York: HarperCollins. **I/NF**

Simon, S. (1994). *Comets, meteors, and asteroids.* New York: Morrow. **I/NF**

Simon, S. (1994). *Winter across America.* New York: Hyperion. **I/NF**

Simon, S. (1997). *Lightning.* New York: Morrow Junior Books. **I/NF**

Simon, S. (1998). *Volcanoes.* New York: William Morrow. **I/NF**

Simon, S. (1999). *Tornadoes.* New York: Morrow Junior Books. **I/NF**

Singer, M. (1989). *Turtle in July.* New York: Macmillan. **I/P**

Sloane, E. (1995). *ABC book of early Americana.* New York: Wings Books. **I/NF**

Smith, H. E. (1990). *Weather.* New York: Doubleday. **I/NF**

Smith, R., & Schmidt, M. (1993). *In the forest with elephants.* San Diego: Harcourt Brace. **I/NF**

Sneve, V. D. H. (1996). *Dancing teepees: Poems of American Indian youth.* New York: Holiday House. **I/P**

Sneve, V. D. H. (1996). *The Cheyennes.* New York: Holiday House. **I/NF**

Soto, G. (1990). *Baseball in April.* San Diego: Harcourt Brace Jovanovich. **I/CB**

Soto, G. (1991). *A fire in my hands.* New York: Scholastic. **I/P**

Soto, G. (1991). *Taking sides.* San Diego: Harcourt Brace. **I/CB**

Soto, G. (1992). *Neighborhood odes.* San Diego: Harcourt Brace Jovanovich. **I/P**

Soto, G. (1993). *Too many tamales.* New York: G. P. Putnam's Sons. **I/PB**

Soto, G. (1993). *The pool party.* New York: Delacorte. **I/CB**

Soto, G. (1995). *Canto familiar.* San Diego, CA: Harcourt Brace. **I/P**

Soto, G. (1995). *Chato's kitchen.* New York: Putnam. **I/PB**

Spier, P. (1982). *Rain.* New York: Doubleday. **B/PB**

Spier, P. (1988). *People.* Garden City, NY: Doubleday. **I/PB**

Spier, P. (1992). *Noah's ark.* New York: Dell. **B/PB**

Stanek, M. (1989). *I speak English for my mom.* Morton Grove, IL: Albert Whitman. **I/PB**

Stanley, D. (1996). *Leonardo da Vinci.* New York: Morrow. **I/PB**

Stanley, D. (1997). *Rumpelstiltskin's daughter.* New York: Morrow. **I/PB**

Stanley, D., & Vennema, P. (1990). *Good Queen Bess: The story of Elizabeth I of England.* New York: Macmillan. **I/PB**

Stanley, J. (1992). *Children of the Dust Bowl: The true story of the school at Weedpatch Camp.* New York: Crown. **I/NF**

Stanley, J. (1994). *I am an American.* New York: Crown. **I/NF**

Staples, S. F. (1989). *Shabanu.* New York: Farrar Straus & Giroux. **I/CB**

Steinbeck, J. (1939/1993). *The grapes of wrath.* New York: Knopf. **A/CB**

Steptoe, J. (1987). *Mufaro's beautiful daughters.* New York: Lothrop, Lee, and Shepard. **I/PB**

Stevens, J. (1995). *Tops and bottoms.* San Diego: Harcourt Brace. **I/PB**

Stock, G. (1988). *The kids' book of questions.* New York: Workman. **I/NF**

Strom, Y. (1996). *Quilted landscape: Conversations with young immigrants.* New York: Simon & Schuster. **I/NF**

Swanson, D. (1994). *Safari beneath the sea, the wonderful world of the North Pacific coast.* San Francisco: Sierra Club. **I/NF**

Taback, S. (1999). *Joseph had a little overcoat.* New York: Viking. **I/PB**

Tafuri, N. (1999). *Snowy, flowy, blowy: A twelve months rhyme.* New York: Scholastic. **B/PB**

Talbot, H., & Greenberg, M. (1996). *Amazon diary: Property of Alex Winters.* New York: Scholastic. **I/CB**

Tashjian, V. (1995). *Juba this and juba that.* Boston: Little Brown. **I/P**

Taylor, C. (1992). *The house that crack built.* San Francisco, CA: Chronicle Books. **A/P**

Taylor, M. (1975). *Let the circle be unbroken.* New York: Dial. **A/CB**

Taylor, M. (1975). *Song of the trees.* New York: Dial. **I/CB**

Taylor, M. (1976). *Roll of thunder, hear my cry*. New York: Dial. **A/CB**

Taylor, M. (1987). *The friendship*. New York: Dial. **I/CB**

Taylor, M. (1987). *The gold Cadillac*. New York: Dial. **I/CB**

Taylor, M. (1990). *Mississippi bridge*. New York: Dial. **I/CB**

Taylor, M. (1995). *The well*. New York: Dial. **I/CB**

Taylor-Cork, B. (1992). *Be an expert weather forecaster*. New York: Gloucester Press. **I/NF**

Teague, M. (1995). *How I spent my summer vacation*. New York: Scholastic. **I/PB**

Tolhurst, M. (1990). *Somebody and the three Blairs*. New York: Scholastic. **I/PB**

Trelease, J. (1992). *Hey, listen to this: Stories to read aloud*. New York: Penguin. **I/CB**

Trelease, J. (1993). *Read all about it! Great read aloud stories, poems, and newspaper pieces for preteens and teens*. New York: Penguin. **I/CB**

Trivizas, E., & Oxenbury, H. (1993). *The three little wolves and the big bad pig*. New York: Scholastic. **I/PB**

Tunnell, M. O., & Chilcoat, G. W. (1996). *Children of Topaz: The story of a Japanese-American internment camp based on a classroom diary*. New York: Holiday House. **I/NF**

Uchida, Y. (1991). *The invisible thread: An autobiography*. Englewood Cliffs, NJ: Messner. **I/NF**

Updike, J. (1999). *A child's calendar*. New York: Holiday House. **I/P**

Usborne science and experiments: The power of nature. (1997). New York: Scholastic. **I/NF**

Valenta, B. (1997). *Pop-o-mania: How to create your own pop-ups*. New York: Dial. **I/NF**

Van Allsburg, C. (1982). *Ben's dream*. Boston: Houghton Mifflin. **I/PB**

VanCleave, J. (1991). *Earth science for every kid: 101 easy experiments that really work*. New York: John Wiley & Sons. **I/NF**

Viorst, J. (1972). *Alexander and the terrible, horrible, no good very bad day*. New York: Atheneum. **I/PB**

Viorst, J. (1994). *The alphabet from z to a (with much confusion along the way)*. New York: Atheneum. **I/P**

Walker, P. R. (1993). *Big men, big country: A collection of American tall tales*. San Diego: Harcourt Brace. **I/CB**

Ward, C. (1988). *Cookie's week*. New York: Putnam. **B/PB**

Waters, J. (1991). *Flood*. New York: Crestwood House. **I/NF**

Webb, S. (2000). *My season with penguins: An Antarctic journal*. Boston: Houghton Mifflin. **I/NF**

Wells, R. (2000). *Emily's first 100 days of school*. New York: Hyperion. **I/PB**

Westridge Young Writers Workshop. (1992). *Kids ex-plore America's Hispanic heritage*. Santa Fe, NM: Jose Muir Publications. **I/NF**

Wiesner, D. (1991). *Tuesday*. New York: Clarion. **B/PB**

Wiesner, D. (1999). *Sector 7*. New York: Clarion. **B/PB**

Wilcox, C. (1988). *Trash*. Minneapolis: Carolrhoda. **I/NF**

Wilcox, C. (1993). *Mummies and their mysteries*. Minneapolis: Carolrhoda. **I/NF**

Wilder, L. I. (1977). *Little house on the prairie*. New York: HarperCollins. **I/CB**

Williams, S. (1990). *I went walking*. San Diego: Harcourt Brace Jovanovich. **B/PB**

Williams, S. A. (1992). *Working cotton*. New York: Trumpet Club. **I/PB**

Withers, C. (1988). *Rocket in my pocket*. New York: Henry Holt. **I/P**

Wolfman, I. (1991). *Do people grow on family trees? Genealogy for kids and other beginners*. New York: Workman. **I/NF**

Wong, J. S. (1994). *Good luck gold and other poems*. New York: Margaret K. McElderry Books. **I/P**

Wong, J. S. (1996). *A suitcase of seaweed*. New York: Margaret K. McElderry. **I/P**

Wong, J. S. (2000). *This next new year*. New York: Farrar, Strauss, Giroux. **I/PB**

Wong, J. (2000). *The trip back home*. San Diego: Harcourt. **I/PB**

Wood, A. (1996). *The Bunyans*. New York: Blue Sky Press. **I/PB**

Wood, J. (1990). *Storms*. New York: Scholastic. **I/NF**

Woodruff, E. (1994). *Dear Levi: Letters from the Overland Trail*. New York: Alfred A. Knopf. **I/CB**

Worth, V. (1987). *All the small poems*. Boston: Little, Brown. **I/P**

Yep, L. (1991). *The lost garden: A memoir*. Englewood Cliffs, NJ: Messner. **I/NF**

Yep, L. (1993). *Dragon's gate*. New York: HarperCollins. **A/CB**

Yep, L. (1995). *Later, gator*. New York: Hyperion. **I/CB**

Yep, L. (1997). *The Khan's daughter*. New York: Scholastic. **I/PB**

Yolen, J. (1992). *Encounter*. San Diego: Harcourt Brace. **I/PB**

Yolen, J. (1993). *Welcome to the Green House*. New York: Putnam & Grosset. **I/PB**

Yolen, J. (1993). *Welcome to the sea of sand*. New York: Putnam & Grosset. **I/PB**

Yolen, J. (1998). *Snow, snow: Winter poems for children*. Honesdale, PA: Boyds Mills Press. **I/P**

Young, E. (1989). *Lon Po Po: A Red Riding Hood story from China*. New York: Philomel. **I/PB**

Zemke, D. (1988). *The way it happened*. New York: Houghton Mifflin. **I/PB**

Zhensun, Z., & Low, A. (1991). *A young painter: The life and paintings of Wang Yani—China's extraordinary young artist*. New York: Scholastic. **I/NF**

INDEX

French, Fiona, 189
Friedberg, B., 57
Friedman, I. R., 186
Fritz, Jean, 96, 224
Froman, R., 201
Fromkin, V., 21
Frost, R., 72
Functions of language, 99

Gagne, E. D., 249
Gallant, Roy, 232
Gallaz, C., 68
Games, 113–114, 117
Gardner, R. C., 30–31
Garelick, M., 260
Garvey, J. J., 21
Garza, Carmen Lomas, 16, 40, 170, 171–172, 174–175, 186
Gasparro, M., 197
Geographic backgrounds of students, 12–13
George, W. T., 219
Gere, A. R., 224
Ghandi, Mahatma, 3
Gibbons, Gail, 39, 73, 110, 220, 233, 254–256, 261
Gibbons, P., 31, 80, 81
Giblin, James Cross, 223–224, 233, 236
Gill, Sharon, 198
Gillard, Jennifer, 86, 204
Gillespie, J. S., 125, 127
Ginsburg, M., 260
Giovanni, Nikki, 201
Glazer, S. M., 193
Goble, Paul, 175
Gold, A. L., 243
Goldberg, R., 126, 243
Gollnick, D. M., 179
Golub, J., 145–146
Gonzales, F., 4, 59
Gonzales, R. D., 169, 182, 183
Gonzalez, L. M., 188
Goodman, B., 263
Goodman, K. S., 55, 107, 142
Goodman, Y., 107, 142
Goor, Nancy, 39
Grabe, W., 106
Graf, M., 263
Graham, Carolyn, 91
Graham, J. B., 201, 259
Graham, Martha, 224
Grammatical knowledge, 23
Graphic organizers, 115, 244–246
Graphs, 247–248
Graves, B., 112–113, 131–132
Graves, Donald, 147, 156
Graves, M., 112–113, 131–132
Greenberg, Mark, 155
Greene, Joshua, 187
Greenfield, Eloise, 72, 200, 205
Greenlaw, M. J., 216
Grutman, Jewel, 155
Gudel, Helen, 155
Guided reading, 59–61

Guiora, A. Z., 30–31
Gunning, T., 64
Guzzetti, B., 43, 216
Gwynne, Fred, 36, 114

Hadaway, Nancy L., 16, 57, 81, 136, 183, 184, 245–246, 252–268
Hade, Dan, 167
Hadingham, E., 243
Hadingham, J., 243
Haggard, M., 120
Hall, 107
Halliday, M. A. K., 24, 80
Hamayan, E., 107
Hamilton, Virginia, 170, 187, 189
Hammond, D., 127
Harris, Violet, 170, 208
Harste, J. C., 92–93
Harwayne, S., 50
Haskins, James, 69, 118
Hawkes, Kevin, 235
Hayes, C. W., 139
Heard, Georgia, 197, 202, 207, 209
Heath, S. B., 136
Henkes, Kevin, 24, 110
Hepler, S., 218
Herber, H., 119
Herman, J. L., 45
Herman, P. A., 114
Herrera, Juan Felipe, 15, 199
Hesse, Karen, 110, 130, 155
Heyde, A., 30–31
Hiebert, E. H., 107, 108
Hillocks, G., Jr., 146
Hindley, J., 54
Hirschi, Ron, 235
Historical fiction, 71–72
Hitler, Adolf, 73
H-maps, 245
Hoban, Tana, 28, 29, 39, 68, 69, 109, 218
Hoberman, M., 27
Hoffman, J. V., 58, 63
Hoffman, M., 187
Hogrogian, Nonny, 187
Holbrook, H. T., 241
Holbrook, Sara, 205
Holdaway, D., 59, 139
Holmes, B. C., 249
Homan, S. P., 248
Home language. See First language acquisition
Hong, Lily Toy, 130, 189
Hooks, W. H., 194
Hopkins, Lee Bennett, 27, 88, 112, 127, 200, 208, 254, 260
Hopson, D. P., 188
Hori, Lillan "Anne" Yamauchi, 220
How-to books, 219–220
Hoyt-Goldsmith, Diane, 186, 219
Hudelson, S., 106, 107, 137–138, 141, 142
Hudson, Wade, 200, 236

Hughes, Langston, 170, 199, 205
Hunt, J., 68
Hutchins, Pat, 29, 68, 109
Hutton, W., 187
Hymes, D., 23
Hynd, C. R., 216

Immigration
impact of, 3
native-born versus immigrant status, 10
newcomer schools, 7
stories of, 13–14
transitional issues, 10–11
Independent reading, 62–63, 125, 259
Informal assessment
of reading development, 132–134
of writing development, 158–160
Innatism, in language acquisition, 25, 26–27
Innocenti, R., 68
Input hypothesis, 27
Instruction methods, 57–63
in literate environment, 51–52
in oral language development, 87–98
in reading development, 57–63, 74, 111–131
using folklore, 183–192
using nonfiction, 239–248
using poetry, 202–208
in writing development, 153–157
Interactionism, in language acquisition, 25–26, 27–28
Interactive read alouds, 126
Intermediate fluency stage, 29–30
Intermediate proficiency level, 34–36, 48
oral language development, 84–86
reading development, 110
writing development, 144–145
Interviews, 95–96
Intrater, Roberta G., 39
Israel, E., 223

Jacobs, J. S., 62
Jacobs, Leland, 262
Jeffers, Susan, 72, 187
Jefferson, Thomas, 231
Jendresen, Erik, 187
Jenkins, Martin, 220
Jenkins, Steve, 42, 234–235
Jenness, Aylette, 245
Jensen, J. M., 138
JimÇnez, M., 59
Jobe, R., 54
Jochum, J., 138
Johnson, D. D., 107, 115, 248–249

Johnston, Tony, 199
Joslin, Sesyle, 24, 40
Jot charts, 246–247, 264
Journals
books, 220
dialogue, 154–156
other formats, 156, 246
reading, 126–127
Just, M., 127

Kahl, L., 259
Karolides, N. J., 127
Kaser, S., 177–178
Keller, Helen, 163
Kennedy, John F., 96
Kessler, C., 229
Kimmel, Eric A., 189, 192
Kindersley, A., 13
King, Martin Luther, Jr., 96, 170
King-Smith, Dick, 71
Kintner, Jolyn, 116
Kipling, R., 189
Knight, Margy Burns, 13, 245
Kobrin, Beverly, 221
Koss, A. G., 262
Kotkin, A. J., 184, 185
Krach, Maywan Shen, 12–13
Krashen, Stephen D., 26–28, 30, 31, 32, 41–43, 47–49, 53, 54, 62, 81, 85, 100, 217, 233
Krensky, S., 24
Kristo, J. V., 226
Krogness, M. M., 182
Kuskin, Karla, 204, 260
Kutiper, K., 200, 201
K-W-L charts, 110, 145, 239, 250

Lambert, W. E., 30–31
Language
Black vernacular, 171
competence in, 23–24
elements of, 21–23
nature of, 21–23
Language acquisition device (LAD), 25
Language Experience Approach (LEA), 41, 143
Language proficiency, 112, 113–114
Lankford, Mary, 29, 188
Lao Tzu, 20
Lapp, D., 138
Lasky, Kathryn, 235
Lauber, Patricia, 96, 226, 232, 233, 238, 241, 245, 263, 265
Lau v. Nichols, 5
Law, B., 265
Lawlor, V., 128
Lawson, Robert, 117, 185
Lay, K., 216
Lazear, D., 242, 243
Legends, 187
Leighton, M. R., 126
L'Engle, Madeleine, 71, 213

291